Power in Modern Societies

8 ☒
9 ☐
10 ☐
12 ☒
14 ☒

15 ☒
16 ☒
19 ☒
20 ☐

23 ☐
24 ☐
26 ☐
28 ☐

21 ☒

Power in Modern Societies

edited by

MARVIN E. OLSEN

&

MARTIN N. MARGER

Michigan State University

WESTVIEW PRESS

Boulder • San Francisco • Oxford

Copyright © 1993 by Westview Press, Inc.

Published in 1993 in the United States of America by Westview Press, Inc., 5500 Central Avenue, Boulder, Colorado 80301-2877, and in the United Kingdom by Westview Press, 36 Lonsdale Road, Summertown, Oxford OX2 7EW

Library of Congress Cataloging-in-Publication Data
Power in modern societies / edited by Marvin E. Olsen, Martin N.
  Marger.
    p.   cm.
  Includes bibliographic references.
  ISBN 0-8133-1288-4 — ISBN 0-8133-1289-2 (pbk.)
    1. Power (Social sciences)   I. Olsen, Marvin Elliot.   II. Marger,
  Martin N.
  HM136.P835   1993
  303.3—dc20   92-28612
                                                                                    CIP

Printed and bound in the United States of America

The paper used in this publication meets the requirements of the American National Standard for Permanence of Paper for Printed Library Materials Z39.48-1984.

10   9   8   7   6   5   4   3   2   1

Contents

Preface   xi
Credits   xiii

PART 1
Power in Social Organization   1

1   Problems in Defining Power, *Dennis H. Wrong*   9

The Intentionality of Power, 9
The Effectiveness of Power, 11
The Latency of Power, or the Actual/Potential Problem, 11
Asymmetry and Balance in Power Relations, 13

2   Power as a Societal Force, *Amitai Etzioni*   18

Power Defined, 18
Power as an Operational Concept, 18
Is Power Universal? 20
Between Power and Coercion, 23
Assets, Power, and Activation, 24
A Classification of Power, 25
Power, Influence, and Authority, 27

3   Forms and Levels of Power Exertion, *Marvin E. Olsen*   29

Four Forms of Social Power, 29
Three Levels of Social Power, 34
References, 36

4   Power, Domination, and Legitimacy, *Max Weber*   37

Power and Domination, 37
Domination and Legitimacy, 38
The Three Pure Types of Authority, 39

5   Power-Dependence Relations, *Richard M. Emerson*   48

The Power-Dependence Relation, 49
Balance and Imbalance, 50
Cost Reduction, 52
Balancing Operations, 52
Conclusion, 56
Notes, 57

6   Power and Distributive Systems, *Gerhard E. Lenski*   59

Two Laws of Distribution, 59
Force and Its Transformation, 61
The Rule of Right, 64
The Varieties of Institutionalized Power, 65
Notes, 67

7   Power in Society as Resource and Problem,
     Robert S. Lynd   68

PART 2
Theoretical Perspectives on Power   75

8   The Materialistic Conception of History, *Karl Marx*   88

9   Inventory of Marx's Ideas, *C. Wright Mills*   90

     References, 100

10   The Materialist Interpretation of History,
     Robert L. Heilbroner   101

     References, 110

11   The Iron Law of Oligarchy, *Robert Michels*   111

Impossibility of Direct Government by the Masses, 111
Psychological Causes of Leadership, 116
Intellectual Factors, 118
The Stability of Leadership, 119
The Struggle Between the Leaders and the Masses, 121
Democracy and the Iron Law of Oligarchy, 121
Final Considerations, 123

CONTENTS   *Elite)*   vii

12   The Ruling Elites, *Kenneth Prewitt and Alan Stone*   125

     The Elite Perspective, 125
     A Difference of Opinion Within the Elite Perspective, 126
     The State Is a Social Contract Between Unequals, 127
     Elite Theory and Social Change, 132
     Democratic Thought and Elite Theory, 134
     Notes, 135

13   Influence of Democracy on the Feelings
     of the Americans, *Alexis de Tocqueville*   137

     Why Democratic Nations Show a More Ardent and Enduring
        Love of Equality Than of Liberty, 137
     Of Individualism in Democratic Countries, 138
     Individualism Stronger at the Close of a Democratic Revolution
        Than at Other Periods, 140
     That the Americans Combat the Effects of Individualism by
        Free Institutions, 141
     Of the Use Which the Americans Make of Public Associations
        in Civil Life, 143

14   Sociopolitical Pluralism, *Marvin E. Olsen* (3)   *pluralism*   146

     Introduction, 146
     The Pluralist Model, 147
     The Mobilization Process, 148
     The Mediation Process, 149
     Problems of Sociopolitical Pluralism, 150
     References, 152

PART 3
National Power Structures   153

15   The Structure of Power in American Society,
     C. Wright Mills   161

16   The American Power Structure, *G. William Domhoff* (4)   170

     My Perspective, 170
     Power Indicators, 173
     Power Networks, 174
     Community Power, 178
     Conclusion, 179
     References, 180

17 The Structure of a National Elite Network, *Gwen Moore* 183

Research Design, 185
Findings: Network Structure, 189
Conclusions, 193
Notes, 195
References, 195

18 Elite Integration in Stable Democracies,
*John Higley, Ursula Hoffmann-Lange, Charles Kadushin,
and Gwen Moore* 196

Elite Integration in Stable Democracies: A Reconsideration, 196
Elite Integration and Elite Circles, 197
Methods and Data, 199
Results, 201
Discussion, 207
References, 208

19 The Structure of Intercorporate Unity
in American Business, *Beth Mintz and Michael Schwartz* 210

Sources of Intercorporate Power and Unity, 211
Interlocks as an Indicator of Intercorporate Power, 213
The Interlock Network, 214
Divisions Within the Interlock Network, 218
Notes, 220
References, 221

20 Upper-Class Power, *Harold R. Kerbo* 223

Upper-Class Economic Power, 223
Upper-Class Political Power, 227
References, 236

21 The Mass Media as a Power Institution,
Martin N. Marger 238

The Societal Role of the Mass Media, 238
Media Control and Accessibility, 239
Mass Media Content, 242
Media Effects, 245
References, 248

PART 4
Power and the State   251

22   Paradigms of Relations Between State and Society, ✐
        Robert R. Alford   258

        Three Paradigms of the State, 258
        Utopian and Pathological Images, 260
        The Strategic Focus of Each Paradigm, 262
        Methodological Implications, 265

23   Marxist Theories of the Capitalist State,
        David A. Gold, Clarence Y.H. Lo, and Erik Olin Wright   268

        The Traditions, 268
        Instrumentalist Theories of the State, 269
        Structuralist Theories of the State, 271
        Hegelian-Marxist Perspectives, 273
        Concluding Remarks, 274
        References, 276

24   The State System and the State Elite, *Ralph Miliband*   277

        References, 285

25   The Reification of the State, *Alan Wolfe*   286

        Public Life in Late Capitalism, 287
        Reification and Resignation, 291
        References, 293

26   The Ruling Class Does Not Rule, *Fred Block*   295

        The Critique of Instrumentalism, 296
        Division of Labor, 297
        Major Structural Mechanisms, 298
        Constraints on State Policies, 299
        Rationalization, 300
        Major Reforms, 303
        Conclusion, 305
        Notes, 305

27   The Potential Autonomy of the State, *Theda Skocpol*   306

        References, 313

28   The Autonomous Power of the State, *Michael Mann*   314

    Defining the State, 314
    Two Meanings of State Power, 315
    Origins of State Power, 319
    Results: Infrastructural Power, 324
    References, 327

About the Book and Editors   328.

Preface

When an earlier version of this book, titled *Power in Societies,* was published in 1970, the topic of social power was still marginal to much sociological thinking. During the ensuing twenty-two years, however, power has become one of the most central concepts in the discipline. The exercise and structuring of social power is now a major concern not only within political sociology but also in general social theory and many other areas such as social stratification, race and ethnic relations, the community, economic sociology, social ecology, and even the family. Sociology has at last rediscovered social power.

This was a rediscovery, because the topic of social power had existed in sociological writings since Karl Marx emphasized it in the 1860s. Power had also been a critical factor in Max Weber's writings in the early 1900s. Most sociologists, however—especially in the United States—paid relatively little attention to power for several decades after that. American sociology was long dominated by two foci that did not involve power: (1) social psychological concerns with the behavior of individuals in society and (2) Parsonian theory with its emphasis on value consensus and normative expectations.

The sociological rediscovery of social power began in the 1950s with the publication of two pivotal books: Floyd Hunter's *Community Power Structure* in 1953, which initiated a long string of studies dealing with the exercise of power in communities, and C. Wright Mills's *The Power Elite* in 1956, which sparked a lively debate about the role of elites in modern societies. Also important was the belated attention American sociologists began giving to Marx's writings during the 1960s, attention that led to innumerable attempts to interpret and reinterpret his theoretical ideas. Finally, the conflicts that erupted in the United States during the 1960s over race relations, poverty, and other critical problems had the effect of "radicalizing" the cohort of sociologists entering the field at that time and making them increasingly aware of the role of power in social affairs. As this rediscovery of social power intensified in sociology during the 1970s and 1980s, it came to dominate much of the discipline and generated a number of important studies.

Our purpose in adding this book to that growing list of publications is to fill a void that remains in the literature. At present, there is no collection of original writings on power that can be used in the classroom to acquaint students with sociological thinking on this topic. (*Power in Societies* is out of print, as are the few other collections of articles on power that appeared during the 1970s.) *Power in Modern Societies* is essentially an updating of that earlier book, based on the experiences that we have had in teaching political sociology courses during the past two decades. It is largely a new work, however: Only a third of its twenty-eight selections are retained from the earlier book. In selecting pieces for this volume, we have sought to present a mixture of classical and contemporary writings, both theoretical and empirical.

There have been so many sociological works on power in recent years that no single volume can encompass an adequate sampling of the literature. Consequently, this book focuses on four major themes: the nature of social power and its role in social organization, the three major theoretical perspectives on social power, current national power structures, and the use of power by the state and political elites. Each of those four parts of the book contains an introduction to its principal concerns and seven selections by other writers.

Although this work is primarily intended to be used as a textbook in upper-level undergraduate and graduate courses in political sociology and social power, it is also designed to serve several other audiences. These include political sociologists, who should find it a useful reference source; sociologists in other specialties who want an overview of recent writings on social power; political scientists who are interested in what sociologists have been saying about social power; graduate students in both sociology and political science who are attempting to become more familiar with the topic of social power; and students in a variety of other sociology and political science courses in which power is a recurring issue.

We therefore hope that many social scientists—both professionals and students—will find *Power in Modern Societies* a valuable addition to their libraries and a useful aid in teaching and learning about social power.

Finally, we want to thank Dean Birkenkamp of Westview Press for his continual encouragement and assistance throughout this endeavor.

Marvin E. Olsen
Martin N. Marger

Credits

The chapters in this book are taken from the following sources. Permissions to reprint are gratefully acknowledged.

1. Excerpted, with notes deleted, from Dennis H. Wrong, *Power: Its Forms, Bases, and Uses* (New York: Harper and Row Publishers, 1979), pp. 2–20, by permission of the author.

2. Excerpted from Amitai Etzioni, *The Active Society* (New York: Free Press, 1968), pp. 314–323, 357–361, by permission of The Macmillan Company and the author. Copyright © by The Free Press, a division of Macmillan, Inc., 1968.

4. Adapted with the premission of The Free Press, a division of Macmillan, Inc., from *The Theory of Social and Economic Organization*, by Max Weber, translated by A. M. Henderson and Talcott Parsons, edited by Talcott Parsons, from pp. 87–423. Copyright ©1947, copyright renewed 1975 by Talcott Parsons.

5. Reprinted from *American Sociological Review* 27 (February 1962): 31–37, 39–41.

6. Excerpted, with notes renumbered, from Gerhard E. Lenski, *Power and Privilege: A Theory of Social Stratification*, pp. 44–46, 50–58, 62–63. Copyright © 1966, 1984 by The University of North Carolina Press. Reprinted by permission of the author and publisher.

7. Excerpted from Robert S. Lynd, "Power in American Society as Resource and Problem," in Arthur Kornhauser, ed., *Problems of Power in American Democracy* (Detroit: Wayne State University Press, 1957), pp. 3–6, 9–14, 20–26, 34–38.

8. Excerpted from Karl Marx, Preface to *A Contribution to the Critique of Political Economy* (Chicago: Charles H. Kerr, 1904), pp. 11–12.

9. Excerpted, with notes deleted, from C. Wright Mills, *The Marxists* (New York: Brandt and Brandt, 1962), pp. 76–94. Copyright © 1962 by

PART 1

Power in Social Organization

"Every social act is an exercise of power, every social relationship is a power equation, and every social group or system is an organization of power" (Hawley, 1963:422). When Amos Hawley wrote that statement in 1963, very few sociologists were giving serious attention to social power. During the succeeding thirty years, however, increasing numbers of writers have argued that *power exertion is the central dynamic within the process of social organization* (cf., Giddens, 1984; Lukes, 1977; Mann, 1986; Wrong, 1979). Michael Mann (1986:1), for instance, began his recent work on the history of social power by asserting that "societies are constituted of multiple overlapping and intersecting sociological networks of power."

NATURE OF SOCIAL POWER

There is no commonly accepted definition of social power, but the essential idea is that *power is the ability to affect the actions or ideas of others, despite resistance*. It is thus a dynamic process, not a static possession, that pervades all areas of social life. Unfortunately, the English language does not contain the verb "to power," so when we discuss power in dynamic terms we must either attach a verb to it (such as exercising or exerting power) or use such verbs as "influence" or "control." Some writers use one or both of those terms as synonyms for social power; others give each of them a distinct meaning. Most commonly, however, they are used to designate the two endpoints of a continuum of power determinateness.

At one end, *influence* is power exertion in which the outcome is highly problematic or indeterminate. When one actor influences another, the recipient retains the ability to exercise power and hence can determine how he or she will respond to that influence, so that the eventual outcome is rather uncertain for the influencer. At the other end of the continuum, the outcome of *control* is rather predictable because the recipient can exercise little power relative to the initiator. In short, the exercise of social power can vary from relatively indeterminate social influence to relatively determinate social control, depending on the

1

type and amount of power being exerted and the relative power of the other actors involved.

The actors who exercise social power can be either individuals or social units of all kinds, from small groups to total societies. In the former case, the activity is sometimes called "personal" (or "interpersonal") power; in the latter case, it is often referred to as "organizational" (or "interorganizational") power. The dynamics of the power exertion process, however, are essentially the same in both cases.

When power relationships become an established feature of any pattern of social ordering, they can be viewed as a structural characteristic of that organization. Max Weber (1978 [1922]:53–54) and more recently Anthony Giddens (1984:28–59) have both referred to such structured patterns of social power as *domination* and have emphasized their perpetuation, stability, and relative predictability in social life.

CHARACTERISTICS OF SOCIAL POWER

1. Because social power is an *interactive process*, it always resides within social interaction and relationships, never in individual actors. A single actor may possess resources that provide a potential basis for exerting social power, but power does not exist until it is expressed in the actions of two or more actors as a dynamic activity. Moreover, both the power attempt made by an exerter and the resistance offered by a recipient are crucial in determining the actual power exercised in any situation.

2. The ability of an actor to exercise social power can be either *potential* or *active* at any given time. An actor exercises potential power when he or she possesses resources, is capable of employing them, and indicates that possibility to others. Power becomes active when those resources are actually converted into actions toward others. Although it is sometimes argued that potential power is only subjective perceptions and should not be considered power exertion, a potential power wielder is never entirely passive. He or she must convey the impression—through either actions or messages (either real or bluffs)—that overt power exertion is a distinct possibility. Hence, the process of exerting power is essentially the same in both cases, except that potential power involves only the manipulation of impressions, whereas active power requires the overt use of resources.

3. Power exertion is a *purposeful activity* that is intended to affect others in certain ways, but it may also have unintended effects. Most sociologists restrict the concept of power to actions that are intended to affect the recipient, because otherwise virtually every action by every actor could be labeled as power exertion. The issue of intentionality is clouded in many situations, however, by three features of many power actions. First, for strategic reasons, actors often attempt to hide or disguise the purpose of their power wielding, attempting to influence others with-

out the others' being aware of it. Second, power can be exerted indirectly through intermediaries, a process that can mask the primary intentions. Third, in addition to its intended outcomes, an exercise of power can have numerous unintended (and sometimes unrecognized) consequences for others.

4. The exercise of social power can affect actions and ideas in either of two directions. It can enable or cause actors to do things they would not otherwise do, or it can hinder or prevent them from doing things they would otherwise do. In other words, power can be used in either a *promotive* or a *preventive* manner. If we wish to emphasize the preventive use of power, we may speak of exercising power *over* others to control them. If we wish to emphasize its promotive use, we may speak of exercising power *with* others to attain common goals. The first expression often conveys the value that power exertion is undesirable because it restricts people's freedom of action, whereas the second expression conveys the value that power is desirable for collective endeavors.

5. The interactions and exchanges that occur between participants when power is exerted can vary from evenly *balanced* to grossly *unbalanced*. In relatively balanced situations, each actor exerts approximately the same amount of influence or control on the other actor(s), so that everyone receives approximately equal benefits. In a highly unbalanced situation, one, or a few actors, exerts much greater influence or control than anyone else and consequently receives most of the benefits. Relatively balanced power is usually more stable and is viewed as more desirable than highly unbalanced power conditions, although, for various reasons, the latter often occur.

FORMS OF SOCIAL POWER

Most instances of social power exertion can be categorized into one of four forms—force, dominance, authority, or attraction—although any specific situation often includes more than one form.

When exerting *force*, an actor brings pressures to bear on the intended recipient by giving or withholding specific resources or threatening to do so. The actor must therefore commit particular resources to that interaction and expend them to whatever extent is necessary to obtain the intended outcomes. Force can be exerted in three different ways (Etzioni, 1968). With *utilitarian* force (also called "inducements," or "compensation"), the recipient is given desired benefits in return for compliance. With *coercive* force (also called "constraint," or "deprivation"), punishments are inflicted or benefits are withheld to obtain compliance. With *persuasive* force (also called "information," or "communication"), messages are conveyed that alter the recipient's beliefs, values, attitudes, emotions, or motivations in an attempt to produce compliance.

When exerting *dominance* (as distinct from domination), an actor effectively carries out a set of established activities or social roles on a regular basis. To the extent that others depend on the performance of those activities, they are vulnera-

ble to being influenced or controlled by that actor. This form of power does not require the commitment of any additional resources to the interaction but relies entirely on the successful performance of the dominant actor's usual activities or
roles. The ability to exert dominance depends heavily on one's position in a social
network or organization, so that the closer an actor's position to the top or center
of a social structure, the greater the possibilities for dominance.

When exercising *authority*, an actor draws on a grant of legitimacy made by
the recipients as a basis for issuing authoritative directives. Because the legitimacy has been voluntarily granted by those subject to the directives, they are expected to comply with them. Legitimacy is sometimes granted to an actor
through direct procedures such as formal votes or informal agreements, but
more commonly it is indirectly expressed as one joins an organization, remains a
member of it, and supports the actions of its leaders who claim legitimacy. Four
bases on which authority often rests are *rational* knowledge or expertise relevant
to the situation, *legal* rights based on formal arrangements, *traditional* beliefs
and values, and *charismatic* appeal by revered leaders (Weber, 1978 [1922]: 215–
254). Authority is by far the most stable form of power exertion.

When exercising *attraction*, an actor draws on the diffuse appeal that he or
she has for others in order to influence them. That appeal, unlike a grant of legitimacy, may have no connection with social power. A skillful actor may be able,
nevertheless, to transform that appeal into power exertion with which others
voluntarily comply. Three common sources of appeal are cognitive *identification* with, positive *feelings* toward, and attribution of *charisma* to an individual
or an organization. Attractive power is often unstable and transitory, but at
times it can become extremely compelling.

LEVELS OF SOCIAL POWER

The exercise of power in social life can occur at three different levels, which
are also called "one-dimensional," "two-dimensional," and "three-dimensional"
perspectives (Lukes, 1974:11–25). These levels or perspectives are cumulative,
so that the second one always includes the first, and the third includes both of
the others.

The first level of power exertion pertains to the actions that actors take as
they attempt to affect others, despite opposition. In particular, this exertion of
power commonly involves making and implementing decisions that are directly
observable and often produce conflict.

The second level of power exertion pertains to the control exercised over situations and other actors that prevents activities from occurring or decisions from
being made. Some actors, especially those who occupy positions that give them
considerable resources, may define certain topics as "nonissues" that are closed
to discussion or certain actions as "illegitimate" that may not be considered.

This level, therefore, involves power exertion that may be partially hidden and results in nondecision making or nonaction by others.

The third level of power exertion pertains to the ways in which actors shape the broad social contexts in which others act, thereby making possible some courses of action and preventing others. To do this, actors must occupy powerful positions and enact critical roles that enable them to structure social situations in particular ways and thus shape the manner in which people view the world and define their interests. This level—which is also termed the exercise of "meta-power" (Baumgartner et al., 1976:Ch. 10)—thus involves overall control of the processes and forms of social organization.

CREATION OF SOCIAL POWER

There are presently two principal and complementary explanations of how social power is created.

The *dependency theory* of power creation, which was formulated by Richard Emerson (1962), is based on the assumption that social power rests on social interdependence. Actor A can exercise power over actor B to the extent that B depends on A for something, and vice versa. This power is activated as A uses B's dependency to make demands on B that result in changes in B's actions or ideas. More formally, the dependency of B on A is directly proportional to B's need for something provided by A, and inversely proportional to its availability to B from other sources. In turn, the power of A over B is directly proportional to the degree of B's dependency on A and inversely proportional to the amount of resistance by B that A cannot overcome. As expressed by Emerson: "The power of A over B is equal to, and based on, the dependency of B upon A" (1962:33).

The *trust theory* of power creation, which was formulated by Talcott Parsons (1963), is based on the assumption that power rests on people's involvement in social relationships in which they trust others. This investment of trust occurs when a participant believes that the other people involved will act responsibly in ways that will benefit their mutual relationship. In relatively small and informal groups, trust normally resides in interpersonal bonds, but in larger and more formal organizations it is often necessary to supplement those bonds with protections such as a constitution, a bill of rights, or a legal contract. Nevertheless, as individuals commit themselves to a collectivity and invest trust in it, that investment generates social power within the collectivity that its members can exercise to attain common goals. More formally, the creation of social power within a collectivity is directly proportional to the investment of trust in it by its participants.

EXERCISE OF SOCIAL POWER

The process of exercising social power involves four distinct but often highly interwoven steps: possessing resources, committing resources, converting resources, and overcoming resistance (Blalock, 1989).

The initial step is *possessing or having access to relevant resources* of some kind. These available resources may be either tangible (e.g., money, property, goods, people, weapons) or intangible (e.g., knowledge, skills, roles, legitimacy, reputation, appeal). Most resources are inherently finite, so that use diminishes their supply; but some (such as knowledge and skills) are not limited and may actually increase with use. To exert any form of social power, an actor must have some kind of resource base on which to draw.

The second step is *committing some or all of one's available resources* to a particular situation. The actor must decide how important this situation is to him or her and consequently how many and what kinds of resources to commit to it. Thus an actor with limited resources who commits all of them to a particular situation may be able to exercise more power than an actor with extensive resources who commits only a small portion of them. The process of exerting potential power ends at this point. If the recipients believe that the power wielder has committed sufficient resources to affect them and is capable of employing those resources, they may alter their actions or ideas even though no power is overtly exerted. Thus potential power equals available and committed resources and a demonstrated willingness to use them.

To actively exercise social power, an actor must carry out the third step of effectively *converting committed resources into power actions*. No amount of committed resources will result in power exertion unless one knows how to transform them into power actions, and considerable skill and finesse may be required to do that. Hence knowing when, where, and how to use one's resources effectively is often more crucial than the amount of those resources. Thus

a power attempt = available and committed resources × one's conversion effectiveness.

The multiplicative nature of this linkage between resources and conversion is critical. If either factor is low, the other one must be quite high if the resulting power attempt is to be effective.

Finally, to successfully affect another actor, social power exertion must to some extent *overcome whatever resistance is made* by the recipient. Not all power attempts are resisted, but most are. If the resistance is sufficient to prevent the initiator from having any effects on the recipient, no power is exercised in that situation. Resistance can take the form of active opposition (which often produces conflict), passive noncompliance, indifference, or withdrawal. The exercise of social power is thus usually a reciprocal process among the involved actors and is rarely completely determined by a single actor, no matter how unbalanced the situation may appear. The complete process of power exertion can therefore be described as

power exertion = available and committed resources × conversion effectiveness − resistance offered.

PERVASIVENESS OF SOCIAL POWER

Because social power exertion is the fundamental dynamic within organized social life, it pervades all domains and forms of social organization. It occurs within the smallest and most personal groups, such as families and friendship cliques; within communities of all sizes; within all goal-oriented associations; within all social institutions, such as the economy and the polity; throughout all societies; and in international relations. It also underlies most social processes such as conflict, stratification, cooperation, and cohesion.

In particular, contemporary sociologists now appreciate the insightfulness of Max Weber's argument made in 1922 that all social inequality rests ultimately on unequal distributions of social power. Marx had made this point in regard to socioeconomic classes in the 1860s, but Weber extended it to all dimensions of stratification. For nearly half a century, however, American sociologists overlooked both Marx and Weber and attributed inequality to differences in the way people perceive and evaluate one another. Not until the publication of Gerhard Lenski's *Power and Privilege* in 1966 was power exertion again seen as the principal cause of social stratification. Today, that "power perspective" pervades all thinking about inequality.

More generally, to understand any aspect of social organization, we must examine its power dynamics. The nature, characteristics, dimensions, types, and exercise of social power vary widely among different social situations. Thus all of the features of power must be empirically determined in every instance of social organization being investigated by social scientists. But social power is always being exerted and is always affecting the actions and ideas of both individuals and collectivities. As expressed by Robert Lynd (1957:3), "It is not primarily the desire of some men to constrain others that makes power, in one form or another, so universal a phenomenon in society; rather, it is the necessity in each society—if it is to be a society, not a rabble—to order the relations of men and their institutional ways of achieving needed ends."

OVERVIEW OF SELECTIONS

The first two selections, by Dennis Wrong and Amitai Etzioni, discuss the basic characteristics of social power. The next two pieces, by Marvin Olsen and Max Weber, distinguish specifically among various forms, levels, and bases of social power. An article by Richard Emerson describes the dependency theory of power creation. The final two selections, by Gerhard Lenski and Robert Lynd, discuss various ways in which power exertion affects social organization.

REFERENCES

Baumgartner, Tom, Walter Buckley, Tom R. Burns, and Peter Schuster. 1976."Meta-Power and the Structuring of Social Hierarchies." In Tom R. Burns and Walter Buckley, eds.,

Power and Control: Social Structures and Their Transformation. London: Sage Publications.

Blalock, Hubert M., Jr. 1989. *Power and Conflict: Toward a General Theory.* Newbury Park, Calif.: Sage Publications.

Emerson, Richard M. 1962. "Power Dependence Relations," *American Sociological Review* 27 (February):31–37.

Etzioni, Amitai. 1968. *The Active Society.* New York: Free Press.

Giddens, Anthony. 1984. *The Constitution of Society: Outline of a Theory of Structuration.* Cambridge: Polity Press; Berkeley: University of California Press.

Hawley, Amos. 1963. "Community Power and Urban Renewal Success," *American Journal of Sociology,* 68 (January):422-431.

Lenski, Gerhard E. 1966. *Power and Privilege: A Theory of Social Stratification.* New York: McGraw-Hill.

Lukes, Steven. 1974. *Power: A Radical View.* London: Macmillan.

―――――. 1977. *Essays in Social Theory.* London: Macmillan.

Lynd, Robert S. 1957. "Power in American Society as Resource and Problem." In Arthur Kornhauser, ed., *Problems of Power in American Democracy,* pp. 3–38. Detroit: Wayne State University Press.

Mann, Michael. 1986. *The Sources of Social Power.* Vol. I. Cambridge: Cambridge University Press.

Parsons, Talcott. 1963. "On the Concept of Political Power," *Proceedings of the American Philosophical Society* 103, no. 3, pp. 232–262.

Weber, Max. 1978 [originally published in 1922]. *Economy and Society: An Outline of Interpretive Sociology,* ed. by Guenther Roth and Claus Wittich. Berkeley: University of California Press.

Wrong, Dennis H. 1979. *Power: Its Forms, Bases and Uses.* New York: Harper & Row.

1

Problems in Defining Power

DENNIS H. WRONG

Although there are hundreds, perhaps thousands, of more recent definitions of social power, or of the power of men over other men, in the literature of social science. I see no reason why we should not make do with older, simpler definitions so long as they are intellectually adequate. I shall therefore adopt a modified version of Russell's definition: *Power is the capacity of some persons to produce intended and foreseen effects on others.* The terms in this definition require detailed analysis to show how they cope with major problems and confusions in the conceptual analysis of power. There are five such problems. First, there is the issue of the *intentionality* of power, and secondly, of its *effectiveness*. The *latency* of power, its dispositional nature to which I have already alluded, is a third problem. The unilateral or asymmetrical nature of power relations implied by the claim that some persons have an effect on others without a parallel claim that the reverse may also be the case is a fourth issue, to be discussed below as the problem of *asymmetry and balance* in power relations. A final question is that of *the nature of the effects produced* by power: must they be overt and behavioural, or do purely subjective, internal effects count also?

THE INTENTIONALITY OF POWER

People exercise mutual influence and control over one another's conduct in all social interaction—in fact, that is what we mean by social interaction. It is essential, therefore, to distinguish between the exercise of power and social control in general—otherwise there would be no point in employing power as a separate concept or in identifying power relations as a distinct kind of social relation. That social control is inherent in all social interaction—at least, in all recurrent or 'patterned' social interaction—has been clearly recognized by contemporary sociologists. ...

9

When social controls have been internalized, the concept of power as a social relation is clearly inapplicable, but to assume that most conformity to norms is the result of internalization is to adopt what I have called an 'over-socialized conception of man.' Moreover, the power of the parent over the child precedes the child's internalization of parental rules; the child's superego is formed by his identification with the parents, whose commands the child eventually issues to himself without reference to their original external source. Submission to power is thus the earliest and most formative experience in human life....

But if to collapse the concept of power into that of social control is to vitiate all need for a separate concept of power, it then becomes necessary to distinguish the diffuse controls exercised by the group over socialized individuals from direct, intentional efforts by a specific person or group to affect another's conduct. Power is identical with *intended* and effective influence. It is one of two subcategories of *influence*, the other, empirically larger subcategory consisting of acts of *unintended* influence. In contrast to several recent writers, I do not see how we can avoid restricting the term power to intentional and effective acts of influence by some persons on other persons. It may be readily acknowledged that intentional efforts to influence others often produce unintended as well as intended effects on their behaviour—a dominating and overprotective mother does not intend to feminize the character of her son. But all social interaction produces such unintended effects—a boss does not mean to plunge an employee into despair by greeting him somewhat distractedly in the morning, nor does a woman mean to arouse a man's sexual interest by paying polite attention to his conversation at a cocktail party. The effects others have on us, unintended by and even unknown to them, may influence us more profoundly and permanently than direct efforts to control our sentiments and behaviour....

The distinction between intentional and unintentional effects on others may seem to be hairsplitting.... Yet rather than equate power with all forms or influence, unintended as well as intended, it seems preferable to stress the fact that the intentional control of others is likely to create a relationship in which the power holder exercises unintended influence over the power subject that goes far beyond what he may have wished or envisaged at the outset....

Intentionality is often understood to include all outcomes that are anticipated or foreseen by the actor. But there is a difference between acting in order to achieve a certain outcome and recognizing that other effects will unavoidably result from the action which are incidental to the outcome sought by the actor. These anticipated but unintended byproducts of the action may from the actor's standpoint be regarded as inconsequential, as undesirable in themselves but a price worth paying to attain the end for which the action was undertaken, or as secondary gains insufficiently attractive to justify undertaking the action. However, so long as the effects were foreseen by the actor even if not aimed at as such, they constitute an exercise of power in contrast to unanticipated (and by definition unintended) effects.

THE EFFECTIVENESS OF POWER

When attempts to exercise power over others are unsuccessful, when the intended effects of the aspiring power-wielder are not in fact produced, we are confronted with an absence or a failure of power.... When an attempted exercise of power fails, although similar attempts may have been successful in the past, we witness the breakdown of the power relation. The effectiveness of power would seem to be so obvious a criterion for its presence as to preclude any need for further discussion.

THE LATENCY OF POWER, OR
THE ACTUAL/POTENTIAL PROBLEM

Power is often defined as a capacity to control or influence others. I have already briefly referred to some of the implications of so defining it: the capacity to perform acts of control and their actual performance are clearly not the same thing—power when thought of as a capacity is a dispositional concept.... The distinction between 'having power' and 'exercising power' reflects the difference between viewing power as a dispositional and as an episodic concept. Unfortunately, power lacks a common verb form, which in part accounts for the frequent tendency to see it as a mysterious property or agency resident in the person or group to whom it is attributed. The use of such terms as 'influence' and 'control', which are both nouns and verbs, as virtual synonyms for power, represents an effort (not necessarily fully conscious) to avoid the suggestion that power is a property rather than a relation.

The evidence that a person or group possesses the capacity to control others may be the frequency with which successful acts of control have been carried out in the past. Thus it makes perfect sense to say that the king or president still 'has' power even when he is asleep in his bed (though not if there has been a successful insurrection since he retired, and armed rebels are guarding the door to his bedroom). Or power may be imputed to an actor when the probability of his intending to achieve and effectively achieving control over another actor is rated high, even though he may not have previously exercised such control.

However, this sense in which power is latent or dispositional is sometimes confused with another, or at least the distinction between them is blurred. Power is sometimes said to be potential rather than actual, to be 'possessed' without being 'exercised', when others carry out the wishes or intentions of the power holder without his ever actually having issued a command to them or even having interacted with them at all to communicate his aims....

The ruler may be asleep in bed while his subjects are not merely engaged in carrying out directives he gave them before retiring but making decisions and taking actions based on their anticipations of what he would wish them to do in the relevant circumstances. It is this that is often called 'latent' or 'potential'

power, as distinct from 'manifest' or 'actual' power where observable communications are transmitted and acted upon. Clearly, more is involved in such cases
than the previously described situation where the ruler may be said to 'have'
power while asleep in the sense that he has an unimpaired capacity to issue
commands in the expectation that they will be obeyed. Both cases, however,
seem to me to indicate essential attributes of all power relationships. ...

But imputations of power based on the 'anticipated reactions' of the power
subject confront a number of difficulties. For A's power over B to be real when it
is not actually exercised, B must be convinced of A's capacity to control him and
must modify his behaviour accordingly. Thus a mother has power over her child
when the child refrains from doing something in anticipation of her displeasure
even when the mother is not present to issue a specific prohibition. Similarly,
the president has power over Congress when congressional leaders decide to
shelve a bill in anticipation of a presidential veto. The consciousness of the
power subject is a crucial consideration in imputations of power on the basis of
anticipated reactions. Max Weber's conception of power as 'the probability that
one actor in a social relationship will ... carry out his own will' may be interpreted as attributing the estimate of probability to the judgment of the power
subject and not merely to that of the observer, say a social scientist. Otherwise,
only overt acts of control or the subsequent imposition of a sanction after the
performance of an act would validate an imputation of power made by an observer, and the distinction between latent and manifest power disappears.

When power is regarded as a capacity, therefore, and when it is understood to
include B's acts based on his anticipation of A's reaction to them, the distinction
between latent and manifest, or potential and actual, power is implicit in the
very definition of power. ...

Those who prefer to equate power with its exercise in a social relationship
fear the subjectivity that appears to be implicit in the view that actors may 'have'
power without exercising it so long as belief in the probability of their exercising
it limits the choices of others. As I have already indicated, treating power as a capacity runs the initial risk of seeing it as vested too exclusively in the power
holder 'from where it radiates to others.' But once we correct this possible over-
emphasis by insisting that power is always a relation between two actors, do we
not then risk going to the opposite extreme of making it dependent entirely on
what is in the mind of the power subject? Are we not in effect saying that someone's belief that someone else has power actually confers power on the latter?...

[T]o avoid such a suggestion, one need only repeat the line of reasoning followed in correcting the opposite inference that power is a kind of force emanat-
ing from the power holder: if an actor is believed to be powerful, if he knows that
others hold such a belief, and if he encourages it and resolves to make use of it by
intervening in or punishing actions by others who do not comply with his
wishes, then he truly has power and his power has indeed been conferred upon
him by the attributions, perhaps initially without foundation, of others. But if

he is unaware that others believe him powerful, or if he does not take their belief seriously in planning his own projects, then he has no power and the belief that he has is mistaken, a misperception of reality. ...

ASYMMETRY AND BALANCE IN POWER RELATIONS

Power relations are asymmetrical in that the power holder exercises greater control over the behaviour of the power subject than the reverse, but reciprocity of influence—the defining criterion of the social relation itself—is never entirely destroyed except in those forms of physical violence which, although directed against a human being, treat him as no more than a physical object.

The asymmetry of power relations, however, is often stressed to a degree that would make it logically contradictory to speak of 'bilateral' power relations or of 'equality of power' in bargaining or conflict. ... Peter Blau maintains that 'interdependence and mutual influence of equal strength indicate lack of power.' Such assertions risk going too far in severing power relations from their roots in social interaction in its generic form, for the asymmetry of power relations is at least immanent in the give and take of dyadic interaction between equals, in which the control of one actor over the other's behaviour is reciprocated by a responsive act of control by the other. Asymmetry exists in each individual act-response sequence, but the actors continually alternate the roles of power holder and power subject in the course of their interaction. In a stable social relation (where there is recurrent interaction between the parties rather than interaction confined to a single occasion) a pattern may emerge in which one actor controls the other with respect to particular situations and spheres of conduct—or 'scopes', as they have often been called—while the other actor is regularly dominant in other areas of activity. Thus a wife may rule in the kitchen, while her husband controls the disposition of the family income. Or a labour union, as in the unions of seamen and longshoremen, controls hiring, while the employer dictates the time and place of work.

Thus if we treat power relations as exclusively hierarchical and unilateral, we overlook an entire class of relations between persons or groups in which the control of one person or group over the other with reference to a particular scope is balanced by the control of the other in a different scope. The division of scopes between the parties is often the result of a bargaining process which may or may not have followed an open struggle for power—a separation in a marriage, a strike against an employer, a lawsuit in commercial rivalry, a war between nations.

The term 'intercursive power' has been suggested for relations characterized by a balance of power and a division of scopes between the parties. It is contrasted with 'integral power', in which decision-making and initiatives to action are centralized and monopolized by one party. Intercursive power exists where the power of each party in a relationship is countervailed by that of the other, with procedures for bargaining or joint decision-making governing their relations when matters affecting the goals and interests of both are involved. ...

Integral power always raises the question *quis custodiet ipsos custodies?*—or who rules the rulers, guards the guardians, oversees the overseers? The assumption behind the query is that the rulers' power to decide at their own discretion cannot be entirely eliminated in human societies. ... Thus where integral power is established and recognized as unavoidable in at least some situations (or scopes), as in the case of the power of the state in modern times, attempts to limit it take a form other than that of transforming integral power into an intercursive power system. Integral power may be restricted without either reducing the decision-making autonomy of the power holder or countervailing it by giving others power over him with reference to particular scopes. Measures designed to limit integral power include periodic reviews of the acts of the power holder (legislative and judicial review), periodic reaffirmations of his power-holding status or his removal and replacement (rules of tenure and succession), the setting of limits to the scopes he can control or to the range of options available to him within each scope ('civil liberties'), and rights of appeal and petition concerning grievances.

If such measures are to be truly effective and not just window dressing, like the impressive constitutions created by so many absolute dictatorships in recent history, there must be sources of power independent of the integral power holder that can be mobilized to enforce them. The law must be a web that catches the lawmaker as well as his subjects. Conditions making this a reality may include the separation of executive, legislative and judicial powers within the government, the creation of different and independent levels of government as in federative states, divided rather than unified elites within society at large, and ultimately, strong support for constitutional guarantees or traditional 'unwritten' rights and liberties on the part of the power subjects. In other words, there must be real countervailing power centres able to enforce limits on the power of the integral power holder, and, insofar as this is required, the distinction between intercursive and integral power is not an absolute one. The checks on integral power, however, are largely negative. ...

There are four broad ways in which power subjects may attempt to combat or resist the power of an integral power holder: (1) they may strive to exercise countervailing power over him in order to transform his integral power into a system of intercursive power; (2) they may set limits to the extensiveness (the number of power subjects), comprehensiveness (the number of scopes), and intensity (the range of options within particular scopes) of his power; (3) they may destroy his integral power altogether, leaving the acts he formerly controlled open to free and self-determined choice; (4) they may seek to supplant him by acquiring and exercising his integral power themselves. ...

Such devices as the initiative, the referendum and impeachment by ballot, as well as the conception of elections as popular mandates, are established ways in which subjects exercise countervailing power over their rulers. The transformation of integral power into intercursive power, however, can never be complete in the case of modern states, in so far as there is an irreducibly integral element in political power that cannot be eliminated altogether. Bills of rights, constitutional guarantees, jurisdictional restrictions, and statutory limits on the options available to the political decision-maker are ways of checking the integral power of the state without eliminating it altogether by depriving the ruler of any scopes in which he can decide and act according to his own discretion. The removal of certain substantive areas of choice by power subjects from any control by the state—such as the 'basic' freedoms of speech, religion, assembly, residence, etc.—has the effect of eliminating the integral power of the state in these areas, though the total elimination of state power—the third choice above—has never been permanently realized in any civilized society. (It has, of course, been the goal of anarchism as a political movement.)

The *extensiveness* of a power relation may be narrow or broad. The former is illustrated by an isolated dyadic relation in which a single person exercises power over a single other, the latter by political regimes in which one man rules over millions of subjects. De Jouvenel mentions only the number of subjects, but the power holder may of course also be plural—there may be many As as well as many Bs. ...

The *comprehensiveness* of a power relation ... refers to the number of scopes over which the power holder holds power, or to the proportion or range of the power subject's total conduct and life-activity that is subject to control. At one extreme there is the power of a parent over an infant or young child, which is very nearly total in its comprehensiveness, extending to virtually everything the child does. At the other extreme, there is the very limited and specific power of the incumbents of highly specialized 'situated roles', such as those of a taxi dispatcher or a high-school student appointed to traffic safety patrol.

A third generic attribute of power relations is the *intensity* of the relation. If I understand correctly de Jouvenel's brief discussion of this attribute, he has in mind the range of effective options open to the power holder *within* each and every scope of the power subject's conduct over which he wields power. What limits are there to the actions which the power holder can influence the power subject to perform? Will the power subject commit suicide or murder under the power holder's influence? What intended effects sought by the power holder will be resisted, producing, at least initially, a breakdown of the power relation? ...

I have previously noted that formal statutory guarantees of 'the rights of man', or civil liberties, set limits both to the comprehensiveness and the intensity of power. In the former case, certain scopes are specifically excluded from the control of power holders, such as the freedoms of speech, assembly, religious worship, travel, and so on. Statutory limits on the intensity of power curtail the range of options available to the power holder within those scopes where he does have control. Thus the courts may possess the power to impose punishments on lawbreakers, but not 'cruel and unusual punishments'; a trade union certified as a collective bargaining agent may require a union shop, but not, under the Taft-Hartley Act, a closed shop. These examples refer to formal legal limitations on the intensity of a power relation within a given scope, but obviously, as the remark of Justice Holmes reflecting his famous legal positivism suggests, *de facto* limits are likely to be present in even the most informal, interpersonal power relations. At the pole of maximum intensity one might locate the relationship between a lover and a loved one where the former declares 'your wish is my command'—and means it. At the opposite pole stands the 'decision-maker' whose choices are confined to a very narrow range: a tax assessor, for example, who by statute can raise or lower tax rates by no more than a few percentage points. The tendency in some social science writing to identify 'decision-making' with the exercise of power can be misleading if the intensity of the decision-maker's power to decide is not taken into account. ...

What interrelationships are there among these three attributes of power relations? The most total and unlimited power, power that is greatest in comprehensiveness and intensity, is likely to be least extensive: namely, dyadic relations in which one person has power over a single other. As far back as Aristotle, the power of a master over a household slave has often served as the standard example of virtually unrestricted power. The power of a parent over a small child is another obvious example. The power of the loved one over the lover in a passionate, 'romantic' love relationship represents the most narrowly extensive and highly individualized form of power relation, since the relation is based entirely on the uniqueness of the particular individuals involved. A love relationship, however, is often a relatively balanced, or bilateral power relation between two individuals. A relationship between a sadist and a masochist best exemplifies a narrowly extensive but highly comprehensive and intensive interpersonal power relation.

A patriarch in the family, a tribal leader or a village despot may also wield highly comprehensive and intensive power over a relatively small number of subjects. The limited extensiveness of his power enables him to dispense with intermediaries to whom power is delegated and who as subordinate power holders may become potential rivals and has to be delegated from the top, and levels of power in a pyramidal or scalar power structure are less likely to emerge. This is a special case of the well-known generalization of organization theory that the larger the group and the more differentiated the activities of its members the greater the number of supervisory levels required if it is successfully to achieve its goals. ...

In summary, there are three main reasons why the greater extensiveness of a power relation sets limits to its comprehensiveness and intensity. First, the greater the number of power subjects, the greater the difficulty of supervising all of their activities. Second, the greater the number of power subjects, the more extended and differentiated the chain of command necessary to control them, creating new subordinate centres of power that can be played off against each other and that may themselves become foci of opposition to the integral power holder. Third, the greater the number of subjects, the greater the likelihood of wide variation in their attitudes toward the power-holder. The power-holder will not be able to wield power with equal comprehensiveness and intensity over all of his subjects. A few may be eager and pliant servants of his will, others will 'go along' less enthusiastically, still others will require constant supervision and threats to keep their performances in line, and there will be some against whom force must be used even to the extent of eliminating them from the ranks of the living.

2

Power as a Societal Force

AMITAI ETZIONI

POWER DEFINED

The realization of most societal goals, even in situations in which the actor's commitment and knowledge are considerable, requires the application of power. That is, under most circumstances, societal goals and decisions not supported by at least some degree of some kind of power will not be implemented. Hence, powerless actors are passive actors. The assumption which underlies these statements is that the realization of a societal goal requires introducing a change into societal relations, either in the societal environment or among the member units, and, as a rule, attempts to introduce changes (as distinct from changes that occur "anyhow," which do not constitute the realization of a goal), encounter some resistance. Unless this resistance is reduced, a course of action set will not be a course of action followed. *Power is a capacity to overcome part or all of the resistance, to introduce changes in the face of opposition* (this includes sustaining a course of action or preserving a status quo that would otherwise have been discontinued or altered).

Power is always relational and relative. An actor by himself is not powerful or weak; he may be powerful in relation to some actors in regard to some matters and weak in relation to other actors on other matters. Here, we are interested chiefly in the macroscopic consequences of the application of power; hence, we are concerned with societal power and not with the power of individuals or small groups, although several of the following statements and propositions apply to these units as well.

POWER AS AN OPERATIONAL CONCEPT

There has been considerable controversy about the definition of power for centuries. Without attempting to review this controversy here or to deal with its

18

many issues, let us briefly indicate our position on the question of whether or not the methodological difficulties involved in the use of the concept can be surmounted. The main methodological objection to the use of the concept of power is that power can be assessed only *post hoc*; we know that x has power only after he overcomes the resistance of y, and whether or not he can do so—it is said—is unknown until after he has done it. Such *post hoc* analysis has no predictive value. To avoid this difficulty, let us use "power" not for a single exercise of it on a single issue over a single subject at one point in time, but rather to refer to a generalized capacity of an actor, in his relations with others, to reduce resistance to the course of action he prefers in a given field (i.e., in the "presence" of other actors) about a set of matters over a period of time. This capacity can be anticipated with a certain degree of probability; on the basis of past instances of the exercise of power, the outcomes of future applications of power can be predicted. Even before an instance of the exercise of power has occurred, we can make probabilistic statements about the expected outcome. These are based on our estimates of the relative assets and the uses made of them by the actors in a given field, which can be studied before power is applied.

All of this is possible once the distinction between assets and power is recognized. Assets are possessions of an actor which *may* be converted into power but are not necessarily so used; hence, there is a systematic difference between the assets of an actor, which may be viewed as a power base or potential, and his actual capacity to reduce the resistance of others, which is the power actually generated. ... If assets and power are viewed as analytically identical, it is impossible to use the one to formulate predictions about the other.

There are three reasons that the concept of power as a generalized capacity that draws on an asset base but is not identical with it, is particularly useful. First, analysis becomes more realistic. When, for a particular line of action, an affluent actor does not mobilize more than a small fraction of his assets and thus loses to a poorer but more mobilized actor, this, in itself, often leads to a greater mobilization of the affluent actor and, in the long run, to his "victory." Atomistic power analysis, focusing on each instance on the exercise of power, would not be able to account systematically for the interplay between the loss of single campaigns and the winning of the whole drive. Collectivistic power analysis, focusing on differences in assets, may expect the affluent actor to prevail initially. Neither approach would alter the observer to the fact that in situation in which there are only a few rounds and the outcome is irreversible, the poor but highly mobilized actor who generated more power in the critical instance will tend to prevail. This applies, for instance, to movements of revolution or national independence (in systems which are poorly integrated) and to the passing of key legislation (in systems which are better integrated).

The second reason that the concept of power as a generalized capacity is particularly useful concerns the cross-sectoral application of power. Much has been said about the sectoral nature of power—that it cannot be deduced that an actor powerful in one area of societal activity will be powerful in other areas; again, the concept has been declared too fragmented to be fruitful. While we agree that power in one sector (e.g., in economic matters) does not necessarily imply power in others (e.g., in religion), there is nonetheless some halo effect; that is, the very capacity to have one's way in one area generates a degree of superordination in another area. ... This, we suggest, is in part because power in one sector tends to invoke some power in other sectors (although, as a rule, not commensurate) and in part because power in one sector can be "cashed" in another sector. ... Thus, an actor whose generalized power is greater will enjoy an advantage over the less powerful actor even in sectors where there is formal equality. The concept of generalized power calls our attention to these power projections.

A third reason that this concept seems useful is that it explains submission even when there is no actual exercise of power. This is because the subjects' considerations—like the application of power—are probabilistic; a small nation or a group of workers refrains from resisting not because it is certain that it will be punished (or, not rewarded) if it were to block the power wielders' course, but because the probability of being treated punitively is higher than it is willing to accept. On the other hand, if the controlling agents cannot exercise sanctions at least occasionally, their power will erode and resistance will rise, as subjective probabilities are adjusted. For all these reasons, in the following discussion "power" means a *generalized* capacity to reduce resistance.

Like energy, power is directly observable only when used. The power of a unit can be predicted by studying its assets, its total structure, and its past performances in this regard. But like the world of physical energy, there is no gain-for-nothing, for power has a cost; assets used to generate it are no longer available to the particular actor. If the asset base is not replenished, the probability of compliance will decline. ...

IS POWER UNIVERSAL?

The concept of power has provoked many debates concerning the socio-political stance it implies. As the concept is used here, the notion of resistance is central. The socio-political world implied is one composed of a plurality of societal actors, many of whom are committed to realizing one or more goals. Scarcity, we assume, prevails in the sense that the total amount of assets available is smaller than that needed to realize all of the goals of all of the actors. (Overcapacity or "affluence" might exist in this or that instrumental realm but is never universal.) Nor are all or even most of the goals of the actors shared or complementary. Hence, while the realization of some goals does not distract from the realization of some others and may even advance them, there is a significant degree of incompatibility among goals (in that the realization of some goals limits the realization of some others) and among means (in that the use of most means for most goals makes these means unavailable for the advancement of any other goal).

From the facts that there is a plurality of actors and of goals and a scarcity of instruments, it follows that societal actors will tend to "resist" each other in the sense of hampering each other's actions. This is not to imply, as has been suggested, that conflict is the prevailing mode of societal relations. Actors often do share some goals and work out a set of priorities among some other goals and a pattern of allocation of scarce instruments. But even if such cooperation and mutual understanding were eventually to encompass the full range of societ action (a situation hard to imagine), the specific pattern of priorities and allocation would still reflect the relative power of the various actors. The agreements reached between an adolescent and his parents, a new nation and a superpower, the poor and City Hall are almost invariably asymmetrical, as indicated both by the respective implementations of divisive (as distinct from complementary and shared) goals and by the respective shares of the scarce instruments and rewards obtained. ... In cooperative relations, power appears in the ability to eliminate all arrangements which differ from those finally reached. It is true that some concessions are made because of non-rational commitments to shared values—for instance, national pride. Also, in part, the arrangements reached reflect the sides' *estimates* of the outcome of a more explicit use of power. But while the outcomes of negotiations or arbitration rarely reflect only the sides' actual relative power, they usually are significantly affected by it—if not in each round, as the rounds accumulate.

Another reason that power and cooperation are fundamentally related is that patterns of cooperation are not worked out on an *ad hoc* basis or completely voluntarily among the actors concerned; cooperation is often imposed by third parties or is institutionalized and enforced as the result of previous arrangements among the actors. For instance, the degree of cooperation among the republics in Central America in part reflects the power the United States has over them; the degree of cooperation between management and labor is affected by the power the national government has over them as well as by enforceable agreements between them. Power and cooperation are, thus, not a mutually exclusive pair of concepts; cooperation often has a power base, and power is exercised through cooperation.

The tendency to associate power with conflict rather than with cooperation is part of a more general tendency to view power negatively. Hence, it should be emphasized that at least in macroscopic social structures, the realization of many values depends on a "proper" power constellation rather than on the elimination of the role of power. Thus, for instance, democratic processes presuppose a plurality of power centers, each strong enough to compete with the others but not so strong as to be able to undermine the societal framework in which the democratic competition takes place. And in societies in which the law prescribes civil and human rights for its members, the effective safeguard of these rights only in part rests with societal education and in the identification of various members with these values; they need also to be supported by at least a latent capacity for any group of citizens whose rights are denied to exert sufficient power to activate the societal mechanisms necessary to restore their rights. The same holds for "free enterprise" and "free" markets; they may exist between units similar in economic power but not between oil companies and gasoline stations or between automobile manufacturers and automobile dealers. To put it differently, the power relations among the member-units of a society and between that society and other societies are a major determinant of the degree to which that societal structure will be consonant or in conflict with the values to which the members "individually" and as a collective unit are committed. In short, effective universalism is not to be expected without an appropriate power distribution.

While power and conflict are not Siamese twins, they are intimately connected and frequently appear together. One reason that conflict is a common mode of societal relations rests in the poor societal knowledge most actors have of their potential power as compared to that of other relevant actors. The sources of societal power are many and varied and include such intangible elements as the capacity of a societal unit to mobilize the loyalties of the membership and the efficacy of its organization and elites. Therefore, it is usually difficult for even a detached observer to assess accurately the power of various actors, and when the assessor is himself an actor in the field, the reasons for misjudgment multiply. If the relative power of various societal units were completely measurable, and if there were a supreme judge who could adjust the patterns of priorities of shared projects and the allocation of assets not committed to shared projects—to the changing power assessments—societal conflict would be greatly reduced; a basic function of societal conflict is to substitute for the lack of such measurements and judges. Societal conflict is, therefore, an inherent element of macroscopic processes. It is a major (although by no means the only) expression of power—of the discrepancy between the capacity of an actor to produce change and the readiness of other actors in the field to agree, between the actual distribution of societal power and that which the prevailing stratification structure and political organization of society assume.

Power relations seem to be an inevitable feature of societal structure. It seems that there will always be a plurality of actors, each with a will of his own that is not completely complementary to, or shared by, all other actors, even if they all are members of one community. While the *intensity* of power declines as the scope of shared values and authentic consensus broadens, so long as there is a scarcity of assets and societal actors have a degree of autonomy, some actors will meet with some resistance from some other actors and will use part of their assets to reduce it in order to further their own goals. ...

To make power a central element of societal analysis is not to assume that other elements—especially goals and values, knowledge and commitment—are less important. On the contrary, we view societal power as a form of the mobilization of societal energy in the service of societal goals. Political elites might seek power for power's sake or, perhaps more accurately, rank the gaining of the instruments of power higher than any other particular goal they seek; but the societal consequences of power lie in the realization of societal goals, whether they be changes in the relations of the societal unit to its environment or the transformation of the societal self. To say that power is a universal feature of society is not to imply that power is omnipotent. A major limitation to power is the values to which actors are committed; actors restrain the use of power under certain circumstances because elites as well as followers *believe* they ought not to use whatever power they command in every situation.

Second, the power of any societal actor, however great, is limited by that of others. Writings in the "power-elite" tradition tend to overestimate the degree to which the power of business or the "military-industrial complex" is autonomous and unchecked. The narrow range of the power of American Presidents is well known, and the limitations of the power of even totalitarian leaders and parties are well documented. Power can be exercised only because—and to the extent that—the power potentials are unevenly distributed among the actors.

BETWEEN POWER AND COERCION

To generate power is not necessarily to rely on force or to be coercive. That there are other sources and means of power—for instance, economic assets—is too obvious to need comment. It is sometimes argued that all other kinds of power "ultimately" rely on force because it is used when economic or moral sanctions fail. While there are cases in which this is true, there are others in which force is not applied even though economic or moral sanctions were not heeded as, for example, in numerous business and interpersonal transactions and relations. Second, even when there is force "in the background," the other sanctions clearly play an autonomous role, for instance, in the likelihood that force will need to be applied.

What is less evident is that although power, by definition, assumes a capacity to reduce resistance, it is not necessarily coercive in the sense of eliminating all or most alternatives to the course imposed on the actors who are subjected to the exercise of power. Of course, power may be coercive; more often, however, power takes effect indirectly by altering the situation. Rather than preventing those subjected to power from following a course of action, it makes the course less attractive (and, by implication, the other alternatives more attractive). Here, the actors still can—if they are willing to pay the higher costs—pursue their original courses. Since few if any acts are without costs (even when these are outweighed by gains), the more common effect of the injection of power into a situation is to alter the costs rather than to destroy the capacity to choose. That is, there is frequently a voluntary element in submission; the unwillingness to pay the cost of not submitting.

Complete coercion occurs when the subjects are, in effect, deprived of the opportunity to choose—e.g., when a parent carries a child away from his toys, or when United States forces physically prevented Cuban exile organizations from raiding Castro's Cuba in 1963 by arresting the leaders and impounding the boats. It has been argued that even in the most coercive situation, the actors have a choice; they can choose to die rather than submit. It is a fact, though, that coercive controls are typically used to foreclose this option, too—to force the subjects to live in jail. The same may be said of collectivities under extreme totalitarian conditions.

There are situations which approximate this extreme case in which, in effect, alternatives are eliminated and the available choices are very skewed—e.g., there are only two alternatives and the penalty of choosing one of them is very high. Therefore, it seems useful to treat the concepts of coercion and noncoercion not as a dichotomy but as points on a continuum. Accordingly, coercion is used to refer to compliance relations in which there is or no effective choice. Noncoercive compliance includes utilitarian and normative reactions. By this definition, some but by no means all or even most power is coercive, initially or "ultimately."

Another reflection of the liberal tendency to evaluate power negatively, apparent in the inclination to make all power seem coercive, is the focusing upon the illicit uses of power. Actually, power might advance any societal goal, from conserving a status quo to altering it. The notion that evil is imposed by power while goodness flies on its own wings assumes an optimistic view of human nature and societal institutions that has little evidence to support it. The application of power is a principal way of getting things done. Its ethical standing depends in part on the ways in which goals are set and attained; these factors, in turn, depend much more on the distribution of power (what proportion of the members of a unit to which power is applied shares in setting the goals?) and on the amounts and kinds of power used (e.g., the degree of coercion) than on the very fact that power was exercised. *Hence, most societal actors must choose not between getting things done voluntarily or through the exercise of power, or between exercising power or not getting things done, but rather among the varying degrees and kinds of power to apply.* ...

ASSETS, POWER, AND ACTIVATION

An exploration of the complicated relations between the assets an actor commands and the power he wields is central for an understanding of the active orientation, because the capacity to act is greatly affected by the possessions of an actor *and* by what he does with these possessions. The common-sense view (and that of some political scientists) tends to estimate the power of an actor by an in-

ventory of his assets. Nations with a large territory, a large population, high production of steel, oil, ship tonnage, or railroad miles are viewed as strong nations.
Or, among sub-societies, the rich are viewed as powerful and the poor as weak.

Actually, the amount of assets an actor has determines only the collectivistic
context of his power, his power *potential* or base—that is, the amount of assets
on which he can draw to support his action. The proportion of these assets he
actually uses to generate power is a different, more organizational, more voluntaristic aspect of societal relations. Each actor constantly chooses, although often not consciously, how many of the assets he controls should be *consumed*
(used to satisfy immediate needs), *preserved* for later consumption, *invested* to increase his assets, and converted into societal power. Assets are, thus, a relatively
"stable" (or structural) aspect of societal relations, while power is more dynamic
(or processual).

The relation of power to assets is analogous to the relation of energy to material. The conversion of assets into power is not an abrupt "jump" but rather a
process of transformation. Various steps may be taken to activate the assets and
bring them closer to a power-yielding state without actually releasing the energy.
Such activation occurs, for instance, when a collectivity or society is preparing
for a conflict—whether it be a war, a strike, or a period of demonstrations. These
preparations are modern analogies to the primitives' war dances. Again, as in
thermodynamics or electronics, while societal assets or power potentials may be
accumulated and stored or activated in anticipation of future use, there are
some costs or "losses" involved since some of the potential energy is "dissi-
pated" and increasingly so as time passes. Thus, arms or means of production
grow obsolescent, and morale and leadership not actively engaged tend gradually to erode. ...

A CLASSIFICATION OF POWER

The conversion of assets into power generates a variety of sanctions, rewards,
and instruments to penalize those who resist, to reward those who assist, to remove those who block, and to provide facilities for those who implement a col-
lectively-set course of action. These sanctions, rewards, and instruments differ
in their substance: They are either physical, material, or symbolic. This makes
for a threefold classification of assets and power: Power is either coercive (e.g.,
military forces), utilitarian (e.g., economic sanctions), or persuasive (e.g., propaganda). The classification is exhaustive. Each concrete application of the use of
power is either one of the three or is composed of their various combinations. ...

Utilitarian assets include economic possessions, technical and administrative
capabilities, manpower, etc. Utilitarian power is generated when these assets are
applied or exchanged in such a fashion as to allow the unit which possesses
them to bring other units to support its line of action.

Coercive assets are the weapons, installations, and manpower which the military, the police, or similar agencies use. There is a thin line between utilitarian and coercive assets; civilians may be inducted into the military and factories might be converted to military use. But so long as such a conversion has not occurred, these means will not be viewed as coercive assets. Coercive power (or force) results when one unit uses coercive assets to impose its preferred course of action on others. Note that coercion refers here to the employment of violent means and not to pressure in a more generic sense. Or, to put it differently, coercive power refers to the use of force and not to other means of enforcement.

Persuasive power is exercised through the manipulation of symbols, such as appeals to the values and sentiments of the citizens, in order to mobilize support and to penalize those who deviate (e.g., by excommunicating them). Unlike utilitarian and coercive power, two concepts which are frequently applied, the concept of persuasive power is not widely used and raises several analytic problems which need to be discussed briefly, especially since the relations between assets and power are less evident in regard to persuasion then with respect to the other two categories.

The normative bonds of societal units, the bases of persuasive power, are often perceived as either resting on personal attitudes and interpersonal relations or as having no structural and organizational base at all. Actually, the capacity to persuade is not randomly distributed in social systems. For instance, in societies in which the church is a main source of persuasive power, the power-holders themselves constitute a hierarchy with a variety of goals, in the pursuit of which the hierarchy brings its power to bear. And the secular authorities which have the church's blessing possess access to a source of power that other secular authorities do not. In the Spanish civil war, for example, Franco was granted such support and the Republicans were undermined. Similarly, in democratic societies, access to the mass media is a source of persuasive power that is more available to political incumbents then to the opposition; in totalitarian societies, this source of persuasive power is largely monopolized by the establishment. In short, persuasive power is structured and organized, allocated and applied, in much the same ways as other kinds of power. ...

The socialization of a people, the values to which they subscribe and the intensity with which they hold them, largely determines the scope and limits of persuasive "assets." At each point in time, we suggest, the values to which actors are committed cannot quickly be changed because these commitments are the result of slow processes. These commitments are assets to those who can appeal to the values and to a power potential not available to those who seek to promote a course of action outside the context of the possible courses of action which these values approve. While commitment to a new value can be developed and then used to support a line of action, this is a much more costly process than appealing to a value that has already been internalized. Hence, the existing distribution of values almost invariably provides an advantage for some lines of action—and of persuasion—over others. The amount of these assets can be measured either in terms of the costs and efforts that were necessary to create and reinforce the relevant commitments (or those which would be required to alter them) or in terms of the scope and amount of action that can be generated by drawing upon them.

The greater the potential appeal of these values and symbols, the larger will be the amount of the persuasive assets of the unit under examination. Persuasive assets are transformed into persuasive power when a member-unit or a system-elite succeeds in demonstrating that a particular course of action which it seeks other units or all member-units to follow is consistent with or an expression of those values and symbols to which the other units are committed.

POWER, INFLUENCE, AND AUTHORITY

Influence and power are often used synonymously. We suggest, however, that it is useful to keep these two terms separate in order to express a significant conceptual distinction. An application of *power* changes the actor's situation and/or his conception of his situation—but not his preferences. Resistance is overcome not because the actor subjected to the use of power changes his "will" but because resistance has been made more expensive, prohibitive, or impossible. The exercise of *influence* entails an authentic change in the actor's preferences; given the same situation, he would not choose the same course of action he favored before influence was exercised. While from the power-wielders' viewpoint, the difference between the two might be relatively small (the exercise of influence also consumes assets though it produces fewer or no counter-currents), from the subjects' viewpoint, it is more significant in that influence involves not suspension or suppression of their preferences but a respecification of their commitments.

Of the three kinds of power, persuasive power is the most similar to influence, since both are symbolic and draw on values and sentiments. The difference between them rests in the depth of their effects; persuasion suppresses the actor's preferences without changing them; it, hence, resembles influence on the surface, but there is really an exercise of power beneath. The difference between persuasion and influence is analogous to the difference between propaganda and education. When persuasive power is very effective and influence is superficial, the two are very similar, but in general, it is not difficult to distinguish one from the other. ...

Both concepts are related to the concepts of authority and legitimation. *Authority* is defined as legitimate power—that is, power that is used in accord with the subject's values and under conditions he views as proper. But even power that is completely legitimate may still support a course of action that is not desired by the subject and is therefore alienating. This is because the course of action, legitimate or not, is still not an expression of the subject's preferences.

Army officers who take their men into battle have the right to do so, a right which the subjects may acknowledge, but this does not necessarily make combat a course of action preferred by the subjects. Illegitimate power is doubly alienating, because the action is both undesirable *and* violates the sense of right and wrong. But if an authorized individual orders the same act, this still would not make the act desirable. Paying taxes to a rejected government, such as a colonial one, after the people's consciousness has been aroused by a national independence movement as compared to paying taxes to one's own government when identification with it is high illustrates the difference. Legitimation and satisfaction are not to be confused. On the other hand, when influence is exercised, the act does become desirable even if the influence were illegitimate (although, as a rule, a full measure of influence would require that it be legitimate in terms of the subject's values). ...

3

Forms and Levels
of Power Exertion

MARVIN E. OLSEN

A broadly inclusive concept such as social power becomes more useful for sociological analysis if it can be divided into several relatively distinct categories. With the process of power exertion, this division is frequently made along two different dimensions: forms and levels. The various forms of power exertion pertain to the manner in which social power is exercised. The levels of power exertion refer to the scope of this process. Four forms and three levels into which power exertion is frequently divided are described in this chapter.

FOUR FORMS OF SOCIAL POWER

Four fairly distinct forms of social power often identified by sociologists are force, dominance, authority, and attraction. The major differences between these forms of power lie in the nature of the resources on which they are based and the manner in which they are exercised. *Force,* the exertion of social pressures, requires the actor to utilize relatively specific resources that were previously uncommitted. *Dominance* results from the performance of established social roles or functions, so that the actor draws on a broad set of resources that have already been committed. *Authority,* the right to issue directives, rests on specific grants of legitimacy to the actor from the recipients of those directives. *Attraction* is the ability to affect others because of who one is, so that the actor draws on an array of personal resources that are already being utilized.

Force

Force is a form of social power that involves *the intentional exertion of social pressures on others to achieve desired outcomes.* To employ force, an actor must commit specific resources to the situation that were not previously being utilized and then convert them into pressures—or convincingly threaten to do so. (Force can involve the threatened or actual withdrawal of resources that were previously flowing to the recipient, but carrying out the threat also requires the expenditure of additional resources.) Even if one successfully bluffs the recipients into following one's wishes, the involved resources are committed to that power relationship for the duration of its existence and cannot simultaneously be used elsewhere. In most situations, however, the actor will have to expend part or all of the committed resources to attain his or her objective. To the extent that many kinds of resources are limited in quantity or availability, an actor's ability to exercise force is correspondingly restricted, although gross disparities obviously occur among actors in the amounts and kinds of resources they possess and hence the amount of force they can exercise.

Force can be exerted in three different ways, depending on the manner in which the involved resources are employed. As suggested by Amitai Etzioni (1968), these are commonly called utilitarian, coercive, and persuasive force. In the following descriptions, the power exerter is referred to as actor A and the power recipient is actor B.

With *utilitarian* force, A provides new or additional desired resources. In return, B does what A requests. This kind of force, which is also called "reward power," or "inducement power," is illustrated by the payment of wages for work. Such arrangements are usually seen as relatively voluntary for B, although if B has no employment opportunities except working for A at whatever wages are offered, it is voluntary only in the sense that B chooses not to starve. As long as B is satisfied with the arrangement, however, it can endure for some time. For A, meanwhile, it can be costly because he or she must continue to supply resources to B.

With *coercive* force, A withdraws (or threatens to withdraw) desired resources that are being transferred to B or transfers (or threatens to transfer) undesired resources to B. To avoid those possibilities, B does what A demands. This kind of force, which is also called "punishment power," or "constraint power," is illustrated by an employee receiving a written reprimand or being demoted. Such an action is often seen as less voluntary for B than utilitarian force, although B usually has the choice of leaving the relationship (unless the punishment involves physical confinement or death). Coercive force can be less costly for A than utilitarian force, especially when threats accomplish the desired end, but in either case, B's obedience is usually given grudgingly and hence remains unreliable.

With *persuasive* force, A transfers verbal messages (which are a type of resource) that convince B to do what A suggests. Those messages may convey information, emotions, beliefs, or values; this kind of force is also called "information power," or "communication power." B accepts and follows A's suggestion because he or she decides that it is rational, beneficial, ethical, or socially responsible to do so. For example, an employer might persuade a worker to perform a task in a different way (because it would be more efficient or acceptable to coworkers) without overtly rewarding or punishing the employee. Persuasion is usually viewed by both A and B as the most desirable way of exerting force. For A, the verbal resources that are transferred are essentially unlimited, so the only cost involved is the effort required to be persuasive. If A is sufficiently persuasive, this may increase B's respect for A and thus enhance A's ability to use persuasion in future situations. Moreover, because persuasion often produces relatively permanent cognitive or attitudinal changes in B, its effects can be quite enduring and reliable and so continue long after the persuasion has occurred. For B, persuasion normally involves the greatest possibility for choice, because he or she usually has complete freedom to decide whether or not to be persuaded. In some situations, however, the persuasive message is so subtle (as in subliminal advertising) that B is not aware of receiving it, and in other situations, B may be essentially incapable of resisting it (as when it evokes very strong emotions).

Dominance

Dominance is a form of social power that results from *the performance of established roles or functions.* To exert dominance, an actor must effectively carry out those functions. Although this requires the ongoing expenditure of already committed resources, the actor need not commit any additional resources to the situation. This process, in other words, relies entirely on the normal performance of existing functional activities. As actors become functionally specialized and hence interdependent, they are vulnerable to the actions of others on whom they depend. To the extent that actors B, C, and D are dependent on the actions of A, A will exert dominance over them through the performance of those actions. Even if A makes no intentional attempt to exercise power, whatever A does will affect B, C, and D. If A intentionally seeks to influence B, C, or D, that can often be accomplished quite easily through small alterations in A's activities that involve shifts in resource flows but require no additional resources.

Dominance is often observed in activities that involve, for example, information flows, economic networks, transportation services, and governmental decision making. Dominance can occur, however, within any organized activity in which the participants are functionally specialized and interdependent. Actors at the top or center of an organization as well as key functionaries such as boundary gatekeepers and communication channelers are often in a particularly advantageous position to exert dominance over a wide range of organizational activities. Nevertheless, any actor within an organization can exercise some amount of dominance to the extent that others are functionally dependent on that actor.

Functional dominance is illustrated by the role that banks play in business networks. Because corporations often find it necessary to borrow large sums of capital from banks, this indebtedness makes them dependent on banks. Banks can, therefore, determine the extent to which corporations grow. In addition, major banks often own large blocks of stock in those corporations to which they loan money. Those banks often place one of their officers on the board of directors of each corporation with which they deal to be able to influence corporate policies if necessary. In these ways, major banks exercise considerable dominance throughout the economy.

In most functional arrangements, all of the participants are interdependent to some extent, so that dominance occurs in all directions in varying ways and degrees. Corporations B, C, and D may depend on bank A for capital loans, but the bank depends on the interest from those loans for its profits. In practice, an actor may use a position of dominance to exert force on others by threatening to withdraw resources from ongoing functional relationships or by actually doing so. Such an action compounds the total process of power exertion that is occurring, but does not erase the distinction between dominance and force.

Authority

Authority involves *the right to issue directives to others who must accept them.* To exercise authority, an actor must be granted legitimacy by the recipients of those directives and must be given the right to make decisions and issue directives in particular situations. That legitimacy, which is usually fairly specific in nature, becomes the resource base for exercising authoritative power. The resource for exercising authority thus originates in the recipients, not in the wielder of power (as occurs with force and dominance). The exerciser of authority then draws on that grant of legitimacy to request or demand compliance with his or her directives, and the recipients are expected to comply voluntarily because they have agreed that those directives are legitimate. Directives by government officials, for instance, are normally authoritative in nature because the citizens have invested legitimacy in the government and the officials are exercising governmental authority. In practice, governmental directives—and most exercises of authority in other realms—are reinforced by the implicit or explicit threat to use force if necessary to enforce those directives. That practice, however, does not eliminate the distinction between authority and force.

The legitimate right to exercise authority can be granted to an actor in many different ways. These include formal procedures (e.g., elections of public officials, legal constitutions, and contracts), semiformal agreements among the members of a group (e.g., that one person will act as chair), and informal understandings among individuals (e.g., a husband who lets his wife choose their furniture). When a person goes to work for a company, that individual implicitly agrees to abide by the decisions of its executives. When a person becomes the patient of a physician, he or she is granting the physician the legitimate right to treat his or her body. Finally, in many voluntary associations, the members implicitly grant legitimacy to the organization and its leaders simply by remaining members of that organization.

Max Weber (1947:324–325) identified four bases on which legitimate authority often rests within societies: *rational knowledge* or expertise relevant to a specific situation; *legal rights* based on formal arrangements; *traditional beliefs and values* sanctified by time; and the *charismatic appeal* of revered leaders to their followers. (Weber combined the first and second bases under the heading of "rational-legal authority" because he thought that they were usually combined in modern societies; but subsequent research has demonstrated that much of the time they are quite separate.) In addition, authority frequently rests on *passive acceptance* resulting from established customs and conventions. The recipients do not overtly grant legitimacy to the authority wielder but simply follow his or her directives out of habit, an act which constitutes an implicit grant of legitimacy. Any one of these bases can be sufficient to give an actor legitimate authority, but if two or more of them can be utilized, the actor's legitimacy is considerably strengthened.

Because authority is a highly stable and reliable form of power exertion, organizational leaders almost invariably seek to protect and extend their legitimacy, no matter how they initially acquired their positions or how extensively they also utilize other forms of power. Even if a government comes to power through a violent revolution and controls its society with coercion, it will still seek to create an image of legitimacy by using tools such as plebiscites and propaganda. It can hardly afford to do otherwise: Without secure legitimacy, its ability to exercise authority is severely restricted and its ability to govern is constantly in jeopardy.

Attraction

Attraction is a form of social power that lies in *the ability of an actor to affect others because of who he or she is.* To use attraction, the actor draws on some kind of appeal that he or she has for others. That appeal usually rests on a diffuse set of personal characteristics that are not necessarily intended to create social power. Nevertheless, if an actor possesses characteristics that are appealing to others, he or she may be able to utilize that appeal to influence those people. As with authority, the recipients of this power give something to the exerciser of power, but in this case it is positive feelings rather than a grant of legitimacy (although appeal can subsequently lead to the granting of legitimacy). Another difference between authority and attraction is that the appeal on which attraction rests occurs independently from any exertion of attractive power, whereas legitimacy is always closely tied to the exertion of authority.

An example of attraction power would be a religious leader who convinces people to join a cult because they believe that the leader is an embodiment of the "divine spirit." Although they follow that leader for religious reasons, they may be willing to do anything he or she says—from donating to the leader all their worldly possessions to committing mass suicide. If they granted the leader only the legitimate right to make decisions about their cult, that would be authority; but if he or she is so appealing that they subordinate themselves entirely, that is a very strong form of attraction. This process is also quite common in political and social movements as well as in interpersonal relations among individuals.

Sometimes attraction is exerted almost entirely unintentionally, as when the fans of an entertainment star copy his or her clothing styles and mannerisms without the star's being aware of the example set for the admirers. Much of the time, however, attraction is intentionally manipulated to influence others. A prominent sports figure, for instance, may be paid a large sum of money by a manufacturer of sports equipment to use its products, in hopes of influencing potential customers.

Three common bases of the appeal that underlies attraction power are cognitive *identification* with, *affective* feelings toward, and attribution of *charisma* to an individual (or sometimes to an organization). Charisma, or the belief by others that a person or organization possesses some kind of special and unique qualities, is by far the strongest of these bases, although the other two bases are more common in ordinary life.

Because attraction rests on these kinds of psychological and emotional appeals, it tends to be quite unstable and unreliable, but at times it can become extremely compelling. In practice, attraction often shades into force (as the appealing actor also rewards or punishes his or her followers) or into authority (as charismatic or affective appeals are used to claim legitimacy).

All four forms of power exertion—force, dominance, authority, and attraction—occur throughout all realms of social life. In practice, they commonly become highly interwoven, as actors convert one form to another or use one form to supplement another. Nevertheless, the four forms of power exertion are quite distinct in their resource bases and the manner in which they are exercised.

THREE LEVELS OF SOCIAL POWER

The process of power exertion can also be categorized into three levels, as determined by its scope. These levels are sometimes referred to as the three "dimensions" of power (Lukes, 1974), but that term is not fully appropriate for this set of categories. Whereas the various dimensions of any phenomenon are presumed to be independent of one another, these three levels of power exertion are cumulative, so that the second level always incorporates the first one and the third level always incorporates both of the other two (Clegg, 1989:90).

First Level

At the first level of power exertion, *actors make decisions and take actions that affect others.* Consequently, this level of power exertion is often referred to as "decision-making power." Most analyses of social power have focused on this level because it is usually fairly observable. First-level power exertion occurs whenever two (or more) actors conflict over interests that they view as incompatible, and one of those actors makes a decision and takes an action that affects the other(s), despite whatever resistance is offered. Robert Dahl's (1956) study of the process through which community decisions are made on controversial public issues is often cited as an example of this level of power. As described by Steven Lukes (1974:15), this first level of power exertion is concerned with "the making of decisions on issues over which there is an observable conflict of (subjective) interests."

Second Level

At the middle level of power exertion, *actors prevent decisions from being made or actions from being taken by others.* Consequently, the second level of power exertion is often referred to as "nondecision-making power." The actors who exercise power at this level are able to prevent others from making decisions or taking actions because of the positions they occupy and the roles they enact within organizations. This level of power exertion may be as common in social life as it is in decision making, although it is less frequently observed because it tends to occur "behind the scenes." The concept of nondecision making was initially applied to politics by Peter Bachrach and Morton Baratz (1962:8) who pointed out that "to the extent that a person or group ... creates or reinforces barriers to the public airing of policy conflicts, that person or group has power." Lukes (1974:20) later expanded the concept to all power exertion when he described it as "the ways in which decisions are prevented from being taken on potential issues over which there is an observable conflict of (subjective) interests."

Third Level

At the highest level of power exertion, *actors shape the overall settings in which issues are defined and decisions are made and hence define the parameters for the exercise of power.* Consequently, the third level of power exertion is often referred to as "agenda setting." The actors who exercise power at this level are able to shape broad social contexts and determine which issues or topics are open to consideration and decision making and which are not. Quite commonly, they occupy powerful positions or enact critical roles at the top or center of established power structures. This level of power exertion is much broader in scope than the first two and probably less common, although its occurrence is always difficult to ascertain because it is usually kept hidden from public view. Lukes (1974:21–25), who formulated this concept of a third level of power exertion, placed heavy emphasis on the distinction between objective and subjective interests. Whereas the first two levels involve perceived (or subjective) interests, the third focuses on actual (or objective) interests. Power exertion at this level, according to Lukes (1974:25), involves "a latent conflict which consists in a contradiction between the interests of those exercising power and the *real interests* of those they exclude."

Tom Baumgartner and colleagues (1976:225) refer to the exercise of power at the third level as "meta-power," which consists of "exercising power to shape the aggregate action and interaction possibilities of those involved in the situation, i.e., to remove certain actions from their repertoires and to create or facilitate others." More recently, Robert Perrucci and Harry Potter (1989:7–8) have suggested that organizational networks can be viewed as interorganizational power structures—or "networks of power"—that exercise considerable meta-power throughout modern societies.

REFERENCES

Bachrach, Peter, and Morton Baratz. 1962. "The Two Faces of Power," *American Political Science Review* 56:947–952.

Baumgartner, Tom, Walter Buckley, Tom R. Burns, and Peter Schuster. 1976. "Meta-Power and the Structuring of Social Hierarchies," in Tom R. Burns and Walter Buckley, eds., *Power and Control: Social Structures and Their Transformation*, Ch. 10. London: Sage Publications.

Clegg, Stewart R. 1989. *Frameworks of Power*. London: Sage Publications.

Dahl, Robert A. 1956. *Who Governs?* New Haven: Yale University Press.

Etzioni, Amitai. 1968. *The Active Society*. New York: Free Press.

Lukes, Steven. 1974. *Power: A Radical View*. London: Macmillan Press.

Perrucci, Robert, and Harry R. Potter. 1989. "The Collective Actor in Organizational Analysis." In Robert Perrucci and Harry R. Potter, eds., *Networks of Power*, pp. 1–15. New York: Aldine de Gruyter.

Weber, Max. 1947. *The Theory of Social and Economic Organization*, trans. by A. M. Henderson and Talcott Parsons. Glencoe, Ill.: Free Press.

4

Power, Domination, and Legitimacy

MAX WEBER

POWER AND DOMINATION

A. "Power" (*Macht*) is the probability that one actor within a social relationship will be in a position to carry out his own will despite resistance, regardless of the basis on which this probability rests.

B. "Domination" (*Herrschaft*) is the probability that a command with a given specific content will be obeyed by a given group of persons. "Discipline" is the probability that by virtue of habituation a command will receive prompt and automatic obedience in stereotyped forms, on the part of a given group of persons.

1. The concept of power is sociologically amorphous. All conceivable qualities of a person and all conceivable combinations of circumstances may put him in a position to impose his will in a given situation. The sociological concept of domination must hence be more precise and can only mean the probability that a *command* will be obeyed.
2. The concept of discipline includes the habituation characteristic of uncritical and unresisting mass obedience.

C. The existence of domination turns only on the actual presence of one person successfully issuing orders to others; it does not necessarily imply either the existence of an administrative staff or, for that matter, of an organization. It is, however, uncommon to find it unrelated to at least one of these. A "ruling organization" (*Herrschaftsverband*) exists insofar as its members are subject to domination by virtue of the established order.

1. The head of a household rules without an administrative staff. A Bedouin chief, who levies contributions from the caravans, persons and

shipments which pass his stronghold, controls this group of changing individuals, who do not belong to the same organization, as soon and as long as they face the same situation; but to do this, he needs a following which, on the appropriate occasions, serves as his administrative staff in exercising the necessary compulsion. (However, it is theoretically conceivable that this type of control is exercised by a single individual.)

2.   If it possesses an administrative staff, an organization is always to some degree based on domination. But the concept is relative. In general, an effectively ruling organization is also an administrative one. The character of the organization is determined by a variety of factors: the mode in which the administration is carried out, the character of the personnel, the objects over which it exercises control, and the extent of effective jurisdiction. The first two factors in particular are dependent in the highest degree on the way in which domination is legitimized.

DOMINATION AND LEGITIMACY

Domination was defined above as the probability that certain specific commands (or all commands) will be obeyed by a given group of persons. It thus does not include every mode of exercising "power" or "influence" over other persons. Domination ("authority") in this sense may be based on the most diverse motives of compliance: all the way from simple habituation to the most purely rational calculation of advantage. Hence every genuine form of domination implies a minimum of voluntary compliance, that is, an *interest* (based on ulterior motives or genuine acceptance) in obedience.

Not every case of domination makes use of economic means; still less does it always have economic objectives. However, normally the rule over a considerable number of persons requires a staff, that is, a *special* group which can normally be trusted to execute the general policy as well as the specific commands. The members of the administrative staff may be bound to obedience to their superior (or superiors) by custom, by affectual ties, by a purely material complex of interests, or by ideal (*wertrationale*) motives. The quality of these motives largely determines the type of domination. *Purely* material interests and calculations of advantages as the basis of solidarity between the chief and his administrative staff result, in this as in other connexions, in a relatively unstable situation. Normally other elements, affectual and ideal, supplement such interests. In certain exceptional cases the former alone may be decisive. In everyday life these relationships, like others, are governed by custom and material calculation of advantage. But custom, personal advantage, purely affectual or ideal motives of solidarity, do not form a sufficiently reliable basis for a given domination. In addition there is normally a further element, the belief in *legitimacy*.

Experience shows that in no instance does domination voluntarily limit itself to the appeal to material or affectual or ideal motives as a basis for its continuance. In addition every such system attempts to establish and to cultivate the belief in its legitimacy. But according to the kind of legitimacy which is claimed, the type of obedience, the kind of administrative staff developed to guarantee it, and the mode of exercising authority, will all differ fundamentally. Equally fundamental is the variation in effect. Hence, it is useful to classify the types of domination according to the kind of claim to legitimacy typically made by each. In doing this, it is best to start from modern and therefore more familiar examples. ...

THE THREE PURE TYPES OF AUTHORITY

There are three pure types of legitimate domination. The validity of the claims to legitimacy may be based on:

1. Rational grounds—resting on a belief in the legality of enacted rules and the right of those elevated to authority under such rules to issue commands (legal authority).

2. Traditional grounds—resting on an established belief in the sanctity of immemorial traditions and the legitimacy of those exercising authority under them (traditional authority); or finally,

3. Charismatic grounds—resting on devotion to the exceptional sanctity, heroism or exemplary character of an individual person, and of the normative patterns or order revealed or ordained by him (charismatic authority).

In the case of legal authority, obedience is owed to the legally established impersonal order. It extends to the persons exercising the authority of office under it by virtue of the formal legality of their commands and only within the scope of authority of the office. In the case of traditional authority, obedience is owed to the *person* of the chief who occupies the traditionally sanctioned position of authority and who is (within its sphere) bound by tradition. But here the obligation of obedience is a matter of personal loyalty within the area of accustomed obligations. In the case of charismatic authority, it is the charismatically qualified leader as such who is obeyed by virtue of personal trust in his revelation, his heroism or his exemplary qualities so far as they fall within the scope of the individual's belief in his charisma.

1. The usefulness of the above classification can only be judged by its results in promoting systematic analysis. ...

2. The fact that none of these three ideal types ... is usually to be found in historical cases in "pure" form, is naturally not a valid objection to attempting their conceptual formulation in the sharpest possible form. ...

Legal Authority

Legal authority rests on the acceptance of the validity of the following mutually inter-dependent ideas.

1. That any given legal norm may be established by agreement or by imposition, on grounds of expediency or value-rationality or both, with a claim to obedience at least on the part of the members of the organization. This is, however, usually extended to include all persons within the sphere of power in question—which in the case of territorial bodies is the territorial area—who stand in certain social relationships or carry out forms of social action which in the order governing the organization have been declared to be relevant.

2. That every body of law consists essentially in a consistent system of abstract rules which have normally been intentionally established. Furthermore, administration of law is held to consist in the application of these rules to particular cases; the administrative process in the rational pursuit of the interests which are specified in the order governing the organization within the limits laid down by legal precepts and following principles which are capable of generalized formulation and are approved in the order governing the group, or at least not disapproved in it.

3. That thus the typical person in authority, the "superior," is himself subject to an impersonal order by orienting his actions to it in his own dispositions and commands. (This is true not only for persons exercising legal authority who are in the usual sense "officials," but, for instance, for the elected president of a state.)

4. That the person who obeys authority does so, as it is usually stated, only in his capacity as a "member" of the organization and what he obeys is only "the law." (He may in this connection be the member of an association, of a community, of a church, or a citizen of a state.)

5. In conformity with point 3, it is held that the members of the organization, insofar as they obey a person in authority, do not owe this obedience to him as an individual, but to the impersonal order. Hence, it follows that there is an obligation to obedience only within the sphere of the rationally delimited jurisdiction which, in terms of the order, has been given to him.

The following may thus be said to be the fundamental categories of rational legal authority:

(1) A continuous rule-bound conduct of official business.

(2) A specified sphere of competence (jurisdiction). This involves: (a) A sphere of obligations to perform functions which has been marked off as part of a systematic division of labor. (b) The provision of the incumbent with the necessary powers. (c) That the necessary means of compulsion are clearly defined and their use is subject to definite conditions. A unit exercising authority which is organized in this way will be called an "administrative organ" or "agency" (*Behörde*). ...

(3) The organization of offices follows the principle of hierarchy; that is, each lower office is under the control and supervision of a higher one. There is a right of appeal and of statement of grievances from the lower to the higher. Hierarchies differ in respect to whether and in what cases complaints can lead to a

"correct" ruling from a higher authority itself, or whether the responsibility for such changes is left to the lower office, the conduct of which was the subject of the complaint.

(4) The rules which regulate the conduct of an office may be technical rules or norms. In both cases, if their application is to be fully rational, specialized training is necessary. It is thus normally true that only a person who has demonstrated an adequate technical training is qualified to be a member of the administrative staff of such an organized group, and hence only such persons are eligible for appointment to official positions. The administrative staff of a rational organization thus typically consists of "officials," whether the organization be devoted to political, hierocratic, economic—in particular, capitalistic—or other ends.

(5) In the rational type it is a matter of principle that the members of the administrative staff should be completely separated from ownership of the means of production or administration. Officials, employees, and workers attached to the administrative staff do not themselves own the non-human means of production and administration. These are rather provided for their use, in kind or in money, and the official is obligated to render an accounting of their use. There exists, furthermore, in principle complete separation of the organization's property (respectively, capital), and the personal property (household) of the official. There is a corresponding separation of the place in which official functions are carried out—the "office" in the sense of premises—from the living quarters.

(6) In the rational type case, there is also a complete absence of appropriation of his official position by the incumbent. Where "rights" to an office exist, as in the case of judges, and recently of an increasing proportion of officials and even of workers, they do not normally serve the purpose of appropriation by the official, but of securing the purely objective and independent character of the conduct of the office so that it is oriented only to the relevant norms.

(7) Administrative acts, decision, and rules are formulated and recorded in writing, even in cases where oral discussion is the rule or is even mandatory. This applies at least to preliminary discussions and proposals, to final decisions, and to all sorts of orders and rules. The combination of written documents and a continuous operation by officials constitutes the "office" (*Bureau*) which is the central focus of all types of modern organized action.

(8) Legal authority can be exercised in a wide variety of different forms which will be distinguished and discussed later. The following ideal-typical analysis will be deliberately confined for the time being to the administrative staff that is most unambiguously a structure of domination: "officialdom" or "bureaucracy." ...

Traditional Authority

Authority will be called traditional if legitimacy is claimed for it and believed in by virtue of the sanctity of age-old rules and powers. The masters are designated according to traditional rules and are obeyed because of their traditional status (*Eigenwürde*). This type of organized rule is, in the simplest case, primarily based on personal loyalty which results from common upbringing. The person exercising authority is not a "superior," but a personal master, his administrative staff does not consist mainly of officials but of personal retainers, and the ruled are not "members" of an association but are either his traditional "comrades" or his "subjects." Personal loyalty, not the official's impersonal duty, determines the relations of the administrative staff to the master.

Obedience is owed not to enacted rules but to the person who occupies a position of authority by tradition or who has been chosen for it by the traditional master. The commands of such a person are legitimized in one of two ways: (a) partly in terms of traditions which themselves directly determine the content of the command and are believed to be valid within certain limits that cannot be overstepped without endangering the master's traditional status; (b) partly in terms of the master's discretion in that sphere which tradition leaves open to him; this traditional prerogative rests primarily on the fact that the obligations of personal obedience tend to be essentially unlimited. Thus there is a double sphere: (a) that of action which is bound to specific traditions; (b) that of action which is free of specific rules.

In the latter sphere, the master is free to do good turns on the basis of his personal pleasure and likes, particularly in return for gifts—the historical sources of dues (*Gebühren*). So far as his action follows principles at all, these are governed by considerations of ethical common sense, of equity or of utilitarian expediency. They are not formal principles, as in the case of legal authority. The exercise of power is oriented toward the consideration of how far master and staff can go in view of the subjects' traditional compliance without arousing their resistance. When resistance occurs, it is directed against the master or his servant personally, the accusation being that he failed to observe the traditional limits of his power. Opposition is not directed against the system as such—it is a case of "traditionalist revolution."

In the pure type of traditional authority it is impossible for law or administrative rule to be deliberately created by legislation. Rules which in fact are innovations can be legitimized only by the claim that they have been "valid of yore," but have only now been recognized by means of "Wisdom" [the *Weistum* of ancient Germanic law]. Legal decisions as "finding of the law" (*Rechstfindung*) can refer only to documents of tradition, namely to precedents and earlier decisions. ...

Gerontocracy and *primary patriarchalism* are the most elementary types of traditional domination where the master has no personal administrative staff.

The term gerontocracy is applied to a situation where so far as rule over the group is organized at all it is in the hands of elders—which originally was understood literally as the eldest in actual years, who are the most familiar with the sacred traditions. This is common in groups which are not primarily of an economic or kinship character. "Patriarchalism" is the situation where, within a group (household) which is usually organized on both an economic and a kinship basis, a particular individual governs who is designated by a definite rule of inheritance. Gerontocracy and patriarchalism are frequently found side by side. The decisive characteristic of both is the belief of the members that domination, even though it is an inherent traditional right of the master, must definitely be exercized as joint right in the interest of all members and is thus not freely appropriated by the incumbent. In order that this shall be maintained, it is crucial that in both cases there is a complete absence of a personal (patrimonial) staff. Hence the master is still largely dependent upon the willingness of the members to comply with his orders since he has no machinery to enforce them. Therefore, the members (*Genossen*) are not yet really subjects (*Untertanen*).

Their membership exists by tradition and not by enactment. Obedience is owed to the mster, not to any enacted regulation. However, it is owed to the master only by virtue of his traditional status. He is thus on his part strictly bound by tradition. ...

Patrimonialism and, on the extreme case, *sultanism* tend to arise whenever traditional domination develops an administration and a military force which are purely personal instruments of the master. Only then are the group members treated as subjects. Previously the master's authority appeared as a pre-eminent group right, now it turns into his personal right, which he appropriates in the same way as he would any ordinary object of possession. In principle, he can exploit his right like any economic asset—sell it, pledge it as security, or divide it by inheritance. The primary external support of patrimonial power is provided by slaves (who are often branded), *coloni* and conscripted subjects, but also by mercenary bodyguards and armies (patrimonial troops); the latter practice is designed to maximize the solidarity of interest between master and staff. By controlling these instruments the ruler can broaden the range of his arbitrary power and put himself in a position to grant grace and favors at the expense of the traditional limitations of patriarchal and gerontocratic structures. Where domination is primarily traditional, even though it is exercised by virtue of the ruler's personal autonomy, it will be called *patrimonial authority*; where it indeed operates primarily on the basis of discretion, it will be called *sultanism*. The transition is definitely continuous. Both forms of domination are distinguished from elementary patriarchism by the presence of a personal staff. ...

Estate-type domination (*ständiche Herrschaft*) is that form of patrimonial authority under which the administrative staff appropriates particular powers and the corresponding economic assets. As in all similar cases, appropriation may take the following forms: (a) appropriation may be carried out by an organized group or by a category of persons distinguished by particular characteristics, or (b) it may be carried out by individuals, for life, on a heredity basis, or as free property.

Domination of the estate-type thus involves: (a) always a limitation of the lord's discretion in selecting his administrative staff because positions or seigneurial powers have been appropriated by an organized group or a status group, or (b) often—and this will be considered as typical—appropriation by the individual staff members of the positions, including in general the economic advantages associated with them; the material means of administration; [and] the governing powers.

Where governing powers are appropriated, the costs of administration are met indiscriminately from the incumbent's own and his appropriated means. Holders of military powers and seigneurial members of the "feudal" army (*ständisches Heer*) equip themselves and possibly their own patrimonial or feudal contingents. It is also possible that the provision of administrative means and of the administrative staff itself is appropriated as the object of a profit-making enterprise, on the basis of fixed contributions from the ruler's magazines or treasury. This was true in particular of the mercenary armies in the sixteenth and seventeenth century in Europe—examples of "capitalist armies."

Where appropriation is complete, all the powers of government are divided between the ruler and the administrative staff members, each on the basis of his personal rights (*Eigenrecht*); or autonomous powers are created and regulated by the special decrees of the ruler or special compromises with the holders of appropriated rights. ...

Charismatic Authority

The term "charisma" will be applied to a certain quality of an individual personality by virtue of which he is considered extraordinary and treated as endowed with supernatural, superhuman, or at least specifically exceptional powers or qualities. These are such as are not accessible to the ordinary person, but are regarded as of divine origin or as exemplary, and on the basis of them the individual concerned is treated as a "leader." In primitive circumstances this peculiar kind of quality is thought of as resting on magical powers, whether of prophets, persons with a reputation for therapeutic or legal wisdom, leaders in the hunt, or heroes in war. How the quality in question would be ultimately judged from any ethical, aesthetic, or other such point of view is naturally entirely indifferent for purposes of definition. What is alone important is how the individual is actually regarded by those subject to charismatic authority, by his "followers" or "disciples." ...

It is recognition on the part of those subject to authority which is decisive for the validity of charisma. This recognition is freely given and guaranteed by what is held to be a proof, originally always a miracle, and consists in devotion to the corresponding revelation, hero worship, or absolute trust in the leader. But where charisma is genuine, it is not this which is the basis of the claim to legitimacy. This basis lies rather in the conception that it is the duty of those subject to charismatic authority to recognize its genuineness and to act accordingly. Psychologically this recognition is a matter of complete personal devotion to the possessor of the quality, arising out of enthusiasm, or of despair and hope. ...

If proof and success elude the leader for long, if he appears deserted by his god or his magical or heroic powers, above all, if his leadership fails to benefit his followers, it is likely that his charismatic authority will disappear. This is the genuine meaning of the divine right of kings (*Gottesgnadentum*). ...

From a substantive point of view, every charismatic authority would have to subscribe to the proposition, "It is written ... but I say unto you. ..." The genuine prophet, like the genuine military leader and every true leader in this sense, preaches, creates, or demands *new* obligations—most typically, by virtue of revelation, oracle, inspiration, or of his own will, which are recognized by the members of the religious, military, or party group because they come from such a source. Recognition is a duty. When such an authority comes into conflict with the competing authority of another who also claims charismatic sanction, the only recourse is to some kind of a contest, by magical means or an actual physical battle of the leaders. In principle, only one side can be right in such a conflict; the other must be guilty of a wrong which has to be expiated.

Since it is "extra-ordinary," charismatic authority is sharply opposed to rational, and particularly bureaucratic, authority, and to traditional authority, where in its patriarchal, patrimonial, or estate variants, all of which are everyday forms of domination; while the charismatic type is the direct antithesis of this. Bureaucratic authority is specifically rational in the sense of being bound to intellectually analysable rules; while charismatic authority is specifically irrational in the sense of being foreign to all rules. Traditional authority is bound to the precedents handed down from the past and to this extent is also oriented to rules. Within the sphere of its claims, charismatic authority repudiates the past, and is in this sense a specifically revolutionary force. It recognizes no appropriation of positions of power by virtue of the possession of property, either on the part of a chief or of socially privileged groups. The only basis of legitimacy for it is personal charisma so long as it is proved; that is, as long as it receives recognition and as long as the followers and disciples prove their usefulness charismatically. ...

The Routinization of Charisma

In its pure form charismatic authority has a character specifically foreign to everyday routine structures. The social relationships directly involved are strictly personal, based on the validity and practice of charismatic personal qualities. If this is not to remain a purely transitory phenomenon, but to take on the character of a permanent relationship, a "community" of disciples or followers or a party organization or any sort of political or hierocratic organization, it is necessary for the character of charismatic authority to become radically changed. Indeed, in its pure form charismatic authority may be said to exist only *in statu nascendi*. It cannot remain stable, but becomes either traditionalized or rationalized, or a combination of both.

The following are the principal motives underlying this transformation: (a) The ideal and also the material interests of the followers in the continuation and the continual reactivation of the community, (b) the still stronger ideal and also stronger material interests of the members of the administrative staff, the disciples, the party workers, or others in continuing their relationship. Not only this, but they have an interest in continuing it in such a way that both from an ideal and a material point of view, their own position is put on a stable everyday basis. This means, above all, making it possible to participate in normal family relationships or at least to enjoy a secure social position in place of the kind of discipleship which is cut off from ordinary worldly connections, notably in the family and in economic relationships.

These interests generally become conspicuously evident with the disappearance of the personal charismatic leader and with the problem of *succession*. The way in which this problem is met—if it is met at all and the charismatic community continues to exist or now begins to emerge—is of crucial importance for the character of the subsequent social relationships. The following are the principal possible types of solution:—

(a) The *search* for a new charismatic leader on the basis of criteria of the qualities which will fit him for the position of authority. ...

In this case the legitimacy of the new charismatic leader is bound to certain distinguishing characteristics; thus, to rules with respect to which a traditional arises. The result is a process of traditionalization in favor of which the purely personal character of leadership is reduced.

(b) *Revelation* manifested in oracles, lots, divine judgments, or other techniques of selection. In this case the legitimacy of the new leader is dependent on the legitimacy of the *technique* of his election. This involves a form of legalization. ...

(c) Designation on the part of the original charismatic leader of his own successor and his recognition on the part of the followers. ...

In this case legitimacy is *acquired* through the act of designation.

(d) Designation of a successor by the charismatically qualified administrative staff and his recognition by the community. In its typical form this process should quite definitely not be interpreted as "election" or "nomination" or anything of the sort. It is not a matter of free selection, but of one which is strictly bound to objective duty. It is not to be determined merely by majority vote, but is a question of arriving at the correct designation, the designation of the right person who is truly endowed with charisma. It is quite possible that the minority and not the majority should be right in such a case. Unanimity is often required. It is obligatory to acknowledge a mistake and persistence in error is a serious offense. Making a wrong choice is a genuine wrong requiring expiation. Originally it was a magical offence.

Nevertheless, in such a case it is easy for legitimacy to take on the character of an acquired right which is justified by standards of the correctness of the process by which the position was acquired, for the most part, by its having been acquired in accordance with certain formalities such as coronation. ...

(e) The conception that charisma is a quality transmitted by heredity; thus that it is participated in by the kinsmen of its bearer, particularly by his closest relatives. This is the case of *hereditary charisma.* The order of hereditary succession in such a case need not be the same as that which is in force for appropriated rights, but may differ from it. It is also sometimes necessary to select the proper heir within the kinship group by some of the methods just spoken of. ...

In the case of hereditary charisma, recognition is no longer paid to the charismatic qualities of the individual, but to the legitimacy of the position he has acquired by hereditary succession. This may lead in the direction either of traditionalization or of legalization. The concept of divine right is fundamentally altered and now comes to mean authority by virtue of a personal right which is not dependent on the recognition of those subject to authority. Personal charisma may be totally absent. ...

(f) The concept that charisma may be transmitted by ritual means from one bearer to another or may be created in a new person. The concept was originally magical. It involves a dissociation of charisma from a particular individual, making it an objective, transferrable entity. In particularly, it may become the *charisma of office.* In this case the belief in legitimacy is no longer directed to the individual, but to the acquired qualities and to the effectiveness of the ritual acts. ...

5

Power-Dependence Relations

RICHARD M. EMERSON

Judging from the frequent occurrence of such words as *power, influence, dominance and submission, status and authority*, the importance of power is widely recognized, yet considerable confusion exists concerning these concepts. There is an extensive literature pertaining to power, on both theoretical and empirical levels, and in small group as well as large community contexts. Unfortunately, this already large and rapidly growing body of research has not achieved the cumulative character desired. Our *integrated* knowledge of power does not significantly surpass the conceptions left by Max Weber.[1]

This suggests that there is a place at this moment for a systematic treatment of social power. The underdeveloped state of this area is further suggested by what appears, to this author, to be a recurrent flaw in common conceptions of social power; a flaw which helps to block adequate theoretical development as well as meaningful research. That flaw is the implicit treatment of power as though it were an attribute of a person or group ("X is an influential person." "Y is a powerful group." etc.). Given this conception, the natural research question becomes "Who in community X are the power holders?". The project then proceeds to rank-order persons by some criterion of power, and this ordering is called the *power-structure*. This is a highly questionable representation of a "structure," based upon a questionable assumption of *generalized power*.[2]

It is commonly observed that some person X dominates Y, while being subservient in relations with Z. Furthermore, these power relations are frequently intransitive! Hence, to say that "X has power" is vacant, unless we specify "over whom." In making these necessary qualifications we force ourselves to face up to the obvious: power is a property of the social relation; it is not an attribute of the actor.[3]

In this paper an attempt is made to construct a simple theory of the power aspects of social relations. Attention is focused upon characteristics of the relationship as such, with little or no regard for particular features of the persons or groups engaged in such relations. Personal traits, skills or possessions (such as wealth) which might be relevant to power in one relation are infinitely variable across the set of possible relations, and hence have no place in a general theory.

THE POWER-DEPENDENCE RELATION

While the theory presented here is anchored most intimately in small group research, it is meant to apply to more complex community relations as well. In an effort to make these conceptions potentially as broadly applicable as possible, we shall speak of relations among *actors*, where an actor can be either a person or a group. Unless otherwise indicated, any relation discussed might be a person-person, group-person or group-group relation.

Social relations commonly entail *ties of mutual dependence* between the parties. A *depends* upon B if he aspires to goals or gratifications whose achievement is facilitated by appropriate actions on B's part. By virtue of mutual dependency, it is more or less imperative to each party that he be able to control or influence the other's conduct. At the same time, these ties of mutual dependence imply that each party is in a position, to some degree, to grant or deny, facilitate or hinder, the other's gratification. Thus, it would appear that the power to control or influence the other resides in control over the things he values, which may range all the way from oil resources to ego-support, depending upon the relation in question. In short, *power resides implicitly in the other's dependency*. When this is recognized, the analysis will of necessity revolve largely around the concept of dependence.[4]

Two variables appear to function jointly in fixing the dependence of one actor upon another. Since the precise nature of this joint function is an empirical question, our proposition can do no more than specify the directional relationships involved:

> *Dependence (Dab)*. The dependence of actor A upon actor B is (1) directly proportional to A's *motivational investment* in goals mediated by B, and (2) inversely proportional to the *availability* to those goals to A outside of the A-B relation.

In this proposition "goal" is used in the broadest possible sense to refer to gratifications consciously sought as well as rewards unconsciously obtained through the relationship. The "availability" of such goals outside of the relation refers to alternative avenues of goal-achievement, most notably other social relations. The costs associated with such alternatives must be included in any assessment of dependency.

If the dependence of one party provides the basis for the power of the other, that power must be defined as a potential influence:

> *Power (Pab)*. The power of actor A over actor B is the amount of resistance on the part of B which can be potentially overcome by A.

Two points must be made clear about this definition. First, the power defined here will not be, of necessity, observable in every interactive episode between A and B, yet we suggest that it exists nonetheless as a potential, to be explored, tested, and occasionally employed by the participants. Pab will be empirically manifest only *if* A makes some demand, and only *if* this demand runs counter to B's desires (resistance to be overcome). Any operational definition must make reference to *change* in the conduct of B attributable to demands made by A.

Second, we define power as the "resistance" which can be overcome, without restricting it to any one domain of action. Thus, if A is dependent upon B for love and respect, B might then draw A into criminal activity which he would normally resist. The reader might object to this formulation, arguing that social power is in fact restricted to certain channels. If so, the reader is apparently concerned with "legitimized power" embedded in a social structure. ...

The premise we began with can now be stated as Pab = Dba; the power of A over B is equal to, and based upon, the dependence of B upon A. Recognizing the reciprocity of social relations, we can represent a power-dependence relation as a pair of equations:

Pab = Dba
Pba = Dab.

Before proceeding further we should emphasize that these formulations have been so worded in the hope that they will apply across a wide range of social life. At a glance our conception of dependence contains two variables remarkably like supply and demand ("availability" and "motivational investment," respectively). We prefer the term *dependency* over these economic terms because it facilitates broader application, for all we need to do to shift these ideas from one area of application to another is change the motivational basis of dependency. We can speak of the economic dependence of a home builder upon a loan agency as varying directly with his desire for the home, and hence capital, and inversely with the "availability" of capital from other agencies. Similarly, a child may be dependent upon another child based upon motivation toward the pleasures of collective play, the availability of alternative playmates, etc. The same generic power-dependence relation is involved in each case. The dependency side of the equation may show itself in "friendship" among playmates, in "filial love" between parent and child, in "respect for treaties" among nations. On the other side of the equation, I am sure no one doubts that mothers, lovers, children, and nations enjoy the power to influence their respective partners, within the limit set by the partner's dependence upon them. ...

BALANCE AND IMBALANCE

The notion of reciprocity in power-dependency relations raises the question of equality or inequality of power in the relation. If the power of A over B (Pab) is confronted by equal opposing power of B over A, is power then neutralized or cancelled out? We suggest that in such a balanced condition, power is in no way removed from the relationship. A pattern of "dominance" might not emerge in the interaction among these actors, but that does not imply that power is inoperative in either or both directions. A *balanced* relation and an *unbalanced* relation are represented respectively as follows:

$$
\begin{array}{ccc}
\text{Pab} & = & \text{Dba} \\
\| & & \| \\
\text{Pba} & = & \text{Dab}
\end{array}
\qquad\qquad
\begin{array}{ccc}
\text{Pab} & = & \text{Dba} \\
\text{v} & & \text{v} \\
\text{Pba} & = & \text{Dab}
\end{array}
$$

Consider two social relations, both of which are balanced, but at *different levels* of dependence. ... A moment's thought will reveal the utility of the argument that balance does not neutralize power, for each party may continue to exert profound control over the other. It might even be meaningful to talk about the parties being controlled by the relation itself.

Rather than cancelling out considerations of power, reciprocal power provides the basis for studying three more features of power-relations: first, a power advantage can be defined as Pab minus Pba, which can be either positive or negative (a power disadvantage); second, the *cohesion* of a relationship can be defined as the average of Dab and Dba, though this definition can be refined; and finally, it opens the door to the study of *balancing operations* as structural changes in power-dependence relations which tend to reduce power advantage.

Discussion of balancing tendencies should begin with a concrete illustration. In the unbalanced relation represented symbolically above, A is the more powerful party because B is the more dependent of the two. Let actor B be a rather "unpopular" girl, with puritanical upbringing, who wants desperately to date; and let A be a young man who occasionally takes her out, while dating other girls as well. (The reader can satisfy himself about A's power advantage in this illustration by referring to the formulation above.) Assume further that A "discovers" this power advantage, and, in exploring for the limits of his power, makes sexual advances. In this simplified illustration, these advances should encounter resistance in B's puritanical values. Thus, when a power advantage is *used*, the weaker member will achieve one value at the expense of other values.

In this illustration of tensions involved in an unbalanced relation need not be long endured. They can be reduced in either of two ways: (1) the girl might reduce the psychic costs involved in continuing the relation by redefining her moral values, with appropriate rationalizations and shifts in reference group attachments; or (2) she might renounce the value of dating, develop career aspirations, etc., thus reducing A's power. Notice that the first solution does *not* of necessity alter the unbalanced relation. The weaker member has sidestepped one painful demand but she is still vulnerable to new demands. By contrast, the second solution alters the power relation itself. In general, it appears that an unbalanced relation is unstable for it encourages the use of power which in turn sets in motion processes which we will call (a) cost reduction and (b) balancing operations.

COST REDUCTION

The "cost" referred to here amounts to the "resistance" to be overcome in our definition of power—the cost involved for one party in meeting the demands made by the other. The process of cost reduction in power-dependence relations shows itself in many varied forms. In the courting relation above it took the form of alteration in moral attitudes on the part of a girl who wanted to be popular; in industry it is commonly seen as the impetus for improved plant efficiency and technology in reducing the cost of production. What we call the "mark of oppression" in the character structure of members of low social castes (the submissive and "painless" loss of freedom) might well involve the same power processes, as does the "internalization of parental codes" in the socialization process. ...

In general, *cost reduction* is a process involving change in values (personal, social, economic) which reduces the pains incurred in meeting the demands of a powerful other. It must be emphasized, however, that these adjustments to not necessarily alter the balance or imbalance of the relation, and, as a result, they must be distinguished from the more fundamental *balancing operations* described below. It must be recognized that cost reducing tendencies will take place even under conditions of balance, and while this is obvious in economic transactions, it is equally true of other social relations, where the "costs" involved are anchored in modifiable attitudes and values. ... We suggest that cost reducing tendencies generally will function to deepen and stabilize social relations over and above the condition of balance.

BALANCING OPERATIONS

The remainder of this paper will deal with balancing processes which operate through changes in the variables which define the structure of the power-dependence relation as such. The formal notation adopted here suggests *exactly four generic types* of balancing operations. In the unbalanced relation

$$Pab = Dba$$
$$v \qquad v$$
$$Pba = Dab,$$

balance can be restored either by an increase in Dab or by a decrease in Dba. If we recall that *dependence* is a joint function of two variables, the following alterations will move the relation toward a state of balance:

1.   If B reduces motivational investment in goals mediated by A.
2.   If B cultivates alternative sources for gratification of those goals.

3. If A increases motivational investment in goals mediated by B.
4. If A is denied alternative sources for achieving those goals.

While these four types of balancing operation are dictated by the logic of the scheme, we suggest that each corresponds to well known social processes. The first operation yields balance through motivational withdrawal by B, the weaker member. The second involves the cultivation of alternative social relations by B. The third is based upon "giving status" to A, and the fourth involves coalition and group formation. ...

In the interest of simplicity and clarity, we will illustrate each of the four generic types of balancing operations in relations among children in the context of play. Consider two children equally motivated toward the pleasures of contributing to such play. These children, A and B, form a balanced relation if we assume further that each has the other as his only playmate, and the give-and-take of their interactions might well be imagined, involving the emergence of such equalitarian rules as "taking turns," etc. Suppose now that a third child C, moves into the neighborhood and makes the acquaintance of A, but *not* B. the A-B relation will be thrown out of balance by virtue of A's decreased dependence upon B. The reader should convince himself of this fact by referring back to the proposition on dependence. Without any of these parties necessarily "understanding" what is going on, we would predict that A would slowly come to dominate B in the pattern of their interactions. On more frequent occasions B will find himself deprived of the pleasures A can offer, thus slowly coming to sense his own dependency more acutely. By the same token A will more frequently find B staying "yes" instead of "no" to his proposals, and he will gain increased awareness of his power over B. The growing self-images of these children will surely reflect and perpetuate this pattern.

Operation Number One: Withdrawal. We now have the powerful A making demands of the dependent B. One of the processes through which the tensions in the unbalanced A-B relation can be reduced is *motivational withdrawal* on the part of B, for this will reduce Dba and Pab. In this illustration, child B might lose some of his interest in collective play under the impact of frustrations and demands imposed by A. Such a withdrawal from the play relation would presumably come about if the other three balancing operations were blocked by the circumstances peculiar to the situation. The same operation was illustrated above in the case of the girl who might renounce the value of dating. It would seem to be involved in the dampened level of aspiration associated with the "mark of oppression" referred to above.

In general, the denial of dependency involved in this balancing operation will have the effect of moving actors away from relations which are unbalanced to their disadvantage. The actor's motivational orientations and commitments toward different areas of activity will intimately reflect this process.

Operation Number Two: Extension of Power Network. Withdrawal as a balancing operation entails subjective alterations in the weaker actor. The second operation takes place through alterations in a structure we shall call a *power network* defined as two or more *connected* power-dependence relations. As we have seen in our illustration, when the C-A relation is connected through A with the A-B relation, forming a simple linear network C-A-B, the properties of A-B are altered. In this example, a previously balanced A-B relation is thrown out of balance, giving A a power advantage. This points up the general fact that while each relation in a network will involve interactions which appear to be independent of other relations in the network (e.g., A and B are seen to play together in the absence of C; C and A in the absence of B), the internal features of one relation are nonetheless a function of the entire network. Any adequate conception of a "power structure" must be based upon this fact.

In this illustration the form of the network throws both relations within it out of balance, thus stimulating one or several of the balancing operations under discussion. If balancing operation number two takes place, *the network* will be extended by the formation of new relationships. The tensions of imbalance in the A-B and A-C relations will make B and C "ready" to form new friendships (1) with additional children D and E, thus lengthening a linear network, or (2) with each other, thus "closing" the network. It is important to notice that the lengthened network balances some relations, but not the network as a whole, while the closed network is completely balanced under the limiting assumptions of this illustration. Thus, we might offer as a corollary to operation number two: Power networks tend to achieve closure.

If the reader is dissatisfied with this illustration in children's play relations, let A be the loan agent mentioned earlier, and B, C, ... , N be home builders or others dependent upon A for capital. This is the familiar monopoly situation with the imbalance commonly attributed to it. As a network, it is a set of relations connected only at A. Just as the children were "ready" to accept new friends, so the community of actors B, C, ... , N is ready to receive new loan agencies. Balancing operation number two involves in all cases the *diffusion* of dependency into new relations in a network. ...

It is convenient at this juncture to take up balancing operation number four, leaving number three to the last.

Operation Number Four: Coalition Formation. Let us continue with the same illustration. When the B-C relation forms, closing the C-A-B network in the process of balancing, we have what appears to be a coalition of the two weaker against the one stronger. This, however, is not technically the case, for A is not involved in the B-C interactions; he simply exists as an alternative playmate for both B and C.

The proper representation of coalitions in a triad would be (AB)-C, (AC)-B, or (BC)-A. That is, a triadic network reduces to a coalition only if two members unite as a single actor in the process of dealing directly with the third. The difference involved here may be very small in behavioral terms, and the distinction may seem overly refined, but it goes to the heart of an important conceptual problem (the difference between a closed "network" and a "group"), and it rests upon the fact that two very different balancing operations are involved. The C-A-B network is balanced through the addition of a third relation (C-B) in operation number two, but it is still just a power network. In operation number four it achieves balance through collapsing the two-relational network into one group-person relation with the emergence of a "collective actor." Operation number two reduces the power of the stronger actor, while number four increases the power of weaker actors through collectivization. If the rewards mediated by A are such that they can be jointly enjoyed by B and C, then the tensions of imbalance in the A-B and A-C relations can be resolved in the (BC)-A coalition.

In a general way, Marx was asking for balancing operation number four in his call to "Workers of the world," and the collectivization of labor can be taken as an illustration of this balancing tendency as an historic process. Among the balancing operations described here, coalition formation is the one most commonly recognized as a power process. However, the more general significance of this balancing operation seems to have escaped notice, for the typical coalition is only one of the many forms this same operation takes. ...

Operation Number Three: Emergence of Status. One important feature of group structure remains to be discussed: status and status hierarchies. It is interesting that one remaining balancing operation provided in this theory takes us naturally to the emergence of status ordering. Operation number three increases the weaker member's power to control the formerly more powerful member through increasing the latter's motivational investment in the relation. This is normally accomplished through giving him status recognition in one or more of its many forms, from ego-gratification to monetary differentials. The ego-rewards, such as prestige, loom large in this process because they are highly valued by many recipients while given at low cost to the giver.

The discussion of status hierarchies forces us to consider *intra*-group relations, and how this can be done in a theory which treats the group in the singular as *an* actor. ... Every intra-group relation involves at once every member of the group. Thus, in a group with members A, B, C, and D, the relations A-B, A-C, etc. do not exist. Any interactions between A and B, for example, lie outside of the social system in question unless one or both of these persons "represents" the group in his actions, as in the coalition pattern discussed at length above. The relations which do exist are (ABCD)-A, (ABCD)-B, (ABCD)-C and (ABCD)-D as a minimum, plus whatever relation of the (ABCD)-(AB) type may be involved in the peculiar structure of the group in question. Thus, in a group of N members we have theoretical reason for dealing with N *group-member* relations rather than considering all of the

N (N-1)/2

possible member-member relations. Each of these group-member relations can now be expressed in the familiar equations for a power-dependence relation:

$$Pgm_i = Dm_ig$$
$$Pm_ig = Dgm_ig.$$

To account for the emergence of a status hierarchy within a group of N members, we start with a set of N group-member relations of this type and consider balancing operations in these relations.

Let us imagine a five-member group and proceed on three assumptions: (1) *status* involves differential valuation of members (or roles) by the group, and this valuation is equivalent to, or an expression of, Dgm_i; (2) a member who is highly valued in other *similar* groups he belongs to or might freely join; and (3) all five members have the same motivational investment in the group at the outset. Assumptions two and three are empirical, and when they are true they imply that Dgm and Dmg are inversely related across the N group-member relations. This in turn implies a state of imbalance of a very precarious nature so far as group stability is concerned. The least dependent member of a group will be the first to break from the group, and these members are precisely the most valued members. It is this situation which balancing operation number three alleviates through "giving status" to the highly valued members, thus gaining the power to keep and control those members. ...

Among the factors involved in status ordering, this theory focuses attention upon the extreme importance of the availability factor in dependency as a determinant of status position and the values employed in status ordering. In considering Dgm (the relative value or importance the group attaches to member roles) it is notably difficult to rely upon a functional explanation. Is the pitcher more highly valued than the center fielder because he is functionally more important or because good pitchers are harder to find? Is the physicist valued over the plumber because of a "more important" functional contribution to the social system, or because physicists are more difficult to replace, more costly to obtain, etc.? The latter considerations involve the availability actor. We suggest here that the *values* people use in ordering roles or persons express the dependence of the system upon those roles, and that the *availability* factor in dependency plays the decisive part in historically shaping those values.[5] ...

CONCLUSION

The theory put forth in this paper is in large part contained implicitly in the ties of mutual dependence which bind actors together in social systems. Its principal value seems to be its ability to pull together a wide variety of social events, ranging from the internalization of parental codes to society-wide movements, like the collectivization of labor, in terms of a few very simple principles. Most important, the concepts involved are subject to operational formulation. Two experiments testing certain propositions discussed above led to the following results:

1.   Conformity (Pgm) varies directly with motivational investment in the group;
2.   Conformity varies inversely with acceptance in alternative groups;
3.   Conformity is high at both status extremes in groups with membership turnover ... ;
4.   Highly valued members of a group are strong conformers *only if* they are valued by other groups as well. (This supports the notion that special status rewards are used to hold the highly valued member who does not depend heavily upon the group, and that in granting him such rewards power is obtained over him.);
5.   Coalitions form among the weak to control the strong (balancing operation number three);
6.   The greatest rewards within a coalition are given to the less dependent member of the coalition (balancing operation number three, analogous to "status giving").

Once the basic ideas in this theory have been adequately validated and refined, both theoretical and empirical work must be extended in two main directions. First, the interaction process should be studied to locate carefully the factors leading to *perceived* power and dependency in self and others, and the conditions under which power, as a potential, will be employed in action. Secondly, and, in the long run, more important, will be study of *power networks* more complex than those referred to here, leading to more adequate understanding of complex power structures. The theory presented here does no more than provide the basic underpinning to the study of complex networks.

NOTES

1. Max Weber, in *The Theory of Social and Economic Organization* (New York: Oxford University Press, 1947), presents what is still a classic formulation of power, authority and legitimacy. However, it is characteristic of Weber that he constructs a typology rather than an organized theory of power.

2. The notion of "generalized power" which is not restricted to specific social relations, if taken literally, is probably meaningless. Power may indeed be generalized, across a finite set of relations in a power network, but this notion, too, requires very careful analysis. Are you dealing with some kind of halo effect (reputations if you wish), or are the range and boundary of generalized power anchored in the power structure itself? These are questions in which must be asked and answered.

3. Just as power is often treated as though it were a property of the person, so leadership, conformity, etc., are frequently referred to the personal traits of "leaders," "conform-

ers" and so on, as if they were distinguishable types of people. In a sociological perspective such behavior should be explicitly treated as an attribute of a relation rather than a person.

4. The relation between power and dependence is given similar emphasis in the systematic treatment by J. Thibaut and H. H. Kelley, *The Social Psychology of Groups* (New York: John Wiley and Sons, 1959).

5. "Motivational investment" and "availability," which jointly determine dependency at any point in time, are functionally related through time. This is implied in our balancing operations. While these two variables can be readily distinguished in the case of Dmg, they are too intimately fused in Dgm to be clearly separated. The values by which a group sees a given role as "important" at time two evolve from felt scarcity in that role and similar roles at time one.

6

Power and Distributive Systems

GERHARD E. LENSKI

TWO LAWS OF DISTRIBUTION

When one seeks to build a theory of distribution on the postulates about the nature of man and society ... , one soon discovers that these lead to a curious, but important, *dualism.* If those postulates are sound, one would predict that almost all other products of men's labors will be distributed on the basis of two seemingly contradictory principles, *need* and *power.*

In our discussion of the nature of man, it was postulated that where important decisions are involved, most human action is motivated either by self-interest or by partisan group interests. This suggests that power alone governs the distribution of rewards. This cannot be the case, however, since we also postulated that most of these essentially selfish interests can be satisfied only by the establishment of cooperative relations with others. Cooperation is absolutely essential both for survival and for the efficient attainment of most other goals. In other words, men's selfish interests compel them to remain members of society and to share in the division of labor.

If these two postulates are correct, then it follows that *men will share the product of their labors to the extent required to insure the survival and continued productivity of those others whose actions are necessary or beneficial to themselves.* This might well be called the first law of distribution, since the survival of mankind as a species depends on compliance with it.

This first law, however, does not cover the entire problem. It says nothing about how any *surplus,* i.e., goods and services are over and above the minimum required to keep producers alive and productive, which men may be able to produce will be distributed. This leads to what may be called the second law of distribution. If we assume that in important decisions human action is motivated almost entirely by self-interest or partisan group interests, and if we assume that many of the things men most desire are in short supply, then, as noted before, this surplus will inevitably give rise to conflicts and struggles aimed at its control. If, following Weber, we define power as the probability of persons or groups carrying out their will even when opposed by others,[1] then it follows that *power will determine the distribution of nearly all of the surplus possessed by a society.* The qualification "nearly all" takes account of the very limited influence of altruistic action which our earlier analysis of the nature of man leads to expect.

This second law points the way to another very important relationship, that between our two chief variables, power and privilege. If privilege is defined as possession or control of a portion of the surplus produced by a society, then it follows that *privilege is largely a function of power, and to a very limited degree, a function of altruism.* This means that to explain most of the distribution of privilege in a society, we have but to determine the distribution of power.

To state the matter this way suggests that the task of explaining the distribution of privilege is simple. Unfortunately, this is not the case since there many forms of power and they spring from many sources. Nevertheless, the establishment of this key relationship reduces the problem to more manageable proportions, since it concentrates attention on one key variable, power. Thus if we can establish the pattern of its distribution in a given society, we have largely established the pattern for the distribution of privilege, and if we can discover the causes of a given distribution of power we have also discovered the causes of the distribution of privilege linked with it.

To put the matter this way is to invite the question of how the third basic element in every distributive system, *prestige,* is related to power and privilege. It would be nice if one could say that prestige is a simple function of privilege, but unfortunately this does not seem to be the case. Without going into a complex analysis of the matter at this point, the best that can be said is that empirical evidence strongly suggests that *prestige is largely, though not solely, a function of power and privilege, at least in those societies where there is a substantial surplus.* If this is true, it follows that even though the subject of prestige is not often mentioned in this volume, its pattern of distribution and its causes can largely be deduced from discussion of the distribution of power and privilege and their causes in those societies where there is an appreciable surplus.

Graphically, the relationship between these three variables, as set forth in the propositions above, can be depicted in this way [as shown in Figure 6.1]. The solid lines indicate major sources of influence, the dashed lines secondary sources.

To make this diagram complete, one other dashed line should probably be added, indicating some feedback from prestige to power. Thus a more accurate representation of the relationships would look like this [as shown in Figure 6.2]. Power is the key variable in the triad from the causal and explanatory standpoint. Hence, it is with this variable that we shall be primarily concerned in the analysis which follows. ...

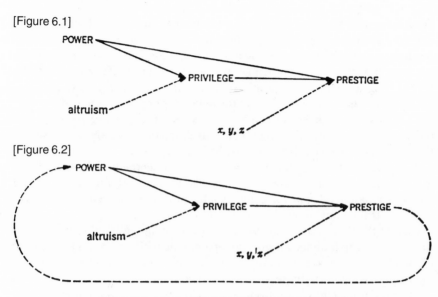

[Figure 6.1]

[Figure 6.2]

FORCE AND ITS TRANSFORMATION

Of the two principles which govern the distributive process, need and power, the first is relatively simple and poses few problems of great importance or difficulty. Unhappily, the same cannot be said of the second. Of all the concepts used by sociologists, few are the source of more confusion and misunderstanding than power. Hence it is necessary to spell out in some detail the nature of this concept and how it functions in the distributive process.

As a starting point, it may be … assumed that survival is the chief goal of the great majority of men. If this is so, then it follows that *the ability to take life is the most effective form of power.* In other words, more men will respond more readily to the threat of the use of *force* than to any other. In effect, it constitutes the final court of appeals in human affairs; there is no appeal from force in a given situation except the exercise of superior force. Hence force stands in the same relationship to other forms of power as trumps to the other suits in the game of bridge, and those who can exercise the greatest force are like those who control trumps …

If force is the foundation of political sovereignty, it is also the foundation of the distributive system in every society where there is a surplus to be divided. Where coercive power is weak, challenges inevitably occur, and the system is eventually destroyed and replaced by another based more firmly on force. Men struggling over control of the surplus of a society will not accept defeat so long as there is a higher court of appeals to which they may take their case with some likelihood of success and profit to themselves. …

Nevertheless, as Edmund Burke, the famed English conservative, recognized, "The use of force alone is but temporary. It may subdue for a moment;

but it does not remove the necessity of subduing again: and a nation is not governed, which is perpetually to be conquered." Though force is the most effective instrument for seizing power in a society, and though it always remains the foundation of any system of inequality, it is not the most effective instrument for retaining and exploiting a position of power and deriving the maximum benefits from it. Therefore, regardless of the objectives of a new regime, once organized opposition has been destroyed it is to its advantage to make increasing use of other techniques and instruments of control, and to allow force to recede into the background to be used only when other techniques fail.

If the new elite has materialistic goals and is concerned solely with self-aggrandizement, it soon discovers that the rule of might is both inefficient and costly. So long as it relies on force, much of the profit is consumed by the costs of coercion. If the population obeys only out of fear of physical violence, a large portion of the time, energy, and wealth of the elite are invariably consumed in the effort to keep it under control and separate the producers from the product of their labors. Even worse, honor, which normally ranks high in the scale of human values, is denied to those who rule by force alone.

If materialistic elites have strong motives for shifting from the rule of might to the rule of right, ideologically motivated elites have even stronger. If the visions and ideals which led them to undertake the terrible risks and hardships of revolution are ever to be fulfilled, the voluntary cooperation of the population is essential, and this cannot be obtained by force. Force is, at best, the means to an end. That end, the establishment of a new social order, can never be fully attained until most members of society freely accept it as their own. The purpose of the revolution is to destroy the old elite and their institutions, which prevent the fulfillment of this dream. Once they are destroyed, an ideological elite strives to rule by persuasion. Thus *those who seize power by force find it advantageous to legitimize their rule once effective organized opposition is eliminated.* Force can no longer continue to play the role it did. It can no longer function as the private resource of a special segment of the population. Rather it must be transformed into a public resource used in the defense of law and order.

This may seem to be the equivalent of saying that those who have at great risk to themselves displaced the old elite must now give up all they have won. Actually, however, this is not at all necessary since, with a limited exercise of intelligence, force can be transformed into authority, and might into right.

There are various means by which this transformation can be effected. To begin with, by virtue of its coercive power, a new elite is in a good position to rewrite the law of the land as it sees fit. This affords them a unique opportunity, since by its very nature law is identified with justice and the rule of right. Since legal statutes are stated in general and impersonal terms, they appear to support abstract principles of justice rather than the special interests of particular men or classes of men. The fact that laws exist prior to the events to which they are applied suggests an objective impartiality which also contributes to their acceptance. Yet laws can always be written in such a way that they favor some particular segment of society. ...

Institutions which shape public opinion serve as a second instrument for legitimizing the position of new elites. Through the use of a combination of inducements and threats, educational and religious institutions, together with the mass media and other molders of public opinion, can usually be transformed into instruments of propaganda for the new regime. A determined and intelligent elite working through them can usually surround itself with an aura of legitimacy within a few months or years.

The concept of "propaganda," or the manipulation of consensus, is an integral element in the synthetic theory of stratification. A recognition of this phenomenon and the special role it plays in the distributive process enables us to avoid the impasse which has driven Dahrendorf and others to despair of ever reconciling the conservative and radical traditions. Consensus and coercion are more closely related than those who preach the Janus-headed character of society would have us believe. *Coercive power can often be used to create a new consensus.* ...

In the short run, propaganda may be used to support a great variety of programs and policies adopted by an elite. In the long run, however, its basic aim is the dissemination of an ideology which provides a moral justification for the regime's exercise of power. Gaetano Mosca put it this way:

> Ruling classes do not justify their power exclusively by *de facto* possession of it, but try to find a moral and legal basis for it, representing it as the logical and necessary consequence of doctrines and beliefs that are generally recognized and accepted.[2]

Most of the theories of political sovereignty debated by philosophers have been intellectualized versions of some popular ideology. This can be seen in the now discredited belief in the divine right of kings. In our own day, the belief in popular sovereignty serves the same justifying function. A basic element in our current American ideology is the thesis expressed by Lincoln that ours is a "government of the people, by the people, for the people." Another basic element is incorporated in Francis Scott Key's oft-sung phrase, "the land of the free." It is difficult to exaggerate the contribution of these beliefs to the political stability of our present political system and of the distributive system based on it.

Finally, the transformation of the rule of might into the rule of right is greatly facilitated by the pressures of daily life, which severely limit the political activities of the vast majority of mankind. Though the majority may become politically active in a significant way for a brief time in a revolutionary era, the necessity of securing a livelihood quickly drives most from the political arena. For better or worse, few men have the financial resources which enable them to set aside their usual economic activities for long. As a result, the affairs of state in any civilized society, and in many that are not, are directed by a small minority.

The majority are largely apolitical. Even in popular democracies the vast majority do no more than cast a ballot at infrequent intervals. The formulation of public policy and the various other tasks required by the system are left in the hands of a tiny minority. This greatly facilitates the task of a new regime as it seeks to make the transition from the rule of might to the rule of right.

THE RULE OF RIGHT

On first consideration it may seem that the rule of right is merely the rule of might in a new guise, and therefore no real change can be expected in the distributive process. Such a view is as unwarranted as that which denies the role might continues to play in support of vested interests, even under the rule of right. The fact is that, as the basis of power is shifted from might to right, certain subtle but important changes occur which have far-reaching consequences.

To begin with, if the powers of the regime are to be accepted as rightful and legitimate they must be exercised in some degree, at least, in accord with the conceptions of justice and morality held by the majority—conceptions which spring from their self-interest and partisan group interests. Thus, even though the laws promulgated by a new elite may be heavily slanted to favor themselves, there are limits beyond which this cannot be carried if they wish to gain the benefits of the rule of right.

Second, after the shift to the rule of law, the interests of any single member of the elite can no longer safely be equated with the interests of the elite as a whole. For example, if a member of the new elite enters into a contractual arrangement with some member of the nonelite, and this turns out badly for him, it is to his interest to ignore the law and break the contract. However, this is not to the interest of the other members of the elite since most contractual arrangements work to their benefit. Therefore, it is to their interest to enforce the law in support of the claims of the nonelite to preserve respect for the law with all the benefits this provides them.

Vilfredo Pareto, the great Italian scholar who has contributed so much to our understanding of these problems, has pointed out a third change associated with the shift from the rule of might to the rule of right. As he observed, those who have won power by force will, under the rule of right, gradually be replaced by a new kind of person and in time these persons will form a new kind of elite. To describe the nature of this change, Pareto wrote of the passing of governmental power from "the lions" to "the foxes."[3] The lions are skilled in the use of force, the foxes in the use of cunning. In other words, the shift from the rule of might means that new skills become essential, and therefore there is a high probability that many of the elite will be displaced because they lack these skills. This displacement is greatly facilitated by the fact that the interests of the elite as a class are no longer identical with the interests of each individual member, which means that individually they become vulnerable. Even those who hang on are forced to change, so that in time the nature of the elite as a class is substantially altered, provided it is not destroyed first by a new leonine revolution or coup. Though this change means increased reliance on intelligence and less on force, as Pareto's choice of the term "fox" and his emphasis on "cunning" indicate, the shift to the rule of right is not the beginning of the millenium when lambs can lie down safely with lions—or foxes. Nor is it the end of the era in which self-interest and partisan group interests dominate human action.

As Pareto's analysis suggests, the rule of the foxes means not merely the rise and fall of individuals, but also changes in the power position of whole classes. Specifically, it means some decline in the position of the military and a corresponding rise by the commercial class and the class of professional politicians, both of which are traditionally skilled in the use of cunning. To a lesser degree, it means some improvement in the status of most of the nonmanual classes engaged in peaceful, civilian pursuits.

Fourth, and finally, the transition from the rule of might to the rule of right usually means greater decentralization of power. Under the rule of might, all power trends to be concentrated in the hands of an inner circle of the dominant elite and their agents. Independent centers of power are viewed as a threat and hence are destroyed or taken over. Under the rule of right, however, this is not the case. So long as they remain subject to the law, diverse centers of power can develop and compete side by side. This development is not inevitable, but it can, and probably will, happen once the elite no longer has to fear for the survival of the new regime. As many observers have noted, the degree of unity within a group tends to be a function of the degree to which the members perceive their existence as threatened by others.

In view of these changes, it becomes clear that shifts from the rule of might to the rule of right and vice versa constitute one of the more important sources of variation within societal types defined in technological terms. In other words, even among societies at the same level of technological development, we must expect differences along the lines indicated above, reflecting differences in their position on the might-right continuum.

THE VARIETIES OF INSTITUTIONALIZED POWER

As the foregoing makes clear, *with the shift from the rule of might to the rule of right, power continues to be the determinant of privilege, but the forms of power change.* Force is replaced by institutionalized forms of power as the most useful resource in the struggle between individuals and groups for prestige and privilege, though force still remains in the picture as the ultimate guarantee of these more general forms.

Institutionalized power differs from force in a number of ways which deserve note. To begin with, it is a socially acceptable form of power, which means that those who exercise it are less likely to be challenged and more likely to obtain popular support than are those who use force. Second, institutionalized power tends to be much more impersonal. Individuals claim the benefits of institution-alized power not because of their personal qualities or accomplishments, which might easily be challenged, but simply because they occupy a certain role or of-fice or own a certain piece of property. To be sure, it is often assumed that those who enjoy the benefits of institutionalized power are entitled to them by virtue of superior accomplishments or personal qualities, but this is not the crucial is-sue and the beneficiary does not have to demonstrate these things. It is enough just to be the occupant of the role or office or the owner of the property. Institu-tionalized power insures that the benefits flow automatically to such persons without regard to their personal qualities or accomplishments. This is, of course, the chief reason why those who gain power by force strive to convert force into institutionalized power.

Institutionalized power takes many forms, but it always involves the posses-sion of certain enforceable rights which increase one's capacity to carry out one's own will even in the face of opposition. It would be impossible to identify and discuss all these many forms here, but it is important to identify some of the more basic and show their varied nature.

One of the basic distinctions within the category of institutionalized power is that between *authority* and *influence*. Authority is the enforceable right to com-mand others. Influence, by contrast, is much more subtle. It is the ability manip-ulate the social situation of others, or their perception of it, by the exercise of one's resources and rights, thereby increasing the pressures on others to act in accordance with one's own wishes. Though these two forms of institutionalized power are quite distinct on the analytical level, they are often hopelessly inter-twined on the empirical.

Institutionalized power varies not only in the mode of its action but also in terms of the foundations on which it rests. Here one can speak of a distinction between *the power of position* and *the power of property*. The power of position means *the power which rightfully belongs to the incumbent of any social role or or-ganizational office possessing authority or influence*. This can be seen in the case of officers of state who enjoy great authority and influence so long as they con-tinue to occupy their post, but who lose it when they are replaced. While this is one of the more impressive examples of the power of position, the same basic phenomenon can be seen in the case of the incumbents of a host of lesser roles. One must include under this heading not merely positions in political organiza-tions, but also those in economic, religious, educational, and military organiza-tions, together with age and sex roles, roles in kin groups, roles in racial and eth-nic groups, and every other kind of role or office with authority or influence.

A second foundation on which institutionalized power commonly rests is the *private ownership of property*. Though property and position have often been closely linked, the connection is neither necessary nor inevitable. The owner-ship of property is frequently dissociated from occupancy of a particular office or role. Since property is, by definition, something in short supply and hence of value, the owner of property controls a resource which can be used to influence the actions of others. The more he owns, the greater is his capacity to influence, and thus the greater his power. In some instances, as in the ownership of slaves or of a political office which has been purchased, the power of property can take the form of authority. It also takes the form of authority to the extent that the owner is entitled to proscribe certain actions by others—that is, order them *not* to do certain things, such as trespass on his land.

Before concluding this brief introduction to institutionalized power, it may be well to take note of Simmel's observation that where the rule of law or right prevails, there is always a two-way flow of influence (and sometimes, one might add, of authority as well) between the more powerful and less powerful.[4] This point is easily forgotten, since the very concept "power" suggests a one-directional flow. To say that there is a two-way flow does not mean that the flow is equally strong in both directions, but it does mean that one should not ignore the secondary flow or the factors responsible for it and the consequences of it.

NOTES

1. See Max Weber, *The Theory of Social and Economic Organization*, translated by A. M. Henderson and Talcott Parsons (New York: Free Press, 1947), p. 152, or Max Weber, *From Wax Weber: Essays in Sociology*, translated by H. H. Gerth and C. Wright Mills (Fair Lawn, N.J.: Oxford University Press, 1946), p. 180.

2. Gaetano Mosca, *The Ruling Class*, translated by Hannah Kahn (New York: McGraw-Hill, 1939), p. 70.

3. See Vilfredo Pareto, *The Mind and Society*, translated by A. Bongiorno and Arthur Livingstone and edited by Livingstone (New York: Harcourt, Brace & World, 1935), vol. III, especially paragraphs 2170–2278.

4. Georg Simmel, *The Sociology of Georg Simmel*, edited and translated by Kurt Wolff (New York: Free Press, 1950), part 3.

7

Power in Society as Resource and Problem

ROBERT S. LYND

It is not primarily the desire of some men to constrain others that makes power, in one form or another, so universal a phenomenon in society; rather, it is the necessity in each society—if it is to be a society, not a rabble—to order the relations of men and their institutional ways of achieving needed ends. ...

Much of the confusion regarding power in contemporary society derives from the transitional identification of power with domination. ... The identification of power with dominance obscures the fact that power in a genuine democracy may be a human resource which can be used for the enlargement of human freedom. It is my purpose to invite clear recognition of power as a social resource and to consider ways in which it may be used and abused. The traditional identification of power with dominance—riveted home in popular thought by the most widely quoted of all statements about power: Lord Acton's dictum that "power corrupts"—renders public reference to organized power in a society professing democratic values furtive and its use awkward. Liberal democracy has, accordingly, tended to resolve the problem of power by quantitative limitation of its use. And the result of this, as I shall note later, has been the progressive transference of this social resource from use for the ends of democratic society to use by private power agencies for their private purposes. If this tendency is to be reversed, it is necessary to remove the concept of power from the dubious limbo in which it now lives, and ask: Under what conditions may this social resource be used in democratic ways for democratic ends? ...

Organized thinking about power arose historically in the context of men's political institutions. ... Man's oldest public preoccupation has been with the burden of tyrants, oligarchies, and other forms of absolute ruling, and with the resulting struggle to establish the rights and freedoms of the citizen under government. The intensity of this preoccupation has deeply prejudiced—right down into the present—consideration of the nature and uses of organized power in society. Under the resulting narrowing of focus to the political model, the tendency has been to view the whole range of reality concerning organized power as equated to, and comprised within, a society's political institutions. In earlier times this often involved exaggeration of the role of leaders and the locating of the "badness" of power in their persons. Latterly, under liberal democracy, the chief villain has been seen as the state.

Political power has historically operated on a scarcity theory. According to this theory, when somebody has power others do not. ... According to this theory—which to some extent survives today—every power assumed by the state reduces by precisely that much the power of the people; for whatever is added to the one is assumed necessarily to be taken from the other. Such scarcity versions of power have meant in no uncertain sense that power is power *over* others. The inherited image is one of struggle against others, of winning or losing the right to dominate and to practice against the losers the skills and wiles that go with domination. ...

The ambiguity I am discussing raises the question whether it is necessary or appropriate to perpetuate in a democratic society this scarcity conception of power conceived in terms of dominance and submission. A thorough-going democracy presumably has a rich resource in the fact that it opens the door to abundance in power by providing opportunity for power *with* others in achieving widely desired ends. ... Politics in such a society performs the double function of affording full opportunity for men to register their areas of agreement, while also providing occasions for clarifying precisely what it is that is important in the differences among them on concrete issues. It may be that such a democracy is unattainable; but if it is attainable, it will be, not through a politics of dominance and submission, but through a use of power which recognizes the resources inherent in both the common humanity and the diversity in human beings. ...

Modern mass society is internally highly interdependent. The maintenance of continuous and reliable webs of relation and of flow may no longer be viewed as primarily private concerns, but are matters of basic concern to our whole society. Many things must be done collectively because they can no longer be done so well—or well enough to be socially dependable—individually and piecemeal. But because of the drag I describe upon the positive exercise of thoroughgoing democratic power, the liberal democratic state has no clear warrant for developing an unambiguous, positive theory of the sustained use of democratic power for collective democratic ends. ...

The suspicion that surrounds state power has not in general extended so acutely to the growth of organized private powers. The growth in size and effective power of private institutions reflects their relative freedom, in fact if not always in visible form, to adapt to changing needs and opportunities. As a result, great corporate industrial blocs, as well as bodies like the American Medical Association, constitute in some very real sense autonomous empires within our liberal democratic society. ...

As we look at the forms and uses of power in society, it is apparent that power-in-use is very widely distributed; persons may be said to have it in varying degrees in their direct relation with others, in their social roles, and in their participation in the making and application of public opinion; institutions have it; values that motivate social action may be said to have it; and likewise power appears in the structure of society. And there can be no doubt that many factors—such as size, organization, wealth, initiative, and access to professional skills, to channels of communication, and to such subtler resources as secrecy and sophistication, as well as the degree of general dependence of the public on the function performed—may *add* to the power of a given unit, however that power may be generated in any larger senses. In this complex and highly dynamic situation it would appear to be extremely difficult to locate any one generating source from which this pervasive phenomenon may be said to stem. Nevertheless, the fact that certain selected emphases recur again and again in the courses that powers take within a given society, and the persistence these emphases exhibit in penetrating and molding seemingly most unlikely aspects of living, suggest that the least probable hypothesis is the pluralistic one. Rather, it would seem that powers in society do not spring up anywhere and anyhow, nor does each develop thereafter on its own autonomous and idiosyncratic terms. Perhaps some tough, enduring factor may be identified as operating fundamentally and persistently to determine the characteristic functions and intensities of organized powers in each specific society. ...

Where, then, does one look for the generating source that gives power its characteristic shape, prominence and direction of thrust in a given society? The answer would appear necessarily to lie either at the level of institutions or at the level of the social structure of a society. ...

Although individual leaders have historically tended to focus the high drama of power in public imagination, it is institutions that have been most widely identified as the place where organized power is and is most truly real. While conditions vary from society to society, the social structure of society has tended to be neither so visible nor so easy to grasp as a whole in its relations to power as have been the institutions that continually exercise control over man's affairs. Reference has already been made to the habit of viewing the state as the great repository of power. From the early Middle Ages to the Reformation and the rise of the nation state, the Church of Rome stood forth as ordering power in Western Europe. More recently attention has focused upon economic institutions as the massive locus of power: Marxism viewed the "mode of production" as determining all other institutions; while liberal capitalism, with its emphasis upon "economic man" in a natural market setting, has factually approached the same end, without directly anticipating it, by largely giving economic institutions their head while reining in the power of the state.

In the United States it has been particularly easy to identify organized power with institutions, rather than with the social structure of American society, because of the absence of an hereditary aristocracy and because of the presence of pronounced individual vertical mobility. Such characteristics, in a setting of formal political democracy preoccupied with its regional differences, have blurred the objective boundaries of classes and thus seemingly emphasized the differentness of American capitalistic democracy from that of the older nations of Europe: This climate of opinion has denied a conspicuous role to our social structure in determining the structure of American power.

And yet, in our society as elsewhere, one should be warned by the thrust—from somewhere behind or beneath institutions—that appears to impart common directions and common limitations in movement to quite diverse institutions. This apparently active selecting and controlling factor does not operate at random; rather, there is in any given society a pattern in what it is "for" and "against." Certain emphases, as regards both favored and opposed lines of action, repeat themselves again and again. The persistence of these broad types of thrust and resistance is impressive. ...

This kind of repeated emphasis in diverse institutions, even in cases where the emphasis is incompatible with the professed aims of a given institution, suggests one of two possibilities: either that institutions do not, so to speak, stand on their own feet and are not primary sources of the power they express but, rather, are agents of something else underlying and controlling them; or that some one institution controls all the others, molding their orientation and actions to support its needs.

The first of these explanations leads directly to the general postulate in contemporary sociology and cultural anthropology that the social structure of a given society conditions and controls the structure and uses of the society's institutions. A social structure is, itself, a structure of power. And since one of the pronounced characteristics of organized power is its tendency to extend into, and to maintain itself in, functions relevant to it, it would be the least likely explanation to say that power relations established in the basic social relations of a society would not repeat themselves in the values and institutions by means of which the society lives and maintains itself.

The second explanation, which postulates the "determination" of all other institutions within a society by one dominant institution, is implicit in the historical tendency to accept the power of the state as supreme. But, as noted earlier, each attribution of primary influence to the state confuses the formality of law with the realities of power which secure the enactment of laws. Nor, for the same reason, does the familiar argument from the state's "monopoly over the legitimized use of force" establish the primacy of the state, other than formally, over all other institutions. Accordingly, the case of state power would appear to support the first of the two explanations above, rather than the second.

A clearer warrant for resort to the second explanation would appear to be the dominance of the economic institutions of capitalist societies over other institutions in such societies. But it is important to note that this dominance results not from the inevitable character of economic institutions, but from the special case of capitalism. Capitalism has operated by an ideology that has had no need for the conception of society; economic institutions have been assumed to rest upon free individuals, predominantly economically motivated and devoid of need of, or responsibility to, society because their self-oriented actions had reference only to the natural, i.e., extra-social, ordering mechanism of the market. Under this natural market theory society was invisible and, when it did obtrude into view, it tended to be regarded as an obtrusive interruption. This has meant under capitalism that society has been submerged in its economic institutions, while the criteria of "success" in the person and the scope of operation of other institutions has tended to be narrowed to terms of functional serviceability to the economy. But this seeming escape of a single institution into autonomy and dominance overlooks an important factor; though liberal capitalism has theoretically rested upon individuals, it has factually rested upon classes of like-circumstanced individuals—the classes being erected fundamentally on economic interest and power; and it has been the fact that this social structure of classes has been primarily economic—despite the avowed democratic equality in the social structure and the democratic professions of the political institutions—that has made it possible for economic institutions so largely to "determine" the other institutions. Accordingly, one may conclude that here, too, the first of our two explanations is correct, i.e., the power expressed by institutions is not primarily autonomous but derives from the social structure. ...

The import of the immediately preceding section is that the generating source of organized power in any society inheres in the social structure of the society; and the locating of this source at the institutional level, however immediately plausible this may seem, tends to confuse both analysis of, and attempts to control the use of, power. This is particularly true where institutional change is at issue. To attempt fundamental change in institutions, of a kind that affects the basic character of organized power in a given society, without changing the social structure of that society is like trying to drive a car forward with the gears set in reverse. ...

So far I have been concerned with ambiguities regarding power and with identification of sources of these ambiguities. Central to my analysis have been the propositions that power is a term that refers to a continuing process that, in one form or another, society cannot dispense with; that the approach to this process has been historically heavily biased by the identification of power with domination conceived as naturally running to arbitrariness and social irresponsibility; and that this combination of necessary use of power with these traditionally imputed unavoidable but deprecated accompaniments of its concrete use has paralyzed direct approach to power as a major social resource capable of adaptation to the values and institutions of a wide variety of social structures. Clearly, a social system stressing thoroughgoing democratic social relations is a test case likely to burst the seams of the traditional conception of power, since a genuinely democratic social structure and a structure of power operating in terms of arbitrary and socially irresponsible dominance are incompatible. ...

Power is no more necessarily a destructive force that needs to be avoided when possible, and otherwise repressed as much as possible, than is emotion in man. The need is to recognize that organized society and organized power are not two discrete things; but that an organized society is, *ipso facto,* organized power. For a society to exist it must be a system of power. The orderly structure of men's relations as they daily go about institutionally channeled ways of achieving needed things also includes ways of resolving differences among them. It is due in part to the unusual visibility of many of these concrete processes of resolving differences that the incidence of power has been associated so largely with that part of social action that concerns men's differences. Power is, of course, no less present in the massive, habitual routines of living. ...

The following five propositions are accordingly suggested as a basis for a positive approach to power as a major social resource:

1. Organized power is not an optional factor in society, but an essential component of social living, always and everywhere present in some form.

2. It is neither inherently, and therefore necessarily, "bad" nor "good." The controls it provides establish and maintain the communities by which a given society lives together in the present and lives toward its version of the future. These controls may range in type, depending upon the fundamental structure of a society, from (a) sustained, arbitrary coercion in the presence of which the maintenance of, and resistance to, the manner of its imposition and the results thereof become a major preoccupation in the life of the society; through (b) various mixed types in which arbitrariness is in varying degrees curbed by law but in which coercion remains in intensities that differ according to what is at stake; to (c) voluntary cooperation for commonly desired ends, in which attention tends to concentrate upon the work itself, while concern over the manner of exercise of control is largely limited to the correction of minor excesses and deficiencies in control as they affect the achievement of the ends sought.

3. Organized power may accordingly be conceived as the process by which whatever is the version of *order* and *disorder* in a given society is continually defined, redefined, and maintained. Order in this sense is the way the major routines of a population's daily actions are channeled toward selected goals in the use of available institutional means. It is a relative term that carries no implication of "goodness" or "efficiency" other than that of serviceability to the given society, or to the controlling segments of the society, in respect to how they identify opportunity and insecurity in view of the concrete resources and preoccupations of the given era and location. Disorderly, likewise a relative term, refers to types of action that are recognized as obstructive to, or destructive of, the main-

tenance of order so defined. What is orderly enough not to be viewed as disorder varies from society to society according to the broad type and concrete detail of its social structure. Order and disorder may vary in detail over time within the same society as a result of change in such factors as size, complexity, technology, and so on.

4. While individual differences in capacities and temperament and the necessarily hierarchical structure of roles in the carrying out of complex social processes will always create some unevenness in ordering society by, for instance, the best conceivable democratic social controls, the issue does not lie at the mercy of such differences among persons and their roles. Different functions, responsibilities and authorities allocated to persons on different levels of a common task need not necessarily create power resentments and antagonisms in a genuinely democratic society. ... What does create resentment and antagonisms is capricious authority and irresponsible power, the arbitrary assignment of status, and the resulting institutionalization of unequal life-chances. Nor does the issue inhere in the sheer fact of controls. ... Ordering controls that stem from the recognition of widely shared needs and are clearly oriented to commonly sought goals relevant to these needs may establish substantial counter-weights against tendencies to abuse power.

5. The fact of the long historical identification of organized power as a corrupting, disordering factor in society may not be interpreted as precluding the possibility of a society in which positive democratic power would be used in democratic ways for collective ends. There is no fundamental incompatibility between democracy and power. Given a system of social relations that expresses unqualified democracy, the structure of power in that society will tend to express similarly unqualified democracy, and likewise the resulting values and modes of operating institutions.

PART 2

Theoretical Perspectives on Power

Three principal theoretical perspectives on social power pervade current sociological thought: Marxian (or class) theory, elite theory, and pluralist theory. Although they are not formal theories, these broad perspectives tend to shape the overall manner in which sociologists view the role of power in social organization. Eventually, all three perspectives will undoubtedly be integrated into a single theory of social power, because in many ways they are complementary rather than contradictory. At present, however, most sociologists are committed to one of these perspectives at the expense of the other two.

THE MARXIAN PERSPECTIVE

Most political philosophers prior to Karl Marx had linked their discussions of power to the state, seeing government and related organizations (such as the military) as the main centers of power in society. Marx broke sharply with that tradition: He argued that social power originates primarily in economic production, that it permeates all aspects of society, that the principal units within power dynamics are social classes, and that government is largely a servant of the dominant social class. He then expanded the conception of social power from a specifically political phenomenon to a ubiquitous social process and offered an explanation of societal development based largely on the exercise of social power. Although contemporary Marxist theorists have expanded, modified, and altered Marx's ideas in countless ways, and several competing schools of Marxist theory presently exist, the following fundamental tenets are generally accepted by most Marxists.

The Marxian theoretical perspective can be divided into three major components: a sociological model based on the primacy of economically generated social power; a historical model describing the process of dialectic social change; and a connecting thesis that unifies the entire thesis, that is, social classes in conflict (Dahrendorf, 1959; Schumpeter, 1962).

The sociological model that underlies all Marxian theory is often called a "materialistic" conception (Heilbroner, 1980), or a "base-superstructure" model (Wacquant, 1985), but both of those terms carry inappropriate connotations. A more precise term might be an "economic-base power model" of society. This model contains two principal arguments.

First, *all societies rest on an economic foundation or base.* Because people must produce goods and services if they are to survive and attain any goals, the economic production processes—which Marx called "modes of production"—that prevail in a society constitute the foundation on which all other aspects of social life rest. Although most societies contain several different modes of economic production, one of them, at any given time, tends to dominate the economy and hence is that society's dominant mode of production. In feudal societies the dominant mode was agriculture; in industrial societies it is manufacturing. The economic base and its dominant mode of economic production shapes and influences all other features of a society—sometimes called its "superstructure"—including its overall structure, its social institutions such as government and education, and its shared cultural ideas, beliefs, and values. The economic base never fully determines the rest of the society, however, for all the other parts retain some functional autonomy and can, to some extent, influence the economic base.

Second, a mode of production contains two components. Its "forces of production" includes all those factors that determine how that kind of economic production is performed: its necessary resources, relevant technology, production techniques, labor force, organizational structures, division of labor, and so on. Although all of these forces are important within the economy, their effects are largely limited to their own realm of activity. The second component, "the relations of production," consists of the social, economic, political, and legal arrangements that define who owns and/or controls that mode of the economic production process. In addition to linking a mode of production with the rest of the society, *the relations of production constitute the primary source of social power* in a society. Because of the functional primacy of the economic base in any society, whoever owns or controls its dominant mode of economic production will have access to its major resource and hence will become the principal wielder of social power in that society.

In short, the Marxian sociological model argues that all societies are shaped (but never totally determined) by the exercise of social power, power that is wielded by those segments of the society who own or control the relations of production in the dominant mode of production within the society's economic base.

The historical model that distinguishes Marxian theory from all other perspectives on human history is usually called "dialectic social change." "Dialectic social evolution" might be more appropriate, however, because the model describes a process through which societies inexorably develop more complex structures and processes. Marx took the dialectic model from the philosopher G.W.F. Hegel, who used it to examine the development of ideas through time and applied it to historical social change. The model consists of three stages: (1) an initial thesis, or existing set of social conditions; (2) an alternative antithesis, or radically different set of conditions that develop from the initial conditions (but are not necessarily the complete opposite of the first stage); and (3) an integrating synthesis, or wholly new set of conditions that emerges from both the thesis and antithesis conditions, contains portions of both of them, and resolves the fundamental contradictions inherent in each of them. That synthesis then becomes the thesis for a succeeding dialectic, so that, theoretically, the process can continue indefinitely. Two features of the dialectic model of social evolution are critical in the Marxian perspective.

First, *the dialectic process is driven by fundamental contradictions that occur within each stage* (Heilbroner, 1980). A social contradiction is not an overt social conflict but rather a deep incompatibility inherent in the structure of a particular economy or other component of society. Regardless of whether people are aware of them, these structural contradictions create critical functional problems within a society that, over time, make it unstable and vulnerable to change. Within capitalism, for example, the private profit motive that underlies all economic activity is fundamentally incompatible with both the expansion of markets in which consumers have the resources to purchase goods and services and with the provision of public goods that do not generate a profit. When the contradictions existing within the thesis stage generate such serious problems that it can no longer function adequately, the antithesis stage is likely to emerge. In that stage, the thesis contradictions are gradually submerged under radically different antithesis conditions that contain their own fundamental contradictions. Over time, those new contradictions will generate their own operational problems that will become increasingly serious. The synthesis stage resolves the contradictions inherent in both the thesis and antithesis stages by integrating the most functionally useful features of both into a wholly new set of social conditions that transcend both preceding stages. To use the dialectic model, therefore, social analysts must uncover the deep structural contradictions that exist within a given society and then determine how they might be negated by antithetical social conditions and eventually resolved within a synthesis set of conditions.

Second, *the dialectic is a useful analytical tool for understanding social change, not an inherent law of history* (Zeitlin, 1967). That is, dialectic change is never inevitable, but when major social changes occur, they tend to follow the dialectic process. Social scientists can use this model to analyze social evolution but must never assume that the process will inevitably occur. The contradictions existing within any particular situation constitute the seeds of social change, but whether (and when) those seeds blossom into radically new social conditions depends on several other factors. The most critical of these factors are: (a) the ability of relatively powerless sectors of the society to challenge and overthrow the existing social arrangements that are being perpetuated and defended by more powerful sectors (those who presently own and control the dominant mode of economic production); and (b) the ability of those currently powerful sectors to prevent such change. Because change is not inevitable, most Marxists insist that social theory must be transformed into "praxis," or theoretically guided action, if it is to have any relevance for real life.

In short, the Marxian dialectic model provides an analytical tool for understanding the process of social change and evolution as based on functional problems that are caused by fundamental structural contradictions and are negated and eventually resolved through a dialectic process.

The unique feature of the Marxian perspective is the manner in which it combines its sociological and historical models into a unified thesis. Marx accomplished this unification with his conception of *social classes and class conflict*. This conception contains two principal arguments.

First, *social classes are defined in terms of their relationship to the dominant mode of economic production* in a society. A social class is a population who have a common relationship to the major means of production and therefore are able to exercise similar amounts of social power. The most powerful, or dominant, class owns or controls the major mode of production; less powerful classes own or control minor modes of production; the middle class lacks such ownership or control but has some power resources in the services it provides to the powerful classes; the working class has no power resources except its labor in operating the various modes of production; and the lowest class is totally powerless because it exists outside of the established economy. These economically based classes thus constitute the basic structure of a society through which social power is exercised. Although most societies contain several social classes, the two most important classes, for analytical purposes, are the small dominant class (the bourgeoisie class in industrial societies) and the large working class (the proletariat class in industrial societies); they are the principal actors within the dynamics of power exertion.

Second, *class conflict is the dynamic process through which dialectic change occurs*. For many reasons—including socialization, social control, economic exploitation and deprivation, political practices, class organization or its absence, and pervasive ideologies—the various social classes cooperate (either voluntarily or involuntarily) with one another much of the time. At other times, however, the structural contradictions and resulting social problems within a society become so severe that the dominant class loses much of its ability to exercise controlling power over the other classes. At that point, class conflict may erupt as one of the subordinate classes—either the middle or the working class—challenges the dominant class. This challenge is most likely to succeed when major changes are occurring in the forces of economic production that result in the development of a new dominant mode of production and hence the creation of a new power resource that can be utilized by a subordinate class. An example of this process is the shift from an agricultural to a manufacturing economy and the resulting conflict between the old land-owning nobility and the newly expanding class of industrialists. The ensuing class conflict and social change can occur peacefully and gradually through cumulative economic and political adjustments. Frequently, however, class conflict erupts into violence as the dominant class uses all means at its disposal to prevent change. Whether or not class conflict results in fundamental social change is difficult to predict; social change depends on the ability of the challenging class to become aware of its position in the social structure, organize itself for collective action, obtain adequate resources for exerting considerable amounts of social power, overcome the established dominant class, and create a new social order. Historically, most attempted social revolutions have been thwarted by the dominant class, but occasionally one does succeed. When that occurs, the economy, polity, and other social institutions within the society are all radically transformed and the society moves to a new stage in the dialectic process.

In short, the Marxian thesis of social classes and class conflict draws on the sociological model of economic-based power to define the nature and structure of social classes. These classes become the actors that carry out the historical model of dialectic social evolution when they engage in class conflict (especially conflict that is generated by the development of a new major mode of production) that results in fundamental social change.

THE ELITE PERSPECTIVE

Many of the ideas of elitism can be found in the writings of Plato, Machiavelli, and numerous other philosophers. As a theoretical perspective on social power, however, elitism was formulated by Vilfredo Pareto (1935), Gaetano Mosca (1939 [1986]), and Robert Michels (1962 [1911]). Writing in the late nineteenth and early twentieth centuries, Pareto, Mosca, and Michels were, in a sense, responding to Karl Marx. Their common thesis was that the concentration of social power in a small set of controlling elites is inevitable in all societies, a thesis that negates Marx's vision of evolutionary change toward a classless society with power equality. At the same time, they held that some social change can occur through the gradual circulation of elites without overt class conflict or societal revolution. Contemporary elite theorists have elaborated, in various ways, the basic ideas of the three formulators of this perspective but have not significantly altered them.

The main tenets of elitism can be placed under six broad headings: a set of basic principles; explanations for the inevitability of elites; descriptions of elite structures; the process of elite circulation; assessments of the role of elites; and concerns about the rights of nonelites.

The *basic principles of the elite perspective* include the following.

1. Within all societies (and other large organizations) that function beyond the subsistence level, there have been—and presumably always will be—one or a few sets of powerful controlling elites. Regardless of the nature of the government or the economy, there is always oligarchy, or rule of the few over the many. The masses cannot and do not govern themselves.

2. Although the elites are always a tiny minority of the population, they control a large proportion of the available resources, are usually well organized, and are quite cohesive. Consequently, the elites are highly effective in wielding power throughout society.

3. Elites commonly employ all available means to protect and preserve their power and to enhance it whenever possible. They share power with others only when it is in their self-interest, and they never voluntarily surrender power.

4. To rule their society, elites employ a wide variety of techniques. These include controlling the government, dominating the economy, using police and military force, manipulating the educational system and the mass media, sanctioning or eliminating those who oppose them, and creating ideologies (beliefs, values, myths, etc.) that legitimize their power and rule.

5. Elites may permit or even encourage limited social change, but only to the extent that they see it as contributing to the goals they seek and not threatening their power. Major social transformations are always strongly resisted by elites.

6. As societies become increasingly large and complex, the power of the elites tends to be less visible because it is embedded within numerous organizational structures. As a consequence, however, their rule becomes more pervasive and effective.

These six principles are summed up in Michels's (1962 [1911]) famous Iron Law of Oligarchy: "Who says organization says oligarchy."

In short, the elites exercise most of the power in any society; the masses do not. Therefore, to understand any society, we must examine its powerful elites, the bases of their power, the manner in which they exercise it, and the purposes for which they exert power.

Although theorists generally agree on the basic principles of the elite perspective, they disagree widely on the *reasons for the inevitability of elites.* Among the many explanations offered by various writers have been the following: (1) elites possess superior personality characteristics; (2) elites are socialized and educated to assume that role; (3) elites come from privileged family backgrounds that give them many advantages over others; (4) elites strive harder than others for success and preeminence; (5) elites are more capable than others of organizing themselves and taking collective action; (6) elites represent the dominant interests prevailing in a society; (7) hierarchical authority structures within all large organizations ensure that there will be elites; (8) elites occupy functionally key positions in the major organizations within society; (9) all organizations require leaders to make decisions and to direct activities; (10) within all organizations, a few central positions necessarily acquire control over critical resources such as finances, personnel, communications, and the distribution of rewards; (11) nonelites perceive elites as functionally indispensable; and (12) nonelites are apathetic and welcome leadership by those who are willing to assume such responsibilities.

These explanations obviously range from highly individualistic to totally structural in nature. Each of them undoubtedly has some validity, but thus far they have not been integrated into any kind of unified explanation. It is noteworthy, moreover, that none of them make explicit reference to the central Marxian concerns with economic production and economically based power. Elitists generally focus primarily on the polity and give little or no attention to the economy as a source of social power.

Early elitists often held a very simplistic conception of the *structure of elites* in society, assuming that there was a single set of elites and a huge mass of nonelites. Contemporary descriptions of elite structures are much more complex, however. Within a modern society or other large organizations, all or most of the following components might be found: (1) a very small set of "top" (or "controlling" or "ruling") elites that exercise power over the entire collectivity; (2) numerous sets of "functionally specialized" (or "segmented") elites, each of whom exercises power within a specific domain of activities; (3) one or more sets of "counterelites" who do not presently exercise significant amounts of power but are potential or actual challengers to the established elites; (4) a "political stratum" of people who occupy powerful but not top positions within the polity; (5) several layers of "subelites" who occupy successively lower levels of positions within all power hierarchies; (6) various sets of "activists" who enact functionally important but not very powerful roles within all power structures; and (7) an "upper" (or "dominant") social class that largely includes, but is not limited to, powerful elites.

The precise structure of power existing in any particular setting must be determined through empirical examination. In most societies and other large organizations, however, that structure is likely to be quite complex. In addition to the formal power structure, there is also an informal structure of power within interpersonal relationships, and this informal structure greatly complicates the total picture.

Although elite theory insists that there will always be elites, it recognizes that, over time, there can be extensive changes in the composition of the elites within any given setting. This process, commonly called *elite circulation*, can occur in at least five different ways.

1. As successive cohorts of young elites experience differing conditions during their formative years, they may bring new ideas and practices into the power structure when they eventually assume key positions in it.

2. Nonelite individuals or sets of individuals who appear to be promising or valuable additions to the elite structure can be recruited into it, often through a process of "sponsorship" by current elites. Generally, this process results in per-

petuating an established power structure across generations, but occasionally the new recruits may bring innovative ideas and practices into the organization.

3. One or more sets of subelites or activists may replace the established ruling elites. Such internal coups d'état change the personnel occupying elite positions but often result in only minor alterations in the activities of the structure.

4. An existing set of counterelites outside the power structure may overthrow the current elites, through either established political or violent procedures. They are likely to bring rather different ideas and practices into the power structure but do not usually alter its basic configuration.

5. A new power resource may become available (anything from a new mode of economic production to a new religion) that gives rise to a new set of powerful actors who displace the existing elites. This method of displacement is similar to the Marxian model, except that it is expanded beyond the economy.

In short, the composition of elites inevitably changes through time, but elite power structures inevitably endure.

Among social scientists there is a rather sharp division in *assessing the role of elites.* One side of this debate views the existence and power of elites as inequitable, unjust, and undesirable. Some holders of this viewpoint attribute the injustice entirely to the manner in which societies and other organizations are structured, whereas others believe that elite individuals are or tend to become self-serving and corrupt. They agree, however, that elite power structures exploit nonelites and thus create unjust inequities in the distribution of social benefits. They believe, therefore, that elite power should be eliminated or at least minimized.

The other side of the debate holds that elites perform many useful services for society and hence are desirable. Some proponents of this viewpoint believe that the preservation of social order is absolutely dependent on the services provided by elites; others merely accept the existence and actions of elites as functionally necessary. They agree, however, that elite power structures must exist, and they believe that elite power should be accepted and protected, although it may be possible to hold elites accountable for their actions.

Because this debate is essentially ideological in nature, it has no totally rational resolution. Current thinking suggests, however, that it may be possible to move the two sides closer by emphasizing procedures for limiting the power of elites and building linkages between them and nonelites.

That possibility leads to the final major concern of elite theorists: the *rights of nonelites.* No elite theorist has argued that elites should be able to control and exploit nonelites to the maximum possible extent; they all believe that to protect the rights of nonelites, there must be limits on the power of elites. Several suggestions have been proposed to accomplish this, including the following.

1.   Ensure the legal rights of nonelites in a constitution or in other basic legal documents (which Mosca, 1939 [1896], called the principle of "juridical defense").

2. Provide open opportunities for recruiting competent nonelites into elite positions, such as public education and appointments based on merit (which Young, 1961, has described as a "meritocracy").
3. Place all elites on probation by periodically requiring them to obtain approval from a majority of nonelites and replacing them with others if they lack such approval (which Schumpeter, 1962, and others have called the "elitist conception of democracy").
4. Establish procedures for empowering nonelites and counterelites so that they can sometimes successfully challenge the power of established elites (which was advocated by Michels, 1962 [1911], and is illustrated by nonelite political parties and labor unions).
5. Create networks of voluntary associations to represent the interests of various nonelites to the elites (which is the essence of the pluralist perspective).

In short, although centralized power structures and powerful elites may be inevitable in organized social life, there are many ways in which their exercise of power can be limited and they can be held at least partially accountable to nonelites for their actions.

THE PLURALIST PERSPECTIVE

Despite the many differences between the Marxian and elitist perspectives, they agree that power has tended to be highly centralized in societies that function beyond the subsistence level. The pluralist perspective, in contrast, holds that in modern, industrialized, democratic societies, power is at least moderately dispersed—and could be extensively decentralized if the pluralist model were fully implemented. Pluralism is thus partially an empirical-descriptive model of what is and partially a theoretical-ideal model of what might be.

The idea of a division of power within government as a means of avoiding tyranny was discussed long ago by Aristotle, and in the eighteenth century Montesquieu stressed the importance of separate bodies for the legislative, executive, and judicial functions. The pluralist model reaches far beyond government, however, emphasizing power dispersal throughout the entire society. James Madison's *The Federalist, Number 10,* sketched the main features of this model, but it was Alexis de Tocqueville's *Democracy in America, Volume 2,* (1961 [1835]), written in the 1830s, that fully developed pluralism as a societal model of power structuring. Tocqueville saw mass equality, created by the breakdown or absence of traditional hierarchies of feudal authority, as providing fertile ground for the emergence of a "tyranny of the majority" in place of a tyranny of the kings or other elites. His conception of sociopolitical pluralism was intended to prevent both forms of tyranny in modern societies.

As the pluralist model has evolved, it has taken three somewhat different forms: elite pluralism, mediation pluralism, and mobilization pluralism.

Elite pluralism, propounded by Robert Dahl (1956) and his colleagues, acknowledges the existence of numerous sets of competing elites in modern communities and societies. It asserts, however, that in most settings, *no single set of elites is powerful enough to dominate critical decision making or exert control over the entire community or society.* On relatively narrow issues, one set of elites may prevail, but its influence is limited to that arena, and other elites prevail in other arenas. On broader issues, the various sets of elites normally compete with one another for dominance, and the winner of those power contests often varies. In both these ways, consequently, power remains at least moderately dispersed. This form of the pluralist model contains no provision for involving nonelites in power exertion, but it nevertheless holds that conflict among numerous sets of relatively separate elites is sufficient to prevent power concentration and ensure political democracy.

Mediation pluralism, which was emphasized by Tocqueville and later by William Kornhauser (1959) and Robert Presthus (1964), also acknowledges the existence of numerous sets of elites but allows for the fact that, in many settings, one set of elites may largely dominate the others. Empirically, therefore, it is closer to the Marxian and elite perspectives. However, it differs sharply from them—and from elite pluralism—in its insistence that power can be structured to allow nonelites to exert some influence on both competing and dominant elites. In practice, the extent of this nonelite involvement varies widely, but in theory it could become quite influential.

To disperse power and involve nonelites in power processes, the pluralist model calls for *a proliferation of autonomous groups, associations, and other organizations* located throughout a society. These are sometimes called "special-interest" associations because they tend to be concerned with fairly specific objectives; they are also sometimes called "intermediate" organizations because they are located between individuals and the government. These associations are private entities, run by their members and possessing their own power resources, and hence are not controlled by the state. Some of them, such as political parties and lobbies, may regularly act as parts of the political system, but most of them are "parapolitical," entering the political arena periodically when their particular concerns are involved.

These intermediate organizations must possess several characteristics if pluralism is to operate effectively. First, the overall network they compose (but not each association) must extend from the grass roots up to the national government. Each organization must also have sufficient resources to exert some amount of influence upward, and those that operate at the national level must wield sufficient power that governmental and other elites pay attention to them and involve them in decision-making processes. Each organization must be relatively specialized in its concerns and activities and limited in its power exertion, so that noone of them becomes so large and powerful that it can dominate the others. In other words, there must be a rough balance of power among all these organizations. The organizations must have crosscutting or overlapping memberships that link them together and prevent individuals from becoming too strongly attached to any single organization. The organizations must be functionally interdependent and interrelated so that they need to cooperate as well as compete with one another. Finally, there must be widespread acceptance of a set of rules specifying how the organizations will operate in their efforts to wield power and influence the government.

All of these intermediate organizations play a mediating role between the citizens and the state, promoting continual flows of information and influence in all directions. They serve their individual members by: providing numerous channels for acquiring information about public issues and activities; enabling persons with similar interests and concerns to generate power resources by organizing for collective action; giving these persons established means through which they can gain access to and exert influence upon governmental decision makers and other elites; supporting spokespersons and leaders who can effectively challenge the actions of rulers; and protecting individuals from direct manipulation by political elites through mass propaganda and state-manipulated associations. At the same time, the intermediate organizations also benefit societal leaders by: giving them numerous sources of information about public interests, concerns, and activities throughout the society; providing established channels through which they can act to maintain adequate social order, control deviant actions, and carry out public programs of all types; and insulating them from direct dependence on mass public opinion and mass movements, thus enabling them to take socially necessary but unpopular actions without fear of riots or other mass uprising. Finally, these mediating organizations benefit the entire society by: keeping the government at least moderately responsive to the citizens; making it possible to resolve conflicts through negotiation and compromise rather than violent confrontation; preventing any single set of elites or organizations from dominating the entire societal power structure; promoting relative social stability; and encouraging gradual but continual social change.

In short, by bringing all members of the society, including national elites, within an established network of powerful interwoven social organizations that mediate between citizens and elites, a pluralistic social structure makes possible effective political democracy.

Mobilization pluralism, as outlined by Gabriel Almond and Sidney Verba (1963) and Marvin Olsen (1982), is essentially an extension of the mediation form of the pluralist model. It addresses the question of how individual citizens can be mobilized to participate in the political system through voting and other political activities. Political participation has become a serious problem in the United States, where less than half of all citizens typically vote in national elections. The turnout rate is even lower in most local elections, and other kinds of political activities such as supporting political parties are normally dominated by less than one-sixth of the people. Although voting turnout is somewhat higher in most other industrial societies, rates of participation in other political activities are generally even lower than in the United States.

The thesis of mobilization pluralism argues that *citizens can be mobilized for active political participation through involvement in all kinds of nonpolitical organizations and activities.* These include not only voluntary special-interest associations but also neighborhood and community affairs and decision-making processes within one's workplace. None of these forms of social involvement need be political in nature; they simply bring people together to express and act on common interests and concerns. As a consequence of such experiences, many individuals become mobilized for participation in political activities. Two features of this mobilization process are especially noteworthy. First, mobilization can occur even when the level of social involvement is not extensive; nonactive membership in one or two local associations will often lead to greater political activity. Second, the mobilization process operates at all social class levels and hence can overcome the political apathy and feelings of powerlessness that are widespread among people with low socioeconomic status.

The political mobilization process occurs for several reasons: social involvement broadens people's sphere of interests and concerns, so that political issues become more salient to them; the social relationships that people create through such involvement draw them into a wide range of new activities, including politics; such involvement gives people training and experience in group processes and collective action that are valuable in the political sphere; social involvement teaches people useful leadership skills; and social involvement provides people with established channels through which they may exert effective political influence.

In short, voluntary associations and other kinds of intermediate organizations perform not only a mediating role between citizens and the state but also a mobilizing function that encourages people to become more involved in all kinds of political activities.

OVERVIEW OF SELECTIONS

The selections in Part 2 of this book present the three theoretical perspectives on social power. The Marxian (or class) perspective is represented by a brief passage from Marx, an overview by C. Wright Mills of Marx's principal ideas, and a discussion by Robert Heilbroner of the relevance of the Marxian perspective to social theory. The elite perspective is represented by Robert Michels's discussions of the Iron Law of Oligarchy and a summary by Kenneth Prewitt and Alan Stone of the main ideas of elite theory. The pluralist perspective is represented by Alexis de Tocqueville's original presentation of the idea and a selection by Marvin Olsen that distinguishes between mediation and mobilization pluralism and critiques the model.

REFERENCES

Almond, Gabriel A., and Sidney Verba. 1963. *The Civic Culture*. Princeton: Princeton University Press.

Dahl, Robert A. 1956. *A Preface to Democratic Theory*. Chicago: University of Chicago Press.

Dahrendorf, Ralf. 1959. *Class and Class Conflict in Industrial Society*. Stanford: Stanford University Press.

Heilbroner, Robert L. 1980. *Marxism: For and Against*. New York: W. W. Norton.

Kornhauser, William. 1959. *The Politics of Mass Society*. New York: Free Press.

Michels, Robert. 1962. [Originally published in 1911.] *Political Parties*, trans. by Eden and Cedar Paul. New York: Free Press.

Mosca, Gaetano. 1939. [Originally published in 1986.] *The Ruling Class*. New York: McGraw-Hill.

Pareto, Vilfredo. 1935. *The Mind and Society*, trans. by A. Bongiorno and A. Livingston; ed. by A. Livingston. New York: Harcourt, Brace, and Co.

Olsen, Marvin E. 1982. *Participatory Pluralism: Political Participation and Influence in the United States and Sweden*. Chicago: Nelson-Hall.

Presthus, Robert. 1964. *Men at the Top: A Study in Community Power*. New York: Oxford University Press.

Schumpeter, Joseph. 1962. *Capitalism, Socialism, and Democracy*. New York: Harper & Row.

Tocqueville, Alexis de. 1961. [Originally published in 1835.] *Democracy in America, Volume 2*, trans. by Henry Reeves. New York: Schocken Books.

Wacquant, Loic. 1985. "Heuristic Models in Marxian Theory," *Social Forces*, 64 (September): 18–36.

Young, Michael. 1961. *The Rise of the Meritocracy: 1879–2033*. Middlesex, England: Penguin Books.

Zeitlin, Irving M. 1967. *Marxism: A Re-Interpretation*. Princeton: Princeton University Press.

8

The Materialistic Conception of History

KARL MARX

In the social production which men carry on they enter into definite relations that are indispensable and independent of their will; these relations of production correspond to a definite stage of development of their material forces of production. The sum total of these relations of production constitutes the economic structure of society—the real foundation, on which rises a legal and political superstructure and to which correspond definite forms of social consciousness. The mode of production in material life determines the social, political and intellectual life processes in general. It is not the consciousness of men that determines their being, but, on the contrary, their social being that determines their consciousness. At a certain stage of their development, the material forces of production in society come in conflict with the existing relations of production, or—what is but a legal expression for the same thing—with the property relations within which they have been at work before. From forms of development of the forces of production these relations turn into their fetters. Then begins an epoch of social revolution. With the change of the economic foundation the entire immense superstructure is more or less rapidly transformed. In considering such transformations a distinction should always be made between the material transformation of the economic conditions of production which can be determined with the precision of natural science, and the legal, political, religious, aesthetic or philosophic—in short, ideological forms in which men become conscious of this conflict and fight it out. Just as our opinion of an individual is not based on what he thinks of himself, so can we not judge of such a period of transformation by its own consciousness; on the contrary this consciousness must be explained rather from the contradictions of material life, from the existing conflict between the social forces of production and the relations of production. No social order ever disappears before all the productive forces for which there is room in it have been developed; and new higher relations of production never appear before the material conditions of their existence have matured in the womb of the old society itself. Therefore, mankind always sets itself only such tasks as it can solve; since, looking at the matter more closely, we will always find that the task itself arises only when the material conditions necessary for its solution already exist or are at least in the process of formation. In broad outlines we can designate the Asiatic, the ancient, the feudal, and the modern bourgeois modes of production as so many epochs in the progress of the economic formation of society. The bourgeois relations of production are the last antagonistic form of the social process of production—antagonistic not in the sense of individual antagonism, but of one arising from the social conditions of life of the individuals; at the same time the productive forces developing in the womb of bourgeois society create the material conditions for the solution of that antagonism. This social formation constitutes, therefore, the closing chapter of the prehistoric stage of human society.

9

Inventory of Marx's Ideas

C. WRIGHT MILLS

The distinctive character of Marx's "scientific socialism," I think, lies in this: his images of the ideal society are connected with the actual workings of the society in which he lived. Out of his projections of the tendencies he discerns in society as it is actually developing he makes up his image of the future society (the post-capitalist society that he wants to come about). That is why he refuses, at least in his maturity, to *proclaim* ideals. Morally, of course, he condemns. Sociologically, he points to the results of that which he condemns. Politically, he directs attention to the agency of historical change—the proletariat—and he argues, with facts and figures, theories and slogans, that this developing connection between human agency and implicit goal is the most important trend in capitalist society. For by the development of this agency within it, capitalist society itself will be overthrown and socialism installed. The historical creation of the proletariat is the central thrust within the capitalist realm of necessity. That thrust is driving capitalism toward the revolutionary leap into the socialist epoch, into the realm of freedom.

This connection of ideal or goal with agency is at once a moral and an intellectual strategy. It sets Marx off from those he characterized as utopian socialists. This connection between built-in agency and socialist ideal is the political pivot around which turn the decisive features of his model of society and many specific theories of historical trend going on within it. It also provides a focus in social theory for the moral discontent registered in socialist aspirations; and on occasion, a new focus for liberal ideals as well. And it leads—as we shall presently see—to the direct ambiguities of marxian doctrine: this connection between ideal and agency has been at the bottom of the continual second thoughts, metaphysical squabbles, and major revisions by marxists who have come after Marx.

To explain the economic and psychological mechanics by which this built-in historical agency is developed, and how this development inevitably leads to the overthrow of capitalism—these are the organizing points of classic marxism. To explain delays in this development and find ways to facilitate and speed it up, or patiently to wait for it—these are the points from which subsequent varieties of marxism depart.

The remarkable coherence of Marx's system, the close correlation of its elements is in large measure a reflection of the consistency with which he holds in view the central thrust toward the development of the proletariat and its act of revolution. If we keep this in mind, we will not violate marxism as a whole. We must now attempt to set forth, for the moment without criticism, a brief inventory of the most important conceptions and propositions of classic marxism.

1. *The economic basis of a society determines its social structure as a whole, as well as the psychology of the people within it.*

Political, religious, and legal institutions as well as the ideas, the images, the ideologies by means of which men understand the world in which they live, their place within it, and themselves—all these are reflections of the economic basis of society.

This proposition rests upon the master distinction within Marx's materialist model of society: the economic base (variously referred to as the mode of economic production, the substructure, the economic foundation) is distinguished from the rest of the society (called the superstructure or institutional and ideological forms). In the economic base, Marx includes the forces and the relations of production. In capitalism the latter means essentially the institution of private property and the consequent class relations between those who do and those who do not own it. The forces of production, a more complex conception, include both material and social elements: (a) natural resources, such as land and minerals, so far as they are used as objects of labor; (b) physical equipment such as tools, machines, technology; (c) science and engineering, the skills of men who invent or improve this equipment; (d) those who do work with these skills and tools; (e) their division of labor, insofar as this social organization increases their productivity.

2. *The dynamic of historical change is the conflict between the forces of production and the relations of production.*

In earlier phases of capitalism, the relations of production facilitate the development of the forces of production. One cannot find a more handsome celebration of the work of capitalists in industrialization that in the pages of Marx's *Capital*. But in due course the capitalist organization of industry—the relations of production—come to fetter the forces of production; they come into objective contradiction with them. "Contradiction" I take to mean a problem that is inherent in and cannot be solved without modifying, or "moving beyond," the basic structure of the society in which it occurs. For Marx, "the basic structure" means the capitalist economy.

Continuous technological development and its full use of production conflicts with the interest of the property owners. The capitalists prohibit the utilization of new inventions, buying them up to avoid the loss of their investment in existing facilities. They are interested in increased productivity and in technical progress only as profits can thereby be maintained or increased. Thus capital itself is "the real historical barrier of capital production."

3. *The class struggle between owners and workers is a social, political and psychological reflection of objective economic conflicts.*

These conflicts lead to different reactions among the members of the different classes of bourgeois society. The "objective" contradiction within the capitalist economy, in brief, has its "subjective" counterpart in the class struggle within capitalist society. In this struggle the wageworkers represent the expanding forces of production and the owners represent the maintenance of the established relations of production (property relations mainly) and with them, the exploitation of the unpropertied class.

History is thus an objective sequence, a dialectic, a series of contradictions and of their resolutions. History is also a struggle between classes. These two ways of thinking are, within marxism, quite consistent. For Marx held that the revolution will result from the developing material forces of production as they come into conflict with the relations of production; this revolution will be realized by the struggle of the classes, a struggle caused by the objective, economic contradiction.

The point may be put more abstractly, in line with the "dialectical" method. In Marx's view, continual change—and change into its opposite—is inherent in all reality, and so in capitalist society. The dialectical method is a way of understanding the history of a social structure by examining its conflicts rather than its harmonies. In brief, and in ordinary language, the "laws of dialectics" are as follows: (a) if things change enough, they become different, qualitatively, from what they were to begin with; (b) one thing grows out of another and then comes into conflict with it; (c) history thus proceeds by a series of conflicts and resolutions rather than merely by minute and gradual changes.

4. *Property as a source of income is the objective criterion of class: within capitalism the two basic classes are the owners and the workers.*

Marx left unfinished his categories of social stratification. A few definitions and remarks are available in *Capital* along with his class analysis of historical events and remarks made in his more abstracted model of capitalist society. From all these, his conceptions and theories appear to be as follows:

The basic criterion of class is the relation of men to the means of production, an objective criterion having primarily to do with economic and legal fact. Those who own the means of production are bourgeoisie, those whom they hire for wages are proletariat. So defined, these terms point to aggregates of people, not to social organizations or psychological matters.

In this objective sense, Marx writes in *The German Ideology,* "the class ... achieves an independent existence over and against individuals, so that the latter find their condition of existence predestined and hence have their position in life and their personal development assigned to them by their class, become subsumed under it."

This statement can be made empirically, as Max Weber later did, in a way that does not violate Marx's meaning. The chances for an individual to achieve that which he values, and even the values themselves, are dependent upon the objective, economic class-position he occupies. At least for statistical aggregates, this is so, irrespective of any psychological opinions or attitudes.

5. *Class struggle rather than harmony—"natural" or otherwise—is the normal and inevitable condition in capitalist society.*

Marx's denial of any theory of natural harmony is an affirmation that in capitalist society conflicts of interest are basic. By "basic" we are to understand: irremediable within the system: if one interest is fulfilled, the other cannot be. For Marx and for most marxists, the general and basic conflict of interest comes from the division between propertied and non-propertied classes. Whether these classes are aware of it or not, there is an inevitable conflict of interest between them, defined by the relation of each to the means of production. A contradiction of their basic interests prevails.

6. *Within capitalist society, the workers cannot escape their exploited conditions and their revolutionary destiny by winning legal or political rights and privileges; unions and mass labor parties are useful as training grounds for revolution, but are not a guarantee of socialism.*

Middle-class democracy is always and necessarily based upon economic inequalities and exploitation. Hence Marx continually warns against reformist illusions, and exposes them by reference to the objective contradiction between productive forces and productive relations. There is only one way out: the wage-workers must themselves, by their successful struggle as a property-less class against the property-owning class, resolve the objective contradiction. They themselves must liberate the constructive forces of production by overturning the entire superstructure that is rooted in the capitalist relations of production. The productive forces, now fettered by capitalist rigidity, will then go forward at an enormously accelerated rate of progress.

7. *Exploitation is built into capitalism as an economic system, thus increasing the chances for revolution.*

Whatever his wages may be, under capitalism the worker is economically exploited. That is the practical meaning of Marx's doctrine of "surplus value." Only human labor, for Marx, can create value. But by the application of his labor power, the worker produces a greater value than he is paid for by the capitalist for whom he works. The "surplus value" thus created is appropriated by the capitalist class, and so the worker under capitalism is exploited.

8. *The class structure becomes more and more polarized, thus increasing the chance for revolution.*

The composition of capitalist society will undergo these changes: (a) the bourgeoise or middle class will decrease in numbers; (b) the wageworkers will in-

crease in numbers; (c) all other "intermediary classes" will fade out of the political picture, as the society is polarized between bourgeoise and proletariat. In
general, by "intermediary" classes Marx means the petty bourgeoise, those of
small property; and not white collar employees.

9. *The material misery of the workers will increase, as will their alienation.*

The increasing misery of the wageworkers refers not only to the physical misery of their life conditions but also to the psychological deprivation arising from
their alienation. It is essential to keep these separate, and to remember that for
Marx the latter seemed the more important, that alienation could exist and
deepen even if material standards of living were improved. However, he expected that the workers will increasingly suffer in both respects, although many
latter-day marxists stress the psychological deprivation, the alienation of men at
work.

It is to misunderstand Marx, I believe, to equate alienation with whatever is
measured as "work dissatisfaction" by industrial psychologists in the USA today.
Behind Marx's difficult conception of alienation there is the ideal of the human
meaning he believes work ought to have and which he believes it will come to
have in a socialist society.

According to Marx, wage work under capitalism is an activity by which men
acquire the things they need. It is an activity undertaken for ulterior ends and
not in itself a satisfying activity. Men are alienated from the process of their work
itself, it is external to them, imposed by social conditions. It is not a source of
self-fulfillment but rather a miserable denial of self. They do not "develop freely" their physical and mental energies by their work, but exhaust themselves
physically and debate themselves mentally.

Moreover, in work the laborer gives over to the owner the control of his activity: "It is not his work, but work for someone else ... in work he does not belong
to himself but to another person." At work, men are homeless; only during leisure do they feel at home.

Finally, work results in the creation of private property; the product of the
work belongs to another. The worker empties himself into this product; the
more he works the greater his product, but it is not his. Private property, accordingly, causes him to be alienated. Thus the alienation of labor and the system of
private property are reciprocal.

Alienation, working together with economic exploitation, leads to increasing
misery—and so in due course, to the formation of the proletariat as a class-for-itself.

10. *The wageworkers—a class-in-itself—will be transformed into the proletariat,
a class-for-itself.*

The first phase—a class-in-itself—refers to the objective fact of the class as
an aggregate, defined by its position in the economy.

The second—a class-for-itself—refers to the members of this class when they
have become aware of their identity as a class, aware of their common situation,

and of their role in changing or in preserving capitalist society. Such class consciousness is not included in the objective definition of the term "class"; it is an expectation, not a definition. It is something that, according to Marx, is going to develop among the members of the classes. How it will develop he does not make as clear as why it will, for according to his analysis of their condition, as the interests of the two classes are in objective and irremediable conflict, their members will eventually become aware of their special interests and will pursue them.

Ideas and ideology are determined (as stated in proposition 1) by the economic bases of a society. The class consciousness of the proletariat will follow this rule. The ideas men come to have are generally determined by the stage of history in which they live, and by the class position they occupy within it. There is not, however, a universal and certainly not an immediate one-to-one correlation. The ideas of the ruling class in a given society are generally the ruling ideas of that epoch. Men who are not in this ruling class but who accept its definitions of reality and of their own interests are "falsely conscious." But in due course, true class consciousness will be realized among the proletariat.

The workers will become increasingly class conscious and increasingly international in their outlook. These economic and psychological developments occur as a result of the institutional and technical development of capitalism itself. In this process, the proletariat will abandon nationalist allegiances and take up loyalties to their own class, regardless of nationality. Like the relations of production, nationalism fetters their true interest which is to release the forces of production.

11. *The opportunity for revolution exists only when objective conditions and subjective readiness coincide.*

Neither the objective conditions for successful revolution nor revolutionary urges within the proletariat, in Marx's view, continuously increase. Both ebb and flow with the development of objective conditions and the resulting political and psychological ones. Sometimes Marx emphasizes the subjective factor of revolutionary class war, sometimes the underlying objective developments. Thus in 1850: "Under the conditions of this general prosperity, when the productive forces of bourgeois society develop as abundantly as is at all possible within the existing bourgeois conditions, there can be no question of a real revolution. Such a revolution is only possible in those periods when the two factors, the modern productive forces and the bourgeois forms of production, come to contradict one another."

The proletariat must do the job by its own revolutionary action as a proletariat, but can succeed only under the correct objective conditions. Sooner or later, the will and the conditions will coincide. Many trends, already indicated, facilitate this. In addition, another rule points toward the proletarian revolution:

12. *The functional indispensability of a class in the economic system leads to its political supremacy in the society as a whole.*

This unstated premise of Marx is the underlying assumption, I believe, of the marxist theory of power. On this premise the capitalists have replaced the nobles, and capitalism has succeeded feudalism. In a similar manner, reasoned Marx, the proletariat will replace the bourgeoise, and socialism replace capitalism. Old rulers who were once functionally indispensable are so no longer. In the course of capitalist development the bourgeoise, like the feudal nobles before them, have become parasitical. They cannot help this. It is their destiny. And so they are doomed.

13. *In all class societies the state is the coercive instrument of the owning classes.*

This of course follows from the theory of power, just stated, and from the conception of the superstructure as economically determined. The state is seen as an instrument of one class and, in advanced capitalism, of a class that is in economic decline. The class of which the state is the coercive instrument is no longer economically progressive, no longer functionally indispensable, and yet it still holds power. It must, therefore, act increasingly by coercion.

14. *Capitalism is involved in one economic crisis after another. These crises are getting worse. So capitalism moves into its final crisis—and the revolution of the proletariat.*

As the proletariat are subjectively readied, the objective mechanics of capitalism moves the system into increasingly severe crises. The economic contradictions that beset it insure increasing crisis. This cannot be halted until the base of capitalism is abolished, for crisis is inherent in the nature of this system.

15. *The post-capitalist society will first pass through a transitional stage—that of the dictatorship of the proletariat; then it will move into a higher phase in which true communism will prevail.*

No one, Marx held, can say exactly what the nature of post-capitalist society will be. Only utopians and dreamers draw up detailed blueprints of the future. Just as he does not like to proclaim ideals, so Marx dislikes to go into explicit detail about the future. Either kind of discussion seems to him "idealistic" in the sense of "irrelevant" or "unrealistic." Nonetheless it is possible to find in the relevant texts, mainly his *Critique of the Gotha Program*, Marx's image of the future society:

The transitional stage may be equated with the revolution. The appropriating class will itself be expropriated, the owners' state will be broken up, the productive facilities transferred to society in order to permit a rational planning of the economy. In this first stage, society will be administered and defended against its enemies by a dictatorship of the revolutionary proletariat. This will probably be something like what he supposed the Paris Commune of 1871 to have been. Still "stamped with the birth-marks of the old society, the newborn society will be limited in many ways by inheritances from the old, capitalist society."

But history will not end there. A higher phase—that of communism—will develop; it will be characterized, first, by the fact that the proletariat as a revolutionary class (not just an aggregate of wageworkers) will form "the immense majority" of the population. The proletariat will be the nation; and so in the nation there will be no class distinctions and no class struggle. More than that, specialization of labor itself, as known under capitalism, with all its deformation of men, will not exist. The inherited opposition of manual and mental labor, the conflict between town and country, will disappear.

Second, the state will wither away, for the only function of the state is to hold down the exploited class. Since the proletariat will be virtually the total population, and thus cease to be a proletariat, they will need no state. Anarchy of production will be replaced by rational and systematic planning of the whole. Only in its second phase, when it has eliminated the remaining vestiges of capitalism and developed its own economic base, will society proceed on principles quite distinct from those of capitalism. Only then will men cease to govern men. Man will administer things. Public authority will replace state power. Only then will the ruling principle of communist society be: "From each according to his abilities, to each according to his needs."

16. *Although men make their own history, given the circumstances of the economic foundation, the way they make it and the direction it takes are determined. The course of history is structurally limited to the point of being inevitable.*

I have noted that in Marx's historical model of society the agency of change is intrinsically connected with socialist ideals. His major propositions and expectations have to do with the development of its historic agency, and with the revolutionary results of that development. Two general questions of interpretation arise when we confront this central view: (a) In general, does Marx believe in historical inevitability? (b) In connection with the mechanics of the central thrust, does he hold that the economic factor is the determining factor in capital society? These questions have been much argued over, as well they might be; for later marxists, notably Lenin, they have been of leading political urgency. Major party strategy has been debated in terms of different answers to them.

My answer to both questions is Yes. Classic marxism contains only one general theory of how men make history. Only in such terms as it provides do all the specific conceptions and theories of Marx make sense. That theory of history-making, very briefly, is as follows:

"... each person follows his own consciously desired end, and it is precisely the resultant of these many wills operating in different directions and of their manifold effects upon the outer world that constitute history ... the many individual wills active in history for the most part produce results quite other than those they intended—often quite the opposite: their motives [of individuals] therefore in relation to the total result are likewise only of secondary significance. On the other hand, the further question arises: what driving forces in turn stand behind these motives? What are the historical causes which translate themselves into these motives in the brains of these actors?" (Engels, 1935:58–59).

In the historical development of marxism, as we shall later see, there is always the tension between history as inevitable and history as made by the wills of men. It will not do, I think, to lessen that tension by "re-interpreting" or "explaining" what Marx plainly wrote on the theme. Politicians who must justify decisions by reference to founding doctrine may need to do that. We do not. It is better to try to keep the record straight, and to designate departures from the classic marxism as departures.

Aside from the documentary evidence, I believe that Marx is a determinist for the following reasons:

(a) The question of the historical agency is clearly bound up with the problem of historical inevitability and with the ideal of socialism. However, ambiguous assorted quotations may make the point seem, classic marxism does differ from utopian socialism and from liberalism precisely on this point. It may be that in arguing against utopian socialism and against liberalism Marx stresses the idea of inevitability. Be that as it may, I am less concerned with *why* he held this view than with the fact that he did.

(b) Marx's refusal to preach ideals and his reluctance to discuss the society of the future makes no sense otherwise. Because he did believe in the historical inevitability, as he saw it, he can treat socialism not as an ideal, a program, a choice of means, or as a matter of or for political decision. He can treat it as a matter for scientific investigation.

(c) He did not try to persuade men of any new moral goals, because he believed that the proletariat would inevitably come to them. "In the last analysis," social existence determines consciousness. Historical developments will implant these goals into the consciousness of men, and men will then act upon them. The individual has little choice. If his consciousness is not altogether determined, his choice is severely limited and pressed upon him by virtue of his class position and all the influences and limitations to which this leads.

(d) Historically, the idea of Progress has been fully incorporated into the very ethos of marxism. Marx re-seats this idea—in the development of the proletariat. This becomes the gauge for moral judgments of progress and retrogression. Generally in his temper and in his theories of the master trends of capitalism in decline Marx is quite optimistic.

17. *The social structure, as noted in proposition number 1, is determined by its economic foundations; accordingly, the course of its history is determined by changes in these economic foundations.*

I have held this point until the end, because it is a point of great controversy. There is a tendency among some marxists to attempt to "defend" Marx's economic determinism by qualifying it. They do this in the manner of Engels' later remarks (made in letters) about the interplay of various factors, or by opposing to it a vague sociological pluralism, by which everything interacts with everything and no causal sequence is ever quite determinable. Neither line of argument, even when put in the abstruse terms of "dialectical materialism," seems very convincing or helpful. Moreover, to dilute the theory in these ways is to transform it from a definite theory, which may or may not be adequate, into equivocation, a mere indication of a problem.

Marx stated clearly the doctrine of economic determinism. It is reflected in his choice of vocabulary; it is assumed by, and fits into, his work as a whole—in particular his theory of power, his conception of the state, his rather simple notions of class and his use of these notions (including the proletariat as the agency of history-making). We may of course assume with Engels that he allows a degree of free-play among the several factors that interact, and also that he provides a flexible time-schedule in which economic causes do their work. But in the end—and usually the end is not so very far off—economic causes are "the basic," the ultimate, the general, the innovative causes of historical change.

To Marx "economic determinism" does *not* mean that the desire for money or the pursuit of wealth, or calculation of economic gain is the master force of biography or of history. In fact, it does not pertain directly to *motives* of any sort. It has to do with the social—the class—context under which motives themselves arise and function in biography and in history. The *causes* of which Marx writes are causes that lie behind the motives which propel men to act. We must understand this in the terms of his model of history-making: "Marx examines the causal nature of the resultants of individual wills, without examining the latter in themselves; he investigates the laws underlying *social* phenomena, paying no attention to their relation with the phenomena of the individual consciousness" (Burkharin, 1927:40).

Such are the bare outlines of classic marxism. In summary, it consists of a model of maturing capitalist society and of theories about the way this society and the men within it are changing. In this society, the productive facilities are owned privately and used to make private profit; the rest of the population works for wages given by those who own. It is a society that is changing because its forces of production come into increasing conflict with the organization of its economy by the owners and by their state.

At bottom, developments of its economic basis—in particular its economic contradictions—are making for changes in all its institutions and ideologies. Increasingly resulting in crisis, increasingly deepening the exploitation of men by men, these contradictions are causing the development of the historical agency which upon maturity is destined to overturn capitalism itself. That agency is the proletariat, a class which within capitalism is being transformed from a mere aggregate of wageworkers into a unified and conscious class-for-itself, aware of its common interests, and alert to the revolutionary way of realizing them.

The objective or institutional conflicts are a fact of capitalist life, but may not yet be reflected fully as the class struggle of owners and workers. Now a minority, concerned only with their immediate interests, the workers are growing more and more exploited, more alienated, more miserable, and more organized; in their ranks what men are interested in is coming to coincide with what is to men's interest; and the workers are becoming more numerous. They are coming to be "the self-conscious independent movement of the immense majority" in pursuit of their real and long-run interests./They are coming to true self-consciousness because of self-consciousness itself is being changed by the relations of production men enter into independent of their will. And having become self-conscious, they cannot pursue their interests, they cannot raise themselves up, "without the whole super-incumbent strata of official society being sprung into the air" (Lowith, 1950:41).

That is why when the time is ripe, when capitalism is mature and the proletariat ready, the revolution of the proletariat by the most politically alert sector of the proletariat is going to occur. Then bourgeois institutions and all their works will be smashed. In turn, the post-capitalist society of socialism will evolve into the communist realm of freedom.

Comprehending every feature of man's activities, human and inhuman, Marx's conception is bitterly filled with sheer intellect and with brilliant leaps of the mind; it is at once analysis, prophecy, orientation, history, program. It is "the most formidable, sustained and elaborate indictment ever delivered against an entire social order, against its rulers, its supporters, its ideologists, its willing slaves, against all whose lives are bound up with its survival" (Berlin, 1959:21).

No sooner were its outlines stated than it began to be revised by other men who were caught up in the torment of history-making. Then the intellectual beauty of its structure, the political passion of its central thrust began to be blunted by the will of political actors and the recalcitrance of historical events.

REFERENCES

Berlin, Isaiah. 1959. *Karl Marx*. New York: Oxford University Press.
Bukharin, Nikolai. 1927. *Economic Theory of the Leisure Class*. New York: International.
Engels, Friedrich. 1935. *Ludwig Feuerbach*. New York: International.
Lowith, Karl. 1950. *Meaning in History*. Chicago:University of Chicago Press.

10

The Materialist Interpretation of History

ROBERT L. HEILBRONER

Marxism ... reflects a particular philosophic stance. But the pursuit of philosophy was never a central task either for Marx or most of his followers. The focal problem has always been the analysis of capitalism, the social order that presented Marx with an endlessly fascinating enigma that demanded understanding, as the unconscious was to present itself to Freud, and the very act of philosophizing to Plato.

Yet it would be an error to proceed directly ... to an examination of what Marx had to say about capitalism. Marx's socioanalysis tries to penetrate the surface appearances of the system and to unveil its concealed essence. [T]he key to Marx's penetrative insight lies ... in his perception that the concealed essence of capitalism is its own forgotten past, its long-disappeared history, preserved in disguise within its existing institutions and beliefs. History thereby becomes the entree for the Marxist study of capitalism, not merely to retrace its emergence from prior societies ... , but to open a perspective without which we cannot understand what capitalism is.

This special historical vantage point is called the materialist interpretation of history, an interpretation that Marx (1978:4) described as follows:

> The general result at which I arrived ... can be briefly formulated as follows: In the social production of their life, men enter into definite relations that are indispensable and independent of their will, relations of production which correspond to a definite stage of development of their material productive forces. The sum total of these relations of production constitutes the economic structure of society, on which rises a legal and political superstructure and to which correspond definite forms of social consciousness. *The mode of production of material life conditions the social, political, and intellectual life process in general.* It is not the conscious-

ness of men that determines their being, but, on the contrary, their social being that determines their consciousness.

We obtain a sharp first impression of this materialist view by comparing it with its opposite, an idealist view. In the eyes of an idealist such as Hegel, history appears altogether differently from the way it appears to Marx. It is not material life, but thought that gives to history its meaning, its intelligibility, its shaping force, its "essence." From such a perspective, ideas "create" history and determine its form, and history itself—that is, the human narrative—must be seen as the embodiment of ideas realized in events.

For Marx it is just the other way around, which is why he claimed to have stood Hegel on his feet. In Marx's view, that which gives meaning, intelligibility, thrust and essence to history is the actual engagement of men and women with their material circumstances, above all with the ever-present necessity to recreate the material requirements of their own continuance. From such a materialist angle, ideas are anchored in, rather than existing independently of, the material setting of history. However much these ideas may act on and shape the material setting, they must in the first instance be produced within it, and must in some general sense be compatible with it.

This raises an immediate problem. Does the materialist interpretation, with its emphasis on production, reduce all of history to an economic determinism? What does Engels mean when he writes in *Anti-Dühring* that "... the ultimate causes of all social changes and political revolutions are to be sought, not in the minds of men, in their increasing insight into eternal truth and justice, but in changes in the mode of production and exchange; they are to be sought not in the *philosophy* but in the *economics* of the epoch concerned" (Burns, 1935:279).

As we shall see, there are very difficult questions associated with the notion that economics is the engine of history—not only difficulties in determining the precise degree of influence to be accorded to economic activities, but difficulties in defining exactly what activities are to be designated as "economic." It will best serve our purposes, however, if we lay these matters aside for the moment, and seek to understand the materialist view by first investigating the central idea used by Marx and Engels to organize their study of history: the idea of *a mode of production*.

A mode of production is not a simple concept. It is used in the first instance to identify and separate clearly different social forms of production and distribution: thus Marx speaks of an Asiatic mode of production, a slave mode, a feudal mode, a capitalist mode, and so on. Thus one meaning of a mode of production is simply a compartmentalization of history that uses as its main criterion different systems of organizing economic, rather than political or religious, life.

Of greater interest is the *internal* construction of these modes. For a common dichotomous aspect applies to all modes of production, however different they may be in other regards. One of these internal divisions Marx called the *forces of production,* referring to society's means of material reproduction—its population, skills, arts, techniques, and artifacts. The other constituent, equally important in the ongoing process of productive activity, is denoted the *relations of production.* This refers to the social arrangements that direct the forces of production and that allocate its output. Here are the institutions of power and hierarchy, embodied in the social classes that we find in all modes of production. These classes are largely defined by the common relationships of their members to the productive and distributive process (lords, serfs, wage-earners, capitalists, etc.), and are characterized by the unequal, and usually antagonistic, relationship that these classes bear to one another.

It can be seen that neither the forces nor the relations of production are narrowly economic concepts. The forces of production embody the skills and arts of the population and are thereby inextricably mixed with its cultural and technical heritage. The relations of production necessarily embrace the legal and political and social bonds that legitimate and enforce the roles of the different classes. Thus political and social, even religious, elements pervade the economic elements. If, then, the entire mode of production gives an "economic" cast to the materialist view of history, it is because it is organized around the overriding necessity of production, not because economic *motives,* as such, are presumed to dominate all others, or because economic *activities,* such as buying or selling, are supposed directly to dictate what men and women will think. ...

The crude "economism" that on occasion has marked Marxist historiography is not, therefore, inherent in its materialist emphasis. What Marx called the economic "base" is conceived as setting *limits* for the kind of sociopolitical arrangements that are compatible with survival—a hunting society will not be able to function with the "superstructure" of a commercial society and vice versa—but a given foundation can underpin numerous variations of the superstructural elements. The mode of production, which describes the way in which social reproduction is assured, thereby helps us understand the prevailing direction of the arrows of causation within society, without imposing a rigid or deterministic relationship of "economic" cause and "social" effect. I do not think, for example, that any Marxist today would argue that the state is just an instrument of the ruling class. On the other hand, all Marxists would claim that the state is generally used to defend the interests of the ruling class. It is this latter view to which non-Marxist history tends to be blind, and it is in that sense that "economic determinism" plays its influential role.

(2)

Materialism in itself, however, does not suffice to identify the Marxist perspective. ... That which gives Marxist historiography its distinctive character is the fusion of a materialist starting point with a dialectical conception of the processes of historical change. That is why, despite the fact that Marx himself never used the phrase, Marxist history has come to be called "dialectical materialism."

The dialectical element within the materialist vision of history emerges from an attribute of the mode of production to which we have not yet paid due notice. This is the relationship of extreme tension resulting from the unequal relations between the superior and inferior classes within any mode. The inequality may take many forms, but it is usually evidenced by the vastly disproportionate access to, or ownership of, wealth that is the prerogative of the ruling class.

From this systemic fact of inequality arises the main driving force of historical change: the *class struggle* through which the existing division of wealth and privilege is attacked by those who are its sufferers and defended by those who are its beneficiaries. Occasionally the struggle is visible as a slave revolt or a peasant uprising. More often it is waged in muted contests over legal entitlements or economic prerogatives. It may indeed be almost completely disguised in the form of battles of ideas, or political or religious disputes, in which the immediate matters under debate conceal, even from the protagonists themselves, the underlying theme of class opposition.

The idea of class struggle is associated with a dialectical view because it reveals a contradiction located within all modes of production. This contradiction involves the interaction between the forces of production and the relations of production. The forces of production require the *cooperation* of the main classes so that material existence can be renewed and sustained. The relations of production reflect the class *antagonisms* we have just described. Thus society reproduces itself, but only under conditions of tension that threaten to disrupt its socioeconomic structure. Therefore, when Marx and Engels write in the *Manifesto* that "the history of all heretofore existing societies is the history of class struggles," they are not merely describing a train of dramatic events in history, but identifying a dialectical process that gives penetration to our understanding of history.

The inherent nature of class struggle is therefore the main theoretical insight that the dialectic imparts to history. It enables us to see that class struggle is rooted in the structural properties of a mode of production, and that it will appear—hidden or overt, focused on one kind of class privilege or another—in all modes. This antagonistic relationship is put under further tension by changes in the forces of production, technical or otherwise, that alter the tasks of different classes, and thus reopen the terms of their mutual dealings. But it would exist, in any case, as a "unity of opposites" that must be sustained to assure the continuity of the mode of production itself.

This insight is the main *aperçu* that Marxist history gives us for the socioanalysis of capitalism. For we can now see that a struggle must exist within capitalism, regardless of the accidents of history or the heartlessness or stupidity of capitalist classes. Although the form and intensity of the struggle may vary widely from one capitalist society to another, from the Marxist view the struggle will be as inescapable and integral a part of all such societies as are the class differences on which they rest. ...

[T]he Marxist depiction of class struggle is not merely that of a never-ending contest that will continue as long as mankind exists. Rather, it is a struggle that eventually achieves the conditions necessary for its own resolution. In the mode of production of capitalism, class antagonisms are finally simplified to two great opposing camps—workers and owners, proletarians and capitalists. The class struggle under capitalism thus leads to the possibility of a final victory by the great masses of individuals who will create a "dictatorship of the proletariat" (words that have since haunted Marxists, but that were not intended by Marx to imply a tyrannical rule). The dictatorship of the proletariat would establish the hegemony of the masses, the domination by the previously dominated. The vanquished class would be absorbed and disappear. A terminus of history would be reached in which a classless society would vindicate the long historical struggle. ...

(3)

Problems abound in this epic conception of history, but I think we should begin by emphasizing its formidable strengths. Here I would place first the leverage given to historical investigation by the adoption of a materialist view. This is not to state, of course, that only from such a perspective can one write good history, or that this perspective unfailingly serves the historian's needs. The perspective is more useful for some periods and for some questions than for others. But an organizing principle of great power emerges from this vantage that is largely absent from other views. This is the emphasis on class struggle, with its focus on the roles, fortunes, and motives of social classes as the red thread of social history.

The theme of class struggle tends to be ignored, glossed over, or denied by many non-Marxist historians—above all when their investigations concern contemporary society. Yet, I find the theme both valid and instructive. There can hardly be a demurrer against the Marxist contention that gross class differences are visible in all socioeconomic formations. The division of wealth and power among social classes, in all societies above the very simplest, displays extreme and systematic inequalities, a fact as true of contemporary advanced capitalist societies (although to a lesser degree) as it was true of societies of feudal or despotic lineage. The disagreement among historians can only arise as to the importance of these differences, and the presence or absence of a "struggle" to resolve them.

Here much of the difficulty is that one imagines class struggle as overt or violent. In fact, however, it is usually latent rather than manifest, potential rather than actual. In most societies the inequalities of class position are obscured or minimized or rationalized—an attitude often fervently supported by the underclasses themselves. Thus a Marxist perspective is of necessity as much interested in centripetal and legitimating social institutions and structures as in centrifugal and disruptive ones. In fact, the need to search for mechanisms that bestow social harmony is emphasized from a Marxist viewpoint, precisely because Marxism, unlike conventional social science, does not hold that harmony is a natural condition for a social order.

The theme of class struggle is therefore powerful because it directs attention to a kind of "secret history"—a history of social activity and ideology of which the protagonists themselves may be unaware. Such central institutions as the military, the law, the schools, and the church come under a scrutiny they would otherwise escape, as participants, willy-nilly, in a struggle to sustain or tear down a given distribution of social rights. In the class struggle, these central institutions are usually to be found on the side of the dominant classes, although they may occasionally play a role in redefining or even in opposing their hegemony. ...

A second source of strength for Marxist historiography lies in its emphasis on dialectics—its insistence that history is not only conflict-laden, but *inherently* conflict-laden, and that its conflictual elements yield their meanings only when we understand them as "contradictions" within a dialectical framework.

Before looking critically at this idea, it is necessary to appreciate its importance. The idea of contradiction, as we have seen, is that social systems may display tendencies that are both necessary for their existence and yet incompatible with it. Such a conception provides a unifying overview with respect to many eras of historic change that otherwise appear only chaotic or patternless. Prime examples of this are the dually destructive and constructive roles of the merchant class during the evolution of feudalism, or the similar roles played by the capitalist class in the process of capitalist development itself. An awareness of dialectical change, embodied in the idea of contradiction, thereby opens another "secret history" of great elucidating significance. ...

A dialectical approach ... is always self-consciously interpretational, because its concern for "essence"—rather than facts—forces it to confront the ambiguous, many-layered, context of events. Contradictions do not present themselves in any pure form; they must be *discovered* within the flux of many conflictive events. The consequent interpretations of a Marxist historian may be inadequate or simply wrong, but at least the crucial task is directly visible, rather than being allowed to exert its influence in unrecognized ways.

One last advantage of the Marxist approach to history must now be given its due. This is its fusion of theory and practice, contemplation and intervention, observation and interposition. This is perhaps the proudest boast of Marxism in general, as well as of Marxist historiography in particular. Marxism is intended to provide more than an understanding of history. It is intended to serve as a guide for making history.

Toward this end, the philosophic, historic, economic, and other theoretical productions of Marxism are each meant to serve a double purpose. By illumining the past, they enlighten mankind as to its heritage: they reveal elements of history congealed in the present; they open consciousness to wholly unsuspected aspects of social existence. Thus, they change the terms by which we accept the present, and thereby change our ability to shape the future. The unity of theory and practice—of knowledge and action—is not, therefore, intended to be a forced unification of two intrinsically different activities; instead, it recognizes that thought and action are inseparably bonded in the experience of life itself. Thought provides the understanding of the past by which we guide our actions, action expresses the translation of thought into our engagement with the future. ...

The laudable element in Marxism is its declaration that the only "meaning" to be ascribed to history is its moral unfolding, or more precisely, its orientation to human freedom. We must not forget that Marxism itself springs from the passionate and unrestrained commitment of Karl Marx to the idea of human emancipation, not to mere inquiry for inquiry's sake. ... Marxism is alone ... in its effort to construct a vision of historical progress, culminating in the idea of a classless and unalienated society. The vision is also alone in its insistence that mankind makes its own history, and thereby makes itself—not just as it pleases, as Marx remarks, but nonetheless wholly by its own efforts. No other study of history is consciously oriented to mastering history, as is Marxism.

(4)

The insights provided by a materialist view of history and by a search for contradictions within the historic process are so compelling that some elements of Marxism have by now penetrated into much conventional historiography, just as a Freudian interpretation of behavior has tinctured much "non-Freudian" psychology. It would be wrong, however, to conclude this résumé without paying careful heed to Marxism's shortcomings; there is an *against* as well as a *for* with respect to Marxist history. Some of its difficulties have already been noted; here I should like to emphasize others of a still more deep-reaching kind.

Let us begin with materialism. According to the materialist view, the key to the course of history lies in the ultimate, dominating influence of mankind's productive activities. We have already taken note of the need to avoid picturing this as a crude "economism," in which a materialist base dominates and wholly determines an ideational superstructure. But that is not the most difficult problem that materialism poses. The challenge, rather, lies in defining the material sphere itself without introducing elements of idealism; or, if you will, in distinguishing activities in the base from those in the superstructure.

Presumably the base of society, where its material forces are to be found, comprises those activities necessary to assure its physical survival and reproduction. Here, of course, we find its economic life, above all the continuous production and distribution of the material output by which it is sustained. The question, however, is whether these activities could assure social continuance without the support of other noneconomic activities. A host of actions that are not "economic" by any conventional definition must be performed if the economic base is to operate. Children must be reared. Some kind of law and order must prevail. Disputes must be adjudicated. ...

These noneconomic activities must no doubt be consonant with certain basic constraints established by the general forces of production: an industrial nation cannot rear its children like a tribe of hunters. But such constraints are so wide as to be of little use for historical analysis. Societies with similar economic bases have displayed striking differences in their political and cultural developments, as the most cursory consideration of the histories of capitalist states makes clear. In addition, the rise and rivalries of nation-states—perhaps the central narrative of modern human history—is only partially and fitfully elucidated by developments in the "bases" of those societies.

I have not developed this argument in order once again to assert the inadequacy of an "economic interpretation" of history. The question, rather, is to know how widely the net must be cast to capture an adequate economic interpretation of events. The intermingling of nonmaterial activities with material ones, the suffusion of ideational elements throughout the body of society, the inextricable unity of "social" and "economic" life, make it difficult to draw boundaries around the material sphere. The problem for a materialist version of history, therefore, is to take into account the influences of law and politics, religion and ideology, and other elements of the ideational realms, without losing the distinctive emphasis that is materialism's claim for superiority. ...

Our second problem returns us once again to dialectics, a subject whose importance within Marxism becomes steadily larger as we penetrate more deeply. Here we must examine two difficulties.

The first is already familiar to use and can be quickly disposed of. It is the tendency to blur the distinction between a "conflict" and a "contradiction." Conflicts abound in history, as they do in nature (in the form of simple oppositions of forces). We do not require a Marxist perspective to recognize them. But for a conflict to merit designation as a contradiction, it must be embedded in the process of social change in a genuinely "contradictory" way. It must bind two antagonistic and incompatible processes into one conceptual unity.

In historiography, as in philosophy, to bestow this designation indiscriminately is to vitiate its force. It is one thing, therefore, to seek a materialist perspective on social change or on the dynamics of various socioeconomic formations, and it is another to label these changes as "dialectical" or "contradictory." *The collisions of history cannot always be dialectical, if we are to preserve an eluci-dating use for that word and not merely to employ it to indicate a universal, and therefore uninteresting, property of things.* Dialectics, like materialism, must remain a hypothesis, an intellectual problematic, not an assumption that would reduce it to the level of a tautology or a metaphysic. The careless use of its terms, in history as in philosophy, only impairs their power when correctly applied.

A second problem posed by dialectics has to do with a matter we have already noted in our examination of the ideas of class struggle ... ; namely, the assumption that the dialectical processes underlying these themes of history would lead to their resolution in a *final* class struggle. ...

At one level, of course, the problem is one of fact. Has the class struggle become simplified and sharpened as the dialectical sequence predicted? Is there, realistically, a prospect of a "realm of freedom" under socialism, whether we define that freedom in social or political terms? The answer to these questions, to date, is clearly No. The temptation is therefore great to dismiss the entire dialectical scheme as falsified by events, or to relegate it to a mere statement of faith, perhaps of inspirational importance but of no scientific value. ...

I do not, however, want to dispose of the problem in this manner. ... At this juncture, I wish to bring to the fore another answer to the charges brought against the dialectical interpretation of events. *The answer denies that a dialectical interpretation of history predicts any climactic or resolutive terminus at all.* All that dialectics gives us is an understanding of class struggle and alienation as intrinsic elements in the movement of societies through time. As to any "finality" to these movements, dialectics says nothing, even though Marx himself (and innumerable Marxists after him) believed in the impending end to class struggle and perhaps to alienation.

Yet this mode of "rescuing" the arguments reveals a very important weakness within dialectics. For the rescue is not one that would be gratefully received by Marxists. As we have already noted, the vision of a dialectical history, *forever* engaged in internecine warfare ... , *never* achieving a transcendence over its historic burden, is one that would strike most Marxists as intolerable. The extreme discomfort that such a view instills reveals for my purposes the telltale weakness of the dialectical view. This is its tacit teleology, its unstated millennial assumptions. The Marxist view of history is not content to declare that ceaseless change is inherent in history as an aspect of the nature of all reality. It imposes a Design on the course of history, a design in no wise less idealistic than the vast mystical resolution attributed to history by Hegel. A view of history as a pageant of ceaseless change without moral transcendence is not one that Marxists can accept. In the end it is Hegel who turns Marx upside down.

Now to turn to the last of the problems associated with a Marxist view of history, a problem that emerges from its commitment to a unity of theory and practice. This is the problem of the relation between the masses of men and women by whose life activities *praxis* will be determined, and the handful of men and women in whose possession *theoria* is to be found.

Few questions have agitated Marxists more violently than the proper relation between thought and action. Opinions still range from the assumption that the masses "know best" about the tactics and strategy of class struggle, to the view that the masses are unreliable and uninformed, and must depend on the guidance and enlightenment of a party elite. ...

Is there a way of combining *theoria* and *praxis* that can utilize the search for scientific insight to inform, but never to dictate, action; and that can create for action the role of validating, but never of dominating, the task of theory? The question is more easily put than answered, and to date the Marxist response has been crude in political life and disappointing in intellectual formulation. Nevertheless, it is here that the political usefulness and the moral validity of the Marxist stance toward history will finally be determined.

REFERENCES

Burns, E., ed. 1935. A *Handbook of Marxism*. New York: Random House.
Marx, Karl. 1978."Preface to a Contribution to the Critique of Political Economy," in Robert C. Tucker, ed., *The Marx-Engels Reader*, 2nd ed. New York: Norton.

11

The Iron Law of Oligarchy

ROBERT MICHELS

IMPOSSIBILITY OF DIRECT GOVERNMENT BY THE MASSES

The practical ideal of democracy consists in the self-government of the masses in conformity with the decision of popular assemblies. But while this system limits the extension of the principle of delegation, it fails to provide any guarantee against the formation of an oligarchical camerilla. Undoubtedly it deprives the natural leaders of their quality as functionaries, for this quality is transferred to the people themselves. The crowd, however, is always subject to suggestion, being readily influenced by the eloquence of great popular orators; moreover, direct government by the people, admitting of no serious discussions or thoughtful deliberations, greatly facilitates *coups de main* of all kinds by men who are exceptionally bold, energetic, and adroit.

It is easier to dominate a large crowd than a small audience. The adhesion of the crowd is tumultuous, summary, and unconditional. Once the suggestions have taken effect, the crowd does not readily tolerate contradiction from a small minority, and still less from isolated individuals. A great multitude assembled within a small area is unquestionably more accessible to panic alarms, to unreflective enthusiasm, and the like, than is a small meeting, whose members can quietly discuss matters among themselves.

It is a fact of everyday experience that enormous public meetings commonly carry resolutions by acclamation or by general assent, whilst these same assemblies, if divided into small sections, say of fifty persons each, would be much more guarded in their assent. ...

The most formidable argument against the sovereignty of the masses is, however, derived from the mechanical and technical impossibility of its realization.

The sovereign masses are altogether incapable of undertaking the most necessary resolutions. The impotence of direct democracy, like the power of indirect democracy, is a direct outcome of the influence of number. In a polemic against Proudhon (1849), Louis Blanc asks whether it is possible for thirty-four millions of human beings (the population of France at that time) to carry on their affairs without accepting what the pettiest man of business finds necessary, the intermediation of representatives. He answers his own question by saying that one who declares direct action on this scale to be possible is a fool, and that one who denies its possibility need not be an absolute opponent of the idea of the state. The same question and the same answer could be repeated today in respect of party organization. Above all in the great industrial centers, where the labor party sometimes numbers its adherents by tens of thousands, it is impossible to carry on the affairs of this gigantic body without a system of representation. ...

It is obvious that such a gigantic number of persons belonging to a unitary organization cannot do any practical work upon a system of direct discussion. The regular holding of deliberative assemblies of a thousand members encounters the gravest difficulties in respect of room and distance; while from the topographical point of view such an assembly would become altogether impossible if the members numbered ten thousand. ...

Hence the need for delegation, for the system in which delegates represent the mass and carry out its will. Even in groups sincerely animated with the democratic spirit, current business, the preparation and the carrying out of the most important actions, is necessarily left in the hands of individuals. ...

Originally the chief is merely the servant of the mass. The organization is based upon the absolute equality of all its members. Equality is here understood in its most general sense, as an equality of like men. ...

This generic conception of equality is, however, gradually replaced by the idea of equality among comrades belonging to the same organization, all of whose members enjoy the same rights. The democratic principle aims at guaranteeing to all an equal influence and an equal participation in the regulation of the common interests. All are electors, and all are eligible for the office. The fundamental postulate of the *Declaration des Droits de l'Homme* finds here its theoretical application. All the offices are filled by election. The officials, executive organs of the general will, play a merely subordinate part, are always dependent upon the collectivity, and can be deprived of their office at any moment. The mass of the party is omnipotent.

At the outset, the attempt is made to depart as little as possible from pure democracy by subordinating the delegates altogether to the will of the mass, by tying them hand and foot. In the early days of the movement of the Italian agricultural workers, the chief of the league required a majority of four-fifths of the votes to secure election. When disputes arose with the employers about wages, the representative of the organization, before undertaking any negotiations, had to be furnished with a written authority, authorized by the signature of every member of the corporation. All the accounts of the body were open to the examination of the members, at any time. ... It is obvious that democracy in this sense is applicable only on a very small scale. In the infancy of the English labor movement, in many of the trade unions, the delegates were either appointed in rotation from among all the members, or were chosen by lot. Gradually, however, the delegates' duties became more complicated; some individual ability becomes essential, a certain oratorical gift, and a considerable amount of objective knowledge. It thus becomes impossible to trust to blind chance, to the fortune of alphabetic succession, or to the order of priority, in the choice of a delegation whose members must possess certain peculiar personal aptitudes if they are to discharge their mission to the general advantage.

Such were the methods which prevailed in the early days of the labor movement to enable the masses to participate in party and trade-union administration. Today they are falling into disuse, and in the development of the modern political aggregate there is a tendency to shorten and stereotype the process which transforms the led into a leader—a process which has hitherto developed by the natural course of events. Here and there voices make themselves heard demanding a sort of official consecration for the leaders, insisting that it is necessary to constitute a class of professional politicians, of approved and registered experts in political life. ...

Even today, the candidates for the secretaryship of a trade union are subject to examination as to their knowledge of legal matters and their capacity as letterwriters. The socialist organizations engaged in political action also directly undertake the training of their own officials. ...

It is undeniable that all these educational institutions for the officials of the party and of the labor organizations tend, above all, towards the artificial creation of an *elite* of the working class, of a caste of cadets composed of persons who aspire to the command of the proletarian rank and file. Without wishing it, there is thus effected a continuous enlargement of the gulf which divides the leaders from the masses.

The technical specialization that inevitably results from all extensive organization renders necessary what is called leadership. Consequently the power of determination comes to be considered one of the specific attributes of leadership, and is gradually withdrawn from the masses to be concentrated in the hands of the leaders alone. Thus the leaders, who were at first no more than the executive organs of the collective will, soon emancipate themselves from the mass and become independent of its control.

Organization implies the tendency to oligarchy. In every organization, whether it be a political party, a professional union, or any other association of the kind, the aristocratic tendency manifests itself very clearly. The mechanism of the organization, while conferring a solidity of structure, induces serious changes in the organized mass, completely inverting the respective position of the leaders and the led. As a result of organization, every party or professional union becomes divided into a minority of directors and a majority of directed.

It has been remarked that in the lower stages of civilization tyranny is dominant. Democracy cannot come into existence until there is attained a subsequent and more highly developed stage of social life. Freedoms and privileges,
and among these latter the privilege of taking part in the direction of public affairs, are at first restricted to the few. Recent times have been characterized by
the gradual extension of these privileges to a widening circle. This is what we
know as the era of democracy. But if we pass from the sphere of the state to the
sphere of party, we may observe that as democracy continues to develop, a back-
wash sets in. With the advance of organization, democracy tends to decline.
Democratic evolution has a parabolic course. At the present time, at any rate as
far as party life is concerned, democracy is in the descending phase. It may be
enunciated as a general rule that the increase in the power of the leaders is directly proportional with the extension of the organization. In the various parties
and labor organizations of different countries the influence of the leaders is
mainly determined (apart from racial and individual grounds) by the varying development of organization. Where organization is stronger, we find that there is
a lesser degree of applied democracy.

Every solidly constructed organization, whether it be a democratic state, a
political party, or a league of proletarians for the resistance of economic oppression, presents a soil eminently favorable for the differentiation of organs and of
functions. The more extended and the more ramified the official apparatus of
the organization, the greater the number of its members, the fuller its treasury,
and the more widely circulated its press, the less efficient becomes the direct
control exercised by the rank and file, and the more is this control replaced by
the increasing power of committees. ...

As organization develops, not only do the tasks of the administration become
more difficult and more complicated, but, further, its duties become enlarged
and specialized to such a degree that it is no longer possible to take them all in at
a single glance. In a rapidly progressive movement, it is not only the growth in
the number of duties, but also the higher quality of these, which imposes a more
extensive differentiation of function. Nominally, and according to the letter of
the rules, all the acts of the leaders are subject to the ever vigilant criticism of the
rank and file. In theory the leader is merely an employee bound by the instruction he receives. He has to carry out the orders of the mass, of which he is no
more than the executive organ. But in actual fact, as the organization increases
in size, this control becomes purely fictitious. The members have to give up the
idea of themselves conducting or even supervising the whole administration,
and are compelled to hand these tasks over to trustworthy persons specially
nominated for the purpose, to salaried officials. The rank and file must content
themselves with summary reports, and with the appointment of occasional special committees of inquiry. Yet this does not derive from any special change in
the rules of the organization. It is by very necessity that a simple employee gradually becomes a "leader," acquiring a freedom of action which he ought not to

possess. The chief then becomes accustomed to dispatch important business on his own responsibility, and to decide various questions relating to the life of the party without any attempt to consult the rank and file. It is obvious that democratic control thus undergoes a progressive diminution, and is ultimately reduced to an infinitesimal minimum. In all the socialist parties there is a continual increase in the number of functions withdrawn from the electoral assemblies and transferred to the executive committees. In this way there is constructed a powerful and complicated edifice. The principle of division of labor coming more and more into operation, executive authority undergoes division and subdivision. There is thus constituted a rigorously defined and hierarchical bureaucracy. In the catechism of party duties, the strict observance of hierarchical rules becomes the first article. The hierarchy comes into existence as the outcome of technical conditions, and its constitution is an essential postulate of the regular functioning of the party machine.

It is indisputable that the oligarchical and bureaucratic tendency of party organization is a matter of technical and practical necessity. It is the inevitable product of the very principle of organization. Not even the most radical wing of the various socialist parties raises any objection to this retrogressive evolution, the contention being that democracy is only a form of organization and that where it ceases to be possible to harmonize democracy with organization, it is better to abandon the former than the latter. ...

In all times, in all phases of development, in all branches of human activity, there have been leaders. It is true that certain socialists, above all the orthodox Marxists of Germany, seek to convince us that socialism knows nothing of "leaders," that the party has "employees" merely, being a democratic party, and the existence of leaders being incompatible with democracy. But a false assertion such as this cannot override a sociological law. Its only result is, in fact, to strengthen the rule of the leaders, for it serves to conceal from the mass a danger which really threatens democracy.

For technical and administrative reasons, no less than for tactical reasons, a strong organization needs an equally strong leadership. As long as an organization is loosely constructed and vague in its outlines, no professional leadership can arise. ... The more solid the structure of an organization becomes in the course of the evolution of the modern political party, the more marked becomes the tendency to replace the emergency leader by the professional leader. Every party organization which has attained to a considerable degree of complication demands that there should be a certain number of persons who devote all their activities to the work of the party. The mass provides these by delegations, and the delegates, regularly appointed, become permanent representatives of the mass for the direction of its affairs.

For democracy, however, the first appearance of professional leadership marks the beginning of the end, and this, above all, on account of the logical impossibility of the "representative" system, whether in parliamentary life or in party delegation. Jean Jacques Rousseau may be considered as the founder of this aspect of the criticism of democracy. He defines popular government as "the exercise of the general will" and draws from this the logical inference that "it can never be alienated from itself, and the sovereign—who is nothing but a collective concept—can only be represented by himself. Consequently the instant a people gives itself to representatives, it is no longer free." A mass which delegates its sovereignty, that is to say transfers its sovereignty to the hands of a few individuals, abdicates its sovereign functions. For the will of the people is not transferable, nor even the will of the single individuals. ...

This criticism of the representative system is applicable above all in our own days, in which political life continually assumes more complex forms. As this complexity increases, it becomes more and more absurd to attempt to "represent" a heterogeneous mass in all the innumerable problems which arise out of the increasing differentiation of our political and economic life. To represent, in this sense, comes to mean that the purely individual desire masquerades and is accepted as the will of the mass. In certain isolated cases, where the questions involved are extremely simple, and where the delegated authority is of brief duration, representation is possible. But permanent representation will always be tantamount to the exercise of dominion by the representatives over the represented. ...

PSYCHOLOGICAL CAUSES OF LEADERSHIP

One who holds the office of delegate acquires a moral right to that office, and delegates remain in office unless removed by extraordinary circumstances or in obedience to rules observed with exceptional strictness. An election made for a definite purpose becomes a life incumbency. Custom becomes a right. One who has for a certain time held the office of delegate ends by regarding that office as his own property. If refused reinstatement, he threatens reprisals (the threat of resignation being the least serious among these) which will tend to sow confusion among his comrades, and this confusion will continue until he is victorious.

Resignation of office, in so far as it is not a mere expression of discouragement or protest (such as distinction to accept a candidature in an unpromising constituency), is in most cases a means for the retention and fortification of leadership. Even in political organizations greater than party, the leaders often employ this stratagem, thus disarming their adversaries by a deference which does not lack a specious democratic color. The opponent is forced to exhibit in return an event greater deference, and this above all when the leader who makes use of the method is really indispensable, or is considered indispensable by the mass. ...

There is no exaggeration in the assertion that among the citizens who enjoy political rights the number of those who have a lively interest in public affairs is insignificant. In the majority of human beings the sense of an intimate relation-

ship between the good of the individual and the good of the collectivity is but little developed. Most people are altogether devoid of understanding of the actions and reactions between that organism we call the state and their private
interests, their prosperity, and their life. ...

In the life of modern democratic parties we may observe signs of similar indifference. It is only a minority which participates in party decisions, and sometimes that minority is ludicrously small. The most important resolutions taken
by the most democratic of all parties, the socialist party, always emanate from a
handful of the members. It is true that the renouncement of the exercise of
democratic rights is voluntary; except in those cases, which are common
enough, where the active participation of the organized mass in party life is prevented by geographical or topographical conditions. Speaking generally, it is the
urban part of the organization which decides everything; the duties of the members living in country districts and in remote provincial towns are greatly restricted; they are expected to pay their subscriptions and to vote during elections in favor of the candidates selected by the organization of the great town. ...

The same thing happens in party life as happens in the state. In both, the demand for monetary supplies is upon a coercive foundation, but the electoral system has no established sanction. An electoral right exists, but no electoral duty.
Until this duty is superimposed upon the right, it appears probable that a small
minority only will continue to avail itself of the right which the majority voluntarily renounces, and that the minority will always dictate laws for the indifferent and apathetic mass. The consequence is that, in the political groupings of
democracy, the participation in party life has an echeloned aspect. The extensive base consists of the great mass of electors; upon this is superposed the enormously smaller mass of enrolled members of the local branch of the party, numbering perhaps one-tenth or even as few as one-thirtieth of the electors; above
this, again, comes the much smaller number of the members who regularly attend meetings; next comes the group of officials of the party; and highest of all,
consisting in part of the same individuals as the last group, come the half-dozen
or so members of the executive committee. Effective power is here in inverse ratio to the number of those who exercise it. ...

Though it grumbles occasionally, the majority is really delighted to find persons who will take the trouble to look after its affairs. In the mass, and even in
the organized mass of the labor parties, there is an immense need for direction
and guidance. This need is accompanied by a genuine cult for the leaders, who
are regarded as heroes. ...

The mass is sincerely grateful to its leaders, regarding gratitude as a sacred
duty. As a rule, this sentiment of gratitude is displayed in the continual re-election of the leaders who have deserved well of the party, so that leadership commonly becomes perpetual. It is the general feeling of the mass that it would be
"ungrateful" if they failed to confirm in his functions every leader of long service. ...

INTELLECTUAL FACTORS

In the infancy of the socialist party, when the organization is still weak, when its membership is scanty, and when its principal aim is to diffuse a knowledge of the elementary principles of socialism, professional leaders are less numerous than are leaders whose work in this department is no more than an accessory occupation. But with the further progress of the organization, new needs continually arise, at once within the party and in respect of its relationships with the outer world. Thus the moment inevitably comes when neither the idealism and enthusiasm of the intellectuals, nor yet the goodwill with which the proletarians devote their free time on Sundays to the work of the party, suffice any longer to meet the requirements of the case. The provisional must then give place to the permanent, and dilettantism must yield to professionalism.

With the appearance of professional leadership, there ensues a great accentuation of the cultural differences between the leaders and the led. Long experience has shown that among the factors which secure the dominion of minorities over majorities—money and its equivalents (economic superiority), tradition and hereditary transmission (historical superiority)—the first place must be given to the formal instruction of the leaders (so-called intellectual superiority). Now the most superficial observation shows that in the parties of the proletariat the leaders are, in matters of education, greatly superior to the led. ...

Whilst their occupation and the needs of daily life render it impossible for the masses to attain to a profound knowledge of the social machinery, and above all of the working of the political machine, the leader of working-class origin is enabled, thanks to his new situation, to make himself intimately familiar with all the technical details of public life, and thus to increase his superiority over the rank and file. In proportion as the profession of politician becomes a more complicated one, and in proportion as the rules of social legislation become more numerous, it is necessary for one who would understand politics to possess wider experience and more extensive knowledge. Thus the gulf between the leaders and the rest of the party becomes ever wider, until the moment arrives in which the leaders lose all true sense of solidarity with the class from which they have sprung, and there ensues a new class-division between ex-proletarian captains and proletarian common soldiers. When the workers choose leaders for themselves, they are with their own hands creating new masters whose principal means of dominion is found in their better instructed minds. ...

The democratic masses are thus compelled to submit a restriction of their own wills when they are forced to give their leaders an authority which is in the long run destructive to the very principle of democracy. The leader's principal source of power is found in his indispensability. One who is indispensable has in his power all the lords and masters of the earth. The history of the working-class parties continually furnishes instances in which the leader has been in flagrant contradiction with the fundamental principles of the movement, but in which the rank and file have not been able to make up their minds to draw the logical consequences of this conflict, because they feel that they cannot get along without the leader, and cannot dispense with the qualities he has acquired in virtue of the very position to which they have themselves elevated him, and because they do not see their way to find an adequate substitute. ...

The incompetence of the masses is almost universal throughout the domains of political life, and this constitutes the most solid foundation of the power of the leaders. The incompetence furnishes the leaders with a practical and to some extent with a moral justification. Since the rank and file are incapable of looking after their own interests, it is necessary that they should have experts to attend to their affairs. From this point of view it cannot be always considered a bad thing that the leaders should really lead. The free election of leaders by the rank and file presupposes that the latter possess the competence requisite for the recognition and appreciation of the competence of the leaders. ...

THE STABILITY OF LEADERSHIP

Long tenure of office involves dangers for democracy. For this reason those organizations which are anxious to retain their democratic essence make it a rule that all the offices at their disposal shall be conferred for brief periods only. If we take into account the number of offices to be filled by universal suffrage and the frequency of elections, the American citizens is the one who enjoys the largest measure of democracy. In the United States, not only the legislative bodies, but all the higher administrative and judicial officials are elected by popular vote. It has been calculated that every American citizen must on an average exercise his function as a voter twenty-two times a year. The members of the socialist parties in the various countries must today exercise similarly extensive electoral activities: nomination of candidates for parliament, county councils, and municipalities; nomination of delegates to local and national party congresses; election of committees; re-election of the same; and so on, *da capo*. In almost all the socialist parties and trade unions the officers are elected for a brief term, and must be re-elected at least every two years. The longer the tenure of office, the greater becomes the influence of the leader over the masses and the greater therefore his independence. Consequently a frequent repetition of election is an elementary precaution on the part of democracy against the virus of oligarchy.

Since in the democratic parties the leaders owe their position to election by the mass, and are exposed to the chance of being dispossessed at no distant date, when forced to seek re-election, it would seem at first sight as if the democratic working of these parties were indeed secured. A persevering and logical application of democratic principles should in fact get rid of all personal considerations and of all attachment to tradition. Just as in the political life of constitutional states the ministry must consist of members of that party which possesses a parliamentary majority, so also in the socialist party the principal offices ought always to be filled by the partisans of those tendencies which have prevailed at the congresses. Thus the old party dignitaries ought always to yield before youthful forces, before those who have acquired that numerical preponderance which is represented by at least half of the membership plus one. It must, moreover, be a natural endeavor not to leave the same comrades too long in occupation of important offices, lest the holders of these should stick in their grooves, and should come to regard themselves as God-given leaders. But in those parties which are solidly organized, the actual state of affairs is far from corresponding to this theory. The sentiment of tradition, in cooperation with an instinctive need for stability, has as its result that the leadership represents always the past rather than the present. Leadership is indefinitely retained, not because it is the tangible expression of the relationships between the forces existing in the party at any given moment, but simply because it is already constituted. It is through gregarious idleness, or, if we may employ the euphemism, it is in virtue of the law of inertia, that the leaders are so often confirmed in their office as long as they like. These tendencies are particularly evident in the German social democracy, where the leaders are practically irremovable. ...

It is in this manner that the leaders of an eminently democratic party, nominated by indirect suffrage, prolong throughout their lives the powers with which they have once been invested. The reelection demanded by the rules becomes a pure formality. The temporary commission becomes a permanent one, and the tenure of office an established right. The democratic leaders are more firmly established in their seats than were ever the leaders of an aristocratic body. Their term of office comes greatly to exceed the mean duration of ministerial life in monarchical states. ...

There is an additional motive in operation. In the working-class organization, whether founded for political or for economic ends, just as much as in the life of the state, it is indispensable that the official should remain in office for a considerable time, so that he may familiarize himself with the work he has to do, may gain practical experience, for he cannot become a useful official until he has been given time to work himself into his new office. Moreover, he will not devote himself zealously to his task, he will not feel himself thoroughly at one with the aim he is intended to pursue, if he is likely to be dismissed at any moment; he needs the sense of security provided by the thought that nothing but circumstances of an unforeseen and altogether extraordinary character will deprive him of his position. Appointment to office for short terms is democratic, but is quite unpractical alike on technical and psychological grounds. Since it fails to arouse in the employee a proper sense of responsibility, it throws the door open to administrative anarchy. ...

In proportion as the chiefs become detached from the mass they show themselves more and more inclined, when gaps in their own ranks have to be filled, to effect this, not by way of popular election, but by cooptation, and also to increase their own effectives wherever possible, by creating new posts upon their own initiative. There arises in the leaders a tendency to isolate themselves, to form a sort of cartel, and to surround themselves, as it were, with a wall, within which they will admit those only who are of their own way of thinking. Instead of allowing their successors to be appointed by the choice of the rank and file, the leaders do all in their power to choose these successors for themselves, and to fill up gaps in their own ranks directly or indirectly by the exercise of their own volition. ...

In the nomination of candidates for election we find, in addition, another grave oligarchical phenomenon, nepotism. The choice of the candidates almost always depends upon a little clique, consisting of the local leaders and their assistants, which suggests suitable names to the rank and file. In many cases the constituency comes to be regarded as a family property. ...

THE STRUGGLE BETWEEN
THE LEADERS AND THE MASSES

Those who defend the arbitrary acts committed by the democracy, point out the masses have at their disposal means whereby they can react against the violation of their rights. These means consist in the right of controlling and dismissing their leaders. Unquestionably this defense possesses a certain theoretical value, and the authoritarian inclinations of the leaders are in some degree attenuated by these possibilities. In states with a democratic tendency and under a parliamentary regime, to obtain the fall of a detested minister it suffices, in theory, that the people should be weary of him. In the same way, once more in theory, the ill-humor and the opposition of a socialist group or of an election committee is enough to effect the recall of a deputy's mandate, and in the same way the hostility of the majority at the annual congress of trade unions should be enough to secure the dismissal of a secretary. In practice, however, the exercise of this theoretical right is interfered with by the working of the whole series of conservative tendencies to which allusion has previously been made, so that the supremacy of the autonomous and sovereign masses is rendered purely illusory. ...

With the institution of leadership there simultaneously begins, owing to the long tenure of office, the transformation of the leaders into a closed caste. ...

DEMOCRACY AND THE IRON LAW OF OLIGARCHY

The only scientific doctrine which can boast of ability to make an effective reply to all the theories, old or new, affirming the immanent necessity for the perennial existence of the "political class" in the Marxist doctrine. In this doctrine the state is identified with the ruling class—an identification from which Bakunin, Marx's pupil, drew the extreme consequences. The state is merely the executive committee of the ruling class, or, to quote the expression of a recent neo-Marxist, the state is merely a "trade-union formed to defend the interest of the powers-that-be." It is obvious that this theory greatly resembles the conservative theory of Gaetano Mosca. ...

The Marxist theory of the state, when conjoined with a faith in the revolutionary energy of the working class and the democratic effects of the socialization of the means of production, leads logically to the idea of a new social order which to the school of Mosca appears utopian. According to the Marxists the capitalist mode of production transforms the great majority of the population into proletarians, and thus digs its own grave. As soon as it has attained maturity, the proletariat will seize political power, and will immediately transform private property into state property. "In this way it will eliminate itself, for it will thus put an end to all social differences, and consequently to all class antagonisms. In other words, the proletariat will annul the state, *qua* state. Capitalist society, divided into classes, has need of the state as an organization of the ruling class, ... whose purpose it is to maintain the capitalist system of production in its own interest and in order to effect the continued exploitation of the proletariat. Thus to put an end to the state is synonymous with putting an end to the existence of the dominant class." But the new collectivist society, the society without classes, which is to be established upon the ruins of the ancient state, will also need elective elements. ... It is none the less true that social wealth cannot be satisfactorily administered in any other manner than by the creation of an extensive bureaucracy. In this way we are led by an inevitable logic to the flat denial of the possibility of a state without classes. The administration of an immeasurable large capital, above all when this capital is collective property, confers upon the administrator influence at least equal to that possessed by the private owner of capital. Consequently the critics in advance of the Marxist social order ask whether the instinct which today leads the members of the possessing classes to transmit to their children the wealth which they (the parents) have amassed, will not exist also in the administrators of the public wealth of the socialist state, and whether these administrators will not utilize their immense influence in order to secure for their children the succession to the offices which they themselves hold. ...

The sociological phenomena whose general characteristics have been discussed in this chapter and in preceding ones offer numerous vulnerable points to the scientific opponents of democracy. These phenomena would seem to prove beyond dispute that society cannot exist without a "dominant" or "political" class, and that the ruling class, while its elements are subject to a frequent partial renewal, nevertheless constitutes the only factor of sufficiently durable efficacy in the history of human development. According to this view, the government, or, if the phrase be preferred, the state, cannot be anything other than the organization of a minority. It is the aim of this minority to impose upon the rest of society a "legal order," which is the outcome of the exigencies of dominion and of the exploitation of the mass of helots effected by the ruling minority, and can never be truly representative of the majority. The majority is thus permanently incapable of self-government. Even when the discontent of the masses culminates in a successful attempt to deprive the bourgeoisie of power, this is after all, so Mosca contends, effected only in appearance; always and necessarily there springs from the masses a new organized minority which raises itself to the rank of a governing class. Thus the majority of human beings, in a condition of eternal tutelage, are predestined by tragic necessity to submit to the dominion of a small minority, and must be content to constitute the pedestal of an oligarchy. ...

FINAL CONSIDERATIONS

Leadership is a necessary phenomenon in every form of social life. Consequently it is not the task of science to inquire whether this phenomenon is good or evil, or predominantly one or the other. But there is great scientific value in the demonstration that every system of leadership is incompatible with the most essential postulates of democracy. We are now aware that the law of the historic necessity of oligarchy is primarily based upon a series of facts of experience. Like all other scientific laws, sociological laws are derived from empirical observation. In order, however, to deprive our axiom of its purely descriptive character, and to confer upon it that status of analytical explanation which can alone transform a formula into law, it does not suffice to contemplate from a unitary outlook those phenomena which may be empirically established; we must also study the determining causes of these phenomena. Such has been our task.

Now, *if* we leave out of consideration the tendency of the leaders to organize themselves and to consolidate their interests, and if we leave also out of consideration the gratitude of the led towards the leaders, and the general immobility and passivity of the masses, we are led to conclude that the principal cause of oligarchy in the democratic parties is to be found in the technical indispensability of leadership.

The process which has begun in consequence of the differentiation of functions in the party is completed by a complex of qualities which the leaders acquire through their detachment from the mass. At the outset, leaders arise SPONTANEOUSLY; their functions are ACCESSORY and GRATUITOUS. Soon, however, they become PROFESSIONAL leaders, and in this second stage of development they are STABLE and IRREMOVABLE.

It follows that the explanation of the oligarchical phenomenon which thus results is partly PSYCHOLOGICAL; oligarchy derives, that is to say, from the psychical transformations which the leading personalities in the parties undergo in the course of their lives. But also, and still more, oligarchy depends upon what we may term the PSYCHOLOGY OF ORGANIZATION ITSELF, that is to say, upon the tactical and technical necessities which result from the consolidation of every disciplined political aggregate. Reduced to its most concise expression, the fundamental sociological law of political parties (the term "political" being here used in its most comprehensive significance) may be formulated in the following terms: "It is organization which gives birth to the dominion of the elected over the electors, of the mandataries over the mandators, of the delegates over the delegators. Who says organization, says oligarchy."

Every party organization represents an oligarchical power grounded upon a democratic basis. We find everywhere that the power of the elected leaders over the electing masses is almost unlimited. The oligarchical structure of the building suffocates the basic democratic principle. ...

From this chain of reasoning and from these scientific convictions it would be erroneous to conclude that we should renounce all endeavors to ascertain the limits which may be imposed upon the powers exercised over the individual by oligarchies (state, dominant class, party, etc.). It would be an error to abandon the desperate enterprise of endeavoring to discover a social order which will render possible the complete realization of the idea of popular sovereignty. In the present work, as the writer said at the outset, it has not been his aim to indicate new paths. But it seemed necessary to lay considerable stress upon the pessimist aspect of democracy which is forced on us by historical study. We had to inquire whether, and within what limits, democracy must remain purely ideal, possessing no other value than that of a moral criterion which renders it possible to appreciate the varying degrees of that oligarchy which is immanent in every social regime. In other words, we have had to inquire if, and in what degree, democracy is an ideal which we can never hope to realize in practice. ...

Democracy is a treasure which no one will ever discover by deliberate search. But in continuing our search, in laboring indefatigably to discover the undiscoverable, we shall perform a work which will have fertile results in the democratic sense. We have seen, indeed, that within the bosom of the democratic working-class party are born the very tendencies to counteract which that party came into existence. Thanks to the diversity and to the unequal worth of the elements of the party, these tendencies often give rise to manifestations which border on tyranny. ...

The democratic currents of history resemble successive waves. They break ever on the same shoal. They are ever renewed. This enduring spectacle is simultaneously encouraging and depressing. When democracies have gained a certain stage of development, they undergo a gradual transformation, adopting the aristocratic spirit, and in many cases also the aristocratic forms, against which at the outset they struggled so fiercely. Now new accusers arise to denounce the traitors; after an era of glorious combats and of inglorious power, they end by fusing with the old dominant class, whereupon once more they are in their turn attacked by fresh opponents who appeal to the name of democracy. It is probable that this cruel game will continue without end.

12

The Ruling Elites

KENNETH PREWITT & ALAN STONE

In all societies—from societies that are very meagerly developed and have barely attained the dawnings of civilization, down to the most advanced and powerful societies—two classes of people appear—a class that rules and a class that is ruled. The first class, always the less numerous, performs all political functions, monopolizes power and enjoys the advantages that power brings, whereas the second, the more numerous class, is directed and controlled by the first.[1]

In this passage, the Italian political sociologist Gaetano Mosca dispelled the previously unchallenged Aristotelian classification of political systems. Aristotle had held that rule was one of three types: rule by the one (monarchy), by the few (aristocracy), or by the many (democracy), each of which a degenerate form—tyranny, oligarchy, mobocracy. For centuries, political theorists had largely accepted this classification and considered it to be accurate and useful.

The Aristotelian concept, however, was not accepted by the elite theorists of the late nineteenth and early twentieth centuries, who denied that there could be rule by the one or by the many. One person could never rule without the active support and involvement of a governing class, whether made up of party bureaucrats, militarists, administrators, or priests. And certainly the people were too disorganized and too incompetent ever to manage themselves and the collective affairs of society. In denying the Aristotelian classification, the elite theorists liberated political sociology from one of its most ancient assumptions. ...

THE ELITE PERSPECTIVE

The history of politics is the history of elites. The character of a society—whether it is just or unjust, dynamic or stagnant, pacifistic or militaristic—is determined by the character of its elite. The goals of society are established by the elite and accomplished under their direction.

The elite perspective does not deny social change; even radical transformations of society are possible. The elitists only point out that most change comes

125

about as the composition and structure of the elite is transformed. History is the interminable struggle among elites to control the society. This struggle results in the circulation of elites, with established elites giving way to new ideas and new interests. Thus is social change wrought.

Elite theory is in conflict with the marxian idea of class struggle. Where the *Communist Manifesto* claims that "The history of all hitherto existing society is the history of class struggles," the elitist manifesto claims that "The history of all hitherto existing society is the history of elite struggles." Moreover, the elitist would add, so matters will remain. The non-elite are passive observers of this struggle, or at best, are pawns to be mobilized for the temporary advantage of a counter-elite battling against the entrenched elite. In the following statement, Pareto summarizes the argument, and dismisses the masses from serious consideration:

> Let A be the elite in power, B the social element seeking to drive it from power and to replace it, and C the rest of the population, comprising the incompetent, those lacking energy, character and intelligence: in short, the section of society which remains when the elites are subtracted. A and B are the leaders, counting on C to provide them with partisans, with instruments. The C on their own would be impotent: an army without commanders. They become important only if guided by the A or B. Very often—in fact, almost always—it is the B who put themselves at the head of C, the A reposing in a false security or despising the C.[2] ...

Although we shall wish to qualify, modify, and criticize features of the elite theory as we proceed, for the present we can summarize the theory in terms of two principles:

First, no matter what the dominant political ideology or the manner of organizing the State, every society can be divided into the small number who rule and the larger number who are ruled.

Second, the character of society and the direction it is taking can be understood in terms of the composition, structure, and conflicts of the ruling group.

A DIFFERENCE OF OPINION WITHIN
THE ELITE PERSPECTIVE

If today many observers of society accept the two principles of the elitist perspective, not all observers draw the same conclusions. Some see the power and privileges of the ruling class and conclude that the rulers exploit and manipulate the ruled for personal benefit. The rulers monopolize power and enjoy advantages by demanding deference and tribute. They live—and live well—from the efforts of others.

There is a contrary view that rulers perform necessary and socially beneficial tasks. If rulers monopolize power, they do so to serve better all the members of society. The general welfare can be provided and protected only if the rulers can give uniform direction to society and have the force necessary to withstand attacks from enemies within or enemies without. And if the rulers enjoy many special advantages, these are only the just rewards for the special skills they bring to the task of governing and for the effort they expend on behalf of the entire society.

We can provide a simple diagram of these two viewpoints [see Figure 12.1]. Both viewpoints accept the fruitfulness of distinguishing between the rulers and ruled, and both recognize that power and privilege are heavily concentrated in the ruling group. They differ sharply, however, in describing the type of relationship that exists between the rulers and the ruled. In these differing views is one of the enduring paradoxes of politics: that these two views can be so divergent and at the same time correct. ...

THE STATE IS A SOCIAL CONTRACT
BETWEEN UNEQUALS

Because the State in the most general sense benefits those who are ruled as well as those who rule, there is good reason for men to enter the social contract and to submit to some central direction. Because the social contract tends always to benefit some men (usually the rulers) more than other men, coercion and conquest are often necessary to establish and maintain the State.

Here, then, is a perspective that allows for the generalized benefits of the social contract and at the same time underscores the fact that these benefits are not equitably distributed. It is appropriate to insist that the social contract is between unequals because societies are arranged so that some men command and others obey. But it can also be insisted that the very fact that society exists is an indication that it is of general benefit. Men flounder and suffer outside society, and their lot can only improve when they join in collective action.

The axiom that titles this section, however, does not answer all of the questions about the function of the ruling class. It only poses in a fresh guise the paradoxical questions with which we began: Do elites exploit or do they serve? Are we to emphasize their privileges or their responsibilities? It is by now evident that contrasting interpretations of politics derive from how one chooses to answer these questions. Let us consider them in greater detail.

Unequal Privileges: The Radical's Emphasis

That the State is a contract between unequals is readily admitted by the radical, and deplored as well. The rulers not only have greater powers than the ruled, which is true by definition, they also enjoy greater privileges. This is because a disproportionately large share of the social surplus produced in the society remains in the hands of the ruling class for their personal enjoyment and benefit. If craftsmen produce artifacts and ornaments, these status symbols become the possessions of the ruling class. If warriors venture forth to conquer and return

[Figure 12.1]

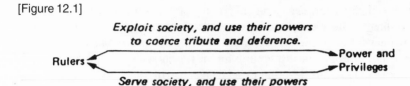

with slaves and women, the slaves will serve in the fields and kitchens of the rulers and the women will be placed in their harems. If the productive labor of society is used to build palaces, temples, and monuments, these edifices will be in-
habited by or dedicated to the members of the ruling class. It has been a
constant fact of history that much more than an equal share of the social surplus
is retained by the rulers for private pleasure.

To the radical, the distinguishing trait of rulers is their inclination to exploit.
Having been granted (or having usurped) certain powers, the rulers seem unable
to refrain from accumulating privileges. They do so through force, fraud, and a
legitimizing ideology. ... For ... [persons] in the radical tradition, the State and
its laws are the instruments of oppression. In the *Communist Manifesto*, Marx
called the executive of the modern State nothing "but a committee for managing the common affairs of the whole bourgeoisie. ... " From the radical viewpoint, rulers rule for their own benefit. ...

The radical perspective contains within it a theory of social change. The two
unequal actors on the political stage stand in an antagonistic relationship to
each other. Social change results from the conflict between then, especially
from the energy released as the oppressed unite and challenge the exploiting
rulers. Marxian theories of class conflict typify this point of view, as do the theories of other political analysts who view the conflict more in terms of authority
relationships than in terms of economic ones.

There are actually two very different results which might derive from the conflict between exploiters and the exploited. And these differences are very important to our analysis. We can use Marx to illustrate one point of view and the
American Declaration of Independence to illustrate the other.

The conflict between the oppressive bourgeoisie and the oppressed proletariat would, according to Marx, ultimately result in a classless society. The inequality between rulers and ruled stemmed from economic arrangements. Terminate
these economic arrangements—specifically private ownership of the means of
production—and the structural division between rulers and ruled would end. It
would probably take a violent revolution to accomplish this, because everywhere
the rulers tenaciously cling to their powers and privileges, but the aftermath
would be well worth the struggle. History would move toward radical egalitarian-
ism, a social community in which none would be more privileged than others.
The long evolution of the State would end, ironically, in the State's demise.

Let us label this viewpoint the attack on the "structure of rule." This is the kernel of truth in the radical perspective: If rulers gain power and enjoy advantages by exploiting, the object of the exploited should be to eliminate all rulers, not just a particular set of rulers. Society must be restructured; it must be classless.

Contrast this doctrine with the Unanimous Declaration of Independence of the Thirteen United States of America, 4 July 1776.

> We hold these truths to be self-evident, that all men are created equal, that they are endowed by their Creator with certain unalienable Rights, that among these are Life, Liberty, and the pursuit of Happiness. ...
>
> That whenever any Form of Government becomes destructive of these ends, it is the Right of the People to alter or to abolish it, and to institute new Government. ...
>
> But when a long train of abuses and usurpations, pursuing invariably the same Object evinces a design to reduce them under absolute Despotism, it is their right, it is their duty, to throw off such Government, and to provide new Guards for their future security.

Thus was proclaimed the "right of revolution," but the practical consequences of the words penned by Thomas Jefferson differ sharply from those of Karl Marx. The American Revolution was aimed at particular rulers and not the structure of rule. It was not to be followed by the "withering away of the State" but by new Guards.

We might label this view the attack on the "composition of the ruling class." This view as well as the Marxist view holds that rulers exploit and oppress, but the differences are more important than the similarities. For Jefferson and his colleagues it was not the "ruling class" in the abstract which was the villain, it was simply those obnoxious Englishmen, especially George III, who would not play by the rules of the game. It was not necessary to change these rules, only to change the rulers. This viewpoint has had a profound significance for American politics, because it effectively isolates American political thought from the more radical tradition which calls into question the very necessity of rulers. As we shall see, it allows for a drift toward the elitist viewpoint that social change is not the product of class tensions but rather results from differing opinions and ambitions within the ruling circles.

Unequal Responsibilities:
The Conservative's Emphasis

The conservative does not deny that the State is a contract between unequals, but he emphasizes not the inequality of privileges but the inequality of responsibilities. The rulers and the ruled make an unequal contribution to the general social order, with the former making much the greater contribution.

This is an old idea, frequently expressed in creation myths. It is the elect who lead the people from darkness, chaos, or slavery into a new and better social order. This elect is then entrusted with the responsibility of preserving the moral and material gains thereby acquired. ...

The conservative is not dismayed that rulers have many special privileges and enjoy advantages denied lesser men. These are the rewards for shouldering responsibilities on behalf of the entire society.

The ruler has two main types of responsibility: moral and material. ... Emile Durkheim ... developed the theme that man cannot do without community and cannot do without the rules implied by community. The quest for company, for community, for social integration is part of human nature. Deny man these things and he loses a sense of direction and meaning. As succinctly stated by one scholar, "The disorder of the community means the disorder of the individual."[3] It is a short step from this comment to observing that man needs rulers: "Those who formulate and apply rules are the leaders of society, not merely because they rule it in a juridical sense, but because they preside over the inner order of man."[4] In short, if there must be rules, there must be rule inventors; if there must be guidance, there must be guidance givers. Thus do leaders provide a moral framework for society, a framework increasingly critical as society grows in complexity and scale. Those who provide this framework merit the powers and privileges they enjoy.

The responsibility for the moral integration of society is particularly evident in the public ceremonies which reaffirm the political beliefs by which men swear. Founding charters, creation myths, constitutions, sacred traditions, and the feats of past rulers express the origin, the growth, and the purpose of the political community. Political elites have responsibility for preserving these beliefs, and for teaching the community their significance. In this way, the solidarity and moral purpose of the society is continually affirmed. ...

In all of these rituals, the rulers are claiming to preserve those hard-earned values and victories of the past, and pledging to apply them to new conditions. They are protecting the political beliefs which men live by. For their willingness to assume such responsibilities, they are entitled to the powers and advantages of office. The pomp and circumstance that surround the rulers are necessary to symbolize to the people the integrity and dignity of the State. To strip the rulers of their eminent status would be to strip them of their significance, and society would be the sorrier for it.

Just as the moral well-being of the society depends on its rulers, so also does the material well-being. The rulers and the ruled are unequals in the sense that the elite have the responsibility for managing the society: They are the ones who get the trains to run on time! The conservative emphasizes that the rulers are indispensable in a complex society. Managing factories and transport systems, providing schools and hospitals, organizing armies and police forces require coordination and regulation, hence there must be coordinators and regulators. Because the material well-being of the populace depends on economic growth, social services, and social protection, the rulers who organize and direct their provision should be given the necessary powers to make things work and should be rewarded for their efforts.

The thesis that elites are necessary for the material well-being of the society can be substantiated by either of two different viewpoints about the masses. Most common is the assertion that the masses are incompetent and thus incapable of "acting in default of an initiative from without and from above." Elite theorist Robert Michels continues, "striking proof of the organic weakness of the mass is furnished by the way in which, when deprived of their leaders in time of action, they abandon the field of battle in disordered flight; they seem to have no power of instinctive reorganization, and are useless until new captains arise capable of replacing those that have been lost."[5] The conception that leaderless people are incompetent receives support with the radical tradition. It was Lenin in *What Is to Be Done* who claimed that "without the 'dozen' tried and talented leaders (and talented men are not born by the hundred), professionally trained, schooled by long experience, and working in perfect harmony, no class in modern society is capable of conducting a determined struggle."[6] Lenin's influential political tract is still used today by communist parties as the justification for the vanguard role, a leadership concept which echoes Michels's pessimism.

In contrast to the view that the masses are incompetent is the proposition that men are rational *and therefore* organize themselves into hierarchies. The people are well aware that their material well-being is furthered by the actions and talents of the rulers, and thus they willingly defer to the judgments of those who command the society. The opportunity costs of an alternative arrangement would be prohibitive, although it is theoretically possible for social action to be organized on the basis of every member of society negotiating with every other member until agreement is reached. But rational men will not pay the costs of such an elaborate negotiating machinery, and prefer to delegate authority to a smaller group of talented and trusted leaders.

Whether you start from the premise that masses are incompetent or that men are rational, you arrive at the same conclusion. It takes leaders to make things go. Thus, there is a very pragmatic reason for a social contract between unequals: Differential responsibilities are assigned and it follows that there will be differential powers and privileges. Those powers must be unequal so that the society can be run efficiently while privileges must be unequal so that the most able will be attracted to the responsible positions.

The conservative sees the relationship between the rulers and ruled in terms not of privilege but of responsibility. The moral significance and material well-being of society rests on the shoulders of the elite. This view is part of a larger perspective which sees society as an "organism" in which each part is mutually interdependent with all other parts. ...

For the conservative, society is not primarily the result of coercion and fraud. It is the result of reciprocity and mutual benefit. The rulers stand at the center of society and provide it with unification, coherence, and direction. Their powers and privileges should not be begrudged. High positions are not gained through force but by superior talent and hard work. Privileges are not stolen but are freely given as fair rewards for the responsibilities assumed. It would be an injustice to deny these rewards, and it would be impractical because how else would men of talent be attracted to positions of responsibility.

ELITE THEORY AND SOCIAL CHANGE

Elitists are sometimes criticized for having no theory of social change. It is true that in their view the interests of the status quo and the established elite are overwhelmingly advantaged in any struggle with new interests or a counter-elite. The clearest statement of this thesis is found in the classic study by Michels of pre-World War I Socialist Parties in Western Europe.[7] He observed the gradual drift of these parties, particularly the German Socialist Party, into the hands of conservative leaders. These leaders were skilled at thwarting any challenge to their powers. The powerful political machines they created virtually precluded their being ousted from office. Moreover, the leaderships had developed life styles and interest different from those of their followers. Generalizing from his investigation, Michels set forth one of the most famous theories of social science—the iron law of oligarchy. In its essentials, the "law" holds that all organizations come to be ruled by self-perpetuating elites with mass participation limited to ritualistically ratifying the actions of the oligarchy. ... Few exceptions to this theory can be found.

Why is this so? A cataloging of the advantages enjoyed within organizations by elites as compared to the advantages of the masses and prospective counter-elites will soon show why the "iron law" describes so many organizations. Those in control of an organization, for example, make use of such resources as its technical staff, publicity and communications machinery, financial resources, and manpower. They also have in their favor a superior knowledge of organization affairs and the opportunity to wrap themselves in the aura of the organization so that criticism of the leadership can be interpreted as an unpatriotic attack on the organization. Additional advantages of elites leading an organization are the important psychological advantages over rivals and potential counter-elites. Custom, the need felt by masses for tried-and-true leadership; the socialized reverence of the masses for extant leadership; and the appeals to experience, indispensibility, and accomplishments are frequently employed by such elites. The element of fear can also be employed by the incumbent elite. This includes both the appeal that dismissal of the leadership would discredit the organization to the outside world and undermine its bargaining position and also the appeal that counter-elites are insufficiently deferential to the accomplishments of the incumbents, and thus perhaps are "unpatriotic" or "traitorous." Intimidation and repression as tactics available to the established elite make the removal of the elite quite difficult.

Michels denies the political significance of any element outside of the ruling minorities. No political initiative comes from the public. The public is best understood as an atomized and fragmented mass, capable only of responding to the leadership of superior elements in society. Only the elite can transcend their own milieux and evolve a vision of a different society. The masses are trapped in their milieux, depending on the visions provided them by an elite.

From this it might be thought that elite theory cannot account for social and political change, and indeed this criticism has often been voiced. But it is misplaced criticism, because elite theorists have a definite explanation of change. ... Because the important conflicts in society are not between classes but within the elite, the dynamic that accounts for social change is the constant struggle between a minority that holds power and another minority seeking power. It is in the process of elite circulation, or rather in blocked circulation, that we must seek one explanation for social change. Thus, Pareto has argued that when elites do not recruit the most able elements in society from outside their ranks and instead restrict entry to their ranks, they eventually become decadent and unable to cope with the tasks they must undertake. At the same time, the excluded talented elements from a counter-elite, organize the masses injured by the incompetence of the elite, and lead a revolution overthrowing the elite. Once this is done the new elite consolidates its power over the masses. ...

It would, however, be foolhardy to assert that all social and political change can be described in this manner, and neither Mosca nor Pareto attempted to. Joseph Schumpeter, the great Austrian economist, has offered an alternative—or rather, a supplementary theory.[8] Although this theory, developed in his important essay *Social Classes*, is discussed in terms of classes, it is best conceived in terms of elites. According to Schumpeter—as adapted—elites' powers and positions in a national structure depend on the significance accorded their function. Thus, under feudalism, manorial lords were pre-eminent in national structure because of the importance of their military, agricultural, and other functions. But, as their decline shows, the continuing influence of an elite depends upon two factors: (1) the continuing significance of their special functions, and (2) the degree to which they successfully perform that function. Thus, changing economic conditions reduced the importance of the manorial lords, causing their relative decline, while capitalist elites gained power because of their enhanced function. Again, a political elite's failure to maintain economic prosperity when it is their announced or implicit task to do so will enable a counter-elite to mobilize and lead masses against them.

The preoccupation of Mosca and Pareto, in particular, with elite circulation reveals a further aspect of elite theory's conservatism. The basic challenge to society is not to reform itself but to keep from disintegrating. The social order is fragile indeed, and must continually be protected from the untutored passions of the masses. To unleash social energies, as the marxist revolutionaries have threatened to do, is sheer folly, because no one can know where this will lead. Indeed, a mob can destroy institutions and accomplishments painfully and slowly evolved over history. The elite theorists wished then for a moderate and paced circulation of elites, sufficient circulation to dampen the tendencies toward mass mobilization by frustrated counter-elites but not so much as to destroy the continuity and stability of society.

Perhaps elite theory's greatest value is that it provides an explanation for why political and social structures change so gradually, if at all. Most of history is not revolutions, but rather the day-in, day-out performance of important tasks by elites and the modest but significant changes in the composition of the ruling groups. When masses are occasionally aroused from their torpor, they are placated by elites granting symbolic benefits or moderate reforms. It is the extremely rare occasion in history that masses cannot be satisfied in this way. Then they are available for the mobilization by counter-elites, and severe breaks in historical continuity can occur. The Communist revolutions of this century are a case in point, as were the democratic revolutions of the eighteenth century.

DEMOCRATIC THOUGHT AND ELITE THEORY

The theory and the practice of democracy can be interpreted as a substantial modification of elite theory. Democratic thought, at least as shaped by two centuries of politics in the United States, accepts the elite thesis that there is always a division of political labor:

> There are some whose task it is to control the actions of others and issue commands, and others who have to allow themselves to be controlled and have to obey. Today as a hundred years ago there are governments, parliaments, and courts the members of which are entitled to make decisions that affect the lives of many citizens, and there are citizens who can protest or shift their vote but who have to abide by the law. Insofar as either of these relations can be described as one of authority, I would claim that relations of domination and subordination have persisted throughout the changes of the past century.[9]

Accepting the inevitability of a division of political labor has not for the democratic theorist meant accepting the many consequences seen by the elitist. Democratic politics is the gradual but certain chipping away of elitist implications of the division of society into rulers and ruled. ...

Stripped of flowery rhetoric, democratic theory reduces to the simple principle that *rulers are on probation*. This fact dramatically rearranges the power relationship between those who rule and those who are ruled. ...

The composition of the ruling group is determined by a voting public, and this leads to an equalization of the power differences between rulers and ruled.

Under the conditions of universal suffrage and competitive elections, the balance of power shifts to the electorate, if only periodically. Because of this, what the rulers decide reflects a wider set of preferences than just those of the (temporary) rulers. Men in power are but transitory representatives of those who put them there. Thus the most fascinating aspect of the democratic revolution concerns the methods and implications of changing leaders, because this becomes the key to an entirely new theory of the "ruling class."

The eliteist points out that even though rulers are elected, they still have all the advantages of the ruling class. For one thing, they are organized and the masses are disorganized. As Mosca puts it, "The domination of an organized minority, obeying a single impulse, over the unorganized majority is inevitable. ... A hundred men acting uniformly in concert, with a common understanding, will triumph over a thousand men who are not in accord, and can therefore be dealt with one by one." Later Mosca explicitly challenges whether elections make much difference:

> The truth is that the representative *has himself elected* by the voters, and if that phrase should seem too inflexible and too harsh to fit some cases, we might qualify it by saying that *his friends have him elected*. In elections, as in all other manifestations of social life, those who have the will and, especially, the moral, intellectual and material *means* to force their will upon others take the lead over the others and command them.[10]

Michels extends this analysis: Not only does organizational ability grant power, the structure of complex society inevitably gives rise to an organized and oligrachical minority.

The ruling class then retains its advantages despite the advances of democratic thinking. The rulers continue to siphon off an undue amount of the social surplus for personal benefit; they continue to make laws which reflect their own world views and which serve their special interests; and they continue to control the selection of the persons who will inherit their positions. ...

Constitutional democracy has not been designed to eliminate the division of political labor between rulers and ruled. It has been designed to provide an instrumentality whereby the public could select its own rulers and whereby the few with immense powers are accountable to the citizens whose lives they affect. ...

NOTES

1. Gaetano Mosca, *The Ruling Class* (New York: McGraw-Hill, 1939), p. 50. This work was initially published as *Elementi di Scienza Politica*, 1896. The version here cited was edited by Arthur Livingston and translated by Hanna D. Kahn.

2. This quotation is taken from *Les Systemes Socialistes*, initially published in 1902, and reproduced in Vilfredo Pareto, *Sociological Writings*, ed. S. E. Finer (London: Pall Mall Press, 1966), p. 134.

3. Renzo Sereno, *The Rulers: The Theory of the Ruling Class* (New York: Harper and Row, 1968), p. 117.

4. Sereno, *The Rulers*, p. 131.

5. Robert Michels, *Political Parties*, trans. Eden and Cedar Paul (New York: Free Press, 1966), p. 90.

6. V. Lenin, *What Is to Be Done*; reprinted in *Essential Works of Lenin*, Henry M. Christman, ed. (New York: Bantam, 1966), p. 145. *What Is to Be Done* was first published in 1902.

7. Michels, *Political Parties, passim*.

8. Joseph Schumpeter, "Social Classes," in *Imperialism, Social Classes* (New York: Meridian, 1951).

9. Ralf Dahrendorf, *Class and Class Conflict in Industrial Society* (Stanford, Calif.: Stanford University Press, 1959), p. 71.

10. Mosca, *The Ruling Class*, pp. 53, 154.

13

Influence of Democracy on the Feelings of the Americans

ALEXIS DE TOCQUEVILLE

WHY DEMOCRATIC NATIONS SHOW A MORE ARDENT AND ENDURING LOVE OF EQUALITY THAN OF LIBERTY

The first and most intense passion which is engendered by the equality of condition is, I need hardly say, the love of that same equality. My readers will therefore not be surprised that I speak of it before all others. ...

The principle of equality may be established in civil society, without prevailing in the political world. Equal rights may exist of indulging in the same pleasures, of entering the same professions, of frequenting the same places—in a word, of living in the same manner and seeking wealth by the same means, although all men do not take an equal share in the government.

A kind of equality may even be established in the political world, though there should be no political freedom there. A man may be the equal of all his countrymen save one, who is the master of all without distinction, and who selects equally from among them all the agents of his power.

Several other combinations might be easily imagined, by which very great equality would be united to institutions more or less free, or even to institutions wholly without freedom.

Although men cannot become absolutely equal unless they be entirely free, and consequently equality, pushed to its furthest extent, may be confounded with freedom, yet there is good reason for distinguishing the one from the other. The taste which men have for liberty, and that which they feel for equality, are, in fact, two different things; and I am not afraid to add, that, amongst democratic nations, they are two unequal things. ...

Freedom has appeared in the world at different times and under various forms; it has not been exclusively bound to any social condition, and it is not

137

confined to democracies. Freedom cannot, therefore, form the distinguishing characteristics of democratic ages. The peculiar and preponderating fact which marks those ages as its own is the equality of conditions; the ruling passion of men in those periods is the love of this equality. Ask not what singular charm the men of democratic ages find in being equal, or what special reasons they may have for clinging so tenaciously to equality rather than to the other advantages which society holds out to them; equality is the distinguishing characteristic of the age they live in; that, of itself, is enough to explain that they prefer it to all the rest. ...

That political freedom may compromise in its excesses the tranquillity, the property, the lives of individuals, is obvious to the narrowest and most unthinking minds. But, on the contrary, none but attentive and clear-sighted men perceive the perils with which equality threatens us, and they commonly avoid pointing them out. They know that the calamities they apprehend are remote, and flatter themselves that they will only fall upon future generations, for which the present generation takes but little thought. The evils which freedom sometimes brings with it are immediate; they are apparent to all, and all are more or less affected by them. The evils which extreme equality may produce are slowly disclosed; they creep gradually into the social frame; they are only seen at intervals, and at the moment at which they become most violent, habit already causes them to be no longer felt.

The advantages which freedom brings are only shown by length of time; and it is always easy to mistake the cause in which they originate. The advantages of equality are instantaneous, and they may constantly be traced from their source. ...

I think that democratic communities have a natural taste for freedom: left to themselves, they will seek it, cherish it, and view any privation of it with regret. But for equality, their passion is ardent, insatiable, incessant, invincible: they call for equality in freedom; and if they cannot obtain that, they still call for equality in slavery. They will endure poverty, servitude, barbarism—but they will not endure aristocracy.

This is true at al times, and especially true in our own. All men and all powers seeking to cope with this irresistible passion will be overthrown and destroyed by it. In our age, freedom cannot be established without it, and despotism itself cannot reign without its support.

OF INDIVIDUALISM IN DEMOCRATIC COUNTRIES

I have shown how it is that in ages of equality every man seeks for his opinions within himself: I am now about to show how it is that, in the same ages, all his feelings are turned towards himself alone. *Individualism* is a novel expression, to which a novel idea has given birth. Our fathers were only acquainted with egotism. Egotism is a passionate and exaggerated love of self, which leads a man to connect everything with his own person, and to prefer himself to every-thing in the world. Individualism is a mature and calm feeling, which disposes each member of the community to sever himself from the mass of his fellow-creatures; and to draw apart with his family and his friends, so that, after he has thus formed a little circle of his own, he willingly leaves society at large to itself. Egotism originates in blind instinct: individualism proceeds from erroneous judgment more than from depraved feelings; it originates as much in the deficiencies of the mind as in the perversity of the heart.

Egotism blights the germ of all virtue: individualism, at first, only saps the virtues of public life; but, in the long run, it attacks and destroys all others, and is at length absorbed in downright egotism. Egotism is a vice as old as the world, which does not belong to one form of society more than to another: individualism is of democratic origin, and it threatens to spread in the same ratio as the equality of conditions.

Amongst aristocratic nations, as families remain for centuries in the same condition, often on the same spot, all generations become as it were contemporaneous. A man almost knows his forefathers, and respects them: he thinks he already sees his remote descendants, and he loves them. He willingly imposes duties on himself towards the former and the latter; and he will frequently sacrifice his personal gratifications to those who went before and to those who will come after him.

Aristocratic institutions have, moreover, the effect of closely binding every man to several of his fellow-citizens. As the classes of an aristocratic people are strongly marked and permanent, each of them is regarded by its own members as a sort of lesser country, more tangible and more cherished than the country at large. As in aristocratic communities all the citizens occupy fixed positions, one above the other, the result is that each of them always sees a man above himself whose patronage is necessary to him, and below himself another man whose co-operation he may claim.

Men living in aristocratic ages are therefore almost always closely attached to something placed out of their own sphere, and they are often disposed to forget themselves. It is true that in those ages the notion of human fellowship is faint, and that men seldom think of sacrificing themselves for mankind; but they often sacrifice themselves for other men. In democratic ages, on the contrary, when the duties of each individual to the race are much more clear, devoted service to any one man becomes more rare; the bond of human affection is extended, but it is relaxed.

Amongst democratic nations new families are constantly springing up, others are constantly failing away, and all that remain change their condition; the woof of time is every instant broken, and the track of generations effaced. Those who went before are soon forgotten; of those who will come after no one has any idea: the interest of man is confined to those in close propinquity to himself.

As each class approximates to other classes, and intermingles with them, its members become indifferent and as strangers to one another. Aristocracy had made a chain of all the members of the community, from the peasant to the king: democracy breaks that chain, and severs every link of it.

As social conditions become more equal, the number of persons increases who, although they are neither rich enough nor powerful enough to exercise any great influence over their fellow-creatures, have nevertheless acquired or retained sufficient education and fortune to satisfy their own wants. They owe nothing to any man, they expect nothing from any man; they acquire the habit of always considering themselves as standing alone, and they are apt to imagine that their whole destiny is in their own hands.

Thus not only does democracy make every man forget his ancestors, but it hides his descendants, and separates his contemporaries, from him; it throws him back for ever upon himself alone, and threatens in the end to confine him entirely within the solitude of his own heart.

INDIVIDUALISM STRONGER AT THE CLOSE OF A DEMOCRATIC REVOLUTION THAN AT OTHER PERIODS

The period when the construction of democratic society upon the ruins of an aristocracy has just been completed, is especially that at which this separation of men from one another, and the egotism resulting from it, most forcibly strike the observation. Democratic communities not only contain a large number of independent citizens, but they are constantly filled with men who, having entered but yesterday upon their independent condition, are intoxicated with their new power. They entertain a presumptuous confidence in their strength, and as they do not suppose that they can henceforward ever have occasion to claim the assistance of their fellow-creatures, they do not scruple to show that they care for nobody but themselves.

An aristocracy seldom yields without a protracted struggle, in the course of which implacable animosities are kindled between the different classes of society. These passions survive the victory, and traces of them may be observed in the midst of the democratic confusion which ensues.

Those members of the community who were at the top of the late gradations of rank cannot immediately forget their former greatness; they will long regard themselves as aliens in the midst of the newly composed society. They look upon all those whom this state of society has made their equals as oppressors, whose destiny can excite no sympathy; they have lost sight of their former equals, and feel no longer bound by a common interest to their fate: each of them, standing aloof, thinks that he is reduced to care for himself alone. Those, on the contrary, who were formerly at the foot of the social scale, and who have been brought up to the common level by a sudden revolution, cannot enjoy their newly acquired independence without secret uneasiness; and if they meet with some of their former superiors on the same footing as themselves, they stand aloof from them with an expression of triumph and of fear.

It is, then, commonly at the outset of democratic society that citizens are most disposed to live apart. Democracy leads men not to draw near to their fellow-creatures; but democratic revolutions lead them to shun each other, and perpetuate in a state of equality the animosities which the state of inequality engendered.

The great advantage of the Americans is that they have arrived at a state of democracy without having to endure a democratic revolution; and that they are born equal, instead of becoming so.

THAT THE AMERICANS COMBAT THE EFFECTS OF INDIVIDUALISM BY FREE INSTITUTIONS

Despotism, which is of a very timorous nature, is never more secure of continuance than when it can keep men asunder; and all its influence is commonly exerted for that purpose. No vice of the human hear is so acceptable to it as egotism: a despot easily forgives his subjects for not loving him, provided they do not love each other. He does not ask them to assist him in governing the state; it is enough that they do not aspire to govern it themselves. He stigmatizes as turbulent and unruly spirits those who would combine their exertions to promote the prosperity of the community; and, perverting the natural meaning of words, he applauds as good citizens those who have no sympathy for any but themselves.

Thus the vices which despotism engenders are precisely those which equality fosters. These two things mutually and perniciously complete and assist each other. Equality places men side by side, unconnected by any common tie; despotism raises barriers to keep them asunder: the former predisposes them not to consider their fellow-creatures, the latter makes general indifference a sort of public virtue.

Despotism then, which is at all times dangerous, is more particularly to be feared in democratic ages. It is easy to see that in those same ages men stand most in need of freedom. When the members of a community are forced to attend to public affairs, they are necessarily drawn from the circle of their own interests, and snatched at times from self-observation. As soon as a man begins to treat of public affairs in public, he begins to perceive that he is not so independent of this fellow-men as he had at first imagined, and, that, in order to obtain their support, he must often lend them his co-operation. ...

The Americans have combated by free institutions the tendency of equality to keep men asunder, and they subdued it. The legislators of America did not suppose that a general representation of the whole nation would suffice to ward off a disorder at once so natural to the frame of democratic society, and so fatal: they also thought that it would be well to infuse political life into each portion of the territory, in order to multiply to an infinite extent opportunities of acting in concert, for all the members of the community, and to make them constantly feel their mutual dependence on each other. The plan was a wise one. The general affairs of a country only engage the attention of leading politicians, who assemble from time to time in the same places; and as they often lose sight of each other afterwards, no lasting ties are established between them. But if the object be to have the local affairs of a district conducted by the men who reside there, the same persons are always in contact, and they are, in a manner, forced to be acquainted, and to adapt themselves to one another.

It is difficult to draw a man out of his own circle to interest him in the destiny of the state, because he does not clearly understand what influence the destiny of the state can have upon his own lot. But if it be proposed to make a road cross the end of his estate, he will see at a glance that there is a connection between this small public affair and his greatest private affairs; and he will discover, without its being shown to him, the close tie which unites private to general interest. Thus, far more may be done by entrusting to the citizens the administration of minor affairs than by surrendering to them the control of important ones, towards interesting them in the public welfare, and convincing them that they constantly stand in need one of the other in order to provide for it. A brilliant achievement may win for you the favour of a people at one stroke; but to earn the love and respect of the population which surrounds you, a long succession of little services rendered and of obscure good deeds—a constant habit of kindness, and an established reputation for disinterestedness—will be required. Local freedom, then, which leads a great number of citizens to value the affection of their neighbours and of their kindred, perpetually brings men together, and forces them to help one another, in spite of the propensities which sever them.

In the United States the more opulent citizens take great care not to stand aloof from the people; on the contrary, they constantly keep on easy terms with the lower classes: they listen to them, they speak to them every day. They know that the rich in democracies always stand in need of the poor; and that in democratic ages you attach a poor man to you more by your manner than by benefits conferred. The magnitude of such benefits, which sets off the difference of conditions, causes a secret irritation to those who reap advantage from them; but the charm of simplicity of manners is almost irresistible: their affability carries men away, and even their want of polish is not always displeasing. This truth does not take root at once in the minds of the rich. They generally resist it as long as the democratic revolution lasts, and they do not acknowledge it immediately after that revolution is accomplished. They are very ready to do good to the people, but they still choose to keep them at arm's length; they think that is sufficient, but they are mistaken. They might spend fortunes thus without warming the hearts of the population around them; that population does not ask them for the sacrifice of their money, but of their pride. ...

OF THE USE WHICH THE AMERICANS MAKE
OF PUBLIC ASSOCIATIONS IN CIVIL LIFE

If each citizen did not learn, in proportion as he individually becomes more feeble and consequently more incapable of preserving his freedom single-handed, to combine with his fellow-citizens for the purpose of defending it, it is clear that tyranny would unavoidably increase together with equality.

Those associations only which are formed in civil life, without reference to political objects, are here adverted to. The political associations which exist in the United States are only a single feature in the minds of the immense assemblage of associations in that country. Americans of all ages, all conditions, and all dispositions, constantly form associations. They have not only commercial and manufacturing companies, in which all take part, but associations of a thousand other kinds—religious, moral, serious, futile, extensive or restricted, enormous or diminutive. The Americans make associations to give entertainments, to found establishments for education, to build inns, to construct churches, to diffuse books, to send missionaries to the antipodes; and in this manner they found hospitals, prisons, and schools. If it be proposed to advance some truth, or to foster some feeling by the encouragement of a great example, they form a society. Wherever, at the head of some new undertaking, you see the Government in France, or a man of rank in England, in the United States you will be sure to find an association. ...

Thus the most democratic country on the face of the earth is that in which men have in our time carried to the highest perfection the art of pursuing in common the object of their common desires, and have applied this new science to the greatest number of purposes. Is this the result of accident? Or is there in reality any necessary connexion between the principle of association and that of equality?

Aristocratic communities always contain, amongst a multitude of persons who by themselves are powerless, a small number of powerful and wealthy citizens, each of whom can achieve great undertakings single-handed. In aristocratic societies men do not need to combine in order to act, because they are strongly held together. Every wealthy and powerful citizen constitutes the head of a permanent and compulsory association, composed of all those who are dependent upon him, or whom he makes subservient to the execution of his designs.

Amongst democratic nations, on the contrary, all the citizens are independent and feeble; they can do hardly anything by themselves, and none of them can oblige his fellow-men to lend him their assistance. They all, therefore, fall into a state of incapacity, if they do not learn voluntarily to help each other. If men living in democratic countries had no right and no inclination to associate for political purposes, their independence would be in great jeopardy; but they might long preserve their wealth and their cultivation: whereas if they never acquired the habit of forming associations in ordinary life, civilization itself would be endangered. A people amongst which individuals should lose the power of achieving great things single-handed, without acquiring the means of producing them by united exertions, would soon relapse into barbarism.

Unhappily, the same social condition which renders associations so neces-sary to democratic nations, renders their formation more difficult amongst those nations than amongst all others. When several members of an aristocracy agree to combine, they easily succeed in doing so: as each of them brings great strength to the partnership, the number of its members may be very limited; and when the members of an association are limited in number, they may easily be-come mutually acquainted, understand each other, and establish fixed regula-tions. The same opportunities do not occur amongst democratic nations, where the associated members must always be very numerous for their association to have any power. ...

A Government might perform the part of some of the largest American com-panies; and several States, members of the Union, have already attempted it; but what political power could ever carry on the vast multitude of lesser undertak-ings which the American citizens perform every day, with the assistance of the principle of association? It is easy to foresee that the time is drawing near when man will be less and less able to produce, of himself alone, the commonest nec-essaries of life. The task of the governing power will therefore perpetually in-crease, and its very efforts will extend it every day. The more it stands in the place of associations, the more will individuals, losing the notion of combining together, require its assistance: these are causes and effects which unceasingly engender each other. Will the administration of the country ultimately assume the management of all the manufactures, which no single citizen is able to carry on? ... The morals and the intelligence of a democratic people would be as much endangered as its business and manufactures, if the government ever wholly usurped the place of private companies.

Feelings and opinions are recruited, the heart is enlarged, and the human mind is developed by no other means than by the reciprocal influence of men upon each other. I have shown that these influences are almost null in demo-cratic countries; they must therefore be artificially created, and this can only be accomplished by associations.

When the members of an aristocratic community adopt a new opinion, or conceive a new sentiment, they give it a station, as it were, beside themselves, upon the lofty platform where they stand; and opinions or sentiments so con-spicuous to the eyes of the multitude are easily introduced into the minds or hearts of all around. In democratic countries the governing power alone is natu-rally in a condition to act in this manner; but it is easy to see that its action is al-ways inadequate, and often dangerous. A government can no more be compe-tent to keep alive and to renew the circulation of opinions and feelings amongst a great people, than to manage all the speculations of productive industry. No sooner does a government attempt to go beyond its political sphere and to enter upon this new track, than it exercises, even unintentionally, an insupportable tyranny; for a government can only dictate strict rules, the opinions which it favours are rigidly enforced, and it is never easy to discriminate between its advice and its commands. Worse still will be the case if the government really believes itself interested in preventing all circulation of ideas; it will then stand motionless, and oppressed by the heaviness of voluntary torpor. Governments therefore should not be the only active powers: associations ought, in democratic nations, to stand in lieu of those powerful private individuals whom the equality of conditions has swept away.

As soon as several of the inhabitants of the United States have taken up an opinion or a feeling which they wish to promote in the world, they look out for mutual assistance; and as soon as they have found each other out, they combine. From that moment they are no longer isolated men, but a power seen from afar, whose actions serve for an example, and whose language is listened to. ...

In democratic countries the science of association is the mother of science; the progress of all the rest depends upon the progress it has made.

Amongst the laws which rule human societies there is one which seems to be more precise and clear than all others. If men are to remain civilized, or to become so, the art of associating together must grow and improve, in the same ratio in which the equality of conditions is increased. ...

14

Sociopolitical Pluralism

MARVIN E. OLSEN

INTRODUCTION

A basic tenet of classical political liberalism ... is that the individual rather than the organized group or community is the fundamental political actor. Participatory democracy accepts this premise and urges all individuals to become highly involved in political affairs. Both classical liberalism and participatory democracy therefore discount the political role of organizations, often viewing them as potentially dangerous "factions" whose special interests will often conflict with the general welfare (Ricci, 1971:11).

As a consequence of this distrust of organizations, traditional democratic theory rests on what Robert Nisbet (1962:253) calls a "unitary conception" of society, in which the only two viable political units are the individual and the national government. Influence is seen as flowing directly from the people to the government through elections, without any intermediate stages of aggregation in interest organizations. This conception of the political state was largely developed in France during the eighteenth century, as an outgrowth of prevailing rationalistic conceptions of man and society, and as an attack on the crumbling feudal social structure. ...

Potential consequences of this unitary conception of society—as observers from Tocqueville onward have often charged—are that individuals are left powerless in the face of government, elections become largely a public popularity contest or the means through which the established regime reaffirms its legitimacy, the people become available for manipulation by elites through mass movements, and the nation drifts toward the model of a "mass society." In Nisbet's (1962:250) words: "By focusing on the abstract political mass, this view of the people becomes administratively committed at the outset to a potentially totalitarian view of the State."

As a response to this unitary conception of the state, the theory of sociopolitical pluralism offers a model of society that emphasizes the crucial political role of private-interest associations. It argues that political democracy in modern nations requires a foundation of strong interest organizations throughout the society that can continually exert influence on the government. "If democracy involves participation and influence in decision-making processes, then the extent to which a society is democratic depends on the degree of citizen participation in associations which are not overtly political as well as in explicitly political associations" (Berry, 1970:16).

THE PLURALIST MODEL

Although the idea of sociopolitical pluralism can be traced back to Plato's *Republic*, it was Alexis de Tocqueville's *Democracy in America* that first presented this model as a necessary social basis for democracy. Tocqueville argued that the breakdown or absence of traditional hierarchies of feudal authority in contemporary societies would lead to conditions of mass equality, which in turn provided fertile ground for a "tyranny of the majority" that would destroy individual freedom in the name of "popular democracy." To replace traditional aristocracies in modern societies, Tocqueville (1961:128–33) called for the creation of multitudes of voluntary associations. "Amongst the laws which rule human societies there is one which seems to be more precise and clear than all others. If men are to remain civilized, or to become so, the art of associating together must grow and improve, in the same ratio in which the equality of conditions is increased."

As elaborated by numerous contemporary writers, the theory of sociopolitical pluralism calls for a complex network of interest organizations throughout society, each of which possesses its own power base and hence can function relatively independently of the government. Sometimes called "intermediate organizations" because of their structural location between the people and the national government, these associations must rest on voluntary membership derived from shared interests and concerns. They must be entirely private, or outside the formal government, to ensure that they remain autonomous sources of power. Each association should be limited in its sphere of activities, so that it cannot become too inclusive of its members' lives. Either separately or in links with one another, these organizations must extend from the grass-roots level of individual participation up to the national level, where they interact with the government. And most important, if they are to affect political decision making, these intermediate organizations must possess sufficient resources of one kind or another to effectively exert influence on governmental bodies and leaders.

Some of these organizations, such as political parties, nonpartisan citizens' associations, political action groups, and lobbies, may participate regularly in the political system. But most of them will normally be nonpolitical, entering the political arena as "parapolitical actors" only when their particular organizational interests are involved. Such parapolitical organizations might include labor unions, business and professional associations, civic organizations, recreational associations, ethnic groups, fraternal associations, "cultural" associations, or churches. Regardless of how frequently or extensively these organizations become politically active, however, the crucial feature of the pluralistic model is that all of them remain voluntary and autonomous, so as to provide citizens with independent power bases outside the formal government.

To prevent a highly pluralistic society from being torn apart by intense conflicts arising among its component organizations as each one seeks to attain its own particular goals, the model also specifies several necessary integrative conditions: (a) crosscutting rather than cumulative interests on various issues, to prevent cleavages among organizations from becoming too deep or irreconcilable; (b) overlapping memberships, with individuals (especially leaders) belonging to several different organizations; (c) interdependent activities, to keep organizations functionally interrelated; and (d) consensus on a set of procedural rules for resolving conflicts and reaching collective decisions. In David Berry's (1970:112) words, "It is the strength of the multiple memberships of associations and the extent to which these are overlapping rather than superimposed upon conflicting interests in society that is significant in maintaining social integration and democracy." None of the major writers on pluralism have specified in any detail how these integrative conditions are to be attained, however, so that the model is more of an ideal than a blueprint for a democratic society.

Although the distinction is not commonly made, there are actually two different versions of pluralist theory. The mobilization version of pluralism focuses on the role of nonpolitical voluntary associations in mobilizing individuals to become active in political affairs. The mediation version of pluralism is concerned, not with individuals' actions, but with the role of intermediate organizations as mediators of political influence between the citizens and the government. Let us examine both versions in greater detail.

THE MOBILIZATION PROCESS

Numerous studies have discovered that people who belong to voluntary associations of all kinds are more likely than others to participate in many forms of political activity (Milbrath, 1965; Verba and Nie, 1972). To explain this widespread relationship, the argument is made that membership and involvement in nonpolitical interest organizations activates people for political participation. The concept of social mobilization is derived from Karl Deutsch (1961), who describes it as "the process in which major clusters of old social, economic, and psychological commitments are eroded or broken and people become available for new patterns of socialization and behavior." He uses this concept in the context of modernizing societies, referring to activities that move people from traditional to "modern" ways of life. However, the idea is equally applicable to modernized societies if we assume that many traditional patterns of social activities in these societies are inimical to involvement in political affairs. People caught in these traditional patterns must be mobilized through involvement in new social contexts such as voluntary associations if they are to become politically active.

Several reasons can be given to explain the dynamic process through which nonpolitical organizational involvement leads to political participation: (1) Association membership broadens one's sphere of interests and concerns, so that public affairs and political issues become more salient to the individual. (2) It brings one into contact with many diverse people, and the resulting social relationships draw the individual into a wide range of new activities, including politics. (3) It gives one training and experience in social interaction and leadership skills that are valuable in the political sphere. (4) It provides one with multiple channels through which he or she can act to exert influence on politicians and the political system.

The importance of this political mobilization process for political democracy has been expressed by Gabriel Almond and Sidney Verba in these words:

> The organization member, compared with the nonmember, is likely to consider himself more competent as a citizen, to be a more active participant in politics, and to know and care about politics. He is, therefore, more likely to be close to the model of the democratic citizen. ... Membership in some association, even if the individual does not consider the membership politically relevant, and even if it does not involve his active participation, does lead to a more competent citizenry. Pluralism, even if not explicitly political pluralism, may indeed be one of the most important foundations of political democracy. [1963:321-22]

THE MEDIATION PROCESS

In addition to mobilizing their members for political activity, the special-interest voluntary associations that pervade a pluralist society enact an influence-mediating process between individual citizens and the government. Each intermediate organization brings together a number of people with similar concerns and goals, provides means through which these members can acquire information about relevant public issues, enables them to pool their resources to generate greater collective influence than could be exercised by a single individual, and provides an established channel through which they can exert this influence "upward" on political decisions and policies. To some extent, they also protect individuals from direct manipulation by elites through the mass media or state-controlled programs (Kornhauser, 1959).

At the same time, intermediate organizations serve governmental leaders by providing necessary information about public interests and needs, as well as an established means through which these leaders can reach "downward" to large numbers of constituents in order to deal effectively with their problems and concerns. Governmental leaders are simultaneously insulated from immediate dependence on mass public opinion and fear of overthrow by mass movements or revolution, which enables them to take socially necessary but unpopular actions (Kornhauser, 1959).

The mediation process thus bridges the influence gap between citizens and the government that is ignored by traditional democratic theory, making it possible for individuals to exercise far more extensive and meaningful influence on political decisions and policies than would ever be possible through occasional mass voting or sporadic mass movements. Robert Presthus expresses the process as follows:

> According to pluralist theory, voluntary groups play a critical role in a democratic system. Linchpins between government and the individual in a complex society, they become the most important means of direct access to those with political power. In the sense that they help shape public policy they are parapolitical. By hammering out a consensus among their members, which then becomes part of the raw material from which political parties manufacture their policies, they become part of the political system. ... In sum, voluntary organizations are essential instruments of pluralism because they make possible citizen influence on government. [1964:241]

PROBLEMS OF SOCIOPOLITICAL PLURALISM

Although pluralism is sometimes described as the unofficial political philosophy of the United States, a number of theoretical criticisms are frequently levied against it. Several of these are briefly mentioned in the following paragraphs.

1. The viability of a pluralist society is questionable when large proportions of the population do not belong to any special-interest voluntary associations, and when a majority of those who do belong to such organizations are only nominal members who take little or no part in the affairs of their organizations. To the extent that this situation prevails—as is presently the case in the United States and most other modern societies—neither the mobilization nor the mediation process can occur. Individuals will not acquire the experiences and skills necessary for political participation, and the organizations will not function as influence channels between citizens and government.

2. The theory implicitly assumes a "natural harmony of interests" among all parts of the society, or consensus on basic values, lack of deep social cleavages, and absence of strong ideologies and extremist politics. Only under such conditions will diverse actions by competing, self-oriented, special-interest organizations result in social unity and promotion of the general welfare. Lacking these conditions, pluralism can either paralyze or destroy a society, since attachment to intermediate associations does not by itself ensure commitment to the total society. As society changes, some organizations are bound to feel adversely af-

fected and deprived, while others will develop new aspirations and goals. In both cases, these organizations may decide that the existing social and political orders are not adequate and reject them in favor of extremist ideologies or bitter intergroup conflict.

3. As new interests arise in a society, new organizations are often formed to promote these interests. But it is often difficult for such organizations to gain legitimacy as accepted players in the political system. This is particularly likely to happen if they advocate radically new ideas or extensive social change. And if such organizations are not recognized by others as representing legitimate collective interests, they cannot enact an influence-mediating role.

4. There is a pervasive tendency in all organizations to drift toward centralized, oligarchic control, as noted over sixty years ago by Robert Michels (1966) in his famous "iron law of oligarchy." To the extent that this process occurs, an organization can neither effectively teach its members political participation skills nor provide an effective influence channel for exerting influence on the government. Some theorists (Lipset, et al., 1956) have argued that internal oligarchy may be necessary if special-interest associations are to speak with a strong voice in political affairs, but this negates the fundamental principle of open participation in decision making and reduces the system to a set of pluralistic elites. Each of these "strategic elites" (Keller, 1963) tends to dominate its own sphere of activity and to encounter little interference from other elites. "A pluralism of elites does not necessarily produce a competitive situation among elites" (Bachrach, 1967:37).

5. In modern nations in which the state tends to predominate over all other sectors of society, private, limited-action associations may have little influence on the government, no matter how well organized they may be. Can such organizations ever exercise any positive influence on public decision making to promote their interests, or are they forever doomed to enacting the role of "veto groups" (Riesman et al., 1954) that can only act negatively to block decisions they oppose? And if most, if not all, of these intermediate organizations lack effective autonomous power resources, they can easily be coopted by the government to become nothing more than agents for carrying out governmental policies.

6. Even if organizations do possess sufficient power resources with which to effectively exert influence on public decision making, they frequently lack viable channels for carrying out this process. The theory of sociopolitical pluralism, as presently envisioned, does not identify any practical influence mechanisms. The theory specifies the role that intermediate organizations should enact in political affairs, but says nothing about how this role is to be carried out. ...

These various criticisms of the pluralist model indicate that it is not an ideal blueprint for promoting political democracy in modern societies. Indeed, if political elites were capable of infiltrating and gaining control of the major interest organizations in a society, they could conceivably convert a pluralist society into a totalitarian state under their complete direction. Nevertheless, the pluralist model does suggest that a viable network of autonomous intermediate organizations throughout a society might provide a means of diffusing the exercise of social power among many different parts of society, thereby giving individual citizens numerous opportunities to participate in the governmental process. If this model were effectively implemented, it could provide an organizational foundation for both political democracy and meaningful involvement by all citizens in the operation and continual transformation of their society.

REFERENCES

Almond, Gabriel, and Sidney Verba. *The Civic Culture*. Princeton, N.J.: Princeton University Press, 1963.

Bachrach, Peter. *The Theory of Democratic Elitism: A Critique*. Boston: Little, Brown and Co., 1967.

Berry, David. *The Sociology of Grass Roots Politics*. London: Macmillan & Co., 1970.

Deutsch, Karl. "Social Mobilization and Political Development." *American Political Science Review* 55 (September 1961): 493–514.

Keller, Suzanne. *Beyond the Ruling Class*. New York: Random House, 1963.

Kornhauser, William. *The Politics of Mass Society*. Glencoe, Ill.: Free Press, 1959.

Lipset, Seymour Martin, Martin Trow, and James Coleman. *Union Democracy*. Garden City, N.Y.: Anchor Books, 1965.

Michels, Robert. *Political Parties*. New York: Free Press, 1966. (Originally published in 1915.)

Milbrath, Lester W. *Political Participation*. Chicago: Rand McNally, 1965.

Nisbet, Robert. *Community and Power*. New York: Oxford University Press, 1962.

Presthus, Robert. *Men at the Top*. New York: Oxford University Press, 1964.

Ricci, David. *Community Power and Democratic Theory: The Logic of Political Analysis*. New York: Random House, 1971.

Riesman, David, et al. *The Lonely Crowd*. New York: Doubleday, 1954.

Tocqueville, Alexis de. *Democracy in America*, Vol. 2, trans, by Henry Reeve. New York: Schocken Books, 1961. (Originally published in French in 1840.)

Truman, David E. *The Governmental Process*. New York: Alfred A. Knopf, 1951.

Verba, Sidney, and Norman H. Nie. *Participation in America: Political Democracy and Social Equality*. New York: Harper and Row, 1972.

PART 3

National Power Structures

An axiom of political sociology is that in all but the most technologically sim-ple societies, power is distributed unequally. Plainly, everywhere and at all times, the few—an elite—rule, whatever the nature of political and economic systems. In modern industrial societies, the gap between elites and masses is especially critical in that elites are able to greatly extend their influence through control of critical societal institutions such as the state, the economy, and the mass media. Much of the debate regarding power in the United States and other industrial societies, therefore, has been concerned with the structure of elite rule.

Analyses of the elite structures of modern societies have focused on two prin-cipal issues. The first concerns the size, composition, and sphere of power of the elite structure. Is there a single power elite or are there multiple elites? Is their power concentrated or dispersed? The second issue concerns the accessibility of elites. To what extent are the masses able to influence elites and hold them ac-countable? Is entrance into elite groups open to those at lower levels of the so-cial hierarchy, or is the power structure relatively closed?

In modern societies like the United States, it is meaningful to speak of a *na-tional* power structure made up of men and women whose decisions render an impact on all individuals and groups in every sphere of societal life. This struc-ture comprises the highest ranking officials of key government agencies, top ex-ecutive officers of giant corporations, media editors and executives, foundation officials, educational leaders, elite lawyers, and others responsible for directing the actions and managing the resources of key organizations and institutions (Dye, 1990). The structure and behavior of elites are particularly important is-sues in democratic societies because it is assumed that a greater concentration of power and elite cohesiveness naturally lead to less accountability and control of elites by citizens—the antithesis of a democratic political order.

The power structure of American society has been studied more extensively than any other, although the observations made about American society are, in a broad sense, applicable to other democratic industrial societies. The structure of elite groups in the United States has usually been interpreted by researchers and analysts through one of the three major theoretical perspectives of societal power described in Part 2.

THE MARXIAN MODEL

Marxian theory, by definition, holds that there is a single dominant class in society consisting of those who own or control the major means of economic production. Marxian-oriented analyses of societal power structures therefore rarely treat the nature of that structure as an empirical question but rather define the structure on theoretical grounds and then investigate its consequences for the rest of the society. Marxian analyses are also likely to assume that the dominant class is relatively cohesive in its interests and concerns and is able to act in a relatively coordinated manner when it becomes necessary to protect those interests.

Most Marxian and neo-Marxian theorists believe that all other conceptions of national power structures are essentially hollow because they fail to take account of the manner in which capitalist political economies shape and constrain all societal institutions. From this perspective, it matters little who the current elites are, how they are organized, or what their social origins may be, because the structure of the political economy transcends the actions of any specific elites. Whatever its composition, the elite class will be driven to act in ways that protect the integrity of the capitalist political economy.

A typical example of the Marxian perspective on societal power structures is the work of Barbara and Gerald Chasin (1974), who assert that the United States contains a ruling class that consists of

> all those who benefit from the earning of capital, whether it be in the form of profits directly, or in the form of dividends and interest. While the society is governed in the interests of the capitalist class, the strings of power are held by a much smaller segment of the bourgeoisie who act as the "executive committee" of their class and perform the political functions necessary to preserve the class interests of the bourgeoisie (p. 146).

THE POWER ELITE TRADITION

A heated debate over the shape and functions of the American power structure arose in the social sciences beginning in the 1950s with the publication of C. Wright Mills's *The Power Elite* (1956) and Floyd Hunter's two works, *Community Power Structure* (1953) and *Top Leadership U.S.A.* (1959). These books presented a radically new view of how American society was ruled, both nationally and at the local level. Mills and Hunter were mavericks among their peers, disputing what had been the generally accepted depiction of power in the United States: a pluralist system in which power was dispersed among many varied interest groups. Mills and Hunter instead portrayed the power structure as socially cohesive and functionally integrated. They claimed that rather than dispersed, power was concentrated among a relatively few people at the very top of the social hierarchy.

Mills described in detail the structure of elites at the national level. Issues calling forth the most consequential and far-reaching decisions—for example, war and peace, economic policy—are made, according to Mills, by a handful of leaders at the pinnacle of three institutions: the giant corporations, the highest echelons of the executive branch of the federal government, and the military. It is here, Mills maintained, that the power to affect the society's critical policies is exercised. The top leaders of each of these three institutions constitute a relatively cohesive power elite, coalescing around the society's major issues and rising above other less significant power wielders.

Mills suggested that the cohesiveness of the power elite stems from three sources. First, its members exhibit similar career paths and have been exposed to common socialization experiences. Second, they maintain close interpersonal and working relationships. And third, their institutions—corporations, government, military—are interdependent and interwoven at various points. The three top groups act as a loose coalition, commonly coming together to decide policy issues of mutual concern.

Mills conceptualized power in the United States as a tri-level arrangement: the power elite at the top, the majority of the citizenry at the bottom, and a middle level of power consisting of legislators, lobbyists, interest group leaders, and lesser political officials and administrators. Those exercising power at the middle level make day-to-day operational decisions and are the major focus of political analysts and the media. None of these groups, however, is able to basically affect essential policies of the state and the economy, policies that are left to be determined by the power elite. Mills maintained that the vast majority of the population has become relatively powerless and is increasingly manipulated by the power elite through its use of mass communications. "The public is merely the collectivity of individuals each rather passively exposed to the mass media," wrote Mills, "and rather helplessly opened up to the suggestions and manipulations that flow from these media" (1956:305).

Though conceived in the 1950s, Mills's thesis remains a thought-provoking model of power in America. Much of the research on power in the United States in the past four decades has been stimulated by Mills's work and can be seen, in large measure, as a response to his thesis. Many theorists have taken their cue from Mills, setting out to confirm or refute his picture.

One who has drawn extensively on the Millsian tradition is G. William Domhoff, who has proposed a ruling class model. Domhoff holds that the upper class in the United States is essentially a ruling class: the major owners of the society's wealth maintain maximum influence in the public policy-forming process (Domhoff, 1967). He sees within this ruling class a power elite, that is, a functional leadership group operating on behalf of the upper class. The membership of this power elite, writes Domhoff, "is made up of active, working members of the ruling class and high-level employees in institutions controlled by members of the ruling class" (Domhoff, 1979:13).

Unlike Mills and Hunter, who emphasized cohesion among elites resulting from the overlapping nature of their activities and organizations, Domhoff argues that elite coalescence is primarily a product of their similar social backgrounds. It is because of the functional and social cohesiveness of the national elite that he refers to it as a "ruling class." Thus, Domhoff draws a very clear connection between the social upper class and those who actually govern the society. Although not all upper-class people are members of the power elite and not all powerful elites belong to the upper class, members of the upper class dominate the policy-making process and are able to groom new members of the power elite recruited from lower social classes. Domhoff does not deny that power is exercised at other levels of society. But it is the upper class, he contends, that is able to "set the terms under which other groups and classes must operate" (Domhoff, 1983:2).

E. Digby Baltzell (1958; 1964) also found evidence of a ruling class. He distinguished among three groups at the top of the social hierarchy: an upper class of wealthy families who retain a sense of communal identity; the "elite" of top functional leaders of various societal institutions; and an "establishment" made up of those who combine their important functional positions with great wealth. Baltzell's "establishment," then, is not unlike Domhoff's "power elite": a relatively cohesive governing unit composed of mostly upper-class members who encourage a kind of elite circulation by recruiting new members from lower social classes.

Unlike Domhoff and the other elitists from the Millsian school of thought, Baltzell believed that an upper class was needed to rule; he viewed the upper class as a group possessing the background, education, and sense of duty to function as a socially beneficent leadership unit. Baltzell contended that ideally, the establishment would be infused with new blood from less privileged groups in the society that are recruited on the basis of talent and ability. Only such elite circulation, he argued, could prevent the upper class from degenerating into a group that neglects its leadership obligations and concerns itself only with enhancing its wealth and power.

THE PLURALIST RESPONSE

Pluralist theorists have generally subscribed to the notion of a plurality of elites in modern societies. Although not denying the existence and functional necessity of elites in modern societies, they see the structure of power and the behavior of the powerful very differently from those in the tradition of Mills. Rather than viewing elites as a socially cohesive group concentrated within the higher confines of the most significant political and economic organizations, pluralists have described elites as more heterogeneous in social origin, dispersed in their duties, and relatively autonomous in their working relations.

One of the first to take a pluralist approach was Suzanne Keller (1963) in her theory of "strategic elites." She contended that because of the complexity of modern societies, no single group of leaders can have the expertise or scope of influence to make critical decisions in every area of societal life. Numerous specialized or "strategic" elites therefore arise, "whose judgments, decisions, and actions have important and determinable consequences for many members of society" (Keller, 1963:20). Business leaders are competent to operate corporations but cannot run governments, which are the domain of political leaders; political leaders in turn know little about educational affairs, which is the specialty of an elite of professional educators; and so on. This view contrasts sharply with the notion of a relatively unified set of elites at the top of the power hierarchy that constitute a single "power elite" or "ruling class."

Arnold Rose (1967) carried this perspective one step further. He agreed with Keller that there are numerous specialized elites. However, he believed that those elites are relatively dispersed throughout society and interlock only sporadically and temporarily in response to specific issues. There is no ensconced ruling class or power elite that thinks and acts with any unity, he argued, but instead a variety of elites who conflict among themselves on particular issues more often than they cooperate.

AN INTEGRATED MODEL

The various theoretical positions regarding elite structure and accessibility can be arranged on the spectrum shown in Table P3.1.

Toward the left end of the spectrum is a condition of a few sets of *unified elites*. The elite structure is visualized as relatively integrated, concentrated, not easily accessible, and not very accountable. In this view, the power elite consists of a single relatively cohesive unit whose members are unified through functional coordination and frequent interaction in social situations. Those who have viewed the power structure in this vein have attempted empirically to document the interlocking nature of elites within various societal spheres (especially the polity and the economy) through common club memberships (Domhoff, 1971; 1974), common schooling experiences, and overlapping organizational activities (Mintz, 1975; Mintz and Schwartz, 1981a, 1981b; Moore, 1979; Useem, 1979; 1984). While they do not imply that members of the power elite deliberately plan their coordination in a conspiratorial fashion or that they invariably act in concert, theorists of this persuasion have tried to show that the parallel organizational needs and interests of elites as well as their common social experiences generally assure their agreement on those economic and political issues that have society-wide impact. In addition, these writers generally hold that access to powerful positions is rather tightly controlled by the established elites, that avenues of mass influence are quite restricted, and that elites

TABLE P3.1   The Spectrum of Elite Structures

	Unified Elites	Interlocking Elites	Autonomous Elites
Location	A few dominant institutions	Major institutions	All organizational spheres
Operation	Consensus	Bargaining and negotiation	Conflict and power struggles
Cohesiveness	Tight	Moderate	Loose
Accessibility	Very closed	Partially open	Very open
Representative theorist	C. W. Mills	S. Keller	A. Rose

are publicly accountable only when they wish to be. In short, the elites extensively control—and exploit—the masses.

Toward the right end of the spectrum depicted in Table P3.1 is a power structure with many sets of *autonomous elites*. This structure is envisioned as constantly shifting, with numerous elites dispersed widely among various societal institutions, in conflict among and within themselves, and exercising only limited power within restricted spheres of activity. Depending on the issue at stake, the power structure will shift from one form to another, with no particular elites ever able to accumulate sufficient power resources to completely override the others. Elite power is dispersed not simply because of functional specialization but also because elites within various institutions are in continual competition with one another. Most issues are therefore settled through negotiation and compromise, not unified concerted action (Dahl, 1967). A few theorists of this school of thought even maintain that elites are so dispersed that they are forced to operate within a kind of political "gridlock." In general, these theorists see the power structure as fairly open to aspiring new elites, as providing numerous avenues for input from the masses, and as at least partially accountable to the public (Presthus, 1964). More specifically, they believe that an intermediate level of power exists between the elites and the masses, made up primarily of special interest associations and their leaders. These "intermediate organizations" enable citizens to participate in the political process through collective action and thus hold elites at least indirectly accountable for their actions.

In recent years, both ends of the spectrum have tended to yield to a middle conception of several sets of *interlocking elites,* a conception that proponents maintain is a more realistic view of modern power structures. Most theorists today acknowledge the existence of several sets of moderately powerful elites who represent diverse societal institutions and spheres of activity. In modern societies, this multiplicity of elites arises as a result of the specialized nature of all organizations and institutions. Within each area of social life, a leadership cadre emerges that is responsible for its specialized function. Because of that specialization, the various elites do not easily link up in a cohesive structure, as unified elitist theorists maintain. This diversity among elites is reflected in internal conflicts not only between members of different institutional elite groups but also among elites of any particular institutional sphere. Corporate executives, for example, are often in conflict with government leaders. Moreover, corporate managers themselves do not see all economic and political issues in the same way, any more than do political officials with different party affiliations (Dye, 1990).

Despite the functional separation of elites, a considerable convergence exists at the top of the national power structure. This convergence is due to two principal factors. First, although specific policy differences are obvious, elites agree on the basic goals of the political economy, goals founded on a broad consensus of values. As Dye puts it, the range of disagreement among elites is relatively narrow, "and disagreement is generally confined to *means* rather than ends" (1990:223). Conflict certainly occurs among top leaders, but such differences do not reflect fundamental rifts in ideology or social perspective.

Second, despite their specialization, elites within the two critical institutions of the political economy—business and government—frequently exchange positions, especially at the upper levels of national power. Some of this movement is a product of overlapping institutional interests, but it is also a result of common organizational skills that may be appropriate for both governmental and corporate organizations. This interchange of personnel further contributes to a common frame of reference and a consensus regarding basic societal issues.

This middle position on the spectrum suggests that the accessibility of elites to the masses will vary, depending on the level of power. At more localized and community levels, democratic processes can be effective in providing the masses with some influence on elite decisions. Moreover, the power elites themselves are not impenetrable to those of lower social origins. At the national level, however, as elites become more remote from the masses, there is greater elite autonomy in decision making. In addition, structural impediments favor those who bring critical class resources to the competition for elite membership. Studies have indicated that both government and corporate elites display social class backgrounds that are considerably higher than the general population. Even those moving into elite positions from lower social origins will usually have been exposed to elite socialization experiences such as higher education and similar occupational roles and affiliations. These experiences provide an additional source of common values and perspectives.

In sum, although the debate regarding national power structures remains unresolved, we should not think of the two ends of the theoretical spectrum as mutually exclusive. Realistically, the structure of elite power in the United States and other industrial societies appears to be neither unified nor dispersed in the extreme. The shape of the power structure and interrelations among its component parts are not static but are continually subject to pressures that, at various times, may pull elites together or drive them apart.

OVERVIEW OF SELECTIONS

The readings in Part 3 reflect the basic issues of the ongoing debate regarding national power structures. Mills and Domhoff describe the American elite structure as relatively unified. In contrast, Higley and colleagues present a conception of multiple elites who are partially unified and partially divided. The selection by Moore and the selection by Mintz and Schwartz approach this issue empirically, tracing linkages among elites at the national level. Kerbo discusses the basis of the power of the upper class. Finally, Marger describes how the media elite play a role that is complementary to government and economic elites in providing the informational and ideological tools to sustain the national power structure.

REFERENCES

Baltzell, E. Digby. 1958. *Philadelphia Gentlemen.* New York: Free Press.

_____. 1964. *The Protestant Establishment.* New York: Random House.

Chasin, Barbara, and Gerald Chasin. 1974. *Power and Ideology: A Marxist Approach to Political Sociology.* Cambridge, Mass.: Schenkman.

Dahl, Robert A. 1967. *Pluralist Democracy in the United States.* Chicago: Rand McNally.

Domhoff, G. William. 1967. *Who Rules America?* Englewood Cliffs, N.J.: Prentice-Hall.

_____. 1971. *The Higher Circles.* New York: Vintage.

_____. 1974. *The Bohemian Grove.* New York: Harper and Row.

_____. 1979. *The Powers That Be: Processes of Ruling-Class Domination in America.* New York: Vintage.

_____. 1983. *Who Rules America Now?* Englewood Cliffs, N.J.: Prentice-Hall.

Dye, Thomas R. 1990. *Who's Running America? The Bush Era,* 5th ed. Englewood Cliffs, N.J.: Prentice-Hall.

Hunter, Floyd. 1953. *Community Power Structure.* Chapel Hill: University of North Carolina Press.

_____. 1959. *Top Leadership U.S.A.* Chapel Hill: University of North Carolina Press.

Keller, Suzanne. 1963. *Beyond the Ruling Class.* New York: Random House.

Mills, C. Wright. 1956. *The Power Elite.* New York: Oxford University Press.

Mintz, Beth. 1975. "The President's Cabinet, 1897–1972," *Insurgent Sociologist* 4:131–148.

Mintz, Beth, and Michael Schwartz. 1981a."Interlocking Directorates and Interest Group Formation," *American Sociological Review* 46(December):851–869.

_____. 1981b. "The Structure of Intercorporate Unity in American Business," *Social Problems* 19(December):87–103.

Moore, Gwen. 1979."The Structure of a National Elite Network," *American Sociological Review* 44(October):673–692.

Presthus, Robert. 1964. *Men at the Top.* New York: Oxford University Press.

Rose, Arnold. 1967. *The Power Structure.* New York: Oxford University Press.

Useem, Michael. 1979."The Social Organization of the American Business Elite," *American Sociological Review* 44(August):553–572.

_____. 1984. *The Inner Circle: Large Corporations and the Rise of Business Political Activity in the U.S. and the U.K.* New York: Oxford University Press.

15

The Structure of Power in American Society

C. WRIGHT MILLS

Power has to do with whatever decisions men make about the arrangements under which they live, and about the events which make up the history of their times. Events that are beyond human decision do happen; social arrangements do change without benefit of explicit decision. But in so far as such decisions are made, the problem of who is involved in making them is the basic problem of power. In so far as they could be made but are not, the problem becomes who fails to make them? ...

How large a role any explicit decisions do play in the making of history is itself an historical problem. For how large that role may be depends very much upon the means of power that are available at any given time in any given society. In some societies, the innumerable actions of innumerable men modify their milieux, and so gradually modify the structure itself. These modifications—the course of history—go on behind the backs of men. History is drift, although in total "men make it." Thus, innumerable entrepreneurs and innumerable consumers by ten-thousand decisions per minute may shape and re-shape the free-market economy. Perhaps this was the chief kind of limitation Marx had in mind when he wrote, in *The 18th Brumaire*, that "Men make their own history, but they do not make it just as they please; they do not make it under circumstances chosen by themselves."

But in other societies—certainly in the United States and in the Soviet Union today—a few men may be so placed within the structure that by their decisions modify the milieux of many other men, and in fact nowadays the structural conditions under which most men live. Such elites of power also make history under circumstances not chosen altogether by themselves, yet compared with other men, and compared with other periods of world history, these circumstances do indeed seem less limiting.

I should contend that "men are free to make history," but that some men are indeed much freer than others. For such freedom requires access to the means of decision and of power by which history can now be made. It has not always been so made; but in the later phases of the modern epoch it is. It is with reference to this epoch that I am contending that if men do not make history, they tend increasingly to become the utensils of history-makers as well as the mere objects of history.

The history of modern society may readily be understood as the story of the enlargement and the centralization of the means of power—in economic, in political, and in military institutions. The rise of industrial society has involved these developments in the means of economic production. The rise of the nation state has involved these developments in the means of violence and in those of political administration. ...

The power to make decisions of national and international consequence is now so clearly seated in political, military, and economic institutions that other areas of society seem off to the side and, on occasion, readily subordinated to these. The scattered institutions of religion, education and family are increasingly shaped by the big three, in which history-making decisions now regularly occur. ... There is no longer, on the one hand, an economy, and, on the other, a political order, containing a military establishment unimportant to politics and to money-making. There is a political economy numerously linked with military order and decision. This triangle of power is now a structural fact, and it is the key to any understanding of the higher circles in America today. For as each of these domains has coincided with the others, as decisions in each have become broader, the leading men of each—the high military, the corporation executives, the political directorate—have tended to come together to form the power elite of America.

The political order, once composed of several dozen states with a weak federal-center, has become an executive apparatus which has taken up into itself many powers previously scattered, legislative as well as administrative, and which now reach into all parts of the social structure. The long-time tendency of business and government to become more closely connected has since World War II reached a new point of explicitness. Neither can now be seen clearly as a distinct world. The growth of executive government does not mean merely the "enlargement of government" as some kind of autonomous bureaucracy: under American conditions, it has meant that the ascendancy of the corporation man into political eminence. Already during the New Deal, such men had joined the political directorate; as of World War II they came to dominate it. ...

The economy, once a great scatter of small productive units in somewhat automatic balance, has become internally dominated by a few hundred corporations, administratively and politically interrelated, which together hold the keys to economic decision. This economy is at once a permanent-war economy and a private-corporation economy. The most important relations of the corporation

to the state now rest on the coincidence between military and corporate interests, as defined by the military and the corporate rich, and accepted by politicians and public. Within the elite as a whole, this coincidence of military domain and corporate realm strengthens both of them and further subordinates
the merely political man. Not the party politician, but the corporation executive, is now more likely to sit with the military to answer the question: what is to
be done?

The military order, once a slim establishment in a context of civilian distrust,
has become the largest and most expensive feature of government; behind smil-
ing public relations, it has all the grim and clumsy efficiency of a great and
sprawling bureaucracy. The high military have gained decisive political and economic relevance. The seemingly permanent military threat places a premium
upon them and virtually all political and economic actions are now judged in
terms of military definitions of reality: the higher military have ascended to a
firm position within the power elite of our time. ...

1. To understand the unity of this power elite, we must pay attention to the
psychology of its several members in their respective milieux. In so far as the
power elite is composed of men of similar origin and education, of similar career
and style of life, their unity may be said to rest upon the fact that they are of similar social type, and to lead to the fact of their easy intermingling. This kind of
unity reaches its frothier apex in the sharing of that prestige which is to be had
in the world of the celebrity. It achieves a more solid culmination in the fact of
the interchangeability of positions between the three dominant institutional orders. It is revealed by considerable traffic of personnel within and between these
three, as well as by the rise of specialized go-betweens as in the new style high-
level lobbying.

2. Behind such psychological and social unity are the structure and the mechanics of those institutional hierarchies over which the political directorate,
the corporate rich, and the high military now preside. How each of these hierarchies is shaped and what relations it has with the others determine in large part
the relations of their rulers. Were these hierarchies scattered and disjointed,
then their respective elites might tend to be scattered and disjointed; but if they
have many interconnections and points of coinciding interest, then their elites
tend to form a coherent kind of grouping. The unity of the elite is not a simple
reflection of the unity of institutions; but men and institutions are always related; that is why we must understand the elite today in connection with such institutional trends as the development of a permanent-war establishment, along-
side a privately incorporated economy, inside a virtual political vacuum. For the
men at the top have been selected and formed by such institutional trends.

3. Their unity, however, does not rest solely upon psychological similarity and
social intermingling, nor entirely upon the structural blending or commanding
positions and common interests. At times it is the unity of a more explicit co-ordination.

To say that these higher circles are increasingly co-ordinated, that this is *one* basis of their unity, and that at times—as during open war—such co-ordination is quite wilful, is not to say that the co-ordination is total or continuous, or even that it is very surefooted. Much less is it to say that the power elite has emerged as the realization of a plot. Its rise cannot be adequately explained in any psychological terms. ...

There are of course other interpretations of the American system of power. The most usual is that it is a moving balance of many competing interests. The image of balance, at least in America, is derived from the idea of the economic market: in the nineteenth century, the balance was thought to occur between a great scatter of individuals and enterprises; in the twentieth century, it is thought to occur between great interest blocs. In both views, the politician is the key man of power because he is the broker of many conflicting powers.

I believe that the balance and the compromise in American society—the "countervailing powers" and the "veto groups," of parties and associations, of strata and unions—must now be seen as having mainly to do with the middle levels of power. It is these middle levels that the political journalist and the scholar of politics are most likely to understand and to write about—if only because being mainly middle class themselves, they are closer to them. Moreover these levels provide the noisy content of most "political" news and gossip; the images of these levels are more or less in accord with the folklore of how democracy works; and, if the master-image of balance is accepted, many intellectuals, especially in their current patrioteering, are readily able to satisfy such political optimism as they wish to feel. Accordingly, liberal interpretations of what is happening in the United States are now virtually the only interpretations that are widely distributed.

But to believe that the power system reflects a balancing society is, I think, to confuse the present era with earlier times, and to confuse its top and bottom with its middle levels.

By the top levels, as distinguished from the middle, I intend to refer, first of all, to the scope of the decisions that are made. At the top today, these decisions have to do with all the issues of war and peace. They have also to do with slump and poverty which are now so very much problems of international scope. I intend also to refer to whether or not the groups that struggle politically have a chance to gain the positions from which such top decisions are made, and indeed whether their members do usually hope for such top national command. Most of the competing interests which make up the clang and clash of American politics are strictly concerned with their slice of the existing pie. Labor unions, for example, certainly have no policies of an international sort other than those which given unions adopt for the strict economic protection of their members. Neither do farm organizations. The actions of such middle-level powers may indeed have consequence for top-level policy; certainly at times they hamper these policies. But they are not truly concerned with them, which means of course that their influence tends to be quite irresponsible.

The facts of the middle levels may in part be understood in terms of the rise of the power elite. The expanded and centralized and interlocked hierarchies over which the power elite preside have encroached upon the old balance and relegated it to the middle level. But there are also independent developments of the middle levels. These, it seems to me, are better understood as an affair of entrenched and provincial demands than as a center of national decision. As such, the middle level often seems much more of a stalemate than a moving balance.

1. The middle level of politics is not a forum in which there are debated the big decisions of national and international life. Such debate is not carried on by nationally responsible parties representing and clarifying alternative policies. There are no such parties in the United States. More and more, fundamental issues never come to any point or decision before Congress, much less before the electorate in party campaigns. ...

The American political campaign distracts attention from national and international issues, but that is not to say that there are no issues in these campaigns. In each district and state, issues are set up and watched by organized interests of sovereign local importance. The professional politician is of course a party politician, and the two parties are semi-feudal organizations: they trade patronage and other favors for votes and for protection. The differences between them, so far as national issues are concerned, are very narrow and very mixed up. Often each seems to be fifty parties, one to each state; and accordingly, the politician as campaigner and as Congressman is not concerned with national party lines, if any are discernible. Often he is not subject to any effective national party discipline. He speaks for the interests of his own constituency, and he is concerned with national issues only in so far as they affect the interests effectively organized there, and hence his chances of reelection. That is why, when he does speak of national matters, the result is so often such an empty rhetoric. Seated in his sovereign locality, the politician is not at the national summit. He is on and of the middle levels of power.

2. Politics is not an arena in which free and independent organizations truly connect the lower and middle levels of society with the top levels of decision. Such organizations are not an effective and major part of American life today. As more people are drawn into the political arena, their associations become mass in scale, and the power of the individual becomes dependent upon them; to the extent that they are effective, they have become larger, and to that extent they have become less accessible to the influence of the individual. This is a central fact about associations in any mass society; it is of most consequence for political parties and for trade unions.

In the 'thirties, it often seemed that labor would become an insurgent power independent of corporation and state. Organized labor was then emerging for the first time on an American scale, and the only political sense of direction it needed was the slogan, "organize the unorganized." Now without the mandate of the slump, labor remains without political direction. Instead of economic and political struggles it has become deeply entangled in administrative routines with both corporation and state. One of its major functions, as a vested interest of the new society, is the regulation of such irregular tendencies as may occur among the rank and file.

There is nothing, it seems to me, in the make-up of the current labor leadership to allow us to expect that it can or that it will lead, rather than merely react. In so far as it fights at all it fights over a share of the goods of a single way of life and not over that way of life itself. The typical labor leader in the U.S.A. today is better understood as an adaptive creature of the main business drift than as an independent actor in a truly national context.

3. The idea that this society is a balance of powers requires us to assume that the units in balance are of more or less equal power and that they are truly independent of one another. These assumptions have rested, it seems clear, upon the historical importance of a large and independent middle class. In the latter nineteenth century and during the Progressive Era, such a class of farmers and small businessmen fought politically—and lost—their last struggle for a paramount role in national decision. Even then, their aspirations seemed bound to their own imagined past.

This old, independent middle class has of course declined. On the most generous count, it is now 40 percent of the total middle class (at most 20 percent of the total labor force). Moreover, it has become politically as well as economically dependent upon the state, most notably in the case of the subsidized farmer.

The *new* middle class of white-collar employees is certainly not the political pivot of any balancing society. It is in no way politically unified. Its unions, such as they are, often serve merely to incorporate it as hanger-on of the labor interest. For a considerable period, the old middle class *was* an independent base of power; the new middle class cannot be. Political freedom and economic security *were* anchored in small and independent properties; they are not anchored in the worlds of the white-collar job. Scattered property holders were economically united by more or less free markets; the jobs of the new middle class are integrated by corporate authority. Economically, the white-collar classes are in the same condition as wage workers; politically, they are in a worse condition, for they are not organized. They are no vanguard of historic change; they are at best a rearguard of the welfare state. ...

Fifty years ago many observers thought of the American state as a mask behind which an invisible government operated. But nowadays, much of what was called the old lobby, visible or invisible, is part of the quite visible government. The "governmentalization of the lobby" has proceeded in both the legislative and the executive domain, as well as between them. The executive bureaucracy becomes not only the center of decision but also the arena within major conflicts of power are resolved or denied resolution. "Administration" replaces electoral politics; the maneuvering of cliques (which include leading Senators as well as civil servants) replaces the open clash of parties.

The shift of corporation men into the political directorate has accelerated the decline of the politicians in the Congress to the middle levels of power; the formation of the power elite rests in part upon this relegation. It rests also upon the semi-organized stalemate of the interest of sovereign localities, into which the legislative function has so largely fallen; upon the virtually complete absence of a civil service that is a politically neutral but politically relevant depository of brainpower and executive skill; and it rests upon the increased official secrecy behind which great decisions are made without benefit of public or even of Congressional debate.

There is one last belief upon which liberal observers everywhere base their interpretations and rest their hopes. That is the idea of the public and the associated idea of public opinion. Conservative thinkers, since the French Revolution, have of course Viewed With Alarm the rise of the public, which they have usually called the masses, or something to that effect. "The populace is sovereign," wrote Gustave Le Bon, "and the tide of barbarism mounts." But surely those who have supposed the masses to be well on their way to triumph are mistaken. In our time, the influence of publics or of masses within political life is in fact decreasing, and such influence as on occasion they do have tends, to an unknown but increasing degree, to be guided by the means of mass communication.

In a society of publics, discussions is the ascendant means of communication, and the mass media, if they exist, simply enlarge and animate this discussion, linking one face-to-face public with the discussions of another. In a mass society, the dominant type of communication is the formal media, and the publics become mere markets for these media: the "public" of a radio program consists of all those exposed to it. When we try to look upon the United States today as a society of publics, we realize that it has moved a considerable distance along the road to the mass society.

In official circles, the very term, "the public," has come to have a phantom meaning, which dramatically reveals its eclipse. The deciding elite can identify some of those who clamour publicly as "Labor," others as "Business," still others as "Farmer." But these are not the public. "The public" consists of the unidentified and the non-partisan in a world of defined and partisan interests. In this faint echo of the classic notion, the public is composed of those remnants of the old and new middle classes whose interests are not explicitly defined, organized, or clamorous. In a curious adaptation, "the public" often becomes, in administrative fact, "the disengaged expert," who, although ever so well informed, has never taken a clear-cut and public stand on controversial issues. He is the "public" member of the board, the commission, the committee. What "the public" stands for, accordingly, is often a vagueness of policy (called "open-mindedness"), a lack of involvement in public affairs (known as "reasonableness"), and a professional disinterest (known as "tolerance").

All this is indeed far removed from the eighteenth-century idea of the public of public opinion. That idea parallels the economic idea of the magical market. Here is the market composed of freely competing entrepreneurs; there is the public composed of circles of people in discussion. As price is the result of anonymous, equally weighted, bargaining individuals, so public opinion is the result of each man's having thought things out for himself and then contributing to the his voice to the great chorus. To be sure, some may have more influence on the state of opinion than others, but no one group monopolizes the discussion, or by itself determines the opinions that prevail.

In this classic image, the people are presented with problems. They discuss them. They formulate viewpoints. These viewpoints are organized, and they compete. One viewpoint "wins out." Then the people act out this view, or their representatives are instructed to act it out, and this they promptly do.

Such are the images of democracy which are still used as working justifications of power in America. We must now recognize this description as more a fairly tale than a useful approximation. The issues that now shape man's fate are neither raised nor decided by any public at large. The idea of a society that is at bottom composed of publics is not a matter of fact; it is the proclamation of an ideal, and as well the assertion of a legitimation masquerading as fact.

I cannot here describe the several great forces within American society as well as elsewhere which have been at work in the debilitation of the public. I want only to remind you that publics, like free associations, can be deliberately and suddenly smashed, or they can more slowly wither away. But whether smashed in a week or withered in a generation, the demise of the public must be seen in connection with the rise of centralized organizations, with all their new means of power, including those of the mass media of distraction. These, we now know, often seem to expropriate the rationality and the will of the terrorized or—as the case may be—the voluntarily indifferent society of masses. In the more democratic process of indifference the remnants of such publics as remain may only occasionally be intimidated by fanatics in search of "disloyalty." But regardless of that, they lose their will for decisions because they do not possess the instruments for decision: they lose their sense of political belonging because they do not belong; they lose their political will because they see no way to realize it.

The political structure of a modern democratic state requires that such a public as is projected by democratic theorists not only exist but that it be the very forum within which a politics of real issues is enacted.

It requires a civil service that is firmly linked with the world of knowledge and sensibility, and which is composed of skilled men who, in their careers and in their aspirations, are truly independent of any private, which is to say, corporation, interests.

It requires nationally responsible parties which debate openly and clearly the issues which the nation, and indeed the world, now so rigidly confronts.

It requires an intelligentsia, inside as well as outside the universities, who carry on the bid discourse of the western world, and whose work is relevant to and influential among parties and movements and publics.

And it certainly requires, as a fact of power, that there be free associations standing between families and smaller communities and publics, on the one hand, and the state, the military, the corporation, on the other. For unless these do exist, there are no vehicles for reasoned opinion, no instruments for the rational exertion of public will.

Such democratic formations are not now ascendant in the power structure of the United States, and accordingly the men of decision are not men selected and formed by careers within such associations and by their performance before such publics. The top of modern American society is increasingly unified, and often seems willfully coordinated: at the top there has emerged an elite whose power probably exceeds that of any small group of men in world history. The middle levels are often a drifting set of stalemated forces: the middle does not link the bottom with the top. The bottom of this society is politically fragmented, and even as a passive fact, increasingly powerless: at the bottom there is emerging a mass society.

These developments, I believe, can be correctly understood neither in terms of the liberal nor the Marxian interpretation of politics and history. Both of these ways of thought arose as guidelines to reflection about a type of society which does not now exist in the United States. We confront there a new kind of social structure, which embodies elements and tendencies of all modern society, but in which they assumed a more naked and flamboyant prominence.

That does not mean that we must give up the ideals of these classic political expectations. I believe that both have been concerned with the problem of rationality and of freedom: liberalism, with freedom and rationality as supreme facts about the individual; Marxism, as supreme facts about man's role in the political making of history. What I have said here, I suppose, may be taken as an attempt to make evident why the ideas of freedom and of rationality now so often seem so ambiguous in the new society of the United States of America.

16

The American Power Structure

G. WILLIAM DOMHOFF

In this chapter I present the main empirical findings and theoretical conclusions that appear in the books and articles that have emerged from my twenty-nine years of studying the American power structure. Because of space limitations I must be extremely brief, so I hope readers will refer to the sources I cite for nuances and the full presentation of the empirical evidence.

MY PERSPECTIVE

By *power* I mean "the capacity of some persons to produce intended and fore-seen effects on others," a definition adapted by Dennis Wrong (1979: 2) from the work of the philosopher Bertrand Russell (1938: 35). This definition leaves open the question of whether force or coercion is always involved in the exercise of power, as most definitions of power seem to imply (Domhoff, 1983: 7–9). By a *power structure*, I mean a network of people and institutions that scores high on a variety of power indicators to be discussed later. This definition is broad enough to encompass whatever kind of power structure is found, whether based in a so-cial class, cross-class coalition, or ethnic group, whether united or divided, whether strong or weak. Power structure networks are constructed with infor-mation found in library reference books, newspapers and periodicals, historical archives, and interviews, or by observing meetings and settings where power people interact. Research on power structures is based in two methodologies: network analysis and content analysis (Domhoff, 1978: Chapter 4).

Because I conclude from my empirical work that the federal government in the United States is dominated by a governing, or ruling, class that is "based upon the national corporate economy and the institutions that economy nourishes"(Domhoff, 1967: 156), it is occasionally assumed that I am a Marxist or neo-Marxist (e.g., Gold, Lo, and Wright, 1975; Skocpol, 1980; Van Den Berg, 1988). Sometimes I am lumped with the instrumentalist Marxist Ralph Miliband (1969), despite the fact that his work appeared after my first books were written. Although I have defended him against his critics who grossly distorted what he actually said (Domhoff, 1986a; 1990: 190–194), I have my own criticisms of his views (Domhoff, 1983: 211–216).

I am not now and never have been a Marxist. The first few pages of my first book made this point apparent: "This book is inspired by the ideas of four very different men—E. Digby Baltzell, C. Wright Mills, Paul M. Sweezy, and Robert A. Dahl" (Domhoff, 1967: 1). Only one of the four, Sweezy, is a Marxist; I draw on a variety of theoretical traditions for testable ideas. "It [this book] is beholden to no theory about the dynamics of history or the structure of society or the future of man. In fact, it is because 'ruling class' is a term that implies a Marxist view of history that the more neutral term 'governing class' is employed" (p. 3).

I went on to say that I was also not part of the classical elitist tradition, stating that "it must be stressed that the term 'governing class' is in no way related to the incorrect usage of that term by Italian social theorist Vilfredo Pareto. Pareto was talking about 'governing elites,' with little or no concern for 'socioeconomic classes' " (p. 3). However, I did switch to the term "ruling class" in the 1970s because the term "governing class" still led some people to identify me with the Italian elitist tradition, and Marxists had by and large abandoned "ruling class" for "dominant class."

For me, a Marxist is a person who begins with the concept of historical materialism, placing primacy on the mode of production and class struggle in all times and places, even to the point of deriving the origins of the state from class struggle. I also think that the labor theory of value is a central element, although I recognize that some Marxists in recent years have argued that it is not essential to the theory of Marxism. In any case, I hold to neither of these concepts.

Put most succinctly, my general theoretical views in the 1960s were closest to those of C. Wright Mills, who argued in his book *The Marxists* (1962: Chapter 6) that there is political determinism and military determinism as well as historical materialism. He criticized Marx for "his economic determinism and his neglect of political and military institutions as autonomous and originative" (p. 118). Mills also stressed that power structures vary greatly from time to time and place to place and that each situation must be studied anew in order to understand the importance of economic, political, and military factors. From this perspective it would be possible through empirical work to conclude, without being a Marxist, that a corporation-based capitalist class—manifesting itself most obviously as a social upper class—dominates the American government. That in fact describes what I have done.

More recently, I have adopted the general framework of Michael Mann (1986; 1992), a framework that goes beyond Mills in positing four networks of organizationally based social power: the economic, the political, the military, and the ideological. Through a detailed consideration of Western civilization from its origins to the early twentieth century, Mann shows that these networks inter-

twine in complex ways and that classes and states only emerged as the dominant
power networks in the past few centuries (Domhoff, 1990: Chapter 1). Mann ob-
serves that by the nineteenth century, some countries had arrived at a "Marxian
result," that is, capitalist-based ruling classes that dominate national governments. Mann's route to this result, however, is a very un-Marxian one. Among
the many reasons I find his general framework useful is that my own earlier speculations on the origins of ruling classes and the state (Domhoff, 1969) stressed
the importance of the ideology network as it manifested itself in religious worship and especially religious sacrifice.

However, my analysis of the American power structure has not dealt at such
rarefied levels. Instead, I used Baltzell's (1958; 1964) findings on the social upper
class as my starting point to show that the owners, managers, and lawyers of the
large corporations and banks were part of this class. I thus established, in Max
Weber's (1946) terms, that the top status group and the major economic class are
one and the same in the United States (Domhoff, 1967: 3-4). I then borrowed
Mill's (1956) concept of a power elite and redefined it as active, working members of the upper class and high-level employees in institutions controlled by
members of the upper class, thereby making it the leadership group of the upper
class (Domhoff, 1967: 8-11; 1979: 13-16; 1983: 2, 109-110). I determined "control" of institutions by origins, financing, and most importantly, the overrepresentation of members of the upper class on the boards of directors of the
organizations and institutions under study.

Thus, my work can be seen most fruitfully as an intertwining of class and organizational perspectives, and the bridge between the two perspectives is the
boards of directors that are in charge of every major institution in America. On
the one hand, the board brings class perspectives and resources to the institution (e.g., Ostrander, 1987). On the other hand, it is at the board level that the
top managers with responsibility for the day-to-day affairs of the institution as-
similate or adapt to the policy desires of upper-class directors as a way to insure
institutional survival and growth. It is a failing of class-oriented theorists that
they have not taken the organizational perspective seriously, but organizational
theorists have fallen short in not seeing boards of directors as something more
than window dressing.

In my work I operationalized the concept of social upper class through listings in social directories, attendance at certain private schools, or membership
in certain social clubs. I noted that such indicators are not perfect because they
sometimes yield false positives or false negatives, but they are serviceable for
large-scale studies (Domhoff, 1970: Chapter 1; 1983: 44-49). After estimating
that this upper class makes up from 0.5 percent to 1 percent of the American
population, I then traced out the networks generated by overlapping school attendance, club memberships, and participation in other social institutions to
show that this upper class is nationwide in scope and socially cohesive
(Domhoff, 1967: Chapter 1; 1970: Chapters 1-4; 1983 Chapter 2). Perhaps my

most convincing study along these lines was a historical, network, and interview study of the famous Bohemian Club in San Francisco. Its annual retreat, held since the 1890s at the Bohemian Grove in the redwoods of Northern California in the last two weeks of July, brings together the rich, celebrities, and government officials for relaxation, merriment, and entertainment (Domhoff, 1974; 1983: 30–31, 48, 70). Following the social psychology literature on small groups, I used my study of the Bohemian Club to argue that social cohesion is one factor in making possible the policy cohesion that is necessary if members of the upper class are to function as leaders within a power elite (Domhoff, 1974: 89–90).

The next step in the research was to see if the social upper class overlaps with what I came to call the "corporate community," which I operationalized most often as all those economic organizations that are linked together by directors who serve on two or more corporate boards (Domhoff, 1983: Chapter 3). Research by myself and many others, sometimes using sophisticated quantitative methods for analyzing social networks, showed that this corporate community contains hundreds and hundreds of closely connected large corporations, with banks at its center, and with men of great wealth or top positions in the biggest banks and corporations forming the inner group or inner circle within this business community (e.g., Sonquist and Koenig, 1975; Dye, 1976; Mintz and Schwartz, 1981; 1985; Useem, 1978; 1980; 1984; Mizruchi, 1982; Salzman and Domhoff, 1983). In turn, this tightly knit corporate community was found to have a large overlap with the social upper class, especially among the inner circle who sit on two or more corporate boards (Domhoff, 1967: Chapter 2; Domhoff, 1975; Bonacich and Domhoff, 1981; and studies summarized in Domhoff, 1983: 66–72). But how do we determine if the overlapping social upper class and corporate community are powerful?

POWER INDICATORS

There are four traditional indicators of power. The first three can be summarized as (1) who *benefits*—who stands highest on such values as great wealth, high income, long life, good health, and so forth; (2) who *sits*—which class or social group is overrepresented in positions of authority in the key power institutions in the society, governmental or elsewhere; and (3) who *wins*—which class or group has its preferences prevail on a wide range of governmental policy decisions (cf., Alford, 1975; Alford and Friedland, 1985). The fourth indicator is a *reputation* for power—who is said to be powerful by a wide range of knowledgeable informants.

All four of these indicators are useful. They all have strengths and weaknesses, and a study is strongest when it can use all four and they all point to the same class or group (Domhoff, 1978: Chapter 4; 1983: 10–13, 221–223). In my own work I have used who benefits, who sits, and who wins as my power indicators. Although I have great respect for the reputational indicator and believe it has been utilized to great profit in many local and national studies (e.g., Hunter, 1953; 1959; Moore, 1979; Higley and Moore, 1981). I have not had occasion to employ it.

All of the "who benefits" indicators point to the upper class as powerful. Its members have great wealth and income. For example, the top 0.5 percent of wealthholders have 25–30 percent of all privately held wealth (Domhoff, 1979: 4–6; 1983: 41–43). Similarly, members of the power elite as I have defined it are disproportionately represented in government at the national level (e.g., Mills, 1956; Mintz, 1975; Zweigenhaft, 1975; Burch, 1980/81; and studies summarized in Domhoff, 1983: 126–130, 137–143). That doesn't mean that they are the majority in each and every agency or department, but they sit in seats of authority tens of times more than would be expected by chance, which is the relevant point in terms of power indicators (Domhoff, 1967: 142–144).

Some critics of the kind of research I do claim that who benefits and who sits are not good indicators of power and that only the decisional indicator (who wins) is valid (e.g., Dahl, 1958; Polsby, 1980). I think that there are good answers to their arguments (Domhoff, 1983: 204–208). Moreover, it can be shown that the decisional method has its own serious weaknesses, including the fact that we can't always obtain the information we need to understand the decision-making process (Domhoff, 1967: 144–145). I demonstrated this point in a restudy of the most respected decisional study of power at the local level, Dahl's (1961) analysis of New Haven, Connecticut. Through a series of follow-up interviews and a content analysis of letters, memos, minutes, and other documents not available at the time of the original study, I was able to show that the decisional process on urban renewal in New Haven was far different from what Dahl thought based on his interviews conducted shortly after the key decisions were made (Domhoff, 1978: Chapter 3; 1983: 184–196).

However, it is possible to provide a theoretical framework for decisional studies that mitigates these problems, and such a framework is one of the major concerns of my work. In terms of Weber's (1946) definition of a "party" as the means by which a class, status group, or coalition of groups tries to influence communal action in a planned manner, the four networks to be discussed in the following paragraphs constitute the real party of the upper class and corporate community. As will be seen, the two major political parties are only one part of a larger picture.

POWER NETWORKS

The first of the four networks through which the power elite dominates the federal government is the *special-interest process*. It deals with the narrow and short-run policy concerns of individuals, families, specific corporations, or specific industries. This network operates through lobbyists, company lawyers, political action committees, and trade associations; it focuses on congressional committees, departments of the executive branch, and regulatory agencies. Many studies of this process by political scientists and journalists show that members of the power elite usually win (Domhoff, 1979: Chapter 2; 1983: 129–131). However, in the best account of how these special interests capture the pieces of the fragmented American government of most concern to them, Grant McConnell (1966) points out that this evidence does not add up to support for the idea of a power elite. It does not show that the power elite is able to work its will on big policy issues. To answer that objection, I have done numerous studies of what I call the policy-planning process.

The second of the power networks is the bipartisan, nonprofit *policy-planning process*. Rooted in the upper class and corporate community through financing and directorships, it consists of interlocked foundations, think tanks, and discussion organizations where business leaders meet with government officials and academic experts to discuss a wide range of issues and attempt to reach policy consensus (Domhoff, 1967: Chapter 3; Domhoff, 1970: Chapters 5–6; Salzman and Domhoff, 1983; Domhoff, 1990: Chapters 3–6; and studies summarized in Domhoff, 1983: Chapter 4). The policy-planning network is not completely unified, however. Within the network are moderately conservative and ultraconservative cliques (Domhoff, 1972: 158–166; 1979: 81–87; 1983: 90–92), but the bases for their differences are not well understood.

The proposals produced in this network reach government in a variety of ways, including reports issued by the organizations and articles published on the opinion pages of the *New York Times, Wall Street Journal,* and *Washington Post.* People from this network also talk with aides to high government officials and serve as governmental advisers. They serve as members of the blue-ribbon presidential commissions that often play a role in major new policies. They also carry their perspectives to government as the business leaders and corporate lawyers who are appointed in great numbers to top positions in government, for the policy-planning network is in fact the main source of the men and women of the upper class and corporate community who are appointed to government (Shoup and Minter, 1977; Salzman and Domhoff, 1980; Useem, 1980; and other work summarized in Domhoff, 1983: 136–143).

If the special-interest and policy-planning processes are to result in positive outcomes for the power elite, there must be business-oriented politicians in government. That leads us to the third power network, which is the *candidate-selection process* that operates through the two major political parties. I argue, following standard political science sources, that the election of a president, along with the system of single-member districts for electing Congress, has generated the structure of strategies and pathways that lead to the two-party system (Domhoff, 1979: Chapter 3; 1983: 117–118). In this context the power elite has been able to dominate both political parties at the national level through campaign financing (Domhoff, 1967: Chapter 4; 1972; 1990: Chapter 9). Large donations are especially important in the primaries, which Alexander Heard (1962:

34) aptly describes as a "choke-point" in the American political system. The two-party system thus results in elected officials who are relatively issueless and willing to go along with the policies advocated by those who work in the special-interest and policy-planning processes. True enough, there are right-wing Republicans and many liberal Democrats who sometimes balk, but they are vastly outnumbered, especially in key leadership positions in Congress. Elections are nevertheless very important, for they keep the power structure from becoming more closed than it already is.

Although members of the power elite are the main financial backers for both parties, this does not mean there are no differences between the two parties. The leadership levels of the two parties have intraclass differences, and the supporters have interclass differences. It is my contention that "the Republican Party is controlled by the largest manufacturers and bankers of the upper class, men who are primarily White Anglo-Saxon Protestant in background and who are from families that became prominent between the Civil War and the Depression," whereas the Democrats are dominated by "very new and very old elements within the upper class, including Southern aristocrats and ethnic rich" (Domhoff, 1967: 86). The Democratic Party, although often billed as the party of the common man, was in fact the party of the Southern segment of the ruling class from its origins until very recently (Domhoff, 1972: Chapter 3; 1990: 235–245). The power of the Southern Democrats was secured in a variety of ways (Potter, 1972), most importantly by the seniority system for selecting committee chairs in Congress. The underlying point, however, is that the one-party system in the South and the exclusion of African-Americans from the voting booth until the mid-1960s gave the Southern planters and merchants power at the national level through the Democratic Party out of all proportion to their numbers or wealth (cf., Key, 1949; and references cited in Domhoff, 1972: 182–184).

The Southerners dominated the party in an alliance with the "machine Democrats" of large Northern cities who were not rooted in labor but rather in the small businesses and real estate interests of their districts. These interests were often Irish, Italian, Jewish, or Polish, which further distinguished them from the Northern Republican business leaders (Domhoff, 1972: 97–99). This alliance between the Southerners and the machines successfully froze out the policy initiatives of the liberal-labor coalition that gives its votes to the party. When this alliance broke down on certain issues where the machine Democrats sided with the liberals and labor, then the Southern Democrats joined with Northern Republicans to create the "conservative coalition." It is my argument that the issues that unite the conservative coalition are the issues that define class struggle in the United States at the legislative level: civil rights, union rights, social welfare, and business regulation (Domhoff, 1990: 240–242). The alliance between the Southern Democrats and the machine Democrats, however, is a prospending alliance based on a common interest in government subsidies to their main backers (Domhoff, 1972: 100; 1990: 240–242). Labor and the poor often benefit from the prospending alliance, which is why they tend to vote Democratic.

The final network through which the power elite dominates government is the ideology, or *opinion-shaping*, process, which tries (often unsuccessfully) to influence public opinion. This process begins with many of the central discussion groups in the policy-planning network, but it also includes hundreds of small organizations that do public relations and "education" in virtually every issue area. These organizations are also linked to the public relations departments of major corporations. At its point of direct contact with the public, the opinion-shaping network is extremely diverse and diffuse. Although the media are in some ways part of this network, my view is that the role of the media in the shaping of public opinion is vastly overstated (except on foreign policy), especially by those theorists who think that there is class domination in the United States (Domhoff, 1983: 107–109).

Unlike those who believe that Americans are brainwashed by elites and the media, I think it is the institutional fit between the daily lives of citizens and the central institutions of the society that gives the social system its acceptance and stability (cf., Mann, 1975). From this perspective, the ideology process is no more basic than the three processes outlined earlier. It is in the special-interest and policy-planning processes that the decisions are made that affect the prosperity of the economy, the success or failure of foreign policy, and hence the stability of overall institutional arrangements. The opinion-shaping process can help to make the other processes function more smoothly and perhaps dampen the protest movements of those who oppose power-elite policies, but it cannot compensate for large-scale failures in the other processes (Domhoff, 1979: 191–198).

Despite all this power at the top, narrow interests or mass movements do have their moments. Business sometimes loses in the special-interest process, and such emotional or religious issues as abortion, school prayer, and gun control, where there is no power-elite interest at stake, are a free-for-all. Some general policy initiatives are altered by the liberal-labor coalition, or even created by it, especially in times of disruption like depression, war, or racial unrest (Piven and Cloward, 1971; 1977). Opponents of the power elite are elected to government, and there is ample criticism of the power elite in speeches, newspapers, and books. But when all is said and done, members of the power elite have enough wealth and income, sit in enough seats of authority, and win enough in the decision-making process for me to conclude that the federal government is dominated (which does not mean complete and total control) by a power elite rooted in the upper class and the corporate community (Domhoff, 1983: 150–151).

Not everyone would agree with me in this conclusion, least of all business leaders themselves. They feel besieged by consumer advocates, environmentalists, and government bureaucrats. However, there are good explanations for the

business leaders' feelings of powerlessness and dislike of government, explanations that are compatible with the fact of their great power (Domhoff, 1967:
152–155; 1983: 146–149). Theorists who believe that the military has independent power also would dispute me (e.g., Hooks, 1991), but I think the evidence for
power elite control of the Pentagon through civilian appointments and other
mechanisms is very strong (e.g., Janowitz, 1960; Huntington, 1961; Bernstein,
1965; 1967; Domhoff, 1967: 115–126; 1968: 257–258; Schwarz, 1981). Finally,
those social scientists who attribute considerable independence to government
officials would disagree with my claims (e.g., Krasner, 1978; Skocpol, 1980), but I
have shown that there are major empirical and interpretive weaknesses in their
case studies of the New Deal and World War II eras (Domhoff, 1990: Chapters
4–8; 1991).

COMMUNITY POWER

One of the first systematic studies of power in the United States was carried
out at the local level (Hunter, 1953), and social scientists have been concerned
with what is called *community power* ever since. Although political scientists dis-
puted sociologist Floyd Hunter's claim that business leaders dominated the
power structure in Atlanta because he did not use the decisional method (Dahl,
1958; Polsby, 1980), later decisional studies by political scientist Clarence Stone
(1976, 1989) came to a very similar conclusion.

Utilizing the pioneering work of Harvey Molotch (1976; 1979; with Logan,
1987), it is my view that community power structures are "growth coalitions," or
"growth machines," that are based in a common concern with the intensifica-
tion of land use in the community or city (cf., Domhoff, 1983: Chapter 6; 1986b).
These landed elites who are also sometimes called "place entrepreneurs," have
somewhat different concerns than the corporate-based power elite because
their interest is in collecting rents (broadly defined) for the use of their land and
buildings, not in selling products or services for a profit. However, there is a
strong basis for cooperation between growth machines and the power elite due
to the fact that corporate investment is one of the major ways to intensify land
use. Thus, growth machines expend considerable energy trying to make the local area attractive to outside corporations. At the same time, this desire to attract
outside investments creates competition among local growth machines. More
generally, growth machines are often rivals for new installations by universities
and government agencies as well.

Conflict between growth machines and corporations is possible over taxes
and other factors that contribute to the local business climate. In many ways,
corporations have the upper hand in any conflict because they have the ability
to leave town if they don't like local conditions, leaving a stalled or broken
growth machine in their wake (Domhoff, 1967: 136–137; Molotch, 1979).

Because government can be essential to growth in a variety of ways, growth machines make every effort to control local governments. Their attempts to shape government usually begin through committees of the Chamber of Commerce, but local charitable foundations or taxpayers associations may also be part of their efforts. The growth machine is the most overrepresented group on local city councils, and it is also well represented on such vital governmental agencies as planning commissions, zoning boards, water boards, and parking authorities (Logan and Molotch, 1987).

The local growth machine sometimes includes a valuable junior partner: the building trades unions. These unions see their fate tied to growth in the belief that growth creates jobs. They are often highly visible on the side of the growth machine in battles against environmentalists and neighborhood groups. However, this does not mean that growth machines win every time. Just as the power elite sometimes loses to the liberal-labor coalition at the national level, so do growth machines sometimes lose to aroused neighborhoods protecting their use values or to coalitions of neighborhoods, environmentalists, and university students—but not very often.

The strength of local governments and the existence of land-based growth machines together add a further dimension to the American power structure. The competition among growth machines and conflicts between growth machines and neighborhoods are further evidence that the American power structure is neither monolithic nor unchallenged.

CONCLUSION

The argument over the structure and distribution of power in the United States has been going on in heated fashion since the publication of Hunter's *Community Power Structure* (1953) and Mills's *The Power Elite* (1956). It has generated a large number of empirical studies, many of which have been cited in this chapter. Some of these studies have been convincing to those who consider themselves disinterested observers.

In the final analysis, however, people's conclusions about the American power structure depend upon their thinking on power indicators, that is, on their philosophy of science (Domhoff, 1983: 221–223). If who benefits and who sits are seen as valid power indicators, on the assumption that power is an underlying social trait that can be indexed by a variety of imperfect indicators, then the kind of evidence briefly outlined in this essay will be seen as a convincing case for the dominant role of a power elite based in the upper class and the corporate community. If who wins on a wide range of government decisions is seen as the only valid indicator of power (as the strict logical positivists among social scientists still seem to believe), the support for my claims will be seen as less impressive. This is because we have not had the time and resources to do enough case studies within the framework of the four networks through which, I believe, the power elite dominates government. A good start has been made in this direction, but it will take far more to convince those who insist that who wins is the only valid power indicator.

Thus, the argument about the American power structure is as much philosophic as it is empirical. While the debate continues, however, we should continue to remind ourselves that members of an upper class making up less than 1 percent of the population own 20 to 25 percent of all privately held wealth and 45 to 50 percent of all privately held corporate stock; they are overrepresented in seats of formal power from the corporation to the federal government; and they win much more often than they lose on issues ranging from the tax structure to labor law to foreign policy.

REFERENCES

Alford, Robert. 1975. "Paradigms of Relations Between States and Societies." In Leon Lindberg, Robert Alford, Colin Crouch, and Claus Offe, eds., *Stress and Contradiction in Modern Capitalism*. Lexington, Mass.: Lexington Books.

Alford, Robert, and Roger Friedland. 1985. *Powers of Theory*. New York: Cambridge University Press.

Baltzell, E. Digby. 1958. *Philadelphia Gentlemen*. New York: Free Press.

_____ . 1964. *The Protestant Establishment*. New York: Random House.

Bernstein, Barton. 1965. "The Removal of War Production Board Controls on Business, 1944–1946." *Business History Review* 39: 243–260.

_____ . 1967. "The Debate on Industrial Reconversion." *American Journal of Economics and Sociology* 26: 159–172.

Bonacich, Phillip, and G. William Domhoff. 1981. "Latent Classes and Group Membership." *Social Networks* 3: 175–196.

Burch, Philip. 1980/81. *Elites in American History*. 3 vols. New York: Holmes and Meier.

Dahl, Robert. 1958. "A Critique of the Ruling Elite Model." *American Political Science Review* 52: 463–469.

_____ . 1961. *Who Governs?* New Haven, Conn.: Yale University Press.

Domhoff, G. William. 1967. *Who Rules America?* Englewood Cliffs, N.J.: Prentice-Hall.

_____ . 1968. "The Power Elite and Its Critics." In G. William Domhoff and Hoyt Ballard, eds., *C. Wright Mills and the Power Elite*. Boston: Beacon Press.

_____ . 1969. "Historical Materialism, Cultural Determinism, and the Origin of the Ruling Classes." *Psychoanalytic Review* 56: 271–287.

_____ . 1970. *The Higher Circles*. New York: Random House.

_____ . 1972. *Fat Cats and Democrats*. Englewood Cliffs, N.J.: Prentice-Hall.

_____ . 1974. *The Bohemian Grove and Other Retreats*. New York: Harper and Row.

_____ . 1975. "Social Clubs, Policy-Planning Groups and Corporations: A Network Study of Ruling-Class Cohesiveness." *Insurgent Sociologist* 5: 173–184.

_____ . 1978. *Who Really Rules: New Haven and Community Power Re-examined*. New Brunswick, N.J.: Transaction Books.

_____ . 1979. *The Powers That Be*. New York: Random House.

_____ . 1983. *Who Rules America Now?* New York: Simon and Schuster.

_____ . 1986a. "State Autonomy and the Privileged Position of Business: An Empirical Attack on a Theoretical Fantasy." *Journal of Political and Military Sociology* 14: 149–162.

_____ . 1986b. "The Power Elite and the Growth Machine." In Robert Waste, ed., *Community Power*. Beverly Hills, Calif.: Sage Publications.

_____ . 1990. *The Power Elite and the State*. Hawthorne, N.Y.: Aldine.

_____ . 1991. "Class, Power, and Parties During the New Deal: A Critique of Skocpol's Theory of State Autonomy." *Berkeley Journal of Sociology* 36: 1–49.

Dye, Thomas. 1976. *Who's Running America?* Englewood Cliffs, N.J.: Prentice-Hall.

Gold, David, Clarence Lo, and Erik Wright. 1975. "Recent Developments in Marxist Theories of the Capitalist State." *Monthly Review* 27: 29–43.

Heard, Alexander. 1962. *The Costs of Democracy*. New York: Doubleday.

Higley, John, and Gwen Moore. 1981. "Elite Integration in the U.S. and Australia." *American Political Science Review* 75: 581–597.

Hooks, Gregory. 1991. *Forging the Military-Industrial Complex*. Urbana: University of Illinois Press.

Hunter, Floyd. 1953. *Community Power Structure*. Chapel Hill: University of North Carolina Press.

_____ . 1959. *Top Leadership U.S.A.* Chapel Hill: University of North Carolina Press.

Huntington, Samuel. 1961. *The Common Defense*. New York: Columbia University Press.

Janowitz, Morris. 1960. *The Professional Soldier*. New York: Free Press.

Key, V. O. 1949. *Southern Politics in State and Nation*. New York: Knopf.

Krasner, Stephen. 1978. *Defending the National Interest*. Princeton, N.J.: Princeton University Press.

Logan, Jonathan, and Harvey Molotch. 1987. *Urban Fortunes*. Berkeley: University of California Press.

Mann, Michael. 1975. "The Ideology of Intellectuals and Other People in the Development of Capitalism." In Leon Lindberg, Robert Alford, Colin Crouch, and Claus Offe, eds., *Stress and Contradiction in Modern Capitalism*. Lexington, Mass.: Lexington Books.

_____ . 1986, 1992. *The Sources of Social Power*. 2 vols. New York: Cambridge University Press.

McConnell, Grant. 1966. *Private Power and American Democracy*. New York: Knopf.

Miliband, Ralph. 1969. *The State in Capitalist Society*. New York: Basic Books.

Mills, C. Wright. 1956. *The Power Elite*. New York: Oxford University Press.

_____ . 1962. *The Marxists*. New York: Dell.

Mintz, Beth. 1975. "The President's Cabinet, 1897–1972." *Insurgent Sociologist* 5: 131–148.

Mintz, Beth, and Michael Schwartz. 1981. "The Structure of Intercorporate Unity in American Business." *Social Problems* 29: 87–103.

_____ . 1985. *The Power Structure of American Business*. Chicago: University of Chicago Press.

Mizruchi, Mark. 1982. *The Structure of the American Corporate Network, 1904–1974*. Beverly Hills, Calif.: Sage Publications.

Molotch, Harvey. 1976. "The City as a Growth Machine." *American Journal of Sociology* 82: 309–330.

_____ . 1979. "Capital and Neighborhood in the United States." *Urban Affairs Quarterly* 14: 289–312.

Moore, Gwen. 1979. "The Structure of a National Elite Network." *American Sociological Review* 44: 673–692.

Ostrander, Susan. 1987. "Elite Domination in Private Social Agencies: How It Happens and How It Is Challenged." In G. William Domhoff and Thomas Dye, eds., *Power Elites and Organizations.* Beverly Hills, Calif.: Sage Publications.

Piven, Frances, and Richard Cloward. 1971. *Regulating the Poor.* New York: Pantheon.

_____ . 1977. *Poor People's Movements.* New York: Random House.

Polsby, Nelson. 1980. *Community Power and Political Theory,* 2nd ed. New Haven, Conn.: Yale University Press.

Potter, David M. 1972. *The South and the Concurrent Majority.* Baton Rouge: Louisiana State University Press.

Russell, Bertrand. 1938. *Power: A New Social Analysis.* London: Allen and Unwin.

Salzman, Harold, and G. William Domhoff. 1980. "The Corporate Community and Government: Do They Interlock?" In G. William Domhoff, ed., *Power Structure Research.* Beverly Hills, Calif.: Sage Publications.

_____ . 1983. "Nonprofit Organizations and the Corporate Community." *Social Science History* 7: 205–215.

Schwarz, Jordan. 1981. *The Speculator.* Chapel Hill: University of North Carolina Press.

Shoup, Laurence, and William Minter. 1977. *Imperial Brain Trust.* New York: Monthly Review Press.

Skocpol, Theda. 1980. "Political Responses to Capitalist Crisis: Neo-Marxist Theories of the State and the Case of the New Deal." *Politics and Society* 10: 155–202.

Sonquist, John, and Thomas Koenig. 1975. "Interlocking Directorates in the Top U.S. Corporations." *Insurgent Sociologist* 5: 196–229.

Stone, Clarence. 1976. *Neighborhood and Discontent.* Chapel Hill: University of North Carolina Press.

_____ . 1989. *Regime Politics.* Lawrence: University of Kansas Press.

Useem, Michael. 1978. "The Inner Group of the American Capitalist Class." *Social Problems* 25: 225–240.

_____ . 1980. "Which Business Leaders Help Govern?" In G. William Domhoff, ed., *Power Structure Research.* Beverly Hills, Calif.: Sage Publications.

_____ . 1984. *The Inner Circle.* New York: Oxford University Press.

Van Den Berg, Axel. 1988. *The Immanent Utopia.* Princeton, N.J.: Princeton University Press.

Weber, Max. 1946. "Class, Status, and Party." In Hans Gerth and C. Wright Mills, eds., *Max Weber: Essays in Sociology.* New York: Oxford University Press.

Wrong, Dennis. 1979. *Power: Its Forms, Bases, and Uses.* New York: Harper and Row.

Zweigenhaft, Richard. 1975. "Who Represents America?" *Insurgent Sociologist* 5: 119–130.

17

The Structure of a National Elite Network

GWEN MOORE

The structure of national elite groups, and particularly the degree to which they are integrated, is a critical issue in political sociology and political science. While considerable integration of elites was generally assumed by the classical elite theorists, Pareto, Mosca and Michels, recent investigators have disagreed strongly about the relative amount, causes and consequences of elite integration in western, industrialized societies.

In the United States a lengthy debate over the structure of power and influence at the national level has centered on the degree to which this structure is unified or diversified. Ruling class and power elite theorists such as Mills and Domhoff find a considerable amount of integration, with various bases, in the national power structure. According to Mills (1956:292):

> The conception of the power elite and of its unity rests upon the corresponding developments and the coincidence of interests among economic, political, and military organizations. It also rests upon the similarity of origins and outlook, and the social and personal intermingling of the top circles from each of these dominant hierarchies.

The existence of a broad, inclusive network of powerful persons with similar social origins, in different institutions, is then one important feature of this view of the power structure.

Pluralists find little integration among elites in diverse sectors. For example, in drawing conclusions from his study of private power and American government, McConnell (1966:339) writes:

> The first conclusion that emerges from the present analysis and survey is that a substantial part of the government in the United States has come under the influ-

ence and control of narrowly based and largely autonomous elites. These elites do not act cohesively with each other on many issues. They do not "rule" in the sense of commanding the entire nation. Quite the contrary, they tend to pursue a policy of noninvolvement in the large issues of statesmanship, save where such issues touch their own particular concerns.

Pluralists argue that each elite group is distinct and narrowly based, with influence confined to the issues most relevant to its membership. ... Elites are seen as fragmented rather than integrated since each is involved primarily with its own relatively narrow concerns and constituencies. ...

The study reported here assesses the extent of integration in a network of political elites in the United States.[1] The concept of political elite integration has several dimensions including, at least, social homogeneity, value consensus and personal interaction (Putnam, 1976:107). Social homogeneity, the extent to which elites share class and status origins and common experiences such as attendance at exclusive private schools, is usually seen as fostering integration. ...

The degree to which leaders agree on political beliefs, both specific public policies and broad ideological orientations, is often used as a measure of value consensus. ... Agreement among elites at least on the "rules of the game" usually is considered essential not only to integration but also to political stability. ...

Personal interaction among elites is probably the crucial dimension of integration. Giddens (1975:120), for instance, defines an integrated elite as one in which members of different elite groups frequently interact as acquaintances, friends or kin. He contends that a highly integrated elite is likely to exhibit both solidarity and relatively little conflict. Many others ... see interpersonal contact among political elites in diverse positions as essential for the development and maintenance of integration at the national level. In a common view, the social organization which is a prerequisite for integration depends in part on a network structured to facilitate interaction and communication among persons in high-level positions in all major institutions. Without extensive connections among persons in different institutions, value consensus could not be achieved or maintained, and the development of solidarity could not occur since it requires trust and familiarity. Elite groups in different sectors would then remain largely encapsuled and fragmented. The investigation of the structure of elite interaction networks thus is a central concern in the assessment of elite integration. ...

Many social scientists have examined sociometric ties among elites in individual communities or groups. ... , but such data rarely have been gathered for major groups at the national level. ... The American Leadership Study, a survey of top position holders in powerful American institutions, which includes data on interpersonal contacts, offers a unique opportunity to examine the extent of integration or fragmentation among political elites in the United States.

I begin with an examination of the structure of an elite interaction network, with particular interest in whether or not it contains many distinct groups individually formed around narrow issue concerns, or, rather, a few large and inclusive groups, each including varying constituencies and concerns. This examination locates one large, cohesive group of leaders, representing all major institutions and issue areas, which serves to integrate the network. Given this finding of integration of American leaders in a large "central circle," two additional issues are addressed. In order to validate the method used, i.e., to be certain that this circle contains the most powerful or influential elites, the members of this central circle are compared with others in similar top-level positions to see if circle members are more influential in ways other than circle membership. Then, the relationship between social origins and current affiliations and membership in the central circle is examined to see if high status origins or influential current affiliations (beyond primary institutional position) are advantageous in achieving connections to this group. Thus, this analysis not only examines the extent of integration but also the social bases for the integration that is found.

RESEARCH DESIGN

The data used are taken from the American Leadership Study, a survey of 545 top position holders in key institutions in American society conducted in 1971–72 by the Bureau of Applied Social Research, Columbia University. Through personal interviews, information was gathered on respondents' policy influencing and policy making activities on major national issues. Extensive attitude and social background data also were collected. The study's wide institutional representation, collection of sociometric data and focus on major issues of the time make it well-suited for evaluating elite integration.

The sample id drawn from persons in the top positions in ten institutional sectors assumed to exercise power in American society. The institutions and positions sampled in each are shown in Table [17.]1. The leaders in the positional sample were asked to name other persons with whom they interact or who they felt were currently influential among leaders in the United States. From the responses to these questions a snowball sample of 61 "opinion-leaders" ... was chosen to correct for important omissions in the positional sample. Most persons in the snowball or reputational sample were in one of the ten positional sectors, especially Congress and the media. A few were not; these include academics, White House staff, governors and mayors. In light of the debate over methods for identifying influential or powerful individuals, it is worth noting that in this case the same persons frequently were identified by the positional and reputational (snowball) techniques. Depending on how many respondents were added in the snowball phase in a given sector, 50 to 60 persons were interviewed in each positional sector.[2] (Because of similarities in function, I combine the industrial corporations, nonindustrial corporations and holders of large fortunes in a sector called business. Likewise, members of the White House staff

TABLE [17.] 1   American Leadership Sample Sectors

Sector	Position
Congress	Senators; members of House of Representatives in following categories: chairman and ranking minority members of all House committees; all members of the Rules, Appropriations and Ways and Means Committees; 50% of sample was drawn from Senate, remainder from House.
Federal Administration— Political Appointees	Secretaries, assistant secretaries, and general counsel of cabinet departments; heads and deputy heads of independent agencies.
Civil Service	Two highest civil service grades from all cabinet departments and independent agencies.
Industrial Corporation	Fortune 500 largest industrial corporations in 1969.
Nonindustrial Corporation	Fortune 300 largest nonindustrial corporations in 1969; 50% of sample is from banks and insurance companies, remainder from utilities, transportation and nonindustrial corporations.
Holders of Large Fortunes	Holders of fortunes worth at least $100 million.
Labor Union	Presidents of unions with at least 50,000 members; officials of the AFL-CIO.
Political Party	Members of Democratic and Republican National Committees; state and city chairpersons of these parties.
Voluntary Organization	Elected head and full-time director of various public affairs organizations including professional societies, farmers' organizations, women's groups, religious organizations, civil rights organizations, business groups and others.
Media	Editors of largest circulation newspapers and public affairs periodicals; syndicated columnists and news executives; broadcasters and commentators of national networks.

are analyzed as part of the political appointees' sector.) The overall completion rate for the interviews is just over 70%.

Each respondent was asked to choose one national issue on which he or she most actively had attempted to influence national policy or inform public opinion in the past few years. The major part of the interview then focused on activities and contacts concerning this issue. A wide variety of issues was chosen, most of which were related to the individual's formal position. ... While respondents usually discussed narrow issues (e.g., prices in the steel industry, U.S. policy toward a specific country), when similar issue concerns were collapsed into more general categories, three major issue areas emerged. The most frequently discussed issue area was the economy (28.6%), a prime concern of government, business and labor at that time. Wage and price controls were instituted by President Nixon during the interviewing period and, as noted, many respondents chose the topic of controls as their issue focus. Other common issues were foreign policy (17.2%), especially the war in Southeast Asia, and a variety of social policy issues (26.6%), including poverty, race relations and urban problems. Less frequently discussed issues include the environment, law and order, and government reform. A series of sociometric questions referring to the respondent's major issue of activity was asked. These questions dealt with both personal contacts (e.g.,"Of the various people you have talked with about this issue, who had the most useful and interesting things to say?") and reputation for influence (e.g.,"Who has the greatest influence among leading Americans on this issue?"). Respondents were allowed an unlimited number of responses to each sociometric question. The network analyzed here is constructed only from those nominations involving direct personal contact; nominations referring to reputation for influence are used subsequently for purposes of validation. A variety of questions on personal contacts was used to elicit each respondent's interaction partners in various sectors and situations within the context of his or her chosen issue area. In the analysis nominations from all questions are combined to yield each person's interpersonal connections in this limited issue context.

The interpersonal network in these data, resulting from interaction related to a specific issue for each respondent, generally reflects informal discussions or day-to-day interaction on these issues. This network is, of course, not identical with networks formed in other contexts and does not include all personal connections which exist among the individuals in this study. Undoubtedly, many persons in this network who are personally acquainted or who interact socially did not report that fact here. ... Also, let me note that given the focus on specific issues, this network does not reflect issues which remain potential or undiscussed (Bachrach and Baratz, 1963; Lukes, 1974). ...

The analysis of these sociometric data utilizes a procedure developed by Alba (1972; 1973) which is well-suited for evaluating network integration since it identifies the more cohesive parts of networks. The cohesive regions are those in which dense interconnections exist among sets of individuals. These connections may be face-to-face, as in cliques, or through short chains of interaction, as in social circles. Since cliques are generally face-to-face groups, they tend to be relatively small. Social circles, on the other hand, may be much larger.

The identification of social circles among political elites in the U.S. seems an appropriate base for studying the extent of their integration. To begin with, given the large size of the totality of American political elites, they could not be integrated through cliques, since these are generally quite small. In addition, social circles have other characteristics making them suitable for the study of political elite integration. Not only are they cohesive groups whose members can easily communicate and interact with one another, albeit often indirectly, but they are also usually informal groups, lacking defined leadership, whose members are drawn together by similar interests and concerns. ... Thus, positing a social circle as the basis for elite integration does not require that its boundaries be visible to its members. Finally, individuals belonging to large, diverse social circles are likely to be more influential than those with more circumscribed connections because they serve as links in elite circles joining persons in high-level positions in a variety of institutions.

If circles can be identified in a network, the nature of their memberships and their relations to each other and the rest of the network are critical for assessing the extent of the network's integration. The existence of cohesive circles (or cliques) does not, in itself, guarantee that the network as a whole is integrated. By definition, an integrated network is one in which "communications" of various kinds can spread easily from one of its parts to another. Crucial then for integration are the ways in which a network's different parts are joined together. One mechanism making for integration is the existence of large circles with diverse memberships, thus drawing together individuals from different institutional areas in a society. Another is the existence of linkages joining these circles to a variety of small, otherwise disconnected cliques and circles. These linkages may take the form of overlapping memberships or direct ties between the members of different circles and cliques. By contrast, evidence of fragmentation is the existence of small, narrowly based circles or cliques which are widely dispersed, i.e., distant from each other in the network.

In specific terms, the procedure for identifying cohesive groups begins with the network of relations formed by all interaction nominations made by sample members. These relations are treated as symmetric since they represent direct communication. ... Also, the intent to locate individuals in their interaction context or social milieu in a large network makes the identities or their connections more critical than the reciprocity or lack of it in reported connections. ... Thus a link between any pair of persons is defined as present if at least one individual in the pair reports talking to the other and absent if neither named the other as an interaction partner. The network formed in this way is not limited to respondents but also includes persons outside of the sample who were named as interaction partners by at least two sample members and thus form a link between them. As a result, the full network is composed of 396 persons outside of the sample and 480 of the 545 sample members. The remaining 65 individuals in the sample are isolates who are connected to none of the persons in the network. All of the 876 persons in this network are connected through chains,[3] but the network is not dense; of the possible direct connections less that 1% (.7%) exist.

Then, cliques and circles are identified in this network. The first step is to identify cliques, i.e., tightly knit, face-to-face groups, which are defined for my purposes as groups of at least three persons, each of whom is directly connected to all of the others. ... [A]n algorithm for locating these subgraphs identified 442 such completely connected groups. The next step is to use these cliques it identify the circles in the network. Circles can be viewed as webs of intricately interlaced cliques, in which indirect communication in facilitated because circle members are also members of these highly overlapping cliques. Thus, circles can be identified by merging highly overlapping cliques. ... When two-thirds or more of the members of a smaller group were also members of a larger group, the

TABLE [17.]2   Network Position by Sector Membership

Sector	Isolates[a]		Not in a Circle or Clique		Circle or Clique Member		Total Network	
	%	N	%	N	%	N	%	N
Congress	1.7	(1)	65.9	(145)	34.1	(75)	25.1	(220)
Political Appts.	4.5	(3)	56.7	(102)	43.3	(78)	20.5	(180)
Civil Service	11.1	(6)	70.8	(51)	29.2	(21)	8.2	(72)
Business	18.9	(25)	68.6	(81)	31.4	(37)	13.5	(118)
Labor	8.3	(4)	60.4	(32)	39.6	(21)	6.1	(53)
Pol. Party	37.3	(19)	69.7	(23)	30.3	(10)	3.8	(33)
Vol. Org.	1.9	(1)	71.9	(41)	28.1	(16)	6.5	(57)
Media	9.5	(6)	57.7	(41)	42.3	(30)	8.1	(71)
Academic	—	(0)	48.6	(17)	51.4	(18)	4.0	(35)
State, Local Govt.	—	(0)	75.0	(18)	25.0	(6)	2.7	(24)
Other	—	(0)	76.9	(10)	23.1	(3)	1.5	(13)
Total	11.9	(65)	64.0	(561)	36.0	(315)	100.0	(876)

[a]Because all isolates are sample members, these percentages are the proportion of isolates in a given sample sector; other percentages in this table are based on the network of 876.

two groups were merged. Thirty-two cliques and circles emerged as the end product of this procedure.[4]

Membership in such cliques and circles is likely to be related to measures of network centrality ... , even though centrality remains an analytically and, to some extent, empirically distinct concept. Centrality reflects, in essence, the number of communication paths which pass through an individual's network location. That an individual is central, however, does not mean that he or she is integrated into a group, and vice versa. ... Cohesion, then, is not simply equatable with greater density of links among circle or clique members, but rather with the integration of each member into tightly knit groups with other members. ...

FINDINGS: NETWORK STRUCTURE

As stated earlier, the procedure for identifying groups located 32 circles and cliques in the connected network from the American Leadership data. This connected part contains 876 persons and the remaining 65 individuals are all isolates, connected neither to each other nor to anyone in the network. Table [17.]2 presents the network locations of individuals—whether they are isolates or, if in the connected network, whether they belong to a circle or clique—by their sector memberships.

As the table shows, just over half of the 876 persons in the connected network hold positions in the three federal political sectors, while the remainder represent a wide variety of nongovernmental institutions. However, in most sector about a third of those in the network are members of circles or cliques. If only those in the original positional sectors are considered, this proportion is much

TABLE [17.]3   Sector and Issue Composition of 32 Elite Circles and Cliques

Group Number	No. of Members	Density[a]	At Least 2/3 of Sample Members in Group Discussed This Issue	At Least 2/3 of Group Members Are in This Sector	Unifying Feature
1	3	100.0	—	media	media sector
2	3	100.0	—	—	?
3	3	100.0	—	media	media sector
4	3	100.0	defense	media	Vietnam
5	3	100.0	defense	media	Vietnam
6	5	70.0	defense	—	defense policy
7	3	100.0	freedom of press	media	freedom of press
8	3	100.0	freedom of press	media	freedom of press
9	3	100.0	social	vol. org.	race relations
10	3	100.0	economy	vol. org.	agriculture
11	5	70.0	ecology	—	ecology and geographic location
12	6	60.0	—	—	geographic location
13	4	83.3	defense	—	Vietnam and geographic location
14	7	52.4	defense	—	defense
15	3	100.0	—	civil service	veterans' affairs
16	3	100.0	social	—	urban affairs
17	3	100.0	economy	—	Dept. of Commerce
18	13	32.1	ecology	—	ecology
19	4	83.3	ecology	pol. appt.	ecology
20	3	100.0	social	pol. appt.	health care
21	6	60.0	social	pol. appt.	Dept. HEW
22	3	100.0	—	pol. appt.	transportation policy
23	5	80.0	defense	Congress	defense
24	3	100.0	—	Congress	?
25	3	100.0	economy	pol. appt.	agriculture
26	3	100.0	economy	Congress	economy
27	3	100.0	economy	—	unions
28	19	26.9	economy	—	agriculture
29	3	100.0	—	—	transportation policy
30	3	100.0	economy	labor	unions
31	227	3.8	—	—	?
32	5	70.0	economy	—	economy

[a]Density is given as percentage of possible ties which are present.

higher only among political appointees and members of the media sector. The isolates—those sample members connected to no one else—come mainly from two sectors, political party and business. In the case of the political party sector, the isolates are local leaders, who have few, if any, ties to national elite groups. The isolated position of these local leaders is not surprising given the frequent description of American political parties as primarily local rather than national organizations. Most of the isolated business leaders are from the smaller organizations among the Fortune 800 corporations. For example, none is the head of

an industrial corporation in the top 100 on the Fortune list and none is from one
of the 20 largest insurance companies.

Of the 32 circles and cliques identified in the network, all but four are unified
around concern with a common issue or through common sector membership,
as Table [17.]3 shows. Most of the groups are quite small. Only three have more
than ten members and two of these are narrowly focused on one issue area each,
ecology and agriculture. The third and most distinctive circle contains 227 persons (of whom 164 are sample members) from all sectors and discussing all issues. It is the only one whose membership is large and inclusive, crossing sector
and issue area boundaries.

Thus, with one prominent exception these are narrow groups of persons with
similar issue concerns. Some are further specified by ideology. For example,
three of the circles concerned with defense policy consist almost entirely of well-
known conservatives in and outside the government, while two other defense
policy groups have only members liberal on foreign policy.

The largest group of 227 persons is quite unlike the others because its membership is so diverse; it is in no way devoted to a single issue, sector or geographic
region. This circle is broad and inclusive rather than narrow and specialized.
Nearly one-third (30.1%) of all persons in the sample are members of this group.
While this circle's density appears low when first compared with the densities of
other groups (Table [17.]3), its membership is in fact well connected, since its
members have an average of 8.7 ties with each other. Also, it is composed of
nearly 350 of the original, highly overlapping cliques and over half of its members belong to at least three of the cliques which have been aggregated to form
it, while nearly 70% belong to at least two of these cliques.

This circle has many bridges connecting it to the more narrowly specialized,
outlying circles and cliques, as Figure [17.]1 clearly shows. The lines in this diagram indicate overlapping membership in each pair of groups connected by a
line. Although not shown here, the proportion of overlap, i.e., the proportion of
all members of the smaller group who are also members of the larger one, varies
from a low of 16.5% to a high of 60.0%. Most of the smaller groups have one, or
occasionally more than one, member in common with the largest circle, although most members of the small groups are connected to the largest circle indirectly (through an intermediary), if at all. The small groups rarely have common members with each other. In the few cases where smaller groups overlap,
the issue area involvement of members of each is generally similar, as in the case
of three groups concerned with agricultural issues.

Ease of communication, then, is particularly true of the largest circle, within
which dense connections among individuals from all sectors and issue areas exist. This circle's overlap with most other circles and cliques also allows members
of the issue-specific groups to communicate directly or through an intermediary
with the diverse membership of that large, generalized circle. Thus, in light of its
size, inclusiveness and relations with the rest of the network, I call it the "central

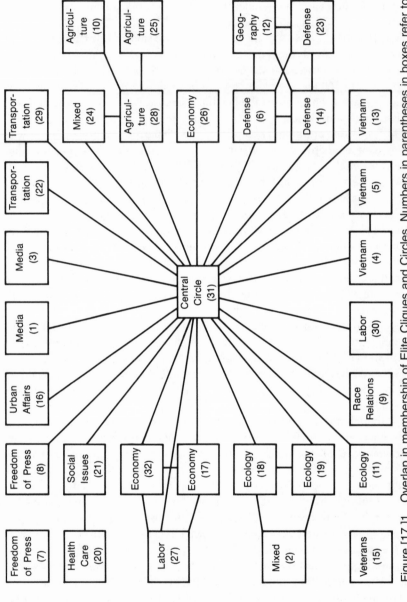

Figure [17.]1 Overlap in membership of Elite Cliques and Circles. Numbers in parentheses in boxes refer to group numbers listed in Table [17.]3.

circle." The existence of the central circle and its connections to issue-based groups indicate that political elites in the United States are integrated not fragmented.

Although the central circle draws its members from all institutional sectors in the sample, representation of the various sectors is not equal, as Table [17.]4 shows. As in the total network, just over half of the central circle members are from the federal political sectors. Aside from business, which has the largest nongovernmental representation, each other sector contributes less than 10% of the members of this circle. A rough assessment of the degree of over- and underrepresentation of sectors in the circle can be made in the following way: if each person in the sample had an equal chance of being a member of the central circle, each sector's proportion in the sample and the circle would be equal and the ratio of these proportions would equal one. When these proportions and ratios are compared it is obvious that this equal probability model is inaccurate.

Two of the three federal political sectors are overrepresented in this circle, partly because specific sociometric questions were asked about contacts with persons in the federal government. In spite of these questions, civil servants are underrepresented in this circle, an indication perhaps that they are rarely included in high-level, broad-based elite circles. Members of the two snowball sectors—academics and state, local government—also are overrepresented in the central circle because in these sectors only persons nominated as influential were interviewed.

While persons in every sector had some chance of being in the central circle, members of the two high-level federal political sectors and persons in the snowball sectors are considerably more strongly represented in the circle than in the sample. Nevertheless, the central circle is a group with broad membership, representing major public and private institutions and organizations. In addition, this circle is representative of the entire sample in terms of political party affiliation, age, sex and education. Democrats and Republicans had an equal chance of membership; nearly three-fourths of the circle and sample members are over 50 years old; 90% attended college; and virtually all (about 95%) of both groups are males. ...

CONCLUSIONS

The purpose of this paper has been to examine the structure of an elite network in major American institutions as a way of assessing the extent of integration among political elites in the United States. No fragmentation of elites in different institutions or issue areas was found. On the contrary, the evidence examined here indicates that considerable integration exists among elites in all major sectors of American society. The existence of a central elite circle facilitates communication and interaction both within that large, diverse group and between its members and those in more specialized elite circles and cliques. ...

TABLE [17.]4   Sector Composition of Central Circle and Sample

Sector	Circle %	Circle N	Sample Members in Circle %	Sample Members in Circle N	Sample %	Sample N	Ratio of Circle Membership to Sample Membership
Congress	22.9	(52)	18.9	(31)	10.6	(58)	1.79
Political Appointees	23.8	(54)	17.7	(29)	12.1	(66)	1.47
Civil Service	5.7	(13)	6.1	(10)	9.9	(54)	.62
Business	15.4	(35)	20.1	(33)	24.2	(132)	.83
Labor	7.0	(16)	7.9	(13)	8.8	(48)	.91
Political Party	2.2	(5)	3.0	(5)	9.4	(51)	.33
Voluntary Organization	5.3	(12)	7.3	(12)	9.5	(52)	.78
Media	7.5	(17)	8.5	(14)	11.6	(63)	.73
Academic	7.5	(17)	8.5	(14)	2.9	(16)	2.97
State, Local Govt.	1.3	(3)	1.8	(3)	.9	(5)	2.00
Other	1.3	(3)	—	(0)	—	(0)	
Total	99.9	(227)	99.8	(164)	99.9	(545)	

$X^2 = 67.6, 9$ d.f., p $<.001$.

[T]he integrated network found in this study is not based on similarities in the social origins and affiliations of its members, to say nothing of upper class origins. While central circle members are more influential than others in similar formal positions, they differ little from the latter in social origins or connections to major private sector organizations. The very diversity of the central elite circle is inconsistent with the expectation that upper class origins and connections are frequently decisive in attaining significant national influence, as it is with the expectation that the solidarity of the highest circles is founded in part on shared origins and mutual upper class affiliations.

This apparent impotence of upper class origins should not be misunderstood. The role of social origins in the attainment of a position in the political elite has been well documented. ... It is at the stage of attainment of an elite position that social origins serve to exclude most Americans from the opportunity to influence national policy making in significant ways. However, once such a position has been achieved, as is true of virtually all persons in this study, these factors are of little subsequent importance. ...

Perhaps the most reasonable interpretation of the network analyzed here is to see it as one involving day-to-day discussions of major issues that have appeared within the public arena. In this light, the structure of the central circle— broad and inclusive, rather than narrow and exclusive—suggests that one of its main functions is the negotiation of conflict among major organized groups in American society. Crucial then are the ways in which the central circle directly and indirectly integrates leaders of a wide variety of institutions into a network capable of discussing and resolving issues of national concern.

NOTES

1. The term *political elite* as used here refers to persons who by virtue of their institutional positions have a high potential to influence national policy making. Thus, the political elite consists not only of high-ranking government officials but also of top position holders in large organizations in the private sector including major corporations, labor unions and other organized interest groups which attempt to influence government policy. ... For stylistic variation, I sometimes use the terms *leaders, influentials* or simply *elites* to refer to political elites.

2. The number of respondents in each sector is shown in Table [17.]4.

3. That is, although there are obviously not direct connections between all 876, it is possible for any one of them to reach any other through one or more intermediaries.

4. Some of the original three-person cliques had insufficient overlap with other cliques (i.e., they shared two or more members with none of the other groups) to be merged at any stage of the procedure.

REFERENCES

Alba, Richard D.
  1972 "COMPLT—a program for analyzing sociometric data and clustering similarity matrices." Behavioral Science 17:566.
Bachrach, Peter and Morton S. Baratz
  1963 "Decisions and non-decisions." American Political Science Review 57:632–42.
Bonacich, Phillip and G. William Domhoff
  1977 "Overlapping memberships among clubs and policy groups of the American ruling class: a methodological and empirical contribution to the class-hegemony paradigm of power structure." Paper presented at the American Sociological Association meetings, Chicago.
Domhoff, G. William
  1967 Who Rules America? Englewood Cliffs: Prentice-Hall.
Giddens, Anthony
  1975 The Class Structure of the Advanced Societies. New York: Harper Torchbooks.
Lukes, Steven
  1974 Power: A Radical View. London: Macmillan.
McConnell, Grant
  1966 Private Power and American Democracy. New York: Knopf.
Mills, C. Wright
  1956 The Power Elite. New York: Oxford University Press.
Putnam, Robert D.
  1976 The Comparative Study of Political Elites. Englewood Cliffs: Prentice-Hall.

18

Elite Integration in Stable Democracies

JOHN HIGLEY, URSULA HOFFMANN–LANGE, CHARLES KADUSHIN, & GWEN MOORE

ELITE INTEGRATION IN STABLE DEMOCRACIES: A RECONSIDERATION

The extent and shape of elite integration in stable democracies are among the most persistent and controversial issues in political analysis. Research from the pluralist perspective typically finds elite fragmentation, with a shifting, roughly balanced power structure overall. ... By contrast, analyses in the power elite tradition ... find considerable elite integration manifested by cohesive nationwide interaction networks. Similarly, class analyses taking an instrumentalist as opposed to a structuralist position ... , though disagreeing with the power elite perspective on certain aspects of the structure and bases of power in capitalist societies, generally agree that elites in these societies are tightly integrated.

In rethinking issues of elite structure, a number of scholars have partly but importantly shifted the focus from fragmented balance or cohesive hegemony to 'consensual unity,' arguing that in stable democracies all important elite groups participate in decisionmaking and agree about informal rules of the game and the worth of existing political institutions (Lijphart, 1969; Field and Higley, 1973, 1980, 1985; Di Palma, 1973; Prewitt and Stone, 1973; Putnam, 1976). Dovetailing with this general contention, but logically separable from the focus on consensual unity, is the claim that several stable democracies originated in 'elite settlements' or 'elite pacts' in which warring elite factions compromised their most basic disputes and established informal networks that secured each other's vital interests, thus laying the basis for political stability and an evolution towards democracy (O'Donnell and Schmitter, 1986; Burton and Higley, 1987a). Converging with both these contentions is Giovanni Sartori's new 'decision-making theory of democracy', which explains how 'a multiplicity of criss-crossing power groups engaged in coalitional maneuvering' nevertheless perceive decisional outcomes as positive-sum and thereby support democracy (Sartori, 1987: 147ff).

These reconceptualizations of elite structure and functioning in stable democracies imply that elites constitute a 'single national power establishment' (Kadushin, 1979) to an extent that is not adequately recognized in the ruling class, power elite and pluralist perspectives, but that is not fundamentally incompatible with them either: national elites are tightly integrated, as in the power elite and class perspectives; at the same time, however, the different elite groups represent sufficiently heterogeneous interests to provide competition among different points of view, as in the pluralist perspective. This image of comprehensive elite integration accords with data on the interaction patterns of national elites in at least three contemporary democracies: the United States, Australia, and West Germany. In this article, we argue that the configurations of *elite circles* in these democracies reveal the ways in which the three familiar perspectives intersect and show why they should be fused in a new and more realistic model. ...

ELITE INTEGRATION AND ELITE CIRCLES

Our general contention is that an interaction structure which provides all important elites with access to central decisionmaking arenas is a precondition of any stable democracy. By elites we mean persons who hold authoritative positions in powerful public and private organizations and influential movements, and who are therfore able to affect strategic decisions regularly (see Burton and Higley, 1987b). If one notes that the pursuit of particularistic interests by elites has routinely led in history to endemic political instability and to numerous autocratic or short-lived democratic regimes (Higley and Burton, 1989), it folows that elites engage in the non-violent, cooperative interactions that are essential for stable democracy only when they believe it is to their mutual benefit (Higley, Field and Groholt, 1976: 59–91). This implies that an interaction structure which enables all important elites to hold and exercise what they regard as more or less satisfactory amounts of influence on decisions of importance to themselves or their organizations underlies any stable democratic order. In short, it is plausible to think that elites in stable democracies engage in power sharing and power competition through a complex but little understood network structure that is a precondition of such democracies. ...

With his new 'decisionmaking theory of democracy', Giovanni Sartori (1987: 214–53) extends and helps concretize this line of reasoning. Sartori theorizes that a stable democracy is possible only if the groups that are most central to its operation perceive decisional outcomes as positive-sum rather than zero-sum. 'Committee' structures—the numerous, small, face-to-face groups of mainly elite actors that persist over time—handle continuous flows of decisions and avoid winner-take-all, majority rule decisionmaking. As relatively invisible entities, committees are the 'real stuff' of politics—the places in which issues are examined, discussed, drafted, and for the most part decided (Sartori, 1987: 228). They function according to the principle of 'deferred reciprocal compensation' whereby committee members who feel less intensely about one issue will go along with a decision which they do not particularly like because they expect to get their way on another issue that is vital to them (Sartori, 1987: 229). This inclines members to view the totality of committee decisions, few of which are ever taken by 'showdown' majority votes, as positive-sum. Further, each committee exists in a web of other committees, all of which interact and coordinate more or less spontaneously on the basis of concessions or 'side payments' that they make to each other. Finally, all this is compatible with democracy to the extent that popularly-elected or otherwise accountable and responsive political leaders hold strategic positions in the committee structure, representing and registering public desires and grievances (Sartori, 1987: 229–35).

Primarily concerned with the workings of explicitly governmental committees. Sartori's insightful scheme can be extended to the larger interaction structure of national elites *tout court*. By substituting the concept of elite circles for committees, we postulate that in stable democracies a relatively tight and at the same time comprehensive integration of national elites permits their members access to decisionmaking and fosters a common perception of mutual interdependence.

Thus, national elites can be thought of as operating through intricate systems of discrete, informal, flexible, but still significantly cohesive influence circles that form around and across issues and institutions. Though they encompass friendships and other personal ties, elite circles do not rest primarily on affect. Rather, they are based on repeated interactions among elite persons who have common policy interests or policy problems to solve. Analytically, these circles are the dense parts of much larger networks of elite contacts and connections. But unlike cliques, committees, and other small bodies which are their constituent parts, elite circles, and even more so the overall elite network, also involve interactions at a distance.

Involving repeated but mainoy informal and often indirect interactions on common policy issues and purposes, elite influence circles achieve a significant amount of integration without, however, having a designated or permanent set of leaders. One reason is that the members of an elite circle usually do not know its entire shape and composition. They know the members of the circle with whom they regularly interact, of course, but they are only dimly aware of the circle's wider membership.

Our theoretical model is not oblivious to inter-personal differences in influence, however, nor does it imply that elite circles are egalitarian structures. First, access to central decision-making arenas is not open to everyone. It presupposes that individuals control power resources or have a reputation for being an expert on the subject matter at hand. Secondly, organizational power resources play an important role in decisionmaking. Although members of decisionmaking committees usually try to reach compromises acceptable to everyone involved, their perceptions of what constitutes a 'fair' compromise depend at least partly on the tacit acceptance of power differentials among the different participants. A final differentiation derives from the strategic positions of individuals in elite circles. Some of their members are more pivotal in the sense that they are more closely connected to large numbers of other circle members, to other important circles, and to other similarly pivotal persons. On the other hand, the multidimensional nature of power and influence resources in a modern society precludes that the various power and influence resources are amenable to a simple rank order and is not compatible with a one-dimensional conceptualization of power and influence.

Given these features of elite power and influence circles, it is plausible to think that they constitute the principal means by which national elites broker their diverse and frequently opposing individual and organizational interests in a modern society. What is at issue, however, is not the existence and importance of elite circles *per se*, but the particular configurations of such circles in stable democracies, for the thrust of our argument is that it is primarily through the informal, flexible, and far-flung interactions which circles permit that elites obtain the mutual access to decisionmaking that is a precondition of stable democracies. Following Sartori's lead, we therefore hypothesize that any stable democracy contains multiple elite circles which overlap each other, which cut across societal sectors, institutional boundaries, and issue arenas, which exist in 'continuous decisional contexts', and which, like Sartori's face-to-face committees, function according to the operational code of *do ut des* (Kadushin, 1981; Sartori, 1987: 228).

But we go one step further than Sartori because we are interested in precisely how the multiple elite circles are themselves finally integrated to facilitate a stable democracy. The answer to this question appears to lie in the existence of a large, overarching elite central circle which links or meshes most other circles and which is the capstone of elite integration in stable democracies. Composed of persons who belong to more specialized circles and who typically are active on several issues or in several decisionmaking arenas simultaneously, this central circle serves as a clearing house for national elite functioning, helping to sift and prioritize decisions, and constituting a key communications structure for arranging and aggregating the trade-offs, compromises, and informal understandings without which a large and diversified national elite would quickly break apart into intransigent and warring factions.

METHODS AND DATA

In the analysis that follows, we investigate the configurations of elite power and influence circles in the US, Australia, and West Germany, and we show the existence of a large elite central circle in each country. Because these central circles are the most novel aspect of our findings, and because of their importance for the overall extent and shape of elite integration, we concentrate on their compositions, internal structures, and social characteristics. It is necessary to begin, however, with a brief discussion of the analytical techniques and data we use in this investigation.

One reason for the inconclusive nature of the debate over elite structure in stable democracies is normative: it has hinged on conflicting images of the 'good society'. But another reason is methodological, involving disputes over how best to study the structure and functioning of national elite or power structures. Systematic research is difficult because these structures are not readily accessible to observation and the content of ties is sometimes secret. Several approaches have been used, each with shortcomings. One ... approach to studying power structures attempts a global mapping of generalized relations between elites. This avoids some of the problems of other approaches since it is not restricted to one sector or policy domain. ... [B]y providing a 'bird's-eye view' of elite structure as manifested in the interaction patterns among numerous powerful groups dealing with scores of policy issues and many issue domains, it allows assessment of degrees of integration or fragmentation overall. For this reason and because it is consistent with our circle model of elite structure, we have adopted the global mapping approach in our research.

Our data are taken from comparable surveys of national elites in the United States in 1971–72, Australia in 1975, and West Germany in 1981. Designed to study elites in institutional sectors with broad impact on national policymaking and political processes, each survey involved interviews with several hundred occupants of key decisionmaking positions in major public and private sectors. Consistent with our theoretical orientation, the interviews gathered data on policy activities, attitudes, involvement in elite communication networks, and social backgrounds. There were 545 respondents in the American survey, 370 in the Australian, and 497 in the West German.

Sample design began with the identification of key organizations in national policy-making. The top position-holders in each institutional sector were sampled: politics, civil service, business, trade unions, mass media, voluntary associations, and the academic sphere. The organizations and positions identified were similar, but not identical, in the three surveys. ... It is important to note that in each survey the positional sample was supplemented by a snowball sample in which persons who were not in the original sample were interviewed if they were mentioned as key actors by three or more respondents.

Each respondent was asked to name the one national issue on which he or she had most actively attempted to influence national policy or public opinion during the preceding twelve months. A wide variety of issues was named in each country. Respondents were questioned extensively about their assessments of and activities on the issue they named. Included were a series of sociometric questions asking the names of the persons with whom they interacted over this issue. Each interaction generated by these questions can be seen as a policy-related communication link.

Our network data thus consists of contacts between respondents and the persons they nameed in answer to the sociometric questions. Because selective memory tends to reveal the 'deep structure' of social networks by blanking out less relevant partners while recalling the more important ones ... , it is reasonable to assume that our data are not merely an ephemeral collection of names. But it is important to understand the limitations of our procedure. These data are an attempt to develop the traces of any system of circles and 'committees' that might exist. Yet the particular contacts reported must not be reified. First, the contacts reported by respondents were hardly the only contacts among elites in the three societies at the time of the surveys because respondents were limited to reporting their interaction partners on only one issue, even though they presumably were active on several issues simultaneously. Thus our data grossly underestimate the actual density of policy-related contacts among elites in the three societies. Should these data reveal an integrated interaction sturcture, one can safely assume not only that such a structure existed, but that it was actually much more dense than our data indicate. Second, the contacts that are reported are those the respondent felt to be in pursuit of legitimate attempts to influence policy. Elite studies conducted by social scientists can never hope to uncover the truly illegitimate. Third, our data are not sufficiently detailed or accurate to distinguish who initiated a contact. For this and another reason to be explained shortly, we must assume that if A talked to B, B talked to A and thus the networks we analyze are nondirectional.

Our analytic procedures are intended not to test the likelihood of a particular connection existing or not existing, nor to gain an estimate of the true density of interaction but rather, consistent with our theory, to recover the overall patterning of interactions. The aim is to test the likelihood that (1) there are various circles and 'committees' and (2) to gain some estimate of the degree to which they overlap. ...

RESULTS

The Central Circles

A procedure developed by Alba (1972, 1973; Alba and Guttmann, 1972) identifies the more cohesive parts of networks. Cliques consisting of three or more persons, all of whom interact on a face-to-face basis, are the basic building blocks. But because a national elite in a large and complex society cannot possibly be connected through face-to-face interactions alone, indirect contacts through intermediaries must also be studied, provided that they involve only one or a few intermediaries. ...

Concretely, our analysis begins with the matrix of links formed by all contacts reported by respondents. This matrix includes respondents as well as non-respondents who were named by two or more respondents and thus constitute a link between those who named them. The inclusion of non-respondents is crucial for two reasons. First, it is not possible to interview all the persons in a national elite, so that the matrix of contact partners is necessarily incomplete. But second and more importantly, the universe of persons actively tyring to influence national policies almost certainly differs from the universe of positionally-defined elites. The former universe is unknown to the researcher at the beginning of a study because it may include influential persons who no longer hold formal elite positions at the time of the study (e.g. 'elder statesmen') as well as persons who are important even though they have not yet reached elite positions ('high fliers'), plus others whose influence primarily rests on personal attributes rather than the formal power resources associated with positions in important organizations. By including non-respondents in the matrix, and by interviewing persons not in the original sample who are frequently named by sample members (i.e. snowball sampling), these problems in elite research are at least partly overcome. … In sum, the first step in our analysis involves reducing the matrix of all reported contacts to a network of persons, all of whom are interconnected directly or through intermediaries [see Table 18.1].

This procedure identified connected networks of roughly 800 persons in each of the national elites studied: 876 in the US, 746 in Australia, and 799 in West Germany. The density of each network is similar and relatively low: the interpersonal ties respondents reported amount to about 1 per cent of all possible ties among network members. However, each of the networks contains a sizable number of cohesive cliques and circles: 32 in the American network, 22 in West Germany, and 11 in Australia. In each country, the majority of these cliques and circles are small, seldom numbering more than a handful of persons. But in each national elite network there is also a large, relatively inclusive circle composed of several hundred persons. This 'central circle' contains 227 persons in the US, 340 in West Germany, and 418 in Australia. The density of each circle is roughly three times that of the national elite network: 3.8 percent in the US, 2.6 percent in Australia, and 2.7 percent in West Germany. Thus central circle members can contact each other more readily than the typical member of the larger network can contact other network members.

Network Centrality

Centrality is another widely used network analytic procedure with an emphasis different from that of clique and circle detection. It denotes, in essence, the number of communication paths which pass through an individual's network location (Freeman, 1977). Thus a highly central individual need not be a member of cohesive cliques and circles since a high centrality score can be achieved through connections to persons who are not themselves connected. … A

TABLE [18.]1   Characteristics of the American (USA), Australian (AUS) and
West German (FRG) Elite Networks

	USA	AUS	FRG
Sample members (n)	545	370	497
Network members (n)	876	746	799
Network density (%)	0.7	1.1	0.9
Cliques (n)	442	1132	739
Circles (n)	32	11	22
Central circle members (n)	227	418	340
Central circle density (%)	3.8	2.6	2.7

'reachability' measure based on the number of persons each network member
could reach within two steps (i.e. through one intermediary) was calculated for
each network member. Persons highly central by this measure could therefore
easily communicate with a large number of other elites. Less central persons
would have to spend more time and effort to reach many others.

This centrality measure allows us to study the core of each national elite by
focusing on the 100 individuals who could reach the largest numbers of others
either directly or through single intermediaries. It is worth noting that the most
central American could reach 389 other persons in the elite network in this way,
his Australian counterpart could reach 462 others, and the most central West
German could reach 436 others. By contrast, the least central person in each national elite network could reach only half a dozen others directly or through single intermediaries. While these centrality scores are calculated for the full networks and are determined by a method different from that by which the central
circles are identified, virtually all of the 100 most central persons in each network are also members of the central circle. To this extent, these 100 most central persons can be thought of as forming the core of each central circle.

Composition of the Central Circles and Circle Cores

Consistent with the thesis of relatively comprehensive integration of national
elites in stable democracies, representatives of all important institutional sectors
belong to the elite networks and central circles in each country. Table [18.]2
shows the sector composition of the original elite sample, the network, the central circle, and the circle core in each country. We interpret the presence of representatives from all sectors in the central circles and their cores as evidence of
relatively comprehensive elite integration.

All sectors, however, are not equally represented in the central circles. The
prevalence of political leaders and government officials in the central circles is a
striking similarity in the three national elites. Roughly half of each central circle
consists of political and civil service elites. While this pattern is most pronounced in the US, it is clear in Australia and West Germany as well.

Lacking direct data on the influence of different sectors in the central circles,
we use as a rough estimate of sectoral over- and under-representation a compari-

TABLE [18.]2 Sector Composition of the Sample, Network, Central Circle and Core in the American (USA), Australian and West German (FRG) Elite Studies (%)

Sector	USA				Australia				FRG			
	Sample	Network	Circle	Core	Sample	Network	Circle	Core	Sample	Network	Circle	Core
Politics	33.0	52.1	50.2	71.0	21.6	28.3	27.2	25.0	27.8	34.2	37.6	38.0
Civil Service	9.9	8.2	5.7	1.0	13.5	17.7	18.4	19.0	11.9	12.4	9.4	5.0
Business	24.2	13.5	16.3	9.0	24.3	17.3	20.8	37.0	29.2	23.9	25.0	27.0
Labor Unions	8.8	6.1	7.0	4.0	13.5	8.9	8.9	4.0	4.6	6.9	9.7	10.0
Media	11.6	8.1	7.5	2.0	10.8	8.1	8.1	6.0	12.1	10.0	10.0	14.0
Vol. Assoc.	9.5	6.5	4.4	6.0	10.8	6.9	4.8	5.0	2.8	2.4	1.8	2.0
Academic	2.9	4.0	7.5	7.0	5.4	10.3	9.8	4.0	6.8	6.5	5.6	4.0
Other	0.0	1.5	1.3	0.0	0.0	2.5	1.9	0.0	4.8	3.8	0.9	0.0
(n)	(545)	(876)	(227)	(100)	(370)	(746)	(418)	(100)	(497)	(799)	(340)	(100)

son of a sector's proportions in the original sample and in the central circle. On the assumption that sample members, in contrast to non-respondents, had equal opportunities to name others, and thus to be members of the central circle, a sector is over-represented if its members are more numerous in the circle than in the sample. As already noted, politicians are over-represented in all three central circles, while civil servants are over-represented only in Australia. Conversely, business elites are numerically under-represented in all three central circles, while trade union leaders are over-represented only in the German circle. Media elites are under-represented in all three circles, which is consistent with the claims of some media respondents that they are observers of, not active participants in, policy-making. Similarly, leaders of voluntary association are weakly represented in all three central circles. By contrast, academics play a more important role.

Conspicuous by their absence in the central circles are military and cultural elites (e.g. religious leaders, intellectuals, artists, entertainment celebrities). Some of these elites were not in the positional samples, and to that extent they had a lower probability of entering the central circles. But this is only part of the explanation for their absence. First, the snowball sampling procedure brings in important elites who were not part of the positional sample. Secondly, the openness of the network analytic procedure allows for the inclusion of non-respondents, and, indeed, quite a few non-respondents ended up in the central circles: 63 in the American, 143 in the Australian, and 110 in the West German. Consequently, well-connected members of the military and cultural elites could have found places in the central circles even though they were not interviewed. In any event, military leaders were included in the West German sample and top-ranking religious leaders were included in both the West German and Australian samples. But even then, no West German military commander belonged to the central circle, and neither did any religious leader in West Germany or Australia. As regards intellectuals, artists, and entertainment figures, a study of the American intellectual elite in the early 1970s found few connections between its members and other elites (Kadushin, 1974). ...

Table [18.]2 shows the sector composition of the central circle core in each country—the 100 persons who could reach the largest numbers of other persons either directly or through single intermediaries. As is true for the central circles, the circle cores contain representatives from all elite sectors. In the US, political-governmental leaders compose nearly three-quarters of the circle core, suggesting their utter centrality in the national elite. In Australia and West Germany, political-governmental leaders also dominate the cores, though not to the same extent. In Australia, the business elite is strongly over-represented in the core which suggests that political-governmental and business leaders form a tightly interconnected and somewhat exclusive 'power elite' formation in that country. However, in contrast to assumptions of power elite theorists, the political-governmental leaders in this formation are associated in more or less equal numbers

with parties sympathetic to and those somewhat hostile towards business interests. In West Germany, the circle core is more diverse. Political-governmental
leaders comprise 43 per cent of the core, but in contrast to Australia, business
leaders are somewhat under-represented, while trade union and media leaders
are somewhat over-represented, with other elites showing up in proportions that
parallel their memberships in the central circle.

Social and Positional Correlates of Circle and Core Membership

Numerous studies have found that occupants of national elite positions are
distinguished by their privileged social origins, higher education, and greater
age. ... Our data are consistent with these findings: In the US, West Germany,
and Australia, only a small proportion of elites have working-class origins, the
bulk of them have university educations, and their average age is in the early fif-
ties (Higley, Deacon and Smart, 1979; Moore, 1979; Hoffmann-Lange, 1985). As
one would expect, the major exception to these general patterns is the trade
union elites: they much more often come from working-class backgrounds and
less often hold university degrees.

Putting trade union elites to one side, do elite persons with privileged backgrounds more frequently end up in the most central network locations as has
been found for business elites in the 'inner circle'? It appears that they do not.
Table [18.]3 shows that social class origins, measured by whether a respondents's
father was a member of the working class, play little, if any, role in determining
where a person is situated in the national elite network. In West Germany and
Australia there is the hint of a slight disadvantage for political leaders from working-class backgrounds in reaching the central circle cores (even though both
countries had left-of-center, trade union-linked governments at the time of the
surveys), but overall, the three networks do not appear to be structured internally in any strong way by the class origins of their members. These results suggest that while upper-class origins remain advantageous for achieving membership in the elite ... , their importance fades once membership has been
achieved.

Far more important for the locations of individuals in the elite circles and
cores are their formal organizational positions as well as their policy-making activities and visibility associated with these formal positions. In all three countries, centrality in the elite network results to a large extent from holding the
most senior positions in important institutions and organizations. For example,
in Australia three-quarters of all federal cabinet ministers belong to the central
circle, while only 18 per cent of their back-bench colleagues in federal Parliament are in the circle. In West Germany all core members hold senior organizational positions: these include, for example, 7 of the 17 members of the federal
cabinet and 7 of the 11 state prime ministers.

TABLE [18.]3   Father Working Class for Sample, Central Circle and Core According to Sector Type for American (USA), Australian (AUS) and West German (FRG) Elites (%)

	Political sectors			Other sectors		
	USA	AUS	FRG	USA	AUS	FRG
Sample	9.4	25.8	30.9	18.8	11.6	20.5
Central circle	11.4	27.1	24.6	16.7	11.5	25.7
Core	15.2	12.9	11.1	13.0	12.9	28.3

Similarly, an analysis of publicly visible policy-making activities, such as testifying before parliamentary or congressional commitees, participating on government advisory committees, giving issue-related speeches, writing articles advocating policies, and the like, shows that central circle members in all three countries are much more heavily involved in such activities than are those outside the central circles (Moore, 1979; Higley and Moore, 1981). ...

DISCUSSION

Proponents of the power elite, ruling class and pluralist perspectives on elite integration in stable democracies have frequently couched their analyses in terms of elite circles. For C. Wright Mills, the American power elite of the 1950s consisted of 'those political, economic, and military circles which as an intricate set of overlapping cliques share decisions having ... national consequences' (Mills, 1956: 18). But while Mills portrayed the power elite in circle terms, he was vague about its configurations, merely alluding to an unspecified number of military, economic and 'public decision-making' circles whose members have common social origins, career patterns, life styles, and thus personality and other psychological affinities (pp. 278–83). Regarding the overall integration of the elite, Mills claimed that some small number of persons who belong to two or more of these 'higher circles' integrate them and constitute the power elite's 'inner core' (pp. 288–9). Meanwhile, pluralists have contended that elites in democracies are arrayed in 'a cluster of interlocking circles, each one preoccupied with its own professionalism and expertise and touching others only at one edge' (Bottomore, 1964: 34). Though they do not specify the number, size, or compositions of these elite circles, pluralists believe that they are basically autonomous, have no central coordinating body other than the government itself, and exist in a kind of natural, enduring balance.

Our findings about the structure of American, Australian, and West German national elite networks and the central circles they contain depict a more comprehensive integration of elites than the familiar perspectives separately envisage. On the basis of survey data covering all important elite sectors and major national policy issues that were being actively considered at the times of our research, we find a funnel-like structure of elite communication and discussion about policy issues which is inclusive of all elite sectors and heterogeneous in the social origins, issue attitudes, and party affiliations of the several hundred persons most centrally located in it. The key feature of this structure in each country is a large, diverse, but significantly integrated central circle which itself narrows into a core of tightly interconnected individuals, each of whom is in close contact with several hundred other elite persons in the central circle and beyond it. The extent of elite integration which this funnel-like structure represents accords with what the power elite and some versions of the ruling class perspective lead one to expect; but the composition of the structure is more in line with pluralist claims about elite inclusiveness and heterogeneity in stable democracies. ...

REFERENCES

Alba R. D. (1972): 'COMPLT—A Program for Analyzing Sociometric Data and Clustering Similarity Matrices', *Behavioral Science*, 17: 566.

_____ (1973): 'A Graph-Theoretic Definition of a Sociometric Clique'. *Journal of Mathematical Sociology*, 3: 113–26.

Alba R. D. Guttmann M P. (1972): 'SOCK: A Sociometric Analysis System', *Behavioral Science*, 17: 326.

Barton A H, Denitch B, Kadushin C. (1985): 'Background, Attitudes, and Activities of American Elites', in Moore g. (ed), *Research in Politics and Society: Studies of the Structure of National Elite Groups (Vol. 1)*, pp. 173–218, Greenwich, CT: JAI Press.

Bottomore T B. (1964): *Elites and Society*, London: Penguin Books.

Burton M G, Higley J. (1987a): 'Elite Settlements', *American Sociological Review*, 52: 295–307.

_____ (1987b): 'Invitation to Elite Theory', in Domhoff G W, Dye T R. (eds), *Power Elites and Organizations*, pp. 133–43, Newbury Park, CA: Sage.

Field L G. Higley J. (1973): *Elites and Non-Elites: The Possibilities and Their Side Effects*, Andover, MA: Warner Modular Publications.

_____ (1980): *Elitism*, Boston: Routledge and Kegan Paul.

_____ (1985): 'National Elites and Political Stability', in Moore G. (ed), *Research in Politics and Society: Studies of the Structure of National Elite Groups (Vol. 1)*, pp. 1–44. Greenwich, CT: JAI Press.

Freeman L C. (1977): 'A Set of Measures of Centrality Based on Betweenness', *Sociometry*, 40: 35–41.

Higley, J. Lowell Field G, Groholt K. (1976): *Elite Structure and Ideology*, New York: Columbia University Press.

Higley, J. Deacon D, Smart D. (1979): *Elites in Australia*, Boston: Routledge and Kegan Paul.

Higley, J. Moore G. (1981): 'Elite Integration in the United States and Australia', *American Political Science Review*, 75: 581–97.

Higley, J. Burton M G. (1989): 'The Elite Variable in Democratic Transitions and Breakdowns', *American Sociological Review*, 54: 17–32.

Hoffmann-Lange U. (1985): 'Structural Prerequisites of Elite Integration in the Federal Republic of Germany', in Moore G, (ed), *Research in Politics and Society: Studies of the Structure of National Elite Groups (Vol. 1)*, pp. 45–96, Greenwich, CT: JAI Press.

Kadushin C. (1968): 'Power, Influence and Social Circles: A New Methodology for Studying Opinion-Makers', *American Sociological Review*, 33: 685–99.

‾‾‾‾‾‾ (1974): *The American Intellectual Elite*, Boston: Little, Brown.

‾‾‾‾‾‾ (1979): 'Power Circles and Legitimacy in Developed Societies', in Denitch B, (ed), *Legitimation of Regimes*, pp. 127–40, Beverly Hills, CA: Sage.

Lijphart, A. (1969): 'Consociational Democracy', *World Politics*, 21: 207–25.

Mills C W. (1956): *The Power Elite*, New York: Oxford University Press.

Moore G. (1979): 'The Structure of a National Elite Network', *American Sociological Review*, 44: 673–92.

O'Donnell G. Schmitter P C. (1986): *Transitions From Authoritarian Rule: Tentative Conclusions About Uncertain Democracies*, Baltimore: Johns Hopkins University Press.

Prewitt K, Stone A. (1973): *The Ruling Elites: Elite Theory, Power, and American Democracy*, New York: Harper and Row.

Putnam R D. (1976): *The Comparative Study of Political Elites*, Englewood Cliffs, NJ: Prentice-Hall.

Sartori G. (1987): *The Theory of Democracy Revisited I: The Contemporary Debate*, Chatham, NJ: Chatham House Publishers.

19

The Structure of Intercorporate
Unity in American Business

BETH MINTZ & MICHAEL SCHWARTZ

Sociologists and political scientists have, for the last 20 years, debated the distributions of power in modern industrial society. Elite unity has been a continuing theme, largely because it is fundamental to the competing theories and because the recent proliferation of structural Marxist analyses has focused
attention on the unity of capitalist enterprise. ...

Although earlier research on power structures emphasized cohesion and
commonality within the business sector, lately, sources of conflict and lines of
cleavage have attracted attention. Within the corporate community interests
differ and needs diverge; examples of potential sources of conflict abound. ...

At the same time, however, a fundamental shared interest persists in preserving the system of private accumulation (O'Connor, 1973; Offe 1973). Given the
contradiction between individual interests and the overriding needs of the capitalist class, ... research has attempted to identify mechanisms capable of transforming individual corporations into a united, hegemonic social force. Structural
Marxists have posited a process in which the state is the focal point of
intercorporate conflict, which it resolves by imposing policies expressing an overall class interest. A state apparatus is created which stands above individual elements of the economy and represents their common interest; thus, class unity is
maintained. ... Conflicts between corporations are forcefully resolved. ...

There are also a significant number of cases in which the corporate community has overcome internal conflicts without the aid of the state. Weinstein
(1968) and Eakins (1966) have demonstrated that social welfare policy developed
within the corporate community before being adopted by government. Shoup
and Minter (1977) make a similar case for the origins of post–Second World War
foreign policy. ...

Policy planning organizations such as the Council on Foreign Relations and the Council for Economic Development define programs which serve the interests of business as a class (Domhoff, 1970, 1971, 1979), while Useem (1978, 1979) has described an inner group within the capitalist class, whose members transcend the narrow interests of individual enterprise. Thus, there are several possible mechanisms for the articulation of a general class interest. This paper concentrates on the structure of intercorporate relations and uses interlocking directories to analyze patterns of interaction which might reflect unifying forces within the corporate world.

SOURCES OF INTERCORPORATE
POWER AND UNITY

Whitt (1979-80) demonstrates that business unity can be achieved, even in the face of visible conflict of interest. What must be explained are the sources of this unity and the basis for the resolution of conflicts. With this in mind, we catalogue the sources of intercorporate power and unity which could suppress the interests of one firm in favor of the needs of another. We then evaluate whether intercorporate interlock patterns reflect any of the following relations and assess whether these relations could be routinely used to coordinate capitalist activity.

Stockholding By Capitalist Families: Although managerialism, the ascendant theory of the firm in U.S. economics and sociology, argues that stockholding is no longer a prevalent instrument of corporate control, stock ownership remains an important source of intercorporate power and coordination. Researchers have demonstrated the inadequacies of managerialist evidence and uncovered new forms of stockholding which were inconsequential when Berle and Means (1968) first enunciated the separation of ownership and control. ... The high level of stock dispersion characterizing the modern corporation means that ownership of a concentrated block of shares in an organization carries with it the potential for control. Ownership of large blocks of stock in *more* than one organization allows an individual capitalist (or a capitalist family) to create a coordinated set of policies among firms. This coordination may suppress competitive behavior among companies, resolve supplier-customer conflicts or encourage cooperation that would otherwise have no reason to exist. In this manner, common stockholding can result in harmonious arrangements among otherwise competitive corporations.

Intercorporate Stock Ownership: Coordinated sets of policies among companies can be established through intercorporate ownership. Any firm which holds a controlling block in another company can impose policies which serve its own interest, even in cases in which the controlled organization suffers. Vertical integration can function in just this manner, helping to suppress intercorporate conflict. No one knows the extent of intercorporate ownership, but most stockholding research suggests it is widespread (Kotz, 1978). Even without systematic research, however, its importance is underscored by the persistence of mergers and conglomerate expansion.

Institutional Stockholding: This device began with the first successes of the Congress of Industrial Organizations' campaign for pension funding after the Second World War. The increasing proportion of investment capital residing in these funds makes them important. Professional managers in the trust departments of major banks make decisions for various clients, pension funds, and endowments. By 1977, institutional investors of this sort accounted for 60 per cent of all stocks traded in the United States. ... This concentration has enormous potential for controlling and coordinating the behavior of individual as well as groups of corporations. ... The policy preferences of large institutional holders have become a major force in determining and directing corporate policies and a potentially important means of suppressing intercorporate conflict.

Lending Relationships: In 1977, non-financial corporations invested $236.5 billion, of which $102 billion (43 per cent) was borrowed, $71 billion of it from financial institutions (*Business Week,* 1978). With more prospective borrowers than available capital, major corporate lenders can decide which projects will be pursued and which will remain unfunded. A corporation in need of capital, therefore, cannot afford to violate the norms set by the lenders. [B]anks regularly use outstanding or prospective loans to intrude into the internal affairs of companies; the power of capital control is an important means of coordinating intercorporate policy.

Joint Ventures: Until the early 1960s, General Motors and Exxon jointly owned the Ethyl Corporation, producer of lead additives for gasoline. This provided an ongoing point of contact and cooperation between the two firms. ... While such a joint effort was unusual before the 1960s, it is commonplace today. ... This tactic is an important means of reducing intercorporate conflict and producing inter-organizational unity.

Lending Consortia: The business press contains daily announcements of lending arrangements between major industrial corporations and consortia of large financial firms, mainly banks and insurance companies. Such arrangements have become normal because even the largest banks cannot independently provide the huge amounts of capital needed for corporate use. Lending consortia demand cooperation from their members. Since it is difficult to withdraw, the interest of each bank is tied to the collective enterprise. The consortium must, therefore, develop and maintain devices for creating and enforcing common policy. This basic structure of corporate financing provides the potential for united action by a large group of banks. Since the number major commercial lenders in the United States is quite small, the existence of large consortia force the financial community to adopt a united policy on any particular corporation. This unity, coupled with the power which comes with capital control, suggests that lending consortia are a source of immense potential and actual power in U.S. corporate life.

Customer-Supplier Relationships: The dependency of borrowing firms on financial institutions makes corporate policy vulnerable to influence from the money supplier. A similar relationship can develop when one company buys goods, raw materials, or finished products from another. ...

The U.S. economy is laced with inter-industry dependencies of this sort. The auto industry depends heavily on the steel industry; steel in turn depends on coal. Individual corporations operate in the context of such broad interdependencies. Each firm must find a way to control and regulate its supply of raw materials and the markets for its products. In so doing a corporation may seek ongoing relationships both with major suppliers and customers, creating still other sources of intercorporate unity and cohesion. Such widespread relationships are often complex. A company may hold stock in a firm upon whom it depends for resources in order to guarantee supplies. A loan relationship between a bank and a non-financial organization may be congruent with institutional stockholding or may coexist with bank holdings in a competing firm. The varieties of relationships are limitless; the issue for researchers is to study the patterns which emerge from these ties.

INTERLOCKS AS AN INDICATOR
OF INTERCORPORATE POWER

Investigating interlocking directorates is a promising, though complicated, way of studying the internal structure of the business community. Although the connection between director interlocks and the exercise of intercorporate unity is not always direct, careful analysis has yielded useful results. ... We use patterns of director interlocks to trace connections among major corporations and to differentiate among the sources of intercorporate unity discussed above. Using this information we analyze the mechanisms which create business structure. We assume that interlocks often reflect power and unity among firms (Mokken and Stokman, 1974). This is a vexing issue at best, requiring further analysis of the correlation between interlocks and intercorporate relationships. Every type of power or unity source discussed above is reflected by interlocks some of the time. ... This imperfect, but consistent, correlation between intercorporate relationships and director interlocks has been demonstrated by researchers representing a variety of viewpoints. ...

There is not sufficient evidence for us to analyze the many different intercorporate relationships directly. The study of interlocks, however, poses two problems: (1) Many of the relationships we seek to study are not represented by director interchanges. (2) There is often no known relationship between firms linked by interlocks. Interlocks often represent friendship ties, or even window dressing, on a prestigious board of directors. ... We do not claim to have solved these problems. Nevertheless, we feel our method extracts the maximum information from these relatively crude indicators and suggests some of the main lines of force within the corporate community.

We try to determine the extent and stability of corporate interlocks, and to discern whether their patterns suggests unifying relationships within the capitalist class. To do this, we focus our attention on those organizations which are central in the corporate network, that is, those companies with the largest number of interlocks and whose interlocks tie them to other highly interlocked corporations. Specifically, we examine: the types of corporations that are most important to determining the structure of the interlock network; the stability of network position over time; different roles within the network; and which firms tend to occupy which positions within the network.

Our population was drawn from *Fortune Magazine,* which publishes an annual list of the largest U.S. coporations of the following types: industrials, utilities, transportation companies, retailers, commercial banks, insurance companies, diversified financials, and miscellaneous firms. We included all companies which appeared in any year from 1962 to 1973. To accommodate the opinion that investment banks are crucial to intercorporate networks, we added to our data the 50 largest bond managers during the 1960s. ... The number of firms in our investigation varied from year to year as certain corporations disappeared because of mergers and bankruptcies while others appeared, often constructed from several firms too small for inclusion in their own right. Using techniques which are now well established (Bearden *et al.,* 1975; Bunting and Barbour, 1971; Mariolis, 1975) we obtained complete listings of the boards of directors for each company for the years 1962 and 1966. For each individual who created an interlock—i.e., who sat on more than one board in our list—we identified specific office and principal affiliation. In 1962, our population included 1,131 of the largest U.S. corporations; in 1966, 1,111 companies were included. Although this is a large data base, it represents only a small proportion of the business world. Nevertheless, we feel that the major corporations are the appropriate sample with which to investigate the question of intercorporate unity.[1]

THE INTERLOCK NETWORK

The corporate network is both extensive and intensive. Of the 1,131 firms in our 1962 data, 989 were tied by varying degrees into a single, continuous network. The average firm was tied directly to 10 other firms. Thus the largest U.S. corporations are linked by a dense network of overlapping directorships. This suggests a degree of collective leadership and information exchange which, by itself, might produce intercorporate unity. ...

We counted the interlocks of each corporation to analyze the roles played by different firms. This revealed great inequalities: besides the 142 companies not tied into the network, there were 111 which interlocked with only one other organization. This group included such prominent institutions as E. F. Hutton & Co., Fidelity Life Insurance, and Singer. Despite their size and fame, these firms appear to be unimportant figures in intercorporate relationships. On the other hand, 39 corporations were tied to more than 30 firms each. Most connected were Equitable Life (78 interlocks to 62 corporations), J. P. Morgan (72 to 59), and Chemical Bank (70 to 57). These companies are the key units in the network. The number of interlocks is not, however, a satisfactory measure of network position. Consider Singer and Fidelity Life, each with one interlock. In 1962, singer interlocked with General Cable, a firm with 72 ties of its own. Fidelity Life, on the other hand, interlocked with Household Finance, which maintained only one other tie. Clearly, Singer was more integrated into the interlock system than Fidelity. However, if we trace the network further, we discover that Household Finance's one tie was to a firm with many interlocks, while General Cable maintained 27 ties to only lightly interlocked companies. This sort of locational complexity makes it impossible to judge the relative importance of all 989 different firms in the network.

Thus, we used a mathematical technique, described in detail by Mariolis *et al.* (1979), Mintz (1978) and Mizruchi and Bunting (1979), set forth by Bonacich (1972), and first used in interlock research by Mariolis and Schwartz (1972) and Mariolis (1975), to evaluate the position of each corporation. We have based our analysis upon this evaluation, which we term centrality.[2] Central corporations are the organizing units of the system and the focal points of the network of intercorporate personnel exchange. From centrality analyses flow our judgments about the relative standing of the major firms in the U.S. economy.

Table [19.]1 shows the 20 most central corporations of 1962, 1966, and 1969, and identifies the focal points in the network of intercorporate relations—the financial institutions.[3] Each year they are dramatically over-represented in the top 20; they hold at least eight of the top 10 positions, and only in 1969 do they fail to hold each of the five top ranks. Thus, the most consistent members of the network elite are financial institutions. If industrial interdependence were a major axis around which intercorporate relations turned, we would expect major utilities, large industrials, and crucial transportation companies to be the stable, central nodes. Instead, only U.S. Steel and American Telephone and Telegraph Co. (AT&T) attain top listing in all three years. The absence of BankAmerica—the largest commercial bank—suggests that corporate lending and institutional stockholding are the bases for inclusion among the most central organizations. BankAmerica is not among the most important corporate lenders or intitutional investors; its size results from its retail business. Indeed, the top corporate banks are

TABLE [19.]1   Twenty Most Central Corporations, 1962, 1966, 1969[a]

Corporation	Type	Centrality Rank 1962	Centrality Rank 1966	Centrality Rank 1969[b]
Morgan (J.P.)	Bank	1	2	8
Chase Manhattan	Bank	2	3	5
Equitable Life Assurance	Ins.	3	1	2
Chemical New York	Bank	4	4	1
New York Life	Ins.	5	12	11
Citibank	Bank	6	5	4
Metropolitan Life	Ins.	7	6	6
Southern Pacific	Trans.	8	19	–
Mellon	Bank	9	11	–
Manufacturers Hanover	Bank	10	–	–
AT & T	Utility	11	7	3
Penn Central	Trans.	12	–	20
I.N.A.	Ins.	13	–	–[c]
Bankers Trust	Bank	14	17	–
General Electric	Ind.	15	–	–
U.S. Steel	Ind.	16	9	7
Westinghouse Electric	Ind.	17	10	–
Charter New York	Bank	18	–	–
Harris Bancorp.	Bank	19	–	–
Phelps Dodge	Ind.	20	–	–
Lehman Bros.	Inv.	–	8	–[c]
United California Bank	Bank	–	13	1
General Motors	Ind.	–	14	17
International Harvester	Ind.	–	15	16
Pacific Mutual	Ind.	–	16	–
First Chicago	Bank	–	18	9
Western Bancorp.	Bank	–	20	–
National City Corp. Cleveland	Bank	–	–	12
General Foods	Ind.	–	–	13
Colgate-Palmolive	Ind.	–	–	14
Cummins Engine	Ind.	–	–	19
I.B.M.	Ind.	–	–	18
Mutual of New York	Ins.	–	–	10
Burlington Northern	Trans.	–	–	15

[a]Centrality scores are assigned to each firm within a data year and range from 1, the most central corporation of the intertie network to n, the least central or most isolated unit present. In 1962, for example, J.P. Morgan was the most central company in the system, Chase Manhattan the second, while Jim Walter Corporation was among the least central organizations with a rank of 1003.

[b]Source: Mariolis (1975)

[c]Not included in the Mariolis data set.

exactly those at the top of our list: Morgan, Chase, Chemical, and Citibank. The life insurance companies are also those most heavily involved in corporate finance.

Financial institutions, it appears, are the organizing units of the interlock network and the most prevalent sources of intercorporate power and unity. Their resource base of institutional stockholding and control of capital gives them the power to mediate intra-class conflict.

High centrality can derive from different sorts of network configurations. A firm is highly central if (1) it is the center of a vast array of interlocking corporations or (2) its interlocks, though few in number, are with companies which are themselves centers. These two sorts of organizations would seem to play rather different roles in the network. The former, which we call a "hub," creates groups of firms around itself; the latter, which we call a "bridge," unites these hubs. Hubs are of the most interest because they are strategically located as organizing elements of the networks. Bridges, although still important to a system as a whole, do not perform the same function of cohesion maintenance.

To determine which highly central corporations were bridges and which were hubs we divided each corporation's interlocks into two categories: those with firms which are less central than the corporation in question, and those with firms which are about as central or more central. By this method, we can judge what proportion of an organization's centrality is hub centrality (derived from less important firms) and what proportion is bridge centrality (derived from firms about as important as itself). Table [19.]2 shows the proportion of hub centrality for the top 20 corporations in 1962 and 1966, grouped according to firm type.[4]

Once again, financial institutions dominate. They derived over 75 percent of their centrality from hub relationships, while non-financials averaged only a little above 50 percent. Even highly central non-financials achieve their importance largely because of their relationships to banks and other financial firms and not primarily from interlocks representing joint ventures or customer-supplier relationships. Thus, the dominant financials—Morgan, Chase, Equitable and Chemical—were all over 70 percent hubs in both years. Chemical had a hub centrality of 99 percent in 1966. On the other hand, the two most consistent industrials—AT&T and U.S. Steel—scored 54 percent and 45 percent respectively in 1962, and 44 percent and 45 percent in 1966. These firms simply did not act as organizing units of the system.

We have already suggested that the pre-eminence of banks and insurance companies in the network may reflect the power of loans and institutional stockholding in intercorporate affairs. The analysis of hub centrality demonstrates that highly central industrials derive their importance within the interlock network from their connection to a handful of financial institutions and not from hub-like connections to a wide variety of companies. This suggests that: (1) major industrial firms act as bridges connecting the financial hubs of the system; and (2) the centrality of the interlock structure is one dimensional: financial institutions form the core organizing centers of the intertie system while highly

TABLE [19.]2   Percent Hub Centrality of the 20 Most Central Corporations, 1962, 1966

	1962	1966
Commercial Banks	83.4%	78.3%
	(N = 9)	(N = 9)
Life Insurance Companies	77.6%	66.3%
	(N = 3)	(N = 4)
Other Financial	58.0%[a]	81.4%[b]
	(N = 1)	(N = 1)
Non-Financial Firms	53.3%	55.5%
	(N = 7)	(N = 6)

[a]Diversified Financial
[b]Investment Bank

central industrial firms link these potential centers of intercorporate coordination and unity. ...

A central, stable core of banks and insurance companies, dominated by the New York "money market" institutions, are the foundation of the interlock system. Commercial banks serve as major hubs which connect a number of less central firms, especially national industrial corporations. Insurance companies, although hubs, maintain strong links with major and minor banks and, therefore, create connecting bridges among them. With some exceptions, large, nationally visible industrials are important only temporarily. Their centrality derives largely from connections to major financial firms. At the same time, they maintain many, less important ties to other, often local, industrials and help unify the system. Their role in the interlock network, then, is two-fold: they bridge the major banks and, at the same time, create links which tie local groupings into the national system.

DIVISIONS WITHIN THE INTERLOCK NETWORK

To identify potential divisions within the interlock network we looked for network "peaks". A peak is a firm which is more central than any firm to which it is directly connected. ... In analyzing the entire network, peaks may appear at the center of a dense and highly interconnected area or in relatively unimportant, sparsely connected sections. Peaks thus provide us with an indication of local dominance without necessarily indicating importance in the network as a whole. ...

Table [19.]3 provides a list of all peaks found among the 100 most central corporations of 1962 and 1966. The pattern is striking; the only firms appearing as peaks in the primary network are financial institutions. This is powerful evidence for the primacy of financials as central, organizing nodes of the interlock network and it is further evidence that financial relationships are the fundamental building blocks of intercorporate unity. Moreover, the list of peaks indicates lines of cleavage in the network. Five of the New York money market banks appear, indicating that they maintain separate relationships with the subordinate

TABLE [19.3]   Corporate Peaks, 1962 and 1966 (Primary Interlocks Only)

		Centrality Rank		
	Location	1962	1966	Years Listed as Peak
New York Market Banks[a]				
J.P. Morgan	NYC	1	2	1962, 1966
Citibank	NYC	2	1	1962, 1966
Chase Manhattan	NYC	3	6	1962, 1966
Bankers Trust	NYC	4	8	1962, 1966
Chemical New York	NYC	5	9	1962, 1966
Manufacturers Hanover				
Other Money Market Banks				
First Chicago	Chicago	6	5	1962, 1966
Continental Illinois	Chicago	8	4	1962, 1966
Mellon	Pittsburgh	15	10	1962, 1966
Regional Banks				
Harris Bancorp	Chicago	10	36	1962
United California Bank	L.A.	36	3	1962, 1966
National City Corporation	Cleveland	52	31	1962, 1966
Northwestern National	Minnesota	58	25	1962, 1966
Cleveland Trust	Cleveland	64	81	1962
Marine Midland	NYC	80	12	1962, 1966
Charter New York	NYC	17	58	1962
National Detroit	Detroit	85	61	1966
Investment Banks				
Lehman Bros.	NYC	9	7	1962, 1966
Goldman Sachs	NYC	16	27	1962, 1966
Lazard Freres	NYC	25	69	1962, 1966
Insurance Companies				
Penn Mutual	Philadelphia	41	13	1966

[a]Money market banks are major commercial lenders who handle the bulk of interbank lending.

firms which act as bridges among them. These special relationships may trace potential lines of competition among the financial units, which are individual spheres of influence exerting pressure against the structural interdependence of these lending institutions.

At the same time, these results reinforce our distinction between commercial banks and insurance companies. Commercial banks account for the vast majority of all system peaks in both 1962 and 1966. Only one insurance company is included in this category. Even investment banks, with relatively low inclusion levels among the most central firms of the intertie system, outnumber insurance firms as network peaks. This suggests that, by and large, insurance companies maintain their centralizing role within the network. Unlike commercial banks which potentially organize individual spheres and demarcate possible cleavage points within the interlock network, insurance companies are conspicuously absent from this category. ...

The portrait which emerges from this analysis reflects both unity and structural cleavage within the community of big business. The main organizing institutions are four major New York commercial banks with national prominence and international presence: Chase Manhattan, J.P. Morgan, Chemical, and Citibank. Each is the hub of a massive network of interlocking and interdependent corporations. The hubs, in turn, are united by common interlocks with three major insurance companies—Equitable Life, Mutual of New York, and Metropolitan Life—each of which has long-term relationships with two or three of the main banks. A select group of nonfinancial firms, including U.S. Steel and AT&T, also help tie the hubs together. Other major industrials create temporary bridges among the major commercial banks. Thus, the centrifugal tendencies of the competing commercial bank hubs are countered by the bridges. ...

Thus, although Baran and Sweezy (1966) assumed that the breakup of interest groups left the corporate world with few mechanisms for conflict resolution, our findings suggest that financial arrangements remain the fundamental source of intercorporate unity, even in the absence of differentiated groupings. We recognized the importance of joint ventures and customer supplier relationships in this regard but view them as secondary. What on the surface looks like an undifferentiated mass of interlocks, we argue, is in fact a highly structured system with the capacity for order. Inter-firm relationships, then, are organized by the predominance and pre-eminence of financial relationships and the clearly defined division between banks and insurance companies. Moreover, the structure of regional-national relations, organized along financial lines, provides further order to the daily and yearly activities of modern U.S. big business.

NOTES

1. For details of data collection, see Bearden, *et al.* (1975); Mintz (1978); and Mintz and Schwartz (1981).

2. Centrality is defined as

$$C_i \sum_{\substack{j=1 \\ i \neq j}}^{n} r_{ij} C_j$$

where r_{ij} = the intensity of the interlock between corporation i and corporation j; C_j = the centrality of corporation j; n = the number of corporations; and $r_{ij} = b_{ij}/\sqrt{d_j}$ where: b_{ij} = the number of interlocks between corporation i and corporation j; d_j = the number of directors on the board of corporation j. For details of this method, see Bearden, *et al.*, (1975); Mariolis (1975, 1978); Mariolis, Schwartz and Mintz (1979). For a comparison of different measures of centrality, see Mizruchi and Bunting (1979).

3. The 1969 figures are taken from Mariolis (1975) and are based upon a restricted sample of 797 firms. Some small inconsistencies between the first two years and 1969 may be due to this difference. ...

4. Hub centrality is defined as: $H_i = C_i - \sum C_j$ when $C_j > .8 C_i$ where H_i = hub centrality of corporation i: C_i = total centrality of corporation i; c_j = total centrality of corpo-

ration j. For the matrices reported in Table [19.]2, therefore, hub centrality is derived from interlocks with firms whose centrality scores were less than 80 percent of the score of the company in question. Data for 1969 were not available.

REFERENCES

Baran, Paul and Paul Sweezy
   1966   Monopoly Capital. New York: Monthly Review Press.
Bearden, James, William Atwood, Peter Freitag, Carolyn Hendricks, Beth Mintz, and Michael Schwartz
   1975   "The nature and extent of bank centrality in corporate networks." Paper presented at the annual meeting of the American Sociological Association, San Francisco, September.
Berle, A. and G. Means
   1968   The Modern Corporation and Private Property. New York: Harcourt, Brace and World. [1932]
Bonacich, Philip
   1972   "Techniques for analyzing overlapping memberships." Pp. 176–86 in Herbert Costner (ed.), Sociological Methodology. San Francisco: Jossey-Bass Inc.
Bunting, David and Jeffrey Barbour
   1971   "Interlocking directorates in large American corporations, 1896–1962." Business History Review 45:317–335.
Domhoff, G. William
   1970   The Higher Circles. New York: Random House.
   1971   "How the power elite set national goals." Pp. 210–219 in Robert Perucci and Marc Pilisuk (eds.,), The Triple Revolution Emerging. Boston: Little Brown.
   1979   The Powers That Be. New York: Random House.
Eakins, David
   1966   "The development of corporate liberal policy research in the United States. Unpublished Ph.D. dissertation, University of Wisconsin.
Kotz, David
   1978   Bank Control of Large Corporations in the United States. Berkeley: University of California Press.
Mariolis, Peter
   1975   "Interlocking directorates and the control of corporations." Social Science Quarterly 56:425–439.
Mariolis, Peter and Michael Schwartz
   1972   "Network analysis of corporate interlocks." Paper presented at the Conference on Network Analysis, Math-Social Science Board of the National Science Foundation. Camden, Maine, October.
Mintz, Beth and Michael Schwartz
   1981   Bank Hegemony, Corporate Networks and Intercorporate Power: A Study of Interlocking Directorates in American Business. Unpublished manuscript. State University of New York, Stony Brook.

Mizruchi, Mark and David Bunting
   1979   "Influence in corporate networks: An examination of four measures." Paper
          presented at the annual meeting of the American Sociological Association, Bos-
          ton, September.
Mokken, R. J. and F. N. Stokman
   1974   "Traces of power I and II: Power influence as political phenomeon." Paper pre-
          sented at the Joint Sessions of the European Consortium for Political Research,
          Strasbourg, France, April.
Shoup, Lawrence H. and William Minter
   1977   Imperial Brain Trust: The CFR and United States Foreign Policy. New York:
          Monthly Review Press.
Useem, Michael
   1979   "The social organization of the American business class." American Sociologi-
          cal Review 44:553-571.
Whitt, J. Allen
   1979- "Can capitalists organize themselves?" Insurgent Sociologist 2(3):51-59.
   1980

20

Upper-Class Power

HAROLD R. KERBO

UPPER-CLASS ECONOMIC POWER

If we have an upper class in this country that, because of its power, can be described as a governing class, by what means does it govern or dominate? ... [T]heorists such as Domhoff consider the upper class dominant in both the economy and politics. But precisely how is this dominance achieved? We will examine first how the upper class is said to have extensive influence over the economy through stock ownership, then turn to the question of economic power through extensive representation in major corporate offices.

Stock Ownership. As some argue, the most important means of upper-class economic power lies in its ownership of the primary means of production. The upper class has power over our economy because of its control of the biggest corporations through stock ownership. ...

Legally, the ultimate control of corporations is found not with top corporate executives, but with major stockholders. In a sense, top corporate executives and boards of directors are charged with managing these corporations for the real owners—the stockholders. Stockholders have the authority to elect corporate directors who are to represent stockholder interests. These directors are then responsible for general corporate policy, including the task of filling top executive positions. The day-to-day management of the corporation is in turn the responsibility of the executive officers, who must generally answer to stockholders and their representatives on the board of directors.

Assuming for now that corporate authority actually operates this way (questions about this ideal power arrangement will be considered below), the largest stockholder or stockholders in a corporation should be in control. Thus, if we find that upper-class families have extensive stock ownership and that this stock is in major corporations, we can say that upper-class families dominate the American economy.

It is clear ... that wealth is very unequally distributed in this country—more so even than family or personal income. One of the most important categories of wealth (because of its usual high return on investment) is corporate stock. ... [One] percent of the people in this country owned *56.5 percent* of the privately held corporate stock, and only 0.5 percent of the people owned *49.3 percent* of the privately held corporate stock in the United States. Thus, from 1 to 0.5 per-cent of the people in this country (roughly equal to the number Domhoff be-lieves is in the upper class) hold most of the privately owned corporate stock.

This concentration of private stock ownership is even more striking when we find that most of the remaining stock is controlled by large financial corpora-tions (see U.S. Senate Committee on Governmental Affairs 1978a, 1980; Kerbo and Della Fave 1983, 1984). To the degree that the upper class also has a lot of in-fluence over these financial corporations (such as banks with large amounts of stock control in other big corporations), the actual stock control of the upper class is much greater (for example, see Figure [20.]1 showing upper-class stock ownership in corporation B plus ownership in corporation A, which also con-trols stock in corporation B). ...

Large amounts of stock held by a family afford economic power in many ways, but the most extensive power flowing from stock ownership comes when this stock is concentrated in a corporation to a sufficient degree to ensure con-trol over the corporation. The amount of stock owned brings an equal number of votes toward electing the board of directors (who can hire and fire the manag-ers) and deciding major issues that come before stockholders. Thus, it becomes important to know how much stock individuals or families hold in each major corporation in determining the control of that corporation.

In the early stages of industrialization in this country the control of corpora-tions was fairly easy to estimate. We knew, for example, that the Rockefeller fam-ily controlled Standard Oil, the McCormick family controlled International Har-vester, the Mellon family controlled Aluminum Company of America, and the Morgan family controlled Morgan Bank by virtue of their extensive stock owner-ship of these companies. But this concentration of stock ownership by specific families in one or a few corporations has changed greatly in recent decades. Few clearly family-controlled corporations ... are found today.

Because of the wide distribution of stockholders in most corporations, gov-ernment agencies and researchers agree that 5 to 10 percent ownership in a par-ticular company by a family will often result in control of that company by the family.

A government study, however, found only thirteen of the top 122 corpora-tions in this country to be clearly controlled by one family (see U.S. Senate Com-mittee on Governmental Affairs 1978a:252). But we must emphasize *clearly* con-trolled. One of the problems in determining control is that the ownership of stock in specific corporations is often hidden. For example, the owner of stock may be listed under meaningless names (such as street names) or under trusts

Figure [20.]1   Upper-Class Economic Power Through Stock
Ownership and Control.

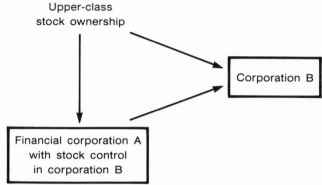

and foundations (Zeitlin, 1974). To make the situation even more complex, corporations (especially banks) control stock in other corporations.

Consider the following situation: A family owns about 2 percent of the stock
in corporation A with other families also owning about 2 percent each. In turn,
this original family owns, say, 5 percent of the stock in corporation B (a bank) and
6 percent in corporation C (an insurance company). We find upon further investigation that company B (the bank) controls 4 percent of the stock in corporation
A, and corporation C (the insurance company) controls 7 percent of the stock in
corporation A. Who controls corporation A?

It *may* be that our original family does, through its stock in corporation A, as
well as B and C. But other families own stock in A who in addition have much
stock in corporations D and E. And (you are probably ahead of me), corporations
D and E also control stock in corporation A! This example is not an exaggeration, as anyone will see in examining the data on stock ownership published in a
Senate study (U.S. Senate Committee on Governmental Affairs 1978a, 1980). In
the face of this complexity of wide stockholdings many researchers simply conclude that top managers of a corporation control by default. ... But, as we will
see below, this generalization also has many drawbacks.

In terms of upper-class dominance in the economy through stock ownership,
all we can say is that its stock ownership is very extensive. But we cannot as yet
arrive at firm conclusions about upper-class control of specific corporations.
The data are hard to obtain, complex, and sometimes of questionable quality.
Therefore, the arguments by ruling-class or governing-class theorists that an upper class dominates the economy through control of stock in major corporations
cannot be completely confirmed.

One argument by ruling-class theorists is given more support; the upper class
today has more extensive *common economic interests* than it once had. Rather
than each family owning and controlling one corporation, today the families
more often have extensive ownership in many corporations. They don't own

each corporation in common, but they do have extensive common interests throughout top corporations in this country. There is a bond of common economic interests that helps cement a unity in defense of the top corporate structure as a whole.

Upper-Class Backgrounds of Economic Elites. Aside from actual stock ownership there is another possible means of upper-class leverage over the economy. After the authority of stockholders in a corporation we find the board of directors and top executive officers. We will call these people *economic elites.* The family backgrounds of these economic elites may be important in how they think, whom they trust, and what group interests they serve while making decisions in their positions of authority in the corporate world. Ruling-class theorists such as Domhoff believe that these economic elites often come from, or have backgrounds in, upper-class families. Thus, even if upper-class families may not own enough stock to control many corporations, their people are there in important positions of authority.

Domhoff (1967) has examined the directors from many top corporations. He has found ... that of the top twenty industrial corporations, 54 percent of the board members were from the upper class; of the top fifteen banks, 62 percent were upper-class members; of the top fifteen insurance companies, 44 percent were upper-class members; of the top fifteen transportation companies, 53 percent were upper-class members; and of the top fifteen utility corporations, 30 percent were upper-class members. Clearly we find much overrepresentation by the upper class on these boards of directors when it is noted that the upper class accounts for only about 0.5 percent of the population.

In another study Soref (1976) took a random sample of board members from the top 121 corporations in the United States. Using Domhoff's definition of upper class, he found upper-class board members had more board positions in other companies (average of 3.49 for upper-class directors, 2.0 for others), and were more often members of board subcommittees that made important long-range decisions in the company.

Finally, in a massive study of institutional elites, Thomas Dye (1979, 1983) obtained background information on the boards of directors *and* top executive officers of the top 201 corporations in 1976 (those corporations controlling 50 percent of the assets in each type of corporation—industrial, financial, insurance, and utilities). This sample included 3,572 people who by our definition were economic elites. Using a list of 37 upper-class social clubs from Domhoff's work, Dye (1979:184) found that *44 percent* of these 3,572 economic elites were members of one or more of these upper-class clubs. ... Thus, by Domhoff's definition, 44 percent of these people were members of the upper class.

In conclusion, we find some evidence supporting the argument that the upper class is able to dominate the economy through positions of authority in major corporations. But this evidence is far from conclusive. A primary reservation raised by Dye (1983) pertains to the validity of upper-class indicators such as elite social clubs. It may be that many economic elites gain club memberships only after they become economic elites. To the extent that this is true, we cannot always say club membership indicates upper-class background or upper-class membership.

There is also the question of whether upper-class members act exclusively to protect the interests of the upper class when in positions of corporate authority. In part, this second reservation pertains to the strength of upper-class unity and consciousness discussed earlier. It is clear that corporate elite membership in social clubs and interlocking directorates through multiple board memberships help unify the structure of large corporations today. However, the question of whose interests (an upper class or corporate elites themselves) are served by this unified corporate structure remains inadequately answered.

UPPER-CLASS POLITICAL POWER

The next questions of importance for ruling-class or governing-class theorists are the degree and means of political power exercised by the upper class. The significance of the state, and especially the federal government, on domestic affairs in this nation has increased rapidly since the 1930s. We find today a federal government with ... programs designed for such things as regulating the economy as well as its traditional job of managing foreign affairs.

The potential impact of the federal government upon upper-class interests is clear. If the upper class is to maintain a position of dominance in the nation it is imperative that it have influence over the state as well as the economy. In this section we will consider evidence suggesting upper-class influence over the government through (1) direct participation by the upper class in politics, (2) the selection of government leaders, (3) the activities of lobby organizations, and (4) organizations established to shape the development of government policy.

Upper-Class Participation in Government. Research on direct participation by the upper class in government is focused heavily on the President's cabinet. Cabinet members are under the direction of the President, but because of the President's many concerns and lack of time in gathering all the needed information in making policy, the President must rely heavily upon cabinet members for advice and information. If these cabinet members represent the interests of the upper class, they can provide the President with information to guide his policy decisions in a way that will ensure that upper-class interests are maintained. ...

Using his definition of upper-class membership outlined earlier, Domhoff (1967:97–99) ... examined the backgrounds of secretaries of state, the treasury, and defense between 1932 and 1964. He found that 63 percent of the secretaries of state, 62 percent of the secretaries of defense, and 63 percent of the secretaries of the treasury could be classified as members of the upper class before assuming office. ... As Domhoff admits, the above represents only a small part of the cabinet for a period of a little more than thirty years. But with these positions we find the upper class represented in proportions far greater than their 0.5 percent of the population would suggest.

Since Domhoff's earlier work, and extensive study of cabinet members has been conducted by Beth Mintz (1975). Using Domhoff's indicators of upper-class membership, Mintz (1975, along with Peter Freitag, 1975) undertook the massive job of examining the backgrounds of *all* cabinet members (205 people) serving between 1897 and 1973. Her most interesting finding at this point is that 66 percent of these cabinet members could be classified as members of the upper class before obtaining their cabinet positions. ... Also interesting is that the member of cabinet members coming from the upper class is fairly consistent between 1897 and 1973. ... Mintz's data show that Republican presidents chose over 71 percent of their cabinet members from the upper class, while Democratic presidents chose over 60 percent from the upper class.

In her background research on these cabinet members Mintz also included information pertaining to the previous occupations of these people. Along with Freitag (1975), she reports that over 76 percent of the cabinet members were associated with big corporations before or after their cabinet position, 54 percent were from *both* the upper class and top corporate positions, and 90 percent either came from the upper class or were associated with big corporations. Focusing on corporate ties of cabinet members, Freitag (1975) shows that these ties have not changed much over the years, and vary only slightly by particular cabinet position. In fact, even most secretaries of labor have been associated with big corporations in the capacity of top executives, board members or corporate lawyers.

Most ruling-class or governing-class theorists consider the cabinet to be the most important position for direct government participation by the upper class. The cabinet allows easy movement into government and then back to top corporate positions. As might be expected, Mintz (1975) found most cabinet members between 1897 and 1973 coming from outside of government, rather than working their way up within government bureaucracies. The United States and England are unique in this aspect of top government elite recruitment. Putnam (1976:48–49) has found that in most other Western industrial societies the top political elites (with positions comparable to those in the United States cabinet) are more likely to come from within government bureaucracies, working their way to the top in a line of career promotions. In the United States and England, this atypical method of political elite recruitment affords the upper class and corporate elite opportunities for political influence lacking in these other industrial nations. ...

There are other political positions of importance. The heads of various government agencies (such as the Federal Aviation Agency), Supreme Court justices, members of the Federal Reserve Board, and top senators and congressmen all represent positions of influence within the government. Although one may agree with C. Wright Mills and others that the cabinet offers more opportunities to influence policy within the federal government, these other positions are of considerable importance. But there is one difference. These other government positions are more often headed or staffed by career bureaucrats or politicians. Thus, they are less open for members of the upper class, who are more often wealthy business leaders. ...

Political Campaign Contributions. Today it costs money, lots of money, to obtain a major elective office. ... In the 1978 U.S. congressional elections, special-interest groups alone contributed $35 million to candidates. This figure increased to $55 million in 1980, and to $150 million in 1988! The average Senate campaign in 1988 cost $4 million.

In his famous work on the power elite just a little over thirty years ago, C. Wright Mills had relatively little to say about campaign contributions. But the subject can no longer be neglected. Especially in an age when political campaigns are won more through presenting images than issues, the image-creating mass media are extremely important and costly. Most presidents and congressional officeholders are wealthy, but they are not super-rich. With a few rare exceptions they cannot afford to finance their own political campaigns. Who, then, pays for these campaigns? Thousands of contributors send $25 or $50 to favored candidates. For the most part, however, the money comes from corporations and the wealthy.

With the nationwide reaction against Watergate and the many illegal campaign contributions to Nixon's reelection committee in 1972, some election reforms were undertaken by Congress in 1974. Among these reforms was the creation of a voluntary $1-per-person campaign contribution from individual income tax reports. A Presidential Election Campaign Fund was established to distribute this money to the major parties and candidates during an election year. In addition, a Federal Election Commission was established to watch over campaign spending, and people were limited to a $1,000 contribution in any single presidential election, with organizations limited to $5,000.

An interesting outcome of the campaign reform law of 1974 is that much of the illegal activity in Nixon's 1972 campaign was *made legal* as long as correct procedures are followed. For example, organizations are limited to $5,000 in political contributions per election. However, if there are more organizations, more money can be contributed. And this is precisely what happened by 1976. There was an explosion in the number of political action committees (PACs) established by large corporations and their executives, an increase far outnumbering those established by any other group, such as labor unions (Domhoff 1983:125). By the 1980 congressional elections, 1,585 corporate, health industry, and other business PACs contributed $36 million to candidates, while $13 million was contributed by 240 labor union PACs. ...

Campaign contributions, therefore, continue to be an important means of political influence. The wealthy are not assured that their interests will be protected by those they help place in office, but they obviously consider the gamble worth taking. Usually, it is hoped that these campaign contributions are placing people in office who hold political views that lead to the defense of privilege when unforeseen challenges to upper-class interests occur along the way. ...

Since the early 1970s a number if studies have been done on this subject (Mintz 1989). For example, Allen and Broyles (1989) examined data pertaining to the campaign contributions of 100 of the most wealthy families (629 individuals) in the United States. They found that about one-half of these individuals made large contributions. And it was the more "visible" and active rich who made these large contributions. By this they mean that the rich were more likely to make contributions if they were corporate directors or executives, listed in "Who's Who," and/or directors of nonprofit foundations. These people were more likely to contribute to Republicans, and this was especially so with the new rich, non-Jews, and people with extensive oil stocks. ...

Congressional Lobbying. If the interests of the wealthy are not ensured by their direct participation in government, and if those the wealthy helped put in office seem to be forgetting their debtors, a third force can be brought into action. The basic job of a lobbyist is to make friends among congressional leaders, provide them with favors such as trips, small gifts, and parties, and, most importantly, provide these leaders with information and arguments favoring their employers' interests and needs. All of this requires a large staff and lots of money.

Oil companies in the United States are among the largest corporations, with Exxon (the largest), Mobil, Texaco, Standard Oil of California, Gulf, and Standard Oil of Indiana holding six of the top ten positions in terms of industrial assets. It may not be surprising, then, that oil companies pay the lowest taxes on profits of all major corporations (Sampson, 1975:205). In 1972, for example, Exxon paid *6.5 percent* of its net profits in income taxes, Texaco paid *1.7 percent,* Mobil paid *1.3 percent,* Gulf paid *1.2 percent,* and Standard Oil of California paid *2.05 percent.* The actual corporate tax rate in the United States was *supposed* to be 48 percent in 1972. But, as a whole, the nineteen top oil companies paid an average of 7.6 percent of profits to taxes in this year (Blair, 1976:187). ...

In one of the first empirical studies of the effects of certain characteristics of corporations on government policies toward these corporations (such as tax policies), Salamon and Siegfried (1977) found that the size of the corporation showed a strong inverse relation to the amount of taxes paid by the corporation. And this inverse relation between size of the corporation and the corporation's tax rate was especially upheld when examining the oil companies and including their state as well as federal taxes paid (Salamon and Siegfried 1977:1039). Thus, the bigger the corporation, the less it tends to pay in corporate taxes.

Later studies have confirmed this relationship between size (and power) and corporate tax rates. Jacobs (1988), however, measured the concentration of powerful corporations within each type of industry. The findings were similar: The more corporate concentration (meaning the size of the firms in the industry and their dominance in the industry), the less the taxes for the corporations in that industry. In examining how this is done in the oil industry and health-care industry, Laumann, Knoke, and Kim (1985) studied 166 government policy decisions relating to these industries, and interviewed 458 lobbyists for these industries. They found that there are leading corporations in these industries which have a reputation for being most politically active in influencing government for the overall industry, and that this reputation is very accurate when measuring their lobbying activity. ...

Lobby organizations, therefore, can be of major importance in ensuring that the special interests of a wealthy upper-class and corporate elite are served. If special favors are not completely ensured through direct participation in the cabinet and campaign contributions, the powerful lobby organizations may then move into action. The upper class and big business are not the only groups that maintain lobby organizations in Washington. The American Medical Association, the National Rifle Association, the Milk Producers Association, and many others have maintained successful lobby organizations. But when considering the big issues such as how to deal with inflation, tax policy, unemployment, foreign affairs, and many others that broadly affect the lives of people in this country, the corporate and upper-class lobbies are most important. ...

Shaping Government Policy. Of the various means of upper-class and corporate political influence, the type least recognized by the general public is referred to as the *policy-forming process* (see Domhoff 1979:61–128, 1983:98–112, 1990; Dye 1983:237–264). As scholars believe, in the long run this means of political influence is perhaps one of the most important. The basic argument is this: The federal government is faced with many national problems for which there are many possible alternative solutions. For example, consider the problem of inflation. The possible government means of dealing with this problem are varied, and a key is that different solutions to the problem may favor different class interests. Some possible solutions (such as wage and price controls) are believed to favor the working class, and thus are pushed by labor unions. Other possible solutions (such as restricting the money supply and raising interest rates on loans) favor the interests of corporations and the upper class and contribute to higher unemployment for the working class. One important means of ensuring that the federal government follows a policy that is favorable to your class interests is to convince the government through various types of research data that one line of policy is the overall best policy. Generating the needed information and spelling out the exact policy required take a lot of planning, organization, personnel, and resources. And there must be avenues for getting this policy information to the attention of government leaders. It is no surprise, ruling-class theorists argue, that the upper class and its corporations are able to achieve the above and guide government policy in their interests.

Far from the eyes of the general public there is a little-known policy-formation process that goes on in this country. The federal government cannot always use its massive resources to generate the information needed in developing policy alternatives with respect to many issues. A mostly private network has developed over the years, supported with upper-class and corporate money and personnel to provide government input when important decisions are to be made. Domhoff (1979:63; also see Dye 1983:240) has charted this process, as shown in Figure [20.]2.

At the heart of this process are (1) upper-class and corporate *money and personnel* (2) that fund and guide *research* on important questions through foundations and universities, (3) then process the information through *policy-planning groups* sponsored by the upper class (4) that make direct recommendations to government, and (5) influence the opinion-making centers, such as the media and government commissions, which in turn influence the population and government leaders in favoring specific policy alternatives.

We will consider briefly the more important steps in this policy-forming process and some of the supporting evidence obtained by various researchers. It is significant to note that although this policy-formation process fits neatly into the ruling-class or governing-class theory, we find much agreement on this process even among these rejecting a ruling-class argument (such as Dye 1983).

Many writers in sociology, political science, and economics have come to stress the increased importance of information and ideas generated through research in guiding the economy and government in advanced or postindustrial societies (see Galbraith 1971; Bell, 1976). As a consequence, some writers argue that an upper-class or wealthy elite is no longer in control of the economy or political system because the ideas and specialized knowledge are in the hands of a new group of elites—strategic elites or technocrats (see Galbraith 1971; Keller 1963).

Others, especially ruling-class theorists, counter by charging that the knowledge and information behind the operation of the economy and government today are not always neutral. Much of this knowledge is generated through upper-class sponsorship, and thus favors its class interests. Increasingly, knowledge needed by corporations and government is generated through research conducted at major universities. Scientific research requires a lot of time, money, and personnel. The upper class and corporations, it is argued, influence the research process through funding and authority positions in major research-oriented universities.

A major source of funds for research is large foundations. These foundations possess extensive wealth that is given to fund research projects (see Lundberg 1968:498–505) that directors of these foundations judge to be important in gen-

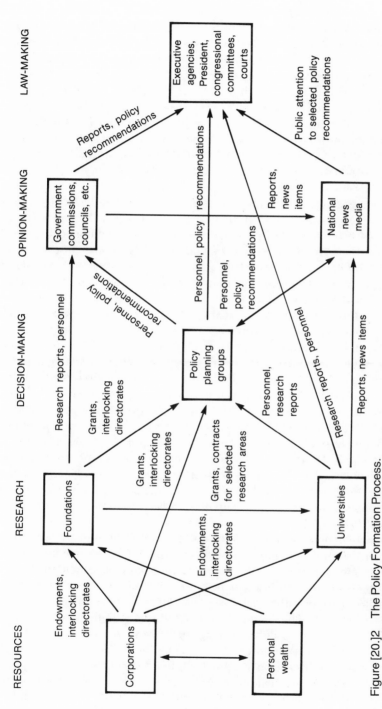

Figure [20.]2   The Policy Formation Process.
Source: G. William Domhoff, *The Powers That Be* (New York: Vintage Press, 1979), p. 63.

erating information needed in guiding political and economic decisions. In most cases, these large foundations were established by wealthy people as a means of reducing taxes. But these families often maintain control of the foundations, influencing their funding policies (see Dye 1979:120). ...

Also important in the research process are the major universities in which much of this research is conducted. Among these universities, for example, are Harvard, Yale, Chicago, Stanford, the Massachusetts Institute of Technology, and the California Institute of Technology. In these universities faculty are often released from their teaching responsibilities to devote most of their time to conducting research sponsored by large corporations and foundations, as well as the federal government. One means of upper-class and corporate influence, therefore, is through guiding what type of research is conducted by the faculty. ...

In this policy-forming process the next important link is through what has been called *policy-planning groups*. The corporate elites and upper class come together in these groups, discuss policy, publish and disseminate research, and, according to Dye and Domhoff, arrive at some consensus about what should be done in the nation. The most important of the policy groups are sponsored directly by the upper class for the purpose of linking the research information discussed above to specific policy alternatives and making certain these policy alternatives find their way to government circles.

Perhaps the most has been written about the Council on Foreign Relations (CFR) and the Committee on Economic Development (CED). Both groups are clearly upper-class institutions (as defined by Domhoff), the former specializing in foreign policy and the latter specializing in domestic issues. The Council on Foreign Relations was established shortly after World War I by upper-class members with the direct intent of influencing the United States government with respect to their business interests overseas (see Shoup, 1975). ... Membership in the CFR is limited to 1,400 people, half of whom are members of the upper class (Domhoff, 1983). The Committee on Economic Development emerged out of the Business Advisory Council in 1942 to continue the input into government by the upper class that began with this earlier organization in the 1930s (Domhoff 1970:123–128, 1979:67–69; Collins 1977). ...

A number of other organizations have been investigated and located among these policy-planning groups sponsored by the upper class. These include the Trilateral Commission (discussed above), the Brookings Institution, the RAND Corporation, and the Business Council. A number of these have been shown sharing memberships with upper-class social clubs on the East and West Coasts (Domhoff 1974:105). The exact influence of these organizations is hard to estimate. Their goals are to decide among themselves what government policy should be and then get the government to adopt the policies. This is a behind-the-scenes process that can be measured only by its outcomes. ...

We have finally to mention briefly the other parts of the policy-forming process described in Figure [20.]2. Various government commissions are established from time to time to make recommendations on such things as civil disorders, the conduct of the CIA, and energy (to list some recent examples). These commissions make public the recommendations of these upper-class policy groups and provide their members with a semiofficial position in the government.

As for the national news media, they are often said to have a liberal slant in their views and to possess much power in shaping public and government opinion. Recent investigations have given some support to these charges (Halberstam 1979; Dye 1983). But the moderate conservative wing of the upper class and corporate leaders most influences the media. The major television networks, magazines, and newspapers are highly concentrated and tied to corporations (see Dye 1983:120). In terms of the backgrounds of top leaders in the national media. Dye (1983:210) found 33 percent had previous careers in big corporations and 44 percent were members of upper-class clubs. Their upper-class backgrounds are not as extensive as those of corporate leaders, but neither are the top media leaders from humble origins.

The backgrounds of media directors, the extensive corporate influence through ownership, and the huge funding from advertising all contribute to making mass media organizations cautious in presenting views that may be overly critical of the upper class and corporate interests. Information critical of these interests is not ignored by the mass media. The upper class might not even want this information to be ignored, for corrective action is often needed to prevent economic problems and corporate abuse from getting out of hand and requiring more drastic solutions that may harm more general corporate interests.
...

One final point requires emphasis. Few theorists writing in this area (on the upper class or, more specifically, on upper-class influence in the mass media) suggest that the upper-class or corporate elites completely control the mass media in the country. Neither do most writers in this area believe that there is some kind of upper-class secret conspiracy to control the mass media—or anything else in the country, for that matter. Rather, they are trying to call attention to an economic structure that allows more influence (in the many ways outlined above) to fall into the hands of groups like the upper-class and corporate elites. Each class or economic interest group tends to have a world view or way of perceiving reality that has been shaped by its own economic and political interests. When one group has more influence over the major means of conveying information, its view of reality often comes to be accepted by more people.

In summarizing the total policy-forming process, we find an underground network in this country that is highly influenced by corporate and upper-class institutions. The federal government and Congress have the authority to adopt or reject the policy recommendations flowing from this process, but most often they accept them, leaving the government to decide exactly how the policy will be carried out (Dye 1979:226). ...

REFERENCES

Allen, Michael Patrick, and Philip Broyles. 1989. "Class Hegemony and Political Finance: Presidential Campaign Contributions of Wealthy Capitalist Families." *American Sociological Review,* 54:275–287.

Bell, Daniel. 1976. *The Coming of Post-Industrial Society.* New York: Basic Books.

Blair, John. 1976. *The Control of Oil.* New York: Vintage Books.

Boies, John L. 1989. "Money, Business, and the State: Material Interests, *Fortune 500* Corporations, and the Size of Political Action Committees." *American Sociological Review,* 54:821–833.

Burch, Philip H. 1981. *Elites in American History,* vols. 1–3. New York: Holmes and Meier.

Collins, Robert. 1977. "Positive Business Responses to the New Deal: The Roots of the Committee for Economic Development, 1933–1942." *Business History Review,* 22:103–119.

Domhoff, G. William. 1967. *Who Rules America?* Englewood Cliffs, N.J.: Prentice-Hall.

Domhoff, G. William. 1970. *The Higher Circles.* New York: Random House.

Domhoff, G. William. 1974. *The Bohemian Grove and Other Retreats.* New York: Harper & Row.

Domhoff, G. William. 1975. "Social Clubs, Policy-Planning Groups, and Corporations: A Network Study of Ruling-Class Cohesiveness." *The Insurgent Sociologist,* 5:173–184.

Domhoff, G. William. 1979. *The Powers That Be.* New York: Vintage Press.

Domhoff, G. William. 1981. "Politics Among the Redwoods: Ronald Reagan's Bohemian Grove Connection." *The Progressive.* (January): 32–36.

Domhoff, G. William. 1983. *Who Rules America Now?: A View for the '80s.* Englewood Cliffs, N.J.: Prentice-Hall.

Dye, Thomas R. 1979. *Who's Running America?* Englewood Cliffs, N.J.: Prentice-Hall.

Dye, Thomas R. 1983. *Who's Running America? The Reagan Years.* Englewood Cliffs, N.J.: Prentice-Hall.

Freitag, Peter. 1975. "The Cabinet and Big Business: A Study of Interlocks." *Social Problems,* 23:137–152.

Galbraith, John Kenneth. 1971. *The New Industrial State.* Boston: Houghton, Mifflin.

Halberstam, David. 1979. *The Powers That Be.* New York: Alfred Knopf.

Jacobs, David. 1988. "Corporate Economic Power and the State: A Longitudinal Assessment of Two Explanations." *American Journal of Sociology,* 93:852–881.

Keller, Suzanne. 1963. *Beyond the Ruling Class: Strategic Elites in Modern Society.* New York: Random House.

Kerbo, Harold R., and L. Richard Della Fave. 1983. "Corporate Linkage and Control of the Corporate Economy: New Evidence and a Reinterpretation." *Sociological Quarterly,* 24:201–218.

Kerbo, Harold R., and L. Richard Della Fave. 1984. "Further Notes on the Evolution of Corporate Control and Institutional Investors: A Response to Niemonen." *Sociological Quarterly,* 25:279–283.

Laumann, Edward, David Knoke, and Yon-Hak Kim. 1985. "An Organizational Approach to State Policy Formation: A Comparative Study of Energy and Health Domains." *American Sociological Review,* 50:1–19.

Lundberg, Ferdinand. 1968. *The Rich and the Super-Rich.* New York: Bantam Books.

Mintz, Beth. 1975. "The President's Cabinet, 1897–1972: A Contribution to the Power Structure Debate." *Insurgent Sociologist*, 5:131–148.

Putnam, Robert. 1976. *The Comparative Study of Elites*. Englewood Cliffs, N.J.: Prentice-Hall.

Salamon, Lester, and John Siegfried. 1977. "Economic Power and Political Influence: The Impact of Industry Structure on Public Policy." *American Political Science Review*, 71:1026–1043.

Sampson, Anthony. 1975. *The Seven Sisters*. New York: Viking.

Shoup, Laurence. 1975. "Shaping the Postwar World: The Council of Foreign Relations and U.S. War Aims During WWII." *Insurgent Sociologist*, 5:9–52.

U.S. Senate Committee on Governmental Affairs. 1978b. *Interlocking Directorates among the Major U.S. Corporations*. Washington, D.C.: U.S. Government Printing Office.

U.S. Senate Committee on Governmental Affairs. 1980. *Structure of Corporate Concentration*. 2 vols. Washington, D.C.: U.S. Government Printing Office.

Zeitlin, Maurice. 1974. "Corporate Ownership and Control: The Large Corporation and the Capitalist Class." *American Journal of Sociology*, 79:1073-1119.

21

The Mass Media
as a Power Institution

MARTIN N. MARGER

In contemporary societies, the two major institutions of power—government and economy—must be joined by a third—the mass media—to complete any scheme of societal power. Although not formally a part of either government or the economy, the mass media are integrally tied to both, and both rely on the mass media to function as they do. Moreover, the mass media have substantial independent resources that make them a formidable institution of power in their own right.

THE SOCIETAL ROLE OF THE MASS MEDIA

The mass media are of two types: print and electronic. Print media are books, magazines, and newspapers; electronic media are television, radio, and films. To refer to them as *mass* media implies that their communicative realm is extremely broad, often encompassing the entire society. In modern societies, the mass media serve several vital functions. They are agents of socialization, instructing people in the norms and values of their society and generally transmitting the society's culture. They are sources of information, supplying citizens with knowledge about their society and especially about the political economy. They function as propaganda mechanisms through which powerful units of the government and economy seek to persuade the public either to support their policies (government) or to buy their consumer products (corporations). Finally, they serve as agents of legitimacy, generating mass belief in (and acceptance of) dominant political and economic institutions.

Given these vital functions, three queries are of fundamental importance in examining the mass media's power in modern societies. The first concerns their control and accessibility: Who owns or controls the mass media, and how much access to them is afforded individuals and groups in the society? The second question pertains to their content: What do the media present to the public, and who makes decisions regarding that content? The third question concerns the effects of mass media on public opinion and political awareness: To what extent do the mass media shape people's views of events and personalities in their society and the world, and how do the media transmit ideology?

Most media research during the past several decades has focused on the United States. The following discussion, therefore, pertains to the power of the mass media primarily in American society. Most of the patterns and tendencies apparent in the United States, however, are increasingly characteristic of the mass media in other industrial societies.

MEDIA CONTROL AND ACCESSIBILITY

Control and accessibility of the mass media in the United States and increasingly in other industrial societies are determined primarily by the economic context within which the media function and by their place in the political economy.

In the United States, the mass media operate almost entirely as privately owned enterprises. In most other industrial societies, newspapers are privately owned but television and radio are at least partially public corporations that compete within a mixed public-private system. Television and radio in Canada, for example, are dominated by the state-run Canadian Broadcasting Corporation (CBC), although there are also several privately owned television and radio networks. A similar system exists in Britain, where the electronic media are a mixture of public and commercial corporations. Only in autocratic societies like China are the media fully state controlled; in these societies, the media are organized and operated to implement the government's social and political policies (Wright, 1986). In recent years, there has been a movement in most societies toward the dominance of privately owned and operated electronic media, although the United States remains unique in the extent of private ownership and control. Moreover, although the electronic media are nominally regulated by government, they operate with far fewer restrictions in the United States than in other societies. Meanwhile, a global trend toward convergence of national networks and companies into transnational units is increasingly evident (Schiller, 1989).

The mass media are huge corporations (or parts of corporate conglomerates) whose primary objective, like all enterprises in a capitalist economy, is to maximize their profits. Like most industries in the American political economy, the mass media are concentrated in a few giant corporate units and thus constitute an oligopoly. Vast multifaceted companies composed of newspaper chains, radio and television stations, and recording, motion-picture, and publishing units dominate the media industry. Among the 1,600 United States daily newspapers, about a dozen corporations control more than half the circulation. The Knight-Ridder chain, for example, owns newspapers throughout the United States with three million in daily circulation, including the *Detroit Free Press*, the *Miami Herald*, the *Philadelphia Inquirer*, and numerous smaller dailies. Gannett owns *USA Today* as well as eighty-eight other dailies with six million in circulation. Although 11,000 individual magazine titles are published in the United States, a handful of corporations derive most of the magazine revenue (Time-Warner alone controls more than 40 percent of magazine business), and among more than 2,500 book publishing companies, a half-dozen corporations sell most books. Three major studios control most of the movie business, and three corporations draw most of the audience and revenue of the television industry (Bagdikian, 1989). Edward Herman and Noam Chomsky have identified twenty-four media giants that basically control the industry. Twenty-three of these companies had assets in excess of $1 billion in 1986 and three-quarters of them earned after-tax profits of over $100 million (Herman and Chomsky, 1988).

One must also consider the scope and diversity of these companies' media holdings and activities. Time-Warner, for example, is made up of Warner Brothers Pictures (movies), dozens of popular mass circulation magazines (including *Time* and *Life*), cable television companies, and book companies. NBC is part of the RCA Corporation, which, in turn, is part of General Electric. CBS and Capital Cities/ABC are massive media conglomerates that own numerous television and radio stations, cable television networks, and magazine, recording, book publishing, and motion picture companies.

Topping off this narrow media concentration are the wire service companies, which accumulate news stories. A large proportion of the items appearing in every mass circulation newspaper in the United States comes from the wires of the Associated Press (AP) or United Press International (UPI). Newspapers subscribe to these services, which become the major source of stories. A few of the larger newspaper companies operate their own wire services and also supply other smaller papers. Thus, in the coverage of national or international news, the difference from one newspaper to another is ordinarily slight. Radio and television news, to a lesser degree, also rely on these wire services.

It is apparent, then, that in the United States, as in most industrial societies, ownership and control of the mass media are extremely concentrated. This concentration parallels the tendency of all political and economic institutions in modern societies to converge into fewer and more powerful units. All other aspects of media power, including their content and effects, are colored by this fact.

In modern societies, to publicly communicate views or ideas requires use of the media. A critical concern, therefore, is not only who owns or controls the media but also who has access to them. In modern societies, only government and big business have the resources—money, authority, and influence—to employ the media regularly and effectively.

As privately owned enterprises, the major goal of the various media is to generate revenue. This objective requires that the media cater primarily to those who can pay to put their views on the air or into print: the major corporations, which use the media primarily to create demand for their products and services through advertising. Consider that a thirty-second television commercial on Super Bowl Sunday in 1992 cost $850,000; or that Procter and Gamble spends almost $1.5 billion each year on media advertising. Advertising not only serves to create demand but also provides corporations with a means of creating a positive public image. General Electric, for example, tells the public that "we bring good things to life." Most corporations convey similar messages in which they are portrayed not as profit-seeking enterprises but as compassionate, publicly responsible citizens.

Government access to the media is founded not on financial power but on the fact that the media are closely interwoven with government, particularly at the national level. Put simply, the relationship between government and media is symbiotic; neither can function effectively without the other. As a regulated industry in the United States, the media must take into account the interests of government elites. More importantly, however, the media are heavily dependent on government elites as their major source of political information, which is the core of news. In fact, it is the actions of government elites that dominate news as presented by both print and electronic media. Moreover, much of the news transmitted by the mass media is prepared by government agencies. Studies have indicated that not only are government officials the source of most news but most news stories are drawn from situations over which newsmakers "have either complete or substantial control" (Sigal, 1973).

Power elites, particularly those in the realm of government, can easily gain access to the mass media simply because they possess credibility among the public as well as among the media elite. Their accounts of events and policies are more likely to be accepted and thus become part of the news format than accounts and interpretations provided by other sources (Gans, 1979). Moreover, in gathering information, the mass media ordinarily follow the path of least resistance; this means relying on official sources for information. As Herman and Chomsky (1988:19) have noted, "Taking information from sources that may be presumed credible reduces investigative expense, whereas material from sources that are not prima facie credible, or that will elicit criticism and threats, requires careful checking and costly research."

Government elites, however, are equally dependent on the mass media. This dependency stems from their need to employ the media to convey their messages to the public and thus shape and influence public opinion. Political leaders today rarely engage in face-to-face communication with the masses. Instead, they speak primarily through the electronic media in soundbites and project their images through photo opportunities. Political dialogue, particularly at the national level, is increasingly reduced to creating impressions (Postman, 1985).

This process reaches a high point in the orchestration of pseudo-events, that is, carefully scripted and staged events that are designed to create favorable public images but that have little basis in reality (Boorstin, 1961).

MASS MEDIA CONTENT

The mass media exercise considerable power independently of both government and business. This power is particularly significant in their role as gatekeepers of political, economic, and social information—what is ordinarily termed "news." As information gatekeepers, it is the media who define what news is or what is socially significant. As suppliers of vital information, the mass media in modern societies are unequalled. They have become our window on the world, and it is through them that we learn about key events, personalities, and other so-called news. The media, in other words, have become a source of reality itself. As Ben Bagdikian (1971:xii–xiii) has put it: "For most of the people of the world, for most of the events of the world, what the news systems do not transmit did not happen. To that extent, the world and its inhabitants are what the news media say they are."

Given the media's strong influence on the molding of political, economic, and social reality, a key power issue concerns the decision-making process of news selection and presentation. Like critical decisions of government and the economy, this process is essentially an elite function. Events become newsworthy, and thus of importance to the society, only after they have been selected by the communications elite—editors, journalists, and media executives (Cohen and Young, 1973; Epstein, 1974; Gans, 1979; Tuchman, 1978). It is the media elite, therefore, who are largely responsible for molding the public's conception of political, economic, and social events and conditions. The media elite must therefore be added to corporate and governmental elites as top decision makers in the United States and other modern societies.

What are the consequences of this concentration of control over the shaping of sociopolitical reality? Here we must consider the political-economic context of the mass media in the United States and most other modern societies. First, because the major media operate as business enterprises, the media elite, when making content decisions, must take into account the interests of the dominant economic groups—the large corporations—that supply them with revenue. Second, given their symbiotic relationship with government, these decisions must be weighed against the interests of political elites. The result is that ideas or movements outside the political and economic mainstream receive little attention. In U.S. elections, for example, minor parties and candidates are generally treated by the mass media as curiosities, not as legitimate contenders. Hence, political debate is narrowly limited to the two major parties in the mainstream political arena, parties that rarely differ fundamentally on policy or philosophical issues. In short, ruling business and political elites are best situated to exercise influence over the content of the mass media.

With maximum access to the mass media as well as the ability to shape news, elites of the political economy are able not only to place their issues on the political agenda but also to define them in ways "likely to influence their resolution" (Bennett, 1988:96). Parties, organizations, and individuals who advocate serious economic or political change but lack financial and political resources have a very difficult time communicating their messages through the mass media. It is true that challenges to established authority are often given attention by newspaper and, particularly, television journalism. But this is due primarily to the fact that "the logic of audience maintenance favors conflict between easily recognizable groups" (Epstein, 1974:269). Coverage is not provided in acknowledgment of the legitimacy of challenging groups or to present the substance of their protest (Gitlin, 1980).

The emphasis on official perspectives results in limited public understanding of the nature of political, economic, and social problems and how they might be resolved. Rarely do the mass media subject the dominant political economy to serious scrutiny and criticism. "The political world," Lance Bennett (1988:96) has explained, "becomes a caricature drawn out of unrealistic stereotypes, predictable political postures, and superficial images." Moreover, even when attention is drawn to societal shortcomings by public affairs or news programs or investigative journalists, it is done in the spirit of the dominant ideology. That is, problems are presented as the products of deviant individuals or groups within the context of an otherwise healthy social system. The *systemic* origins of chronic problems are rarely explained or even acknowledged. As David Paletz and Robert Entman (1981:167) have observed, "The mass media have never given powerless Americans the necessary information to link the ubiquitous rotten apples to the structure of the barrel." Questioning the structure and functioning of dominant political and economic institutions is clearly beyond the capabilities of the mass media (Gans, 1979; Gitlin, 1980; Parenti, 1986).

The bias of mass media content toward the dominant system should not be seen, however, as the result of government and economic elites conspiring with media editors, journalists, and executives. The media elite express dominant values largely unconsciously: They see themselves as objective news commentators, not bearers of opinion. As Herbert Gans (1979:39–40) has noted, "The values in the news are rarely explicit and must be found between the lines—in what actors and activities are reported or ignored, and in how they are described." Political objectivity, therefore, is not political neutrality. Critical information presented by the media, in the form of news and public affairs, is framed by dominant values and shaped by power elites, no matter how seemingly objective the presentation may be (Iyengar and Kinder, 1987). Moreover, the very notion of objectivity among the media is illusory. As Paletz and Entman (1981:22) have explained, "to edit is to interpret, to speak is to define, to communicate is to structure reality." Hence, the media, by their very nature, cannot be objective.

The inability of the mass media to present issues to the public in a thorough and critical manner is largely a result of their commercial imperatives. News, like other aspects of mass media, must be sold as a consumer product. This requires that it be presented in an entertainment format, and, as Bennett (1988) has explained, be personalized, dramatized, fragmented, and normalized. It is personalized in the sense that it "gives preference to the individual actors and human-interest angles in events while downplaying institutional and political considerations that establish the social contexts for those events" (p. 26). Similarly, the media seek out dramatic events and personalities to which viewers and readers can relate, rather than events and personalities that may be more politically significant though less glamorous and fascinating. The entertainment format of news forces it to be presented in unrelated bits and pieces rather than as a meaningful whole. As a result, news becomes a series of what Neil Postman (1985) has called "decontextualized facts," comparable to background music. Finally, information presented as news is filtered through traditional themes and images of the society, thereby assuring the viewer or reader of the merit of dominant institutions and discrediting challenges to them.

In short, although they may engage in social criticism, the mass media frame their presentations in a way that legitimizes the prevailing political economy. Although there is no blatant censorship of media content in the United States as there is in a totalitarian society, an implicit understanding exists on the part of the media elite regarding their role in upholding the status quo. Self-censorship by the media is reinforced when they anticipate the reactions of political and economic elites and alter their presentations in advance. At times, of course, more blatant attempts at censorship may arise, as when corporate advertisers exert direct pressure to influence the content of the media or when government elites pressure the media to "toe the line" (Gans, 1979). Although the media elite may resist these pressures, more often their ideological perspectives are fully compatible with those of political and economic elites, and they may therefore have little inclination to follow a path not basically in line with those views. Moreover, although the media commonly present opposing sides of social and political issues, the two perspectives are only narrowly divergent and the issues are presented in ideologically safe stereotypes. The irony of modern communications systems is that despite the profusion of messages with which the citizenry is bombarded daily, the absence of a thorough exploration of issues by the mass media results in an increasingly uninformed public.

It is also important to consider the essentially passive role of the citizenry in the communications system of most modern societies. In essence, political communication flows only in one direction. The media are virtually unchallenged by consumers. There is little effective feedback from those who read newspapers and especially from those who watch television. Thus, as Mills explained almost four decades ago, there is a growing tendency for mass media to be tools of manipulation rather than channels for the interchange of opinion: "In the primary public the competition of opinions goes on between people holding views in the service of their interests and their reasoning. But in the mass society of media markets, competition, if any, goes on between the manipulators with their mass media on the one hand, and the people receiving their propaganda on the other" (1956:305).

Although viewers and readers, as consumers, can choose not to buy a newspaper or watch a television program, the mass media operate in an oligopolistic market domestically and, increasingly, in an integrated international market. Hence, consumer choices are limited and, in the end, it is the producers—in this case the newspapers and television networks—who make critical decisions about the product and who exercise control over its supply and demand.

MEDIA EFFECTS

Concentrated media power, in the form of constricted ownership and control of content, does not necessarily guarantee to the users of the media—primarily government and big business—that the effects they desire, that is, public acceptance and internalization of their messages, will be produced. To what extent are the media effective in molding public opinion and shaping people's versions of political and social reality?

Although sociologists and communications experts are not certain about the precise effects of the mass media on socialization or how the media modify the influences of other socializers like the family and the school (Comstock, 1980; Gerbner, 1967), it appears that the media are becoming the chief means through which people construct their versions of social reality. Well before the advent of television, Walter Lippmann (1922) explained how the mass media, by selectively reporting and interpreting events and personalities, determine the pictures in our heads (stereotypes, as he referred to them) that shape our social worlds. With the predominance of television, this "reality-shaping" function of the mass media has become much more complete. Television serves increasingly in this capacity because few can escape its influence. Only sleep and work occupy more of Americans' time than television viewing. Most important, the mass media serve as the primary organs of political communication, setting the framework of public discourse, solidifying the legitimacy of powerful institutions and elites, and transmitting the society's dominant ideology.

The mediated version of social reality presented by television, newspapers, and other media is most evident in the communication of news. "News," as has been suggested, is hardly a complete or precise picture of societal or world events. Rather, it is a picture constructed by the media elite who select and interpret events, processes, and personalities. From an almost infinite number of happenings that occur each day, only a few are chosen for transmission as news.

Beyond the realm of our personal lives, the issues that concern us are therefore the issues defined for us by the media elite as important and worthy of our attention.

In the early years of research on the effects of mass media on public attitudes and beliefs, the prevalent view was that media had a direct and significant influence. Starting in the 1940s, research seemed to reverse this view, concluding instead that the power of the mass media had been exaggerated. The new perspective held that viewers and readers were not to be seen as a "mass," but rather as individual consumers whose interpretations of media presentations were modified by social class, ethnicity, religion, and other social variables (Lazarsfeld et al., 1948). People exposed themselves to the media selectively, it was suggested, so that media messages generally had the effect of simply reaffirming people's prior beliefs and views. V. O. Key (1964:357) warned against overestimating the effectiveness of the mass media in conveying the same messages to all people: "The flow of the messages of the mass media," he wrote, "is rather like dropping a handful of confetti from the rim of the Grand Canyon with the object of striking a man astride a burro on the canyon floor. In some measure chance determines which messages reach what targets." This "minimal-effects" view remains today among some media observers. Albert Gollin (1988:43), for example, has written that: "People bring to their encounters with the mass media a formidable array of established habits, motives, social values and perceptual defenses that screen out, derail the intent or limit the force of media messages. The media certainly do affect people in obvious and subtle ways. But no simple 1:1 relationship exists between content or intent and effects."

More recently, researchers have pointed out that the minimal-effects view was based on perceived changes, brought about by the media, in attitudes about political issues. What was overlooked, however, was the impact of mass media on creating a public *awareness* of issues. This has become known as the "agenda-setting function" of the mass media (McCombs and Shaw, 1972). Communications researchers have explained that although television and other mass media may not be overly effective in telling us *what* to think, they are extremely effective in telling us what and whom to think *about* (Shaw and McCombs, 1977; Iyengar and Kinder, 1987). Issues emphasized by the media become the issues regarded by viewers and readers as significant. As the media shift their emphasis to new issues, public perceptions change correspondingly. Moreover, Iyengar and Kinder (1987) have suggested a kind of media power that goes one step beyond agenda setting, which they call "priming." Priming refers to changes in the standards that people use in making political choices and judgments. As news, especially television news, shifts its attention from one issue to another, governments and political leaders are judged on their performance regarding those issues. Thus, by drawing attention to some aspects of political life at the expense of others, television helps bring to mind certain bits of political memory while others are ignored.

The mass media not only transmit descriptions of events and personalities but, more importantly, they convey the society's dominant ideology. It is in this sense that the media are agents of social control, used by power elites not only to communicate and legitimize their policies and actions but to stabilize the political and economic systems by generating allegiance among the public. As Todd Gitlin has explained:

> The media bring a manufactured public world into private space. From within their private crevices, people find themselves relying on the media for concepts, for images of their heroes, for guiding information, for emotional charges, for a recognition of public values, for symbols in general, even for language. Of all the institutions of daily life, the media specialize in orchestrating everyday consciousness—by virtue of their pervasiveness, their accessibility, their centralized symbolic capacity. They name the world's parts, they certify reality as reality—and when their certifications are doubted and opposed, as they surely are, it is those same certifications that limit the terms of effective opposition. To put it simply: the mass media have become core systems for the distribution of ideology (1980:1–2).

We should not assume that the presentation of news is the mass media's only way of creating support for the society's dominant ideology and institutions. In modern societies, news and public affairs represent only a small portion of all media fare, particularly of television. The remaining entertainment, and especially the advertising that constantly accompanies it, is no less reflective and supportive of the society's prevailing value system (Bagdikian, 1983; Goldsen, 1977; Parenti, 1986).

In recognizing the enormous power of mass media in modern societies to portray a particular version of reality, it should be understood that this is not consummate power. The ability of the media to propagate dominant values and shape political reality is by no means absolute. More specialized media (i.e., non–mass media), especially books and magazines, regularly present alternative and dissenting views. Moreover, dissident views are given coverage by the mass media once those views have gained at least some credibility. Nor can the media create problems that are nonexistent or conceal those that do exist (Iyengar and Kinder, 1987).

Acknowledging the less-than-total power of mass media to influence people's social and political worlds, however, should not lead to an underestimation of the power of this institution. In all modern societies, control of information is critical: Whoever controls the means of communication has great power. Marx posited that those who control the society's means of material production are the most powerful. It might be claimed that in modern societies, great power hinges on control of the means of information—the media. This is the reason that political and economic elites make great efforts to dominate the media and to control the flow of information. Those who exert significant control over the media or who can freely gain access to them are able to exercise great influence in determining the views, images, and ideas that will become part of the public consciousness.

REFERENCES

Bagdikian, Ben. 1971. *The Information Machines.* New York: Harper & Row.

———. 1983. *The Media Monopoly.* Boston: Beacon.

———. 1989. "Missing From the News," *The Progressive* 53 (August): 32–34.

Bennett, W. Lance. 1988. *News: The Politics of Illusion,* 2nd ed. New York: Longman.

Boorstin, Daniel J. 1961. *The Image: A Guide to Pseudo-Events in America.* New York: Harper & Row.

Cohen, Stanley, and Jock Young, eds. 1973. *The Manufacture of News.* London: Constable.

Comstock, George. 1980. "The Impact of Television on American Institutions." In Michael Emery and Ted Curtis Smythe, eds., *Readings in Mass Communication: Concepts and Issues in the Mass Media,* 4th ed. (pp. 28–44). Dubuque, Iowa: Wm. C. Brown.

Epstein, Edwin Jay. 1974. *News from Nowhere.* New York: Vintage.

Gans, Herbert J. 1979. *Deciding What's News.* New York: Pantheon.

Gerbner, G. 1967. "An Institutional Approach to Mass Communications Research." In L. Thayer, ed., *Communication: Theory and Research* (pp. 429–451). Springfield, Ill.: Charles C. Thomas.

Gitlin, Todd. 1980. *The Whole World Is Watching.* Berkeley: University of California Press.

Goldsen, Rose K. 1977. *The Show and Tell Machine: How Television Works and Works You Over.* New York: Dell.

Gollin, Albert E. 1988. "Media Power: On Closer Inspection, It's Not That Threatening." In Ray Eldon Hiebert and Carol Reuss, eds., *Impacts of Mass Media,* 2nd ed. (pp. 41–44). New York: Longman.

Herman, Edward S., and Noam Chomsky. 1988. *Manufacturing Consent: The Political Economy of the Mass Media.* New York: Pantheon.

Iyengar, Shanto, and Donald R. Kinder. 1987. *News That Matters: Television and American Opinion.* Chicago: University of Chicago Press.

Key, V. O., Jr. 1964. *Public Opinion and American Democracy.* New York: Knopf.

Lazarsfeld, Paul, Bernard Berelson, and H. Gaudet. 1948. *The People's Choice.* New York: Columbia University Press.

Lippmann, Walter. 1922. *Public Opinion.* New York: Macmillan.

McCombs, Maxwell, and Donald Shaw. 1972. "The Agenda-Setting Function of Mass Media," *Public Opinion Quarterly* 36:176–187.

Mills, C. Wright. 1956. *The Power Elite.* New York: Oxford University Press.

Paletz, David L., and Robert M. Entman. 1981. *Media Power Politics.* New York: Free Press.

Parenti, Michael. 1986. *Inventing Reality: The Politics of the Mass Media.* New York: St. Martin's.

Postman, Neil. 1985. *Amusing Ourselves to Death: Public Discourse in the Age of Show Business.* New York: Penguin.

Schiller, Herbert I. 1989. *Culture, Inc.: The Corporate Takeover of Public Expression.* New York: Oxford University Press.

Shaw, Donald L., and Maxwell E. McCombs. 1977. *The Emergence of American Political Issues: The Agenda-Setting Function of the Press.* St. Paul: West Publishers.

Sigal, Leon V. 1973. *Reporters and Officials: The Organization and Politics of News Reporting.* Lexington, Mass.: Heath.

Tuchman, Gaye. 1978. *Making News.* New York: Free Press.

Wright, Charles R. 1986. *Mass Communication: A Sociological Perspective,* 3rd ed. New York: Random House.

PART 4

Power and the State

Statelessness is a condition that characterizes only technologically simple societies with correspondingly simple divisions of labor. Political decisions are made and conflicts are resolved in those societies through family, kinship, or religious institutions rather than through the state. In modern societies, in contrast, the state is the dominant institution concerned with power and conflict.

NATURE OF THE STATE

In modern usage, the state is generally understood as that institution in society through which authority, or legitimate power, is exercised within a given territory. Definitions of the state vary among theorists, but in all cases, its uniqueness lies in its monopoly of the use of force to accomplish its objectives (Weber, 1968). The "state," however, should not be confused with "government," which, as Alford and Friedland (1985:1) have noted, is "merely the specific regime in power at any one moment—the governing coalition of political leaders." The state, then, transcends any particular group of political officials or bureaucrats and remains the basis of authority despite frequent changes in power personnel.

Michael Mann (1988) has suggested two types of state power: despotic and infrastructural. Despotic power is the power of the state to exert its will through the application of coercion, primarily through military and police force. This type of power has declined among states in modern societies, having been replaced by infrastructural power. Infrastructural power is the state's power to coordinate and influence all areas of social life, especially the distribution of economic resources, and at the same time provide for the protection of life and property. In performing these functions, the state becomes an increasingly centralized institution. Political authority rests with a relatively small set of coordinated elites who are supported by complex and far-reaching bureaucratic organizations.

Mann has pointed out that defining the state can be confounding because two dimensions can be analyzed: what the state *looks like* (the institutional dimension) and what the state *does* (the functional dimension). Both, of course, relate to the unique societal power of the state. In considering the structure and function of the state, sociological analysis can be reduced to four broad queries: (1) In whose interests does the state act? (2) Who influences and controls the state? (3) To what extent do the masses hold state leaders (political elites) accountable? and (4) How do states change?

In responding to these questions, political sociologists have put forth several sweeping theories, each of which has given rise to a number of specific variations. Those theories can be grouped under the three models of power described in Part 2. Although none would deny the prominence of the state as a locus of power at all levels of society, there is much disagreement among theorists and researchers regarding the power of the state relative to other institutions, especially the economy. Much of the theoretical and empirical literature, therefore, has concerned this issue.

THE MARXIAN PERSPECTIVE
ON THE STATE

Although not intended as a theory of the state per se, the model formulated by Marx and others who followed his general line of thought represents one of the most comprehensive explanations of the state and its power. The essence of the Marxian model is the overriding role of economic resources in determining the nature of the state and its influence on social life. According to Marx's model, the state, like all other institutions, is shaped by the society's mode of economic production. Because power flows most effusively from economic activities, those who control the means of production—the bourgeoisie in capitalist societies—also control the state. The state in capitalist societies becomes, in traditional Marxian parlance, a tool of the owners of capital. "The executive of the modern representative State," wrote Marx and Engels, "is but a committee for managing the common affairs of the whole bourgeoisie" (Tucker, 1972:337). Traditional Marxian theory is therefore unequivocal concerning who controls the state and in whose interests the state rules: The state is controlled by and acts in the interests of the productive property-owning class.

Traditional Marxian theorists hold that all politics is "class politics" in that owners and workers, the two major classes in modern society, are in conflict over the distribution of economic resources. The pursuit of power, therefore, is essentially a struggle for control of the means of production, the source of a society's economic wealth. Political power, as Marx and Engels put it, "is merely the organized power of one class for oppressing another" (Tucker, 1972:337). It is through class struggle, moreover, that political changes are effected. In capitalist societies, this struggle—if successful—will eventually result in victory by the workers, giving rise to a socialist state. With the establishment of socialism, the state continues to exist but acts in the interests of the proletariat. Later, with the creation of a communist classless society, the state will wither and eventually disappear.

Undoubtedly the most important idea in the traditional Marxian model of the state is the notion of political economy—the meshing of the state and economy in both structure and function. To fully understand the power of the state and the actions of its officials, one must recognize it as an institution shaped fundamentally by the system of economic production and therefore by the dominant economic class. The state, therefore, is not an arbitrary enforcer of order among competing interest groups, nor is it an autonomous institution that acts on behalf of the society as a whole.

Contemporary neo-Marxian theorists have reexamined this traditional model of political power and more precisely analyzed the relationship of the dominant economic class to the shape and functions of the state. During the past several decades, three principal neo-Marxian conceptions of the state have emerged: the instrumental, structural, and state-autonomy theses.

The instrumentalist view, stated most clearly by Ralph Miliband (1969), maintains that the dominant economic class does not directly rule in the sense that its members actually function as state officials but that it rules indirectly by controlling those officials. The state functions "in terms of the instrumental exercise of power by people in strategic positions, either directly through the manipulation of state policies or indirectly through the exercise of pressure on the state" (Gold, Lo, and Wright, 1975:34). Neo-Marxian theorists who espouse this perspective have analyzed the close functional and social relations that exist among members of the corporate elite and the political elite (Mills, 1956; Mintz, 1975; Useem, 1984).

The structural view, which is closely associated with Nicos Poulantzas (1973), contends that close working relations between corporate and state elites are not necessary for the state to act in the interests of the capitalist class. Rather, the basic structure of the political economy dictates that those interests will be served by the state. Because the society is so thoroughly dependent on the functioning of the economy, state officials must act to protect the economic system and, in so doing, serve the ends of those who own and control the majority of the society's productive wealth (Block, 1977; Poulantzas, 1973). Indeed, state leaders may at times act to protect capitalist interests more effectively than capitalists themselves. Because the capitalist class is internally divided, the state assumes the function of protecting broad capitalist interests. The state, therefore, exercises some autonomous power that transcends particular segments of the capitalist class.

The instrumental and structural perspectives agree that the state in modern capitalist societies usually facilitates the accumulation of capital. By sponsoring investment, subsidizing industries, and providing services such as education whose benefits redound to the corporate class, the state intervenes in economic life in countless ways. In this process, it contributes to perpetuating the unequal distribution of property and wealth. As Miliband (1969:78) has written, capitalist enterprise "depends to an ever greater extent on the bounties and direct support of the state, and can only preserve its 'private' character on the basis of such public help." This capital accumulation role of the state is especially important in modern corporate-dominated economies like that of the United States; it enables the state to maintain partial autonomy from the dominant economic institutions. Alan Wolfe has argued, however, that the capital accumulation function of the state in advanced capitalist societies constitutes a fundamental contradiction with the expectations of ordinary citizens that the state will promote economic and political democracy. In attempting to resolve this contradiction, the state is assigned "a wide variety of mythic powers," which Wolfe has referred to as the "reification of the state" (1977:279). The fundamental contradiction remains unresolved, however.

The state autonomy view, which has been propounded most extensively by Theda Skocpol (1979, 1981), holds that the state functions as a relatively independent institution in society and is not necessarily linked with the economy. Skocpol refutes the conventional Marxian notion that the state is shaped by and functions on behalf of a society's dominant class, arguing instead that the state has both power resources and interests that do not depend on the dominant economic class. She has suggested that the state gains further autonomy through its conflicts with other states within the international political system. Rather than viewing the state as a reflection of class interests, she contends that the state is an independent social institution that may find itself in conflict not only with other states but with different classes within its society, including even the dominant class. Skocpol calls her theory "realist," refusing to accept the idea of the state as merely a creation of a society's mode of production and its attendant class relations. States, in her view, "are actual organizations controlling (or attempting to control) territories and people" (Skocpol, 1979:31).

Although the traditional Marxian and the three neo-Marxian perspectives on the state differ in many ways, the general Marxian framework remains the most discerning and cohesive conceptualization of the state and societal power. It has generated far more extensive and detailed theoretical analysis than either the elitist or pluralist perspectives on the state. Moreover, both of those viewpoints have essentially been responses to the Marxian model.

THE ELITIST PERSPECTIVE ON THE STATE

Elite theorists, like Marxian theorists, recognize the concentrated nature of state power but do not see it as a function of economic power. Instead, elite theory has traditionally viewed social power as an outcome of control of organizations. In this view, power is exercised by elites who control the vast bureaucratic organizations that dominate all activities within a society. In modern societies, the state and its attendant organizations are the most important loci of power.

As societies industrialize, they create what Max Weber called "legal-rational authority," so that power wielding is based on formalized standard procedures. Rationalized systems of power typify all large organizations, making them quite functionally efficient. The leaders of these organizations, however, are able to mobilize vast resources and control the actions of all subordinate members. As the state becomes bureaucratized it also becomes highly centralized, exercising power throughout virtually every sphere of societal life. Consequently, the most critical source of power in modern societies is control over the state's vast bureaucratic organizations. As was seen in Part 2, modern elite theory centers on the state and the powerful elites who control it.

Elite theory views ordinary citizens as having virtually no ability to influence the state. The classical elite theorists—Mosca, Pareto, and Michels—and more recent theorists in this tradition—for example, Mills (1956) and Domhoff (1971)—have all seen state leaders as relatively insular and rarely influenced by other members of society. Mills described the majority of the American population as a "mass" that has been increasingly deprived of influence by the remoteness of the power elite as well as by the ability of the elite to manipulate political thought and action through the mass media.

The bureaucratic structure of modern states also creates a natural barrier to mass influence. Familiar expressions such as "red tape" and "bureaucratic maze" reflect the inability of citizens to penetrate state organizations and to have any meaningful effect upon them. Elites who head public bureaucracies are not only far removed from citizens, but they also erect structural barriers that make them immune to public control.

The elite perspective, therefore, views the state as acting fundamentally in the interests of powerful organizations and individuals in the society. The state's leaders interact only with heads of other major institutions, producing a centralized coordinated power structure. Disagreements among elite theorists concern primarily the relation of state elites to those in other institutions, particularly the economy, and the relative cohesion of the elite structure.

THE PLURALIST PERSPECTIVE ON THE STATE

In contrast to both Marxian and elitist perspectives, the pluralist perspective posits that the state in modern democratic societies acts essentially as an impartial clearinghouse for resolving disputes among contending interest organizations and social institutions. Its major function, in other words, is to negotiate and mediate among all other components of the society, enabling contending interests to come together and play out their competing power dynamics. The state is neither a representative of one particular class, as in Marxian theory, nor a relatively impermeable and remote set of leaders and organizations, as in the elite view. It is, rather, an impartial arbiter among competing pressure groups. It provides a set of rules and a playing field upon which organizations representing diverse interests and goals can exchange power resources.

Pluralists view the state as the major institution through which societal power flows, but they contend that the state has no interests of its own, serving only to referee conflicts among competing interests. Nor does the state represent any particular segment of society. In addition, citizens are able to maintain control over state leaders, at least indirectly, through elections and interest-group activity. According to the pluralist perspective, the separation of governmental powers among a number of different branches, agencies, and divisions further assures that no single set of state elites can dominate the government.

OVERVIEW OF SELECTIONS

The first selection in Part 4, by Robert Alford, presents a summary of the three theoretical perspectives on the state: Marxian, elitist, and pluralist. The other chapters all reflect the predominance of Marxist-oriented theories of the state in contemporary sociology. Gold, Lo, and Wright discuss the three major neo-Marxian conceptions of the state. The chapter by Miliband is perhaps the seminal statement of the instrumentalist view. Wolfe holds an essentially structural view of the state, emphasizing its fundamental contradiction with the ideal of political democracy. Block presents a revision of the structural model, arguing that the state maintains some autonomy as it functions to protect the capitalist economy. Finally, the state autonomy thesis is more fully developed by both Skocpol and Mann.

REFERENCES

Alford, Robert R., and Roger Friedland. 1985. *Powers of Theory: Capitalism, the State, and Democracy*. Cambridge: Cambridge University Press.

Block, Fred. 1977. "The Ruling Class Does Not Rule: Notes on the Marxist Theory of the State," *Socialist Review* 7 (May–June): 6–28.

Domhoff, G. William. 1971. *The Higher Circles*. New York: Vintage.

Gold, David A., Clarence Y.H. Lo, and Erik Olin Wright. 1975. "Recent Developments in Marxist Theories of the Capitalist State," *Monthly Review* 27 (October): 29–43.

Mann, Michael. 1988. *States, War and Capitalism*. New York: Basil Blackwell.

Miliband, Ralph. 1969. *The State in Capitalist Society*. New York: Basic Books.

Mills, C. Wright. 1956. *The Power Elite*. New York: Oxford University Press.

Mintz, Beth. 1975. "The President's Cabinet, 1897–1972: A Contribution to the Power Structure Debate," *Insurgent Sociologist* 5(Spring): 131–148.

Poulantzas, Nicos. 1973. *Political Power and Social Classes*. London: New Left Books and Sheed and Ward.

Skocpol, Theda. 1979. *States and Social Revolutions*. Cambridge: Cambridge University Press.

_____ . 1981. "Political Response to Capitalist Crisis: Neo-Marxist Theories of the State and the Case of the New Deal," *Politics and Society* 10: 155–201.

Tucker, Robert C., ed. 1972. *The Marx-Engels Reader*. New York: Norton.

Useem, Michael. 1984. *The Inner Circle*. New York: Oxford University Press.

Weber, Max. 1968. *Economy and Society: An Outline of Interpretive Sociology*, ed. and trans. by Guenther Roth and Claus Wittich. New York: Bedminster Press.

Wolfe, Alan. 1977. *The Limits of Legitimacy: Political Contradictions of Contemporary Capitalism*. New York: Free Press.

22

Paradigms of Relations Between State and Society

ROBERT R. ALFORD

Three paradigms of the relations between the state and the society in industrialized capitalist democracies can be labeled *pluralist, elite,* and *class.* ... [T]he three paradigms focus upon distinct social and political forces that shape the state and legitimate its actions: individuals and groups for the pluralist paradigm, bureaucratic organizations for the elite paradigm, and social classes for the class paradigm. ... [E]ach paradigm gains its explanatory power by focusing upon a particular context of action—a situational context within which individuals and groups choose to mobilize to influence political decisions, for the pluralist paradigm; an organizational context within which bureaucracies deploy their resources, for the elite paradigm; and a societal context within which social classes shape institutions that reinforce their rule, for the class paradigm. ...

THREE PARADIGMS OF THE STATE

The *pluralist* paradigm assumes that diverse groups and interests intermittently present demands to political parties and other elite coalitions that in turn aggregate and represent those demands to leaders and officials. The state comprises a mosaic of agencies and organizations, each of which is an institutionalized response to the historic sequence of demands and responses by elites to those demands. Through a complicated process of political, social, and economic competition, these demands are filtered or screened in order to define the essential commitments and goals of the various components of the state. The highest level of authorities—political leaders and statesmen—mediate and compromise between those demands that attain the visibility and level of support to warrant reaching the level of authority that can make binding decisions. The issues entering the political arena for decision are relatively limited in number, scope, and intensity because they occur within the narrow boundaries of a fundamental consensus among all social groups on basic values and the institutions embodying those values. Power is held by those who win in a particular struggle within the legitimate political arena.

In the pluralist view the state is not a single "bureaucracy" but a multiplicity of overlapping jurisdictions, each competing for more resources—manpower, functions, and money. Each is linked to a public and private constituency and seeks to broaden its constituency to the maximum degree while simultaneously retaining maximum autonomy.

In the pluralist paradigm bureaucratic organizations are assumed to be ultimately responsive to a clientele, controlling agency, or democratic political process. If such organizations act in ways that seriously violate popular or elite expectations of justice, equality, and freedom, they will be forced to change in the long run. Social classes in the pluralist paradigm are assumed to be one of many clusters of interests in the society, with more political resources than some groups, but counterbalanced by the adult franchise and capacity of minorities to mobilize public opinion and influence political elites, even in the absence of decisive majority support.

The *elite* paradigm assumes that large-scale complex organizations tend to form in almost every sphere of social life in these societies: factories, universities, government agencies, labor unions, and political parties. All interest groups, in order to have an impact in such a bureaucratized society, must themselves reach some threshold of size, homogeneity, and organizational capability, or else they will be helpless. Unorganized groups must thus be represented by organized ones. The combination of expertise, hierarchical control, and the capacity to allocate human, technological, and material resources gives the elites of bureaucratic organizations power not easily restrained by the mechanisms of pluralistic competition and debate. The competition between organizational elites is held to be, if not the hallmark, then at least an essential requirement for democratic politics in societies dominated by industrial and political bureaucracies. Power is held by those who hold dominant positions within the organizations that control key resources.

In the elite paradigm the pluralistic diversity of social groups and demands is assumed to result in a political arena in which few decisions of real consequence for the structure of power are made. Social classes in the elite paradigm are assumed to be a crucial base of power for certain elites, but have lost their independent control over both the economy and the state because of the emergence of a social stratum possessing expertise and managerial skill that are functionally required for such a society. The state is thus seen as a cluster of large-scale organizations, each based upon a separate institutional sector, the elites of which have come to manipulate and control their political base, not the other way around.

The *class* paradigm views neither the debates and decisions occurring in pluralistic political arenas nor the battles of organizational elites to maintain their control over material and human resources as exhausting the crucial facts about the relations between the state and the society. Both group interests and organizational elites are operating within a framework of economic appropriation and cultural hegemony that seldom challenges the principles defining the basic structure of the society. These principles guarantee the continued disproportionate allocation of the social product as well as its control to a relatively small portion of the population of the society that constitutes the "ruling class." Power is held by those classes benefiting from the structure of society in a given historical period.

In the class paradigm a pluralistic diversity of social groups representing a wide variety of interests and values is real but relatively unimportant since the issues and demands that arise seldom challenge the basic institutional framework. The "consensus" applauded by the pluralists as preventing "demand overload" is, in this view, a manifestation of the cultural domination of intellectual and political life by ideas and attitudes congruent with the maintenance of that institutional framework. Bureaucratization in the class paradigm is a technological requirement for the necessary coordination and administration of a class society, but seldom, if ever, do the elites manning bureaucracies challenge the premises of the institutional allocation of the social product.

To summarize, within the *pluralist* paradigm the core function of the state is to achieve *consensus* and thus social order through continuous exchanges of demands and responses by social groups and government and a continuous sequence of bargaining processes. Within the *elite* paradigm the core function of the state is the maintenance of *domination* by existing elites. Within the *class* paradigm the core function of the state is the reproduction and management of existing class relationships, via both formal processes (the operations of courts, police, army, administrative and legislative agencies) and informal processes (socialization within schools and family to accept the limits of political participation and political action as inevitable, pragmatic, and even desirable).

UTOPIAN AND PATHOLOGICAL IMAGES

Each paradigm has both a utopian and a pathological image of state-society relationships, and each has both empirical (predictive) and normative (ideological) aspects.

The utopian image of the pluralist paradigm might be called *pluralist democracy*. Groups can freely form within the larger society and have open access to authoritative bodies to express their interests and values and seek support for them. The political process as a whole consists of a moving equilibrium of demands and responses, resulting in a gradual evolution toward a more just, more humane, more equalitarian society. No group has a dominant role in the society as a whole.

The pathological variant might be called *mass society*. Groups have lost their capacity to act as intermediaries between their members and other groups, to soften the demands of their members, or to negotiate reasonable bargains with other groups. As a result, some groups present unrestrained demands upon other groups and upon the leaders of the largest group of all, the society. The societal leaders become unable to mediate or negotiate effectively between the groups, and the "rules of the game" governing the bargaining process break down. The pluralist paradigm, being a model essentially of the "normal" processes of group formation and representation, cannot deal with these pathological developments except to criticize them from a normative perspective.

The elite paradigm also has its utopian and pathological images. Its utopian image might be called the *planned society*. In such a society elites are not so bound by the short-term demands of the groups that keep them in office or in power that they cannot develop long-range rational planning of the direction of investment of the social resources that they command. The elites of the many giant organizations that dominate the society are responsible and farsighted enough to realize that they must coordinate their activities with others and work out arrangements for the orderly exchange of needed personnel, services, and other resources because they realize that they are dependant upon each other in the long run, regardless of how competitive they may be in the short run. Thus, the elites of various organizations cooperate in supporting the overall development of societal resources that benefits them all: education, science, technology, transportation, health care. These resources are sometimes to be developed by the state and sometimes by private action, depending upon the most rational use of social resources. Through the coordinated activity of these elites, economic growth continues, and basic group demands are met.

The pathological image is *totalitarianism*. The top elites lose any effective sanctions over their behavior, and they begin to act in such a way as to maximize the benefits accruing either to them personally or to their organization, rather than to work together with other elites. Also, they begin to manipulate the opinions and preferences of mass publics in order to maintain their own control. In the extreme case this manipulation takes the form of outright repression and terror and use of police or military force against any attempts to replace them. Within the elitist paradigm it is very difficult for elites who have attained this degree of control to be overthrown (this is almost Max Weber's image of "normal" bureaucracy), and it is only counter-elites who have even this potential. The best safeguard against elitist totalitarianism is thus the maintenance of a system of competitive elites. Mass democracy is merely utopian in an era when the society is basically controlled by giant corporations, and decisions are inevitably made by relatively few people because of the lack of interest and information among the mass electorate about the complex and technical grounds of decision making.

The class paradigm also has utopian and pathological images. The utopian image is *anarchism*. The enormous productive capacity of a capitalist society is assumed to be convertible to rational human uses instead of being consumed by military production, advertising, packaging, useless commodities, and the various social expenditures such as those on police and television that may be necessary to mystify and control a population potentially aware of alternative possibilities. It assumes that a complex division of labor based on advanced technology can be based on rational knowledge and thus consent, not authority and domination. It assumes that the common interests of the entire society can be translated into resource investments without requiring either a structure of authority relationships—with the problems of selecting and training elites associated with such structures—or a diversity of specialized interest groups whose needs and demands would necessitate some structure of participation, representation, and access to ultimate decision makers. This is the classic image of a communist society and is essentially an anarchist image of a simultaneously decentralized and cooperative society.

The pathological image of the class paradigm is *fascism*. In such a society the ruling class, no longer capable of maintaining its rules through the peaceful political processes of parliamentary debate and electoral competition, resorts either to repression of dissent and organized opposition by various techniques— wiretapping, bribery, legal harassment, agents provocateurs, co-optation or intimidation of opponents—or to open abolition of representative institutions. More subtly, the political culture is manipulated by symbolic distortions of events through the mass media to turn, in Orwellian language, repression into law and order and defeats into victories—resulting first in popular revulsion, then depoliticization, and finally apathy, all dubbed consensus and mass support.

THE STRATEGIC FOCUS OF EACH PARADIGM

Aside from its political and ideological content, each paradigm can be regarded as an analytic strategy allowing a focus upon what are assumed to be key relationships, ignoring other factors. The class, elite, and pluralist paradigms identify societal, organizational, and situational contexts of action, respectively. The pluralist paradigm focuses upon the conditions of mobilization of particular groups and individuals for political action and upon the strategies of influence and the outcomes of action in particular situations. As already noted, power is defined as the winner in a pluralist combat between potentially equal opponents. The elite paradigm focuses upon the stable coalitions of resources in organizations manned by elites and emphasizes the limited range of possible decisions within the organizational parameters. Power is defined as the long-range capacity to deploy organizational resources. The class paradigm focuses upon the basic institutions of property and the objective class relations arising from those institutions. Power is held by those who continuously benefit from the functioning of those institutions, regardless of what their particular structural forms are or who makes decisions within them.

The explanatory power generated by focusing upon a particular context of action is gained at the cost of neglecting certain questions. Because these definitions of state-society relations are paradigms and not merely models or theories, each tends to explain away the independence of the phenomena of central concern to the other paradigms or to subsume them under its core concepts and variables.

The pluralist paradigm neglects some important questions: First, the origins of those "preferences" (interests and values) of individuals that lead them to form groups: These are essentially taken as given, and their historical or institutional origins are not problematic. Second, the sources of inequalities in the basic resources or capabilities of groups to act in defense of their core interests or values: No inherent institutional or resource barriers to the formation of any groups are assumed to exist if potential members have some felt interests or values in common. Third, the extent to which groups are actually created and then sustained by the actions of other groups, or by institutions at the level of the society as a whole, mainly the state: The voluntaristic image of group creation neglects the extent to which positive legal or political action at higher levels actually generates social groups.

The elite paradigm also ignores some questions that are crucial to the other paradigms. First, because it assumes that the structures of power commanded by elites have become severed from their possible origins in group demands and needs, it tends to ignore the concrete social and economic interests actually served by bureaucratic organizations. The maintenance of power and domination by elites is seen as having become an end in itself, and the consequences of elite decisions and policies for social groups and classes tend to be slighted. Second, the differences in power of different bureaucratic organizations are neglected. Because the focus tends to be upon separate organizations with relations between them defined as exchanges of resources, rather than upon the consequences of the operation of the bureaucratic organizations for specific social groups, the social origins of the differences in the amount of resources and what they are used for tends not to be analyzed. Third, the origin of bureaucracies in past critical decisions and outcomes of social conflicts is not seen as an analytic problem. Once in existence, giant organizations become social actors, but their origins in past conflicts as attempts by social groups or social classes to solve their problems or to establish a claim upon a part of the social product tend to be neglected.

Thus, both the pluralist and class paradigms would criticize the elite paradigm for artificially isolating giant organizations—whether corporations, trade unions, universities, or government agencies—from their social milieu or context. The pluralist paradigm sees organizations as arising from and representing the legitimate needs of social groups; the class paradigm sees organizations as attempts by segments of social classes to defend their interests within the range of possibilities and limits imposed by a given set of class relations and type of productive system.

The class paradigm also fails to deal with some important questions. First, the extent of social and cultural diversity within classes is played down, although this class heterogeneity may have decisive implications for the potential for class consciousness, solidarity, and conflict. Second, the persistence of authority relationships and the requirements of hierarchical and disciplined organization of labor under conditions of high technology and industrial production are minimized, if not ignored. If these requirements are not in fact simply an epiphenomenon of capitalism, but are endemic to industrial organization, both the image of the future society and the means to get there would have to change sharply. Third, the problem of stable representation of diverse group interests is neglected or simply assumed to be easily solvable, once the fundamental distortions resulting from class rule are done away with. However, even given a productive system capable of meeting everyone's basic needs, there would still have to be mechanisms for articulating, representing, mediating, and ultimately deciding between alternative forms and modes of satisfying human needs. These potential modes of participation and response are neglected in the class paradigm.

Each paradigm has a tendency to claim more explanatory power than it possesses and to extend the domain of its concepts to answer those questions it is actually unable to deal with. For example, the pluralist paradigm sometimes collapses the societal and organizational contexts of action into the situational context, regarding no causal factor as being important if it is not reflected in overt, current behavior. This occurs when class hegemony over the definition of public versus private spheres of activity, for example, is regarded as a cultural consensus, manifest in an acceptance of the limits of action by all participants in the political arena. This also occurs when organizational dominance over key resources such as money, personnel, and legality is regarded as only an attribute of individuals who choose whether or not to use their resources. In such instances the historically developed societal and organizational constraints upon action are denied as such or are reinterpreted as cultural values internalized by actors. In the pluralist paradigm the potent analytic emphasis upon the contingencies of action in the *present*, the varying motives of actors, and the widely varying probabilities of different outcomes can thus become a way of concealing organizational and societal constraints.

Similarly, the class paradigm can lead to a merging of the three levels or contexts of action if it is assumed that class interests are always perfectly reflected in class organizations, which in turn always act in ways that serve underlying and long-range class interests. The reputational school in the study of community power, for example, comes close to assuming that discovery of a banker sitting on a city council is not only evidence of his personal interests and motives (as the pluralists would conclude), but also evidence for the power of the banks as organizations and even for the power of the capitalist class in the society.

METHODOLOGICAL IMPLICATIONS

Two sets of methodological implications can be drawn from the previous argument, suggesting either an additive or an interaction model of relations between different levels of social organization. In the additive model, individual, organizational, and societal levels are not perfectly correlated with each other. An important element of contingency or "slippage" exists between these levels, each of which is causally important and cannot be reduced to the others. This independence provides each paradigm with its explanatory potential within its own level or context.

The variance in the predictability of the behavior of historically specific, concrete actors, even within similar class and organizational contexts, gives the pluralist paradigm its independent analytic potential. The elite paradigm derives its independent analytic potential from the narrow range of possible alternatives for action once a set of organizations and their elites exists, and because the class relations in a society do not absolutely determine the possible forms or mode of organization of political parties, trade unions, legal structure, etc. Because neither pluralist combat nor elite domination frequently challenges the underlying class relations of production in a given capitalist society, and because the actions of the state can plausibly be interpreted as reinforcing those relationships, the class paradigm also has independent analytic potential.

Using an additive model, each level of "structure" sets limits upon the other levels, but does not completely determine structures within them. That is, the class structure of a society sets broad limits upon the types of organizations that can easily arise and those that are deterred, fought, or opposed by economic, legal, and political power. However, one cannot predict from the fundamental character of the class structure the particular array of organizations that will exist in a given historical period: political parties, a particular form of state agency. Nor can one predict the life history and internal dynamics of those organizations; they behave according to "laws" of organizations, not of societies. Nor can one predict the ways organizations will act in particular situations or the ways individuals within groups will act. The organizational structure of a society in a given period sets broad limits upon the kinds of situations that are likely to arise, but does not predetermine the outcome of those situations.

Thus, within an additive model of the three paradigms, a pluralist paradigm is a powerful tool for analyzing the situational context of action and the conditions of mobilization of individuals and groups to influence particular political decisions within a framework of a cultural consensus. The elite paradigm provides a means for understanding the structures of power of complex organizations constituting the state and their bargains, exchanges of resources, personnel, and impact on general policies that set the parameters for particular decisions. The class paradigm enables us to understand the limits of policy formation and of the state structure within the class relations of a given society. The translation of class interests (or a cultural consensus) into organizational form and then into action is problematic and contingent, as are the consequences of specific actions and events that may challenge and change only particular decisions in some circumstances, the structure of organizations under other conditions, and the general structure of social relations under other conditions.

This formulation contains, however, an unresolved ambiguity in the possible relations between these "levels." If each level of structure sets limits on the other levels but does not completely constrain their internal relations, then the relationships between levels are additive. That is, social class variables affect some organizational variables, and both organizational and class variables affect some situational variables. Social class variables do not affect the relations among the organizational variables, nor do class and organizational variables affect the relations among situational variables. If these conditions in fact hold empirically, then legitimate grounds exist for analyzing the three levels in isolation. Although an isolated analysis results in only a partial view of the system, the results can at least be generalized to similar parts of other systems.

However, an interaction model can be specified starting from any of the paradigms. Within the class paradigm the internal relations within organizations change as the class structure changes, and political situations become fundamentally different if both the elite/organizational structures and the class structure change.

Within the pluralist paradigm a change of political circumstances and situations alerts the outcomes of action not merely temporarily, or within the confines of an overdetermined set of structural relationships, but permanently, and the probabilities of such contingent outcomes cannot be predicted from a knowledge of organizational and class structures. From this viewpoint the diversity, complexity, and variation between empirical situations of action produce a prediction of intense interaction effects from the other "direction" than that which the class paradigm predicts. The complex combination of situational factors changing almost from moment to moment produces gross consequences not predictable from knowledge of structure.

The degree of independence of the three different levels is not a question that can or should be resolved by sheer assertion or theoretical assumption but is ultimately an empirical question to be addressed by systematic comparative studies that include variations in each level as part of the research design. The additive model hypothesizes that the internal relations between variables is the same at different levels although the probability for the occurrence of conditions under which those variables will be found together may differ, depending on the context. The interaction model hypothesizes that not only will the probability of the variables occurring together differ, but also the correlations between them will be sharply different, even reversed.

To settle the claim of each paradigm to be a truly general description and explanation of state-society relations in these types of societies may require an interaction model of the relations between levels of analysis. If pluralism is a valid general theory and not just a set of decision rules for analysis of specific political situations and decisions, then organizations and classes, regarded by the other paradigms (under certain historical conditions) as homogeneous social and political actors, are really temporary coalitions of diverse groups and individuals held together by a fragile consensus and a set of beliefs that successfully cause them to act as a coalition. That is, the apparent unity of resources and interests that we label an "organization" or a "class" is actually created by the successful strategies of elites and leadership and has no "structural" reality. Conversely, if class theory is valid generally, then the apparent diversity of individual and group interests conceals an underlying logic of an institutional structure that imposes similar principles of action upon all components of the society, and in fact the surface diversity and complexity may be highly functional in legitimating and reproducing a given set of class relations. ...

23

Marxist Theories of the Capitalist State

DAVID A. GOLD, CLARENCE Y.H. LO,
& ERIK OLIN WRIGHT

While Marxists have always had much to say about the state, it has only been fairly recently that the creation of a theory of the state has been considered an explicit task. Recent attempts at theorizing have drawn heavily on conceptualizations of the state that were largely implicit in earlier work. Three such implicit perspectives, which may be characterized as the instrumentalist, the structuralist, and the Hegelian-Marxist traditions, have been especially important in guiding current Marxist work on the state. ...

This paper will focus first on the traditional approaches. While, as we shall argue below, there is no necessary incompatibility among these various strands of thinking, many Marxists have treated them as quite irreconcilable, and much of the recent work on the state has taken the form of a polemic against one or another alternative perspective. It will therefore be useful, as a point of departure, to lay out the basic logic of these orientations. This discussion will be followed by an explication and brief analysis of some of the recent developments that have attempted to move beyond the more traditional frameworks. We will conclude with some general remarks on theoretical work that remains to be done.

THE TRADITIONS

Very few Marxist works on the state can be considered pure examples of an instrumentalist, structuralist, or Hegelian-Marxist perspective. The logic behind identifying a theoretical perspective as structuralist, instrumentalist, or Hegelian-Marxist is not to imply that every statement which it contains can be neatly pigeonholed into a single category. The point is that in any theory certain parts are systematically organized and integrated into a coherent set of propositions whereas other parts have more the status of ad hoc amendments. What we mean, therefore, by an "instrumentalist theory" of the state is a theory in which the ties between the ruling class and state are systematically examined, while the structural context within which those ties occur remains largely theoretically unorganized. A "structuralist theory," in a complementary way, systematically elaborates how state policy is determined by the contradictions and constraints of the capitalist system, while instrumental manipulation remains a secondary consideration. Finally, a "Hegelian-Marxist theory" places its emphasis on consciousness and ideology, while the link to accumulation and instrumental manipulation stays in the background.

Regardless of which of these traditions is drawn upon most heavily, virtually all Marxist treatments of the state begin with the fundamental observation that the state in capitalist society broadly serves the interests of the capitalist class. Marx and Engels stated this premise in its classic form in *The Communist Manifesto*: "The executive of the modern state is but a committee for managing the common affairs of the whole burgeoisie."

Given this axiom, Marxist theories of the state generally attempt to answer two complementary questions: "*Why* does the state serve the interests of the capitalist class?" and "*How* does the state function to maintain and expand the capitalist system?" But while Marxist works on the state have generally shared these underlying questions, they have dealt with them with varying degrees of sophistication, have formulated them at different levels of abstraction and with different methodological principles, and have given considerably different emphases to one or the other.

INSTRUMENTALIST THEORIES OF THE STATE

The instrumentalist perspective provides a fairly straightforward answer to the question, "Why does the state serve the interests of the capitalist class?" It does so because it is controlled by the capitalist class. Ralph Miliband (1969: 22) expresses this position clearly:

> In the Marxist scheme, the "ruling class" of capitalist society is that class which owns and controls the means of production and which is able, by virtue of the economic power thus conferred upon it, to use the state as its instrument for the domination of society.

... The research agenda associated with this perspective has focused primarily on studying the nature of the class which rules, the mechanisms which tie this class to the state, and the concrete relationships between state policies and class interests. The method consists of detailed studies of the sociology of the capitalist class, in the first instance simply to show that it exists; studies of the direct personal links between this class and the state apparatus, and links between the capitalist class and intermediary institutions (such as political parties, research organizations, and universities); specific examples of how government policy shaped; and reinterpretations of episodes from the annals of history. ...

While most of ... [Miliband's] analysis ... centers on the patterns and consequences of personal and social ties between individuals occupying positions of power in different institutional spheres, Miliband stresses that even if these personal ties were weak or absent—as sometimes happens when social democratic parties come to power—the policies of the state would still be severely constrained by the economic structure in which it operates. Furthermore, he moves away from a voluntaristic version of instrumentalism by stressing the social processes which mold the ideological commitments of the "state elite." Nevertheless, in spite of these elements in Miliband's work, the systematic aspect of his theory of the state remains firmly instrumentalist. ...

The functioning of the state is ... fundamentally understood in terms of the instrumental exercise of power by people in strategic positions, either directly through the manipulation of state policies or indirectly through the exercise of pressure on the state.

The instrumentalist perspective has made a number of important contributions to a Marxist theory of the state. It has generated much research that has helped to build a sociology of the capitalist class. In particular, it has contributed to piercing the veil of legitimacy that hangs over many of the specific institutions that systematically link the capitalist class to the state. Instrumentalist research has also been of great importance in bringing to light the conflicts that exist within the capitalist class. Such work has made a considerable contribution toward an understanding of the local basis of capitalist class power and of the interrelationships between local, regional, and national institutions of the capitalist class.

Despite these successes, the instrumentalist perspective has some major deficiencies which make it unsuitable as a general theory of the capitalist state. Much of the empirical work represents an explicit attempt to confront the conclusions of pluralists. While largely successful in such confrontations, this work has failed to transcend the framework that the pluralists use. The emphasis, especially in American power-structure research, has been on social and political groupings rather than classes defined by their relationship to the means of production. Furthermore, like most pluralists, instrumentalist writers tend to see social causes simply in terms of the strategies and actions of individuals and groups. While in pluralist theory there are many such groups, all working for their interests and influencing the state, in instrumentalist theory there is only one overwhelmingly dominant group. But the logic of social causation remains the same. With rare exceptions, there is no systematic analysis of how the strategies and actions of ruling-class groups are limited by impersonal, structural causes. At times the exercise of power and the formation of state policy seem to be reduced to a kind of voluntarism on the part of powerful people.

In a slightly different vein, there are numerous examples of state activity that appear not to fit even the sophisticated variants of instrumentalism. On a number of occasions, reforms undertaken by the state were opposed by large segments of the business community, as, for example, during the New Deal. Even when such reforms are ultimately co-optive, to treat all reforms as the result of an instrumentalist use of the state by capitalists is to deny the possibility of struggle over reform. There are also state policies which cannot easily be explained by direct corporate initiatives but which may come from within the state itself. These tend to speak to broad, rather than specific, capitalist interests. To explain these fully there is the need for a logic of the capitalist state, both in terms of its relations to civil society and in terms of its internal operations.

Finally, there are important realms of state-related activity which are clearly not manipulated by specific capitalists or coalitions, such as culture, ideology, and legitimacy. These possess a degree of autonomy which tends to place them outside the realm of simple manipulation. ...

STRUCTURALIST THEORIES OF THE STATE

The structuralist analysis of the state categorically rejects the notion that the state can be understood as a simple "instrument" in the hands of a ruling class. In a critique of the work of Miliband, Nicos Poulantzas, a French structuralist Marxist, wrote that:

> the *direct* participation of members of the capitalist class in the state apparatus and in the government, even where it exists, is not the important side of the matter. The relation between the bourgeois class and the state is an *objective relation*. This means that if the *function* of the state in a determinate social formation and the *interests* of the dominant class in this formation coincide, it is by reason of the system itself: the direct participation of members of the ruling class in the state apparatus is not the *cause* but the *effect*, and moreover a chance and contingent one, of this objective coincidence (1969: p. 245).

The fundamental thesis of the structuralist perspective is that the functions of the state are broadly determined by the structures of the society rather than by the people who occupy positions of state power. Therefore, the starting point of the structuralist analysis is generally an examination of the class structure in the society, particularly the contradictions rooted in the economy. Structuralists then analyze how the state attempts to neutralize or displace these various contradictions. The structuralist theory of the state thus attempts to unravel the functions the state must perform in order to reproduce capitalist society as a whole. These functions determine the specific policies and organization of the state. According to the structuralists, the concrete ways in which the state meets the functions vary with such factors as the level of capitalist development and the forms of class struggle.

The most elaborate structuralist-Marxist model of the state is presented by Poulantzas, especially in his book *Political Power and Social Classes*. Following Marx, Poulantzas argues that in capitalist society the crucial economic contradiction centers on the ever-increasing social character of production on the one hand and the continuing private appropriation of the surplus product on the other. This contradiction poses two complementary threats to the reproduction of the system as a whole. On the one hand, the contradiction between social production and private appropriation poses the threat of *working-class unity*, which becomes potentially stronger as the social nature of the production process deepens, and which eventually contains the possibility of the destruction of capitalism itself. On the other hand, this contradiction poses the threat of *capitalist-class disunity*, fostered by the continued private and competitive appropriation of surplus. This lack of unity threatens the ability of the capitalist class to contain struggles by the working class. The state plays the decisive role of mediating this contradiction, of providing the "factor of unity in a social formation" operating to counteract the combined threats of working-class unity and capitalist disunity.

Poulantzas analyzes this function of the capitalist state, the promotion of unity in a social formation, in terms of its impact on the working class and the capitalist class:

(a) *The working class*. The state serves the function of atomizing the working class, of disintegrating its political unity through the transformation of workers into individualized citizens while at the same time representing itself as the integrated, universal interest of the society as a whole. This is accomplished through the institutions of bourgeois democracy and justice, which create the appearance of equality, fair play, due process, etc., and through various kinds of economic concessions made by the state which help to transform the political struggle of the working class as a whole into narrow, economistic interest-group struggles of particular segments of the working class.

(b) *The capitalist class*. The state serves the function of guaranteeing the long-run interests of the capitalist class as a whole. Poulantzas stresses that the bourgeoisie cannot be considered a homogeneous ruling class with an unambiguous class-wide interest. Rather, the bourgeoisie is a highly fractionated class, with divergent interests as the political as well as economic levels. These diverse class fractions are organized into what Poulantzas (following Gramsci) calls the "power bloc," a political coalition under the domination of a particular hegemonic fraction. Such a power bloc, however, is always precarious, possessing only limited ability to enforce the concessions to the working class which are so necessary for the stability of the long-term interests of the capitalist class as a whole. The only way that these interests can be protected, therefore, is through the relative autonomy of the state, through a state structure which is capable of transcending the parochial, individualized interests of specific capitalists and capitalist class fractions. A state which was the tool of one capitalist grouping would be utterly incapable of accomplishing this.

This relative autonomy, however, is not an invariant feature of the capitalist state. Particular capitalist states will be more or less autonomous depending upon the degree of internal divisiveness, the contradictions within the various classes and fractions which constitute the power bloc, and upon the intensity of class struggle between the working class and the capitalist class as a whole.

The absence of any real discussion of how social mechanisms regulate these various functional relationships seriously weakens Poulantzas's structural analysis. Although there is a fairly rich discussion of *how* the relative autonomy of the state protects the class interests of the dominant class, and of the functional *necessity* for such a state structure, there is no explanation of the social mechanisms which guarantee that the state will in fact function in this way.

One obvious way out of this difficulty would be to employ some notion of "class consciousness." It could then be argued that class-conscious capitalists guide the development of state structures which accomplish the needed functional patterns. Structuralist writers, however, have almost completely rejected the usefulness of consciousness as an explanation for any aspect of social structure. They insist that class consciousness is a catch-all residual category used by Marxists to "explain" things that more systematic theory fails to resolve. Consciousness, the structuralists argue, explains nothing; the point is to explain consciousness through an analysis of the dynamics of society. But if class consciousness doesn't provide a way out, structuralists have not advanced any more suitable way to deal with these theoretical difficulties. While the instrumentalist perspective has tended toward voluntarism to explain state activities, the structuralists have almost entirely eliminated conscious action from their analysis. ...

HEGELIAN-MARXIST PERSPECTIVES

There are many Marxists who derive their primary inspiration from Hegel and the early writings of Marx and Engels, and more recently from Lukacs and writers such as Habermas, Marcuse, and others in the tradition of the Frankfurt School (or what is sometimes called "critical theory"). Instead of focusing on the *why* and *how* of the relationship between the state and the capitalist class, the Hegelian-Marxist perspective operates at a somewhat higher level of abstraction. The key question appears to be, "*What* is the state?" The basic answer is that the state is a mystification, a concrete institution which serves the interests of the dominant class, but which seeks to portray itself as serving the nation as a whole, thereby obscuring the basic lines of class antagonism. Thus, the state represents a universality, but a false one, an "illusory community."

Most of the writings in this perspective take off from this point and examine how the mystification occurs. They have placed great emphasis on ideology, consciousness, legitimacy, and the mediating role of institutions and ideas, thereby contributing significantly to current thinking on politics. However, the Hegelian-Marxist perspective has not developed a coherent theory of the state or even a well-defined logic of the relation between state and society. There is little analysis of specific states actions or concrete politics in these writings, so it is difficult to connect these ideas with an empirical reality. Perhaps because of this, the key notions of false consciousness and false ideology remain incomplete; it is unclear how and why they remain false when they are being continually confronted with the reality of daily life under capitalism.

Antonio Gramsci, who is difficult to classify within any one perspective, can be considered as one thinker emerging from the Hegelian-Marxist tradition who avoids the pitfalls of over-abstraction. Gramsci analyzed capitalist ideology both theoretically and empirically, studying cultural changes in Italy and America induced by changes in production relations. His theory of civil society and the state, and his concrete discussions of fascism and the collapse of political parties in interwar Europe are examples of a Marxist analysis that is developed in both the political-economic and ideological dimensions. "The southern Question," Gramsci's essay on the ideological and political factors that produce alliances between classes stands as a Marxist classic. Through his examination of the groups that could possibly support the interests of the industrial bourgeoisie of northern Italy, Gramsci developed the notion of "hegemony," a key concept in the analysis of capitalist domination through the state. His work has been an important influence on Poulantzas, among others, who has attempted to incorporate such political phenomena into a more systematic theory of capitalist society. ...

CONCLUDING REMARKS

A number of general propositions can be made which define the contours within which ... a general theory of the capitalist state might be developed. We offer these only as a preliminary formulation reflecting the current stage of our own thinking rather than as actual elements of a complete synthesis of the ideas discussed in this paper.

(1) The capitalist state must be conceived both as a structure constrained by the logic of the society within which it functions and as an organization manipulated behind the scenes by the ruling class and its representatives. *The extent to which actual state policies can be explained through structural or instrumental processes is historically contingent.* There are periods in which the state can be reasonably understood as a self-reproducing structure which functions largely independently of any external manipulation, and other times when it is best viewed as a simple tool in the hands of the ruling class. Certain parts of the state apparatus may be highly manipulated by specific capitalist interests while other parts may have much more structural autonomy. But in no situation can state activity be completely reduced to either structural or instrumental causation. The state is always *relatively* autonomous: it is neither completely autonomous (i.e., free from active control by the capitalist class) nor simply manipulated by members of the ruling class (i.e., free from any structural constraints). As Marx

put it so eloquently in his analysis of the French state in the mid-nineteenth century: "Men make their own history, but they do not make it just as they please; they do not make it under circumstances chosen by themselves, but under circumstances directly encountered, given and transmitted from the past."

(2) *The internal structures of the state, as well as the concrete state policies shaped within those structures, are the objects of class struggle.* A theory of the state must not regard the structures of the state as historical givens but must attempt to explain the development of the structures themselves. Otherwise, the analysis takes on a static quality. ...

As in much of Marxist theory, explanations based on "history" or "class consciousness" or "class struggle" often have a residual quality to them. To say that the structures of the state are the objects of class struggle and that class struggle explains the specific evolution of structures is only a starting point. It is further necessary to develop a proper theory of such political class struggle itself.

(3) The notion of the "relative autonomy of the state" needs further theoretical development. Structuralist writers have conceptualized this notion by treating the state as relatively autonomous with respect to direct, instrumental manipulations by the capitalist class. ... The word "relative" is crucial; there is no implication that the capitalist state can ever be emancipated from the constraints of a capitalist social formation. But there is the implication that as the state becomes more and more implicated in the productive sphere itself, as larger realms of social activity become decommodified (in the sense that production becomes organized around politically determined use-values rather than exchange-values), the state can develop a much greater degree of autonomy than is understood by the conventional Marxist notion of "relative autonomy." This further suggests that it may make sense to talk of the state as such having an emergent "interest," rather than simply seeing the state as in some sense reflecting the interests of the bourgeoisie. The analysis of an interest of the state is undeveloped within the Marxist perspective. But it is a line of thought which we feel is worth pursuing.

(4) With the development of capitalism from the early phases of monopoly capitalism into advanced monopoly capitalism the reproduction of favorable conditions for accumulation depends more and more upon the active intervention of the state. There is no guarantee that the state will in fact discover the correct forms of such intervention, nor even that it will avoid making catastrophic mistakes. The only certainty is that the requirements for such an expanded role of the state will increase, particularly in the direction of increasingly direct involvement in the accumulation process.

It is especially important that future theoretical and empirical work on the capitalist state should attempt to understand the relationship of the internationalization of capital to the dynamics of state involvement in accumulation. Work on the theory of the capitalist state is now developing the tools for analyzing the relationship of the state to accumulation within a national context; it is only beginning to explore the implications of the continuation of the nationally based state in the face of an accumulation process which is increasingly supranational. ...

(5) The increasing pressure on the state to become involved in the accumulation process has a number of contradictory consequences which in turn will shape the further development of state structures and state policies:

(a) The institutional mechanisms that evolved in earlier periods of capitalist development become less and less effective as mechanisms for policy formation under the newer requirements for accumulation. ... This points to the likelihood that there will be a period of greater instrumental manipulation of the state by ruling-class groups in attempts to restructure the state in ways more compatible with the new requirements for accumulation. An increasingly instrumental relationship of the ruling class (or fractions of the ruling class) to the state is a critical mechanism for the development of new state structures which, if successful, make further direct manipulation less necessary.

(b) Simultaneously, however, the increasing involvement of the state directly in the accumulation process has the effect of politicizing the accumulation process itself in the sense that more and more decisions about accumulation are at least partially made in public agencies rather than in private corporate offices. Explicit or implicit political criteria increasingly enter into the organization of production and the allocation of resources in the accumulation process, replacing more purely market criteria. The result is that class struggle in turn tends to become more politicized. It becomes increasingly difficult to contain working-class demands at the level of firms and industries; demands tend to become increasingly directed toward the state and toward state structures.

Ruling-class groups organized to restructure the state apparatus thus have to respond to quite contradictory forces: on the one hand there is the necessity of creating structures more capable of directly planning and managing the accumulation process; on the other hand, there is the necessity of containing or reversing the growing politicization of class struggle which has resulted from the increasing role of the state in the economy.

While we are still in the middle of this transitional period of state restructuring, some of the elements of the "solution" are becoming apparent. In particular, the combination of executive centralization and the growth of technocratic legitimations for state policies can be interpreted as at least partial attempts to handle these contradictions. It is perhaps characteristic of the dialectical quality of the development of Marxist theory itself that the new directions in the theory of the state are emerging at precisely the time when the capitalist state is undergoing such qualitative change.

REFERENCES

Miliband, Ralph. 1969. *The State in Capitalist Society.* New York: Basic Books.
Poulantzas, Nicos. 1969. "The Problem of the Capitalist State," *New Left Review* 58 (November/December).

24

The State System and the State Elite

RALPH MILIBAND

I

There is one preliminary problem about the state which is very seldom considered, yet which requires attention if the discussion of its nature and role is to be properly focused. This is the fact that 'the state' is not a thing, that it does not, as such, exist. What 'the state' stands for is a number of particular institutions which, together, constitute its reality, and which interact as parts of what may be called the state system.

The point is by no means academic. For the treatment of one part of the state—usually the government—as the state itself introduces a major element of confusion in the discussion of the nature and incidence of state *power*; and that confusion can have large political consequences. Thus, if it is believed that the government is in fact the state, it may also be believed that the assumption of governmental power is equivalent to the acquisition of state power. Such a belief, resting as it does on vast assumptions about the nature of state power, is fraught with great risks and disappointments. To understand the nature of state power, it is necessary first of all to distinguish, and then to relate, the various elements which make up the state system.

It is not very surprising that government and state should often appear as synonymous. For it is the government which speaks on the state's behalf. It was the state to which Weber was referring when he said, in a famous phrase, that, in order to be, it must 'successfully claim the monopoly of the legitimate use of physical force within a given territory'. But 'the state' cannot claim anything: only the government of the day, or its duly empowered agents, can. Men, it is often said, give their allegiance not to the government of the day but to the state. But the state, from this point of view, is a nebulous entity; and while men may choose to give their allegiance to it, it is to the government that they are required to give their obedience. A defiance of its orders is a defiance of the state, in whose name the government alone may speak and for whose actions it must assume ultimate responsibility.

This, however, does not mean that the government is necessarily strong, either in relation to other elements of the state system or to forces outside it. On the contrary, it may be very weak, and provide a mere façade for one or other of these other elements and forces. In other words, the fact that the government does speak in the name of the state and is formally *invested* with state power, does not mean that it effectively *controls* that power. How far governments do control it is one of the major questions to be determined.

A second element of the state system which requires investigation is the administrative one, which now extends far beyond the traditional bureaucracy of the state, and which encompasses a large variety of bodies, often related to particular ministerial departments, or enjoying a greater or lesser degree of autonomy—public corporations, central banks, regulatory commissions, etc.—and concerned with the management of the economic, social, cultural and other activities in which the state is now directly or indirectly involved. The extraordinary growth of this administrative and bureaucratic element in all societies, including advanced capitalist ones, is of course one of the most obvious features of contemporary life; and the relation of its leading members to the government and to society is also crucial to the determination of the role of the state.

Formally, officialdom is at the service of the political executive, its obedient instrument, the tool of its will. In actual fact it is nothing of the kind. Everywhere and inevitably the administrative process is also part of the political process; administration is always political as well as executive, at least at the levels where policy-making is relevant, that is to say in the upper layers of administrative life. That this is so is not necessarily due to administrators' desire that it should be so. On the contrary, many of them may well wish to shun 'politics' altogether and to leave 'political' matters to the politicians; or alternatively to 'depoliticise' the issues under discussion. Karl Mannheim once noted that 'the fundamental tendency of all bureaucratic thought is to turn all problems of politics into problems of administration' (Mannheim, 1952:105). But this, for the most part, merely means that political considerations, attitudes and assumptions are incorporated, conscious or not, into the 'problems of administration', and correspondingly affect the nature of administrative advice and action. Officials and administrators cannot divest themselves of all ideological clothing in the advice which they tender to their political masters, or in the independent decisions which they are in a position to take. The power which top civil servants and other state administrators possess no doubt varies from country to country, from department to department, and from individual to individual. But nowhere do these men *not* contribute directly and appreciably to the exercise of state power. If the regime is weak, with a rapid ministerial turnover, and with no possibility of sustained ministerial direction, as happened under the French Fourth Republic, civil servants will step into the vacuum and play an often dominant part in decision-making. But even where the political executive is strong and stable, top administrators are still able to play an important role in critical areas of policy by tendering advice which governments often find it very difficult, for one reason or another, to discount. However much argument there may be over the nature and extent of bureaucratic power in these societies, the range of possibilities must exclude the idea that top civil servants can be reduced to the role of mere instruments of policy. ...

Some of these considerations apply to all other elements of the state system. They apply for instance to a third such element, namely the military, to which may, for present purposes, be added the para-military, security and police forces of the state, and which together form that branch of it mainly concerned with the 'management of violence'.

In most capitalist countries, this coercive apparatus constitutes a vast, sprawling and resourceful establishment, whose professional leaders are men of high status and great influence, inside the state system and in society. Nowhere has the inflation of the military establishment been more marked since the second world war than in the United States, a country which had previously been highly civilian-oriented. And much the same kind of inflation has also occurred in the forces of 'internal security', not only in the United States; it is probably the case that never before in any capitalist country, save in Fascist Italy and Nazi Germany, has such a large proportion of people been employed on police and repressive duties of one kind or another.

Whatever may be the case in practice, the formal constitutional position of the administrative and coercive elements is to serve the state by serving the government of the day. In contrast, it is not at all the formal constitutional duty of judges, at least in Western-type political systems, to serve the purposes of their governments. They are constitutionally independent of the political executive and protected from it by security of tenure and other guarantees. Indeed, the concept of judicial independence is deemed to entail not merely the freedom of judges from responsibility to the political executive, but their active duty to protect the citizen *against* the political executive or its agents, and to act, in the state's encounter with members of society, as the defenders of the latter's rights and liberties. This, as we shall see, can mean many different things. But in any case, the judiciary is an integral part of the state system, which affects, often profoundly, the exercise of state power.

So too, to a greater or lesser degree, does a fifth element of the state system, namely the various units of sub-central government. In one of its aspects, sub-central government constitutes an extension of central government and administration, the latter's antennae or tentacles. In some political systems it has indeed practically no other function. In the countries of advanced capitalism, on the other hand, sub-central government is rather more than an administrative device. In addition to being agents of the state these units of government have also traditionally performed another function. They have not only been the channels of communication and administration from the centre to the periphery, but also the voice of the periphery, or of particular interests at the periphery; they have been a means of overcoming local particularities, but also platforms for their expression, instruments of central control and obstacles to it. For all the centralisation of power, which is a major feature of government in these countries, sub-central organs of government, notably in federal systems such as that of the United States, have remained power structures in their own right, and therefore able to affect very markedly the lives of the populations they have governed.

Much the same point may be made about the representative assemblies of advanced capitalism. Now more than ever their life revolves around the government; and even where, as in the United States, they are formally independent organs of constitutional and political power, their relationship with the political executive cannot be a purely critical or obstructive one. That relationship is one of conflict *and* cooperation.

Nor is this a matter of division between a pro-government side and an anti-government one. *Both* sides reflect this duality. For opposition parties cannot be wholly uncooperative. Merely by taking part in the work of the legislature, they help the government's business. This is one of the main problems of revolutionary parties. As they enter existing parliamentary bodies, so are they also compelled, however reluctantly, to take a share in their work which cannot be purely obstructive. They may judge the price worth paying. But by entering the parliamentary arena they make at least a particular political game possible, and must play it according to rules which are not of their own choosing.

As for government parties, they are seldom if ever single-minded in their support of the political executive and altogether subservient to it. They include people who, by virtue of their position and influence, must be persuaded, cajoled, threatened or bought off.

It is in the constitutionally-sanctioned performance of this cooperative and critical function that legislative assemblies have a share in the exercise of state power. That share is rather less extensive and exalted than is often claimed for these bodies. But, as will be further argued presently, it is not, even in an epoch of executive dominance, an unimportant one.

These are the institutions—the government, the administration, the military and the police, the judicial branch, sub-central government and parliamentary assemblies—which make up 'the state', and whose interrelationship shapes the form of the state system. It is these institutions in which 'state power' lies, and it is through them that this power is wielded in its different manifestations by the people who occupy the leading positions in each of these institutions—presidents, prime ministers and their ministerial colleagues; high civil servants and other state administrators; top military men; judges of the higher courts; some at least of the leading members of parliamentary assemblies, though these are often the same men as the senior members of the political executive; and, a long way behind, particularly in unitary states, the political and administrative leaders of sub-central units of the state. These are the people who constitute what may be described as the state elite.

Of course, the state system is not synonymous with the political system. The latter includes many institutions, for instance parties and pressure groups, which are of major importance in the political process, and which vitally affect the operation of the state system. And so do many other institutions which are not 'political' at all, for instance, giant corporations, Churches, the mass media, etc. Obviously the men who head these institutions may wield considerable power and influence, which must be integrated in the analysis of political power in advanced capitalist societies.

Yet while there are many men who have power outside the state system and whose power greatly affects it, they are not the actual repositories of state power; and for the purpose of analysing the role of the state in these societies, it is necessary to treat the elite, which does wield state power, as a distinct and separate entity.

It is particularly necessary to do so in analysing the relationship of the state to the economically dominant class. For the first step in that analysis is to note the obvious but fundamental fact that this class is involved in a *relationship* with the state, which cannot be *assumed*, in the political conditions which are typical of advanced capitalism, to be that of principal to agent. It may well be found that the relationship is very close indeed and that the holders of state power are, for many different reasons, the agents of private economic power—that those who wield that power are also, therefore, and without unduly stretching the meaning of words, an authentic 'ruling class'. But this is precisely what has to be *determined*.

II

Writing in 1902, Karl Kautsky observed that 'the capitalist class rules but does not govern', though he added immediately that 'it contents itself with ruling the government' (Kautsky, 1903:13). This is the proposition which has to be tested. But it is obviously true that the capitalist class, as a class, does not actually 'govern'. ... [T]he capitalist class has generally confronted the state as a separate entity—even, in the days of its rise to power, as an alien and often hostile element, often under the control and influence of an established and land-owning class, whose hold upon the state power had to be broken by revolution, as in France, or by erosion, as in England in the nineteenth century, that process of erosion being greatly facilitated, in the English case, by the constitutional and political changes wrought by violence in the seventeenth century.

Nor has it come to be the case, even in the epoch of advanced capitalism, that businessmen have themselves assumed the major share of government. On the other hand, they have generally been well represented in the political executive and in other parts of the state system as well; and this has been particularly true in the recent history of advanced capitalism.

This entry of businessmen in the state system has often been greatly underestimated. Max Weber, for instance, believed that industrialists had neither the time nor the particular qualities required for political life (Bendix, 1960:436). ... Raymond Aron has more recently written of businessmen that 'they have governed neither Germany, nor France, nor even England. They certainly played a decisive role in the management of the means of production, in social life. But what is characteristic of them as a socially dominant class is that, in the majority of countries, they have not themselves wanted to assume political functions' (Aron, 1964:280).

Businessmen themselves have often tended to stress their remoteness from, even their distaste for, 'politics'; and they have also tended to have a poor view of politicians as men who, in the hallowed phrase, have never had to meet a payroll and who therefore know very little of the *real* world—yet who seek to interfere in the affairs of the hard-headed and practical men whose business it is to meet a payroll, and who therefore do know what the world is about. What this means is that businessmen, like administrators, wish to 'depoliticise' highly contentious issues and to have these issues judged according to the criteria favoured by business. This may look like an avoidance of politics and ideology: it is in fact their clandestine importation into public affairs.

In any case, the notion of businessmen as remote from political affairs, in a direct and personal way, greatly exaggerates their reluctance to seek political power; and equally underestimates how often the search has been successful.

In the United States, businessmen were in fact the largest single occupational group in cabinets from 1889 to 1949; of the total number of cabinet members between these dates, more than 60 per cent were businessmen of one sort or another (Lasswell, et al., 1952:30). Nor certainly was the business membership of American cabinets less marked in the Eisenhower years from 1953 to 1961. As for members of British cabinets between 1886 and 1950, close to one-third were businessmen, including three prime ministers—Bonar Law, Baldwin and Chamberlain. Nor again have businessmen been at all badly represented in the Conservative cabinets which held office between 1951 and 1964. And while businessmen have, in this respect, done rather less well in some other advanced capitalist countries, nowhere has their representation been negligible.

But the government itself is by no means the only part of the state system in which businessmen have had a direct say. Indeed, one of the most notable features of advanced capitalism is precisely what might be called without much exaggeration their growing colonisation of the upper reaches of the administrative part of that system. ...

Much the same kind of business predominance over other economic groups is to be found in the financial and credit institutions of the state, and in the nationalised sector. The creation of that sector has often been thought of as removing an important area of economic activity from capitalist control and influence. But quite apart from all the other forces which prevent a subsidiary nationalised sector from being run on other than orthodox lines, there is also the fact that business has carved out an extremely strong place for itself in the directing organs of that sector; or rather, that business has been invited by governments, whatever their political coloration, to assume a major role in the management and control of the public sector. In comparison, representatives of labour have appeared as very poor parents indeed—not, it should be added, that the entry of a greater number of 'safe' trade union leaders would make much difference to the orientation of institutions which are, in effect, an integral part of the capitalist system.

The notion that businessmen are not directly involved in government and administration (and also in parliamentary assemblies) is obviously false. They are thus involved, ever more closely as the state becomes more closely concerned with economic life; wherever the state 'intervenes', there also, in an exceptionally strong position as compared with other economic groups, will businessmen be found to influence and even to determine the nature of that intervention.

It may readily be granted that businessmen who enter the state system, in whatever capacity, may not think of themselves as representatives of business in general or even less of their own industries or firms in particular. But even though the *will* to think in 'national' terms may well be strong, businessmen involved in government and administration are not very likely, all the same, to find much merit in policies which appear to run counter to what they conceive to be the interests of business, much less to make themselves the advocates of such policies, since they are almost by definition most likely to believe such policies to be inimical to the 'national interest'. It is much easier for businessmen, where required, to divest themselves of stocks and shares as a kind of *rite de passage* into government service than to divest themselves of a particular view of the world, and of the place of business in it.

Notwithstanding the substantial participation of businessmen in the business of the state, it is however true that they have never constituted, and do not constitute now, more than a relatively small minority of the state elite as a whole. It is in this sense that the economic elites of advanced capitalist countries are not, properly speaking, a 'governing' class, comparable to pre-industrial, aristocratic and landowning classes. In some cases, the latter were able, almost, to dispense with a distinct and fully articulated state machinery and were themselves practically the state. Capitalist economic elites have not achieved, and in the nature of capitalist society could never achieve, such a position.

However, the significance of this relative distance of businessmen from the state system is markedly reduced by the social composition of the state elite proper. For businessmen belong, in economic and social terms, to the upper and middle classes—and it is also from these classes that the members of the state elite are predominantly, not to say overwhelmingly, drawn. The pattern is monotonously similar for all capitalist countries and applies not only to the administrative, military and judicial elites, which are insulated from universal suffrage and political competition, but to the political and elective ones as well, which are not. Everywhere and in all its elements the state system has retained, socially speaking, a most markedly upper- and middle-class character, with a slowly diminishing aristocratic element at one end, and a slowly growing working-class and lower-middle-class element at the other. The area of recruitment is much more narrow than is often suggested. As Professor Dahrendorf notes, 'the "middle class" that forms the main recruiting ground of the power elite of most European countries today, often consists of the top 5 per cent of the occupational hierarchy in terms of prestige, income and influence, (1964:238). ...

The picture is not appreciably different for the United States, where ... inequality of educational opportunity ... has also helped to narrow the area of recruitment to the state service. As Professor Matthews notes:

> Those American political decision-makers *for whom this information is available* are, with very few exceptions, sons of professional men, proprietors and officials, and farmers. A very small minority were sons of wage-earners, low salaried workers, farm labourers or tenants ... the narrow base from which political decision-makers appear to be recruited is clear. (Matthews, 1954: 23–24)

... While inequality of educational opportunity, based on social class, helps to account for this pattern, there are other factors which contribute to its formation. Here too, as in the case of access to elite positions outside the state system, there is also the matter of connections. Certainly, the more spectacular forms of nepotism and favouritism associated with an unregenerate aristocratic and preindustrial age are not part of the contemporary, middle-class, competitive state service: the partial liberation of that service from the aristocratic grip was indeed one of the crucial aspects of the extension of bourgeois power in the state and society. But it would, all the same, be highly unrealistic to think that even in an examination-oriented epoch membership of a relatively narrow segment of the population is not a distinct advantage, not only in terms of entry into the higher levels of the state service, but also, and hardly less important, of chances of upward movement inside it. Such membership affords links of kinship and friendship, and generally enhances a sense of shared values, all of which are helpful to a successful career. ...

Those who control and determine selection and promotion at the highest level of the state service are themselves most likely to be members of the upper and middle classes, by social origin or by virtue of their own professional success, and are likely to carry in their minds a particular image of how a high-ranking civil servant or military officer ought to think, speak, behave and react; and that image will be drawn in terms of the class to which they belong. No doubt, the recruiters, aware of the pressures and demands of a 'meritocratic' age, may consciously try to correct their bias; but they are particularly likely to overcome it in the case of working-class candidates who give every sign of readiness and capacity to adapt and conform to class-sanctioned patterns of behaviour and thought. 'Rough diamonds' are now more acceptable than in the past, but they should preferably show good promise of achieving the right kind of smoothness. ...

What the evidence conclusively suggests is that in terms of social origin, education and class situation, the men who have manned *all* command positions in the state system have largely, and in many cases overwhelmingly, been drawn from the world of business and property, or from the professional middle classes. Here as in every other field, men and women born into the subordinate classes, which form of course the vast majority of the population, have fared very poorly—and not only, it must be stressed, in those parts of the state system, such as administration, the military and the judiciary, which depend on appointment, but also in those parts of it which are exposed or which appear to be exposed to the vagaries of universal suffrage and the fortunes of competitive politics. In an epoch when so much is made of democracy, equality, social mobility, classlessness and the rest, it has remained a basic fact of life in advanced capitalist countries that the vast majority of men and women in these countries has been governed, represented, administered, judged, and commanded in war by people drawn from other, economically and socially superior and relatively distant, classes.

REFERENCES

Bendix, R. 1960. *Max Weber: An Intellectual Portrait*. Garden City, N.Y.: Anchor Doubleday.

Dahrendorf, R. 1964. "Recent Changes in the Class Structure of European Societies." In Stephen R. Graubard, ed., *A New Europe?* Boston: Houghton Mifflin.

Kautsky, K. 1913. *The Social Revolution*. Chicago: Charles H. Kerr.

Lasswell, H. D., D. Lerner, and C. E. Rothwell. *The Comparative Study of Elites*. Stanford, Calif.: Stanford University Press.

Mannheim, K. 1952. *Ideology and Utopia*. New York: Harcourt Brace Jovanovich.

Matthews, D. R. 1954. *The Social Background of Political Decision-Makers*. New York: Doubleday.

25

The Reification of the State

ALAN WOLFE

It is neither size per se nor specific policies that are central to an analysis of the late capitalist state, but changes in the *character* of government. ... What happens to the character of government when the available methods of resolving the contradiction between liberal needs and democratic desires have been utilized? That is the question I want to address [here]. The activity of the state has increased to the point where it has become a major producer and certainly the major consumer, but often forgotten is that the growth in the potential power of the state is matched by a decline in the options that the state has at its command. For this reason the increased activity of the state reflects, not an expansion of alternatives, but the exhaustion of them. The enormous political power in the hands of the leaders of Western societies is accompanied by a generalized inability to use that power toward purposive ends. The more the state does, in short, the less it can do. ... The single most important effect that the arrival of late capitalism has had on the structure of the state is this peculiar tendency for greater power to bring about greater impotence.

Class struggle is thus the root cause of the political stagnation of the late capitalist state. At home vested interest block reforms favorable to powerless groups while the majoritarian residue of liberal democracy formally prevents the state from serving as an unmediated arm of the ruling class. Internationally, struggles against hegemonic powers make the latter ineffective for all the weapons at their command, while a bureaucracy developed in response to political needs prevents those needs from being realized. In addition, political immobility creates its own contradictions. The decline in the ability of the private accumulation system to generate capital necessitates that the state play more of a role in the accumulation process, granting subsidies to giant corporations, helping multinationals subdue populations, supporting research and development costs, and warping the tax structure to help private companies increase their profits. Then, if the balance between class forces is not to be disrupted, welfare and repressive functions must continue or be increased. And as hegemonic powers lose control, their arms budgets, searches for new weapons, and corresponding state expenditures go up also. Inertia pushes one way while necessity pushes the other. The late capitalist state is caught in a bind, in which the more functions government must perform, the greater the inability to perform them. Damned if it does and damned if it doesn't, the state approaches the point at which its utility for reproducing social relationships is nil. ...

PUBLIC LIFE IN LATE CAPITALISM

The single most noteworthy feature of the public life of late capitalism is the intransigence of bureaucracy. While bureaucracy is an old phenomenon it assumes a unique aspect in the late capitalist era due to the exhaustion of political alternatives. So long as the state was concerned predominantly with an accumulation function, government bureaus were small and easily managed, or in the case of the United States, easily mismanaged. The need to reconcile accumulation with legitimation changed this uncomplicated situation; out of this need the modern bureaucratic state began to grow. ...

The creation of new bureaus was tantamount to a confession that no solution to the basic contradiction of advanced capitalism existed within the sphere of private life, forcing the state to assume the role of conflict resolver of last resort. State intervention, however, did not solve the problem but transformed it in two significant, and contradictory, ways. On the one hand, each failure of a public agency to routinize class conflict with finality led to demands for new bureaus, intensifying the failure even more. There is no better symbol of the inability of the late capitalist state to extricate itself from its own dilemmas than the sprawling, irrational, contradictory, and wasteful bureaucractization it engenders. But while this was taking place, new demands on the state were *incompatible* with further bureaucratization. A distinction that Claus Offe (1974) makes between allocative and productive state activity is helpful in this context. According to Offe, the capitalist state can act in two ways: distributing existing resources to all the contending parties, and creating new resources directly by participating in the accumulation process. Under late capitalism, there is a turn in the direction of state productive activity to generate solutions to economic and political stagnation. But productive activity, contrasted with allocative, is incompatible with a bureaucratic mode of organization. Productive activity, Offe notes, assumes a range of questions that bureaucracies are not equipped to answer: What is the end goal of the activity? What is the most efficient way of obtaining it? How should it be financed? For this reason, the emergence of late capitalism brings about new needs that bureaucracy cannot satisfy at the same time that it encourages greater bureaucratization. In other words, the most noticeable feature of late capitalism is the tendency of the bureaucracy to become caught in a bind between what it must do and what it is inherently incapable of doing.

An alternative way to express this situation is to suggest that, under conditions of late capitalism, public administration is called upon to resolve questions that at one time were left to the market. Habermas calls this tendency the repoliticization of the relations of production, as the state assumes the fourfold task of constituting and maintaining the mode of production, complementing the market, replacing the market when necessary, and compensating for the market under pressure from disadvantaged groups (Habermas, 1975: 53–54). When the state assumes the task of allocating and even producing resources within a capitalist economy, a devastating contradiction emerges. If the state is to uphold the conditions necessary for capitalist accumulation, as Offe suggests, it must be organized according to a noncapitalist logic. If, on the other hand, it denies capitalist logic too strenuously, it undermines the capitalism that it is supposed to be supporting (Offe, 1972). ... Because of these polar imperatives, public life under late capitalism becomes a hodgepodge of conflicting urges. The late capitalist state supports certain bureaucratic alternatives that it must then suppress, only to find that the suppression of them causes once again a need for their existence. In the remainder of this section, I will argue that this simultaneous need for but despair of bureaucratizaton colors the public life of late capitalism and gives it a decidedly confused character. This can be done by examining four consequences of this ambiguity toward state action: politicization, centralization, decentralization, and rationalization.

Because the growth of new bureaus does not solve the problems for which they were created, the state faces an administrative crisis of which its much publicized fiscal crisis is only a part. Volker Ronge has shown how this administrative crisis is due to the conflicting needs of accumulation and legitimation, which push state policy makers in contrary directions. The major consequence of this duality, he argues, is to break down the traditional distinction that capitalist societies make between politics and administration. Since "more and more administrations must strive for specific support for their policies" when faced with contradictory expectations, the bureaucracy finds itself unable to resist building support for its decisions, thereby becoming as political as it is administrative (Ronge, 1974). ...

A second consequence of the ambiguity of the late capitalist state toward bureaucracy involves centralization. For a considerable period of time, the monopolization in the private sector was not matched by a similar cartelization in the public. As firms eliminated competition and subjected the economy to a thorough rationalization, bureaus within the state remained parochial, competitive, and inefficient by capitalist criteria. This was the period when industrialists looked at the public sector with dismay, wondering aloud why government did not seem as efficient as monopoly capital. But given the monopoly sector's eventual reliance on the state, such a disparity between the principles that were organizing the two sectors could not be tolerated, and the result was an attempt to organize public bureaus in monopolistic fashion. Centralization into super-administrative units became the public administrator's watchword. ...

When competitive capitalism was transformed into monopoly capitalism, the market was destroyed as an allocation mechanism, replaced by administered pricing. Similarly, attempts to centralize bureaus within the state may eliminate waste and duplication (although the points is highly debatable) but they do so at the cost of eliminating self-generated standards of propriety. As Offe has pointed out, the firm and the state operate by different standards; because the latter is not a unit of capitalist accumulation, the criterion by which it makes decisions is not bounded by considerations such as profit or the market (Offe, 1974). And with the adoption of Keynesian fiscal policies, not even a balanced budget constitutes a limitation on state activity. Centralization under these conditions leads the state into an endless spending cycle, much as conservative economists charge, with limits established only by the political process. ...

If centralization had become counterproductive because it could not provide a means of control, the obvious solution was to call for decentralization. The fact that this alternative was diametrically opposed to the one just tried was not a problem, for solutions to the difficulties of the capitalist state have traditionally been eclectic: if tariffs can go up and down rapidly, bureaus can be created and dismantled at the same rate. Decentralization eventually became as attractive as centralization as a way out of the *cul-de-sac* of contradictory bureaucratization.

Decentralized departments might be less "efficient" by the standards of monopoly capitalism, but their virtues were touted nonetheless. Political scientists like Martin Landau tried to show how duplication and overlap need not necessarily produce chaos; in his view, a certain redundancy works to foster coordination by encouraging extensive communication (Landau, 1969). In addition, competitive departments, like firms in a competitive economy, must bargain with each other for scarce resources, and the bargaining process, like the market, could be relied on to produce policies that were the best available compromise among all the different interests. In opposition to the centralizers, a school of thought developed holding that approximation to a marketplace system of allocation *within the state* was the best option. For every conglomerate department, there were calls for vouchers, local initiatives, creative federalism, and voluntary programs. Centralization and decentralization were even advocated by the same men at the same time. ... In this confused ideological context, one must see both solutions as not being answers in themselves. The fact that political thought could swing with such abandon from one pole to the other is testimony to how intractable the problem of bureaucracy in late capitalism was becoming. ...

A fourth indication of the ambiguous role of bureaucratization in late capitalism emerges out of attempts at rationalization. In the 1960s, new strategies designed to bring order out of the chaos of administrative procedure began to fascinate policy makers in one country after another. Planning-programing-budgeting systems (PPBS) in the United States, the Public Expenditure Survey

Committee, Program Analysis and Review, and Central Policy Review Staff in the United Kingdom, and the *rationalisation des choix budgetaires* in France all spoke a new mood, one in which criteria of rationality would be applied to the budgetary process, hopefully bringing order to all other processes as well. ... [C]ritics of reform like Wildavsky are correct to point out that such proposals are political, not administrative, for they involve not changes in procedure but in the distribution of power (Wildavsky, 1969). What appears to be a process of rationalization could just as easily be interpreted as a process of politicization.

Have reform proposals like PPBS been successful? In general, such ventures have not made any inroads into the vested power of bureaucratic elites; like recalcitrant businessmen before World War I, immediate interest was found to be more valuable than long-range gain. Such reforms had an impact only when they were tailored to, and did not try to counter, traditional methods of performing the public business, which is precisely what was supposed to have been reformed in the first place. ... In other words, the anarchy of the marketplace that businessmen found intolerable remains, but it is an anarchy caused by sprawling government bureaus and not one brought about by competitive firms. The late capitalist state operates by principles once thought to be appropriate, but later found wanting, to the nineteenth-century economy.

The problems associated with politicization, centralization, decentralization, and rationalization reinforce the point that in late capitalism public administration assumes many of the contradictions once existing in the economy. To phrase this another way, the process of absorbing the class struggle within the state means that the bureaucracy must confront within itself the irresolvable tensions that at one time lay within the province of the entire society. In late capitalism the bureaucracy becomes more than unwieldy—it becomes the one place to which the most impossible tasks are assigned. The class struggle and the political process once decided who gets what, when, and how; in late capitalism, the bureaucracy performs this function. But public life is not organized for this task; indeed, the formal ideology of bureaucracy is that it is nonpolitical, conflict-free, and concerned only with administrative rationality. Caught between its politicized tasks and its depoliticized rationale, public administration in late capitalism searches for answers to its intractable task wherever it can find them, only to discover that each possible option causes as many problems as it solves.

Bureaucratization is therefore symbolic of the closing of political options characteristic of the late capitalist state. One could generalize and say that the greater the class conflict in any late capitalist society, the more paralyzed will be the bureaucracy. Yet at the same time, the greater the amount of class conflict, the greater also will be the need for state intervention to keep it in check. In this double-bind situation, the nature of government undergoes a change, best described by Offe's concept of selectiveness (1972: 10). Offe argues that the fundamental problem for the late capitalist state can be viewed, not as promoting certain activities over others, but as excluding from the agenda questions and policies that would disturb the class character of the state. Selective mechanisms, which he describes as a "system of filters," are created, designed to exclude claims and interests on a number of different levels. Whereas the early capitalist state served the interests of the bourgeoisie by acting in certain ways, the late capitalist state tends to serve that interest by not acting in others, which is why the literature on "nondecisions" has more applicability to the public administration than the literature on decision making as such. Under late capitalism, selectivity may become so important that there is little left from which to select.

This politicization of administration is a most important development, given the tendency of the public bureaucracy to assume the consequences of class struggle and political conflict. But at the same time that administrative life becomes politicized ... , political life increasingly becomes administered, as the political process loses its content and become subject to rules of predictability. Ever since Saint-Simon, radical writers have been fascinated by his vision that the government of men would be replaced by the administration of things, but under late capitalism the opposite occurs: the administration of men and the government of things. Because the attempt to administer more and more areas of social life can be understood only as part of the desperation of a state that is running out of options, government ... means not to choose but to choose not to choose. As choices decline in a state of exhausting options, public life, as symbolized by the bureaucracy, becomes a swamp in which attempts to act are matched by the inability to act. Their enormous power tied up in knots, the rulers of late capitalism tend to decide what they will not decide, not what they will. The public administration of late capitalism becomes weaker the stronger it appears to be, a contradiction ultimately caused by the gap between its political requirements and its administrative ideology. ...

REIFICATION AND RESIGNATION

The ambiguities, confusions, and irrationalities of the late capitalist state adversely affect the quest for legitimation. In order to continue to rule without challenge, late capitalist elites need an institution that can make it appear that the political contradictions of the society either do not exist or are being resolved. But where is such an institution to be found? The firm cannot be called upon, because it is ordered by the logic of private property, which, by definition, precludes a public role. The Church cannot do it, because the mode of production has rationalized the society in increasingly secular fashion. The family cannot perform the task because of its particularity. Consequently, the only institution that can be called upon to resolve the contradictions taking place within the state is the state itself, and each time it tries to do this, it further intensifies these contradictions, thus requiring even more state intervention. The state is called upon to prove that class tensions do not exist at the moment when the state is immobilized by those very tensions. Only the state, the object of class struggle, can appear to be above class struggle. The self-proclaimed spokesmen for each class, businessmen as well as labor leaders, wish the state to be both partisan and nonpartisan, to serve their specific interests and to serve the general interest at the same time. Hence the late capitalist state can satisfy its class interest only by being universal and can be universal only by fulfilling its class character. The state is part of the problem and part of the solution at the same time.

The task of the late capitalist state, in short, is an impossible one, to be both one thing and another simultaneously. Its Sisyphean character leads to a transformation in the way it is perceived. One would think that an institution charged with an impossible mission would be denigrated, and to some extent this is true. A school of thought, which I will call the political theory of resignation, develops, holding that state action is incapable of bringing about any fundamental change. But many of the members of this school once held the opposite position, and in their writings is a sureness of position that converts so often possess. The fact is that before disenchantment with the state set in, affirmation was the more likely reaction. The more common argument is that the state can do what no other institution is capable of doing, which is to ensure social peace in a class society. In general, defenders of public order ascribe more and more power and ability to the state, hoping that it can perform an alchemy that will magically quell all tensions and bring about a utopia within the existing class structure. Thus, the contradictions of the late capitalist state bring about, not unexpectedly, a contradictory response; the state is praised and the state is blamed; the state is the answer to all problems and the answer to none. In both cases, the state is no longer accepted for what it is but is assigned extrahuman powers, the sublimity of heaven or the intractability of hell. For this reason, both alternatives can be seen as similar responses to an identical problem, no matter how divergent their prescriptions.

A central political development of late capitalist society has been an increase in the tendency to view the state as capable of solving problems that lie outside its competence. As the ascription of ability and magical powers to the state fails to solve these problems, advocates of statization press their claim for even stronger potions, producing a cycle in which impotence results in calls for greater potency, which bring about higher levels of impotence. The more the state fails, the more it is worshipped, and the more it is worshipped, the greater will be its failure. I will call the process by which the state is assigned a wide variety of mythic powers the reification of the state.

The reification of the state is a key aspect of the political life of late capitalist societies. To be sure, there has long been a tendency to worship the state by assigning it extraordinary powers. ... One of Max Weber's contributions to political sociology was to show how the process of rationalization stripped away these justifications, leaving the state naked as an instrument of power, the monopoly of the legitimate means of violence. In this context, reification takes place when state power is justified as an end in itself and not as a means to some other end.

To defend the state because it promotes the preservation of order is to engage in this type of reification; since the definition of the state is that it alone preserves order, to justify it on this ground is tautological. The state is good because it is the state. The same kind of reasoning applies to those who defend the state as the embodiment of the national interest, when they also view that interest as codeterminous with the state. Such kinds of modern, secularized reification will most likely occur when two conditions are present: first, extensive social conflict forces a reliance on the state that makes questions of government authority important; and, second, an element of democratization requires a theory of legitimation. These conditions are associated with late capitalism, which is why the reification of the state is not a relic of feudal society but a matter of importance to modern capitalist life. The reification of the state can become the tangible expression of the exhaustion of political alternatives. ...

In contrast with personification, the *objectification* of the state takes place when the state is assigned characteristics that make it seem a concrete thing as opposed to the instrument of the people's will. Mechanistic conceptions of society are generally associated with the objectification of the state, for if society is conceived of as a machine, then the state becomes a homeostatic valve, making adjustments here and there in order to keep the machine in operation. ...

Finally, the *epicization* of the state refers to the process by which political figures, rather than being seen as public *servants*, are transformed into public *heroes*, generally of epic dimensions. There is something quaint and also positive about the notion of a public servant, for it expresses the idea that those who hold power do so at the bidding of the people who put them there. As subordinates, power holders should be grateful for whatever favors the public chooses to give them. With the reification of the state, the concept of a public servant undergoes a thorough transformation into its opposite. The power holder is the master, and the general public the servant. ...

As the opposite of reification of the state, the political theory of resignation also completes it. Both views of the state are reactions to the political contradictions of late capitalism, for both indicate how problematic the political search for answers to economic and social contradictions has become. So long as the late capitalist state is expected to resolve irresolvable tensions, the contradictions of its existence will produce contradictory expectations about its performance. A cycle of praise and blame for the state is likely to be a conspicuous feature of the political life of late capitalism, reflecting a cycle of increased power and decreased options. The modern state is indeed a unique phenomenon, but its particularity lies more in its contradictions than in its capabilities.

REFERENCES

Habermas, Jürgen. 1975. *Legitimation Crisis*. Boston: Beacon Press.

Landau, Martin. 1969. "Redundancy, Rationality, and the Problem of Duplication and Overlap," *Public Administration Review* 34 (July–August): 346–358.

Offe, Claus. 1972. "Class Rule and the Political System: On the Selectiveness of Political Institutions," mimeographed translation of Ch. 3 of *Strukturprobleme des Kapitalistischen Staates* (Frankfurt: Suhrkamp).

_____ . 1974. "The Theory of the Capitalist State and the Problem of Policy Formation," unpublished paper.

Ronge, Volker. 1974. "The Politicization of Administration in Advanced Capitalist Societies," *Political Studies* 22 (March): 86–93.

Wildavsky, Aaron. 1969. "Rescuing Policy Analysis from PPBS," *Public Administration Review* 34 (April): 189–202.

26

The Ruling Class Does Not Rule

FRED BLOCK

The Marxist theory of the state remains a muddle despite the recent revival of interest in the subject. Substantial progress has been made in formulating a critique of orthodox Marxist formulations that reduce the state to a mere reflection of economic interests. However, the outlines of an adequate alternative Marxist theory are not yet clear. This is most dramatically indicated by the continued popularity in Marxist circles of explanations of state policies or of conflicts within the state that are remarkably similar to orthodox formulations in their tendency to see the state as a reflection of the interests of certain groups in the capitalist class. ... These earlier formulations—even when they have been carefully criticized and dismissed—sneak back into many current analyses because they remain embedded in the basic concepts of Marxist analysis.

This essay proposes two elements of an alternative Marxist theory of the state. The first element is a different way of conceptualizing the ruling class and its relationship to the state. This reconceptualization makes possible the second element—the elaboration of a structural framework which specifies the concrete mechanisms that make the state a capitalist state, whereas other structural theories have tended to analyze structures in an abstract and mystifying way.

Although these two elements do not provide a complete Marxist theory of the state, they do provide a new way of thinking about the sources of rationality within capitalism. Contemporary Marxists have been forced to acknowledge that despite its fundamental irrationality, capitalism in the developed world has shown a remarkable capacity to rationalize itself in response to the twin dangers of economic crisis and radical working-class movements. Since the present historical period again poses for the left the threat of successful capitalist rationalization, the understanding of the sources of capitalism's capacity for self-reform is of the utmost political importance. The traditional Marxist explanation of capitalist rationality is to root it in the consciousness of some sector of the ruling class. In this light, capitalist reform reflects the conscious will and understand-

295

ing of some sector of the capitalist class that has grasped the magnitude of the problem and proposes a set of solutions. The alternative framework being proposed here suggests that capacity of capitalism to rationalize itself is the outcome of a conflict among three sets of agents—the capitalist class, the managers of the state apparatus, and the working class.[1] Rationalization occurs "behind the backs" of each set of actors so that rationality cannot be seen as a function of the consciousness of one particular group.

This argument and its implications will be traced out through a number of steps. First, I intend to show that critiques of orthodox Marxist theory of the state are flawed by their acceptance of the idea of a class-conscious ruling class. Second, I argue that there is a basis in Marx's writing for rejecting the idea of a class-conscious ruling class. Third, I develop a structural argument that shows that even in the absence of ruling-class class consciousness, the state managers are strongly discouraged from pursuing anti-capitalist policies. Fourth, I return to the issue of capitalist rationality and describe how it grows out of the structured relationship among capitalists, workers, and state managers. Finally, I briefly analyze the implications of this argument for capitalism's current difficulties in the United States.

THE CRITIQUE OF INSTRUMENTALISM

The major development in the Marxist theory of the state in recent years has been the formulation of a critique of instrumentalism. A number of writers have characterized the orthodox Marxist view of the state as instrumentalism because it views the state as a simple tool or instrument of ruling-class purposes. First, it neglects the ideological role of the state. The state plays a critical role in maintaining the legitimacy of the social order, and this requires that the state appear to be neutral in the class struggle. In short, even if the state is an instrument of ruling-class purpose, the fact that it must appear otherwise indicates the need for a more complex framework for analyzing state policies. Second, instrumentalism fails to recognize that to act in the general interest of capital, the state must be able to take actions against the particular interests of capitalists. Price controls or restrictions on the export of capital, for example, might be in the general interest of capital in a particular period, even if they temporarily reduced the profits of most capitalists. To carry through such policies, the state must have more autonomy from direct capitalist control than the instrumentalist view would allow.

The critics of instrumentalism propose the idea of the relative autonomy of the state as an alternative framework. In order to serve the general interests of capital, the state must have some autonomy from direct ruling-class control. Since the concept of the absolute autonomy of the state would be un-Marxist and false, the autonomy is clearly relative. However, the difficulty is in specifying the nature, limits, and determinants of that relative autonomy. Some writers have attempted to argue that the degree of autonomy varies historically, and that "late capitalism" is characterized by the "autonomization of the state apparatus." But these arguments have an ad hoc quality, and they share an analytic problem derived from the phrase "relative autonomy from ruling-class control."

The basic problem in formulations of "relative autonomy" is the conceptualization of the ruling class. Relative autonomy theories assume that the ruling class will respond effectively to the state's abuse of that autonomy. But for the ruling class to be capable of taking such corrective actions, it must have some degree of political cohesion, an understanding of its general interests, and a high degree of political sophistication. In sum, the theory requires that the ruling class, or a portion of it, be class-conscious, that is, aware of what is necessary to reproduce capitalist social relations in changing historical circumstances. Yet if the ruling class or a segment of it is class-conscious, then the degree of autonomy of the state is clearly quite limited. At this point the theory of relative autonomy collapses back into a slightly more sophisticated version of instrumentalism. State policies continue to be seen as the reflection of inputs by a class-conscious ruling class.

The way out of this theoretical bind, the way to formulate a critique of instrumentalism that does not collapse, is to reject the idea of a class-conscious ruling class. Instead of the relative autonomy framework the key idea becomes a division of labor between those who accumulate capital and those who manage the state apparatus. Those who accumulate capital are conscious of their interests as capitalists, but, in general, they are not conscious of what is necessary to reproduce the social order in changing circumstances. Those who manage the state apparatus, however, are forced to concern themselves to a greater degree with the reproduction of the social order because their continued power rests on the maintenance of political and economic order. In this framework, the central theoretical task is to explain how it is that despite this division of labor, the state tends to serve the interests of the capitalist class. It is to this task—the elaboration of a structural theory of the state—that I will turn after a brief discussion of the division of labor between capitalists and state managers.

DIVISION OF LABOR

The idea of a division of labor between non-class-conscious capitalists and those who manage the state apparatus can be found in Marx's writings. Two factors, however, have obscured this aspect of Marx's thought. First, Marx did not spell out the nature of the structural framework in which that division of labor operated, although he hinted at the existence of such a framework. Second, Marx's discussion of these issues is clouded by his polemical intent to fix responsibility for all aspects of bourgeois society on the ruling class. Even when Marx recognizes that the ruling class lacks class consciousness, he still formulates his argument in such a way as to imply that the ruling class as a whole is in conscious control of the situation. Marx used the idea of a conscious, directive ruling class as a polemical shorthand for an elaboration of the structural mechanisms through which control over the means of production leads to control over other aspects of society. ...

Marx's idea of representation suggests the general structural links between the capitalists and those who manage the state apparatus. Marx recognized that those in the state apparatus tended to have a broader view of society than the capitalists, although their view is still far short of a general understanding of what is necessary to reproduce the social order. After all, the state managers' preoccupation with the struggle for political power distorts their understanding. ... But if neither the ruling class nor its representatives know what is necessary to preserve and reproduce capitalist social relations, why then does the state tend to do just that? The answer is that such policies emerge out of the structural relationships among state managers, capitalists, and workers. ...

MAJOR STRUCTURAL MECHANISMS

A viable structural theory of the state must do two separate things. It must elaborate the structural constraints that operate to reduce the likelihood that state managers will act against the general interests of capitalists. An understanding of these constraints is particularly important for analyzing the obstacles to reformist socialist strategies. But a structural theory must also explain the tendency of state managers to pursue policies that are in the general interests of capital. It is not sufficient to explain why the state avoids anti-capitalist policies; it is necessary to explain why the state has served to rationalize capitalism. Once one rejects the idea of ruling-class class consciousness, one needs to provide an alternative explanation of efforts at rationalization.

Both tendencies can be derived from the fact that those who manage the state apparatus—regardless of their own political ideology—are dependent on the maintenance of some reasonable level of economic activity. This is true for two reasons. First, the capacity of the state to finance itself through taxation or borrowing depends on the state of the economy. If economic activity is in decline, the state will have difficulty maintaining its revenues at an adequate level. Second, public support for a regime will decline sharply if the regime presides over a serious drop in the level of economic activity, with a parallel rise in unemployment and shortages of key goods. Such a drop in support increases the likelihood that the state managers will be removed from power one way or another. And even if the drop is not that dramatic, it will increase the challenges to the regime and decrease the regime's political ability to take effective actions.

In a capitalist economy the level of economic activity is largely determined by the private investment decisions of capitalists. This means that capitalists, in their collective role as investors, have a veto over state policies in that their failure to invest at adequate levels can create major political problems for the state

managers. This discourages state managers from taking actions that might seriously decrease the rate of investment. It also means that state managers have a
direct interest in using their power to facilitate investment, since their own continued power rests on a healthy economy. There will be a tendency for state
agencies to orient their various programs toward the goal of facilitating and encouraging private investment. In doing so, the state managers address the problem of investment from a broader perspective than that of the individual capitalist. This increases the likelihood that such policies will be in the general interest
of capital.

CONSTRAINTS ON STATE POLICIES

This is, of course, too simple. Both sides of the picture—constraints and rationalization—must be filled out in greater detail to make this approach convincing. One problem, in particular, stands out—if capitalists have a veto over
state policies, isn't this simply another version of instrumentalism? The answer
to this question lies in a more careful analysis of the determinants of investment
decisions. The most useful concept is the idea of business confidence. Individual capitalists decide on their rate of investment in a particular country on the
basis of a variety of specific variables such as the price of labor and the size of the
market for a specific product. But there is also an intangible variable—the capitalist's evaluation of the general political/economic climate. Is the society stable; is the working class under control; are taxes likely to rise; do government
agencies interfere with business freedom; will the economy grow? These kinds
of considerations are critical to the investment decisions of each firm. The sum
of all of these evaluations across a national economy can be termed the level of
business confidence. As the level of business confidence declines, so will the
rate of investment. Business confidence also has an international dimension
when nations are integrated into a capitalist world economy. Multinational corporations, international bankers, and currency speculators also make judgments
about a particular nation's political/economic climate which determine their
willingness to invest in assets in that nation. This, in turn, will affect the internal
level of business confidence and the rate of productive investment.

Business confidence is, however, very different from "ruling-class consciousness." Business confidence is based on an evaluation of the market that consid-
ers political events only as they might impinge on the market. This means that it
is rooted in the narrow self-interest of the individual capitalist who is worried
about profit. Business confidence, especially because of its critical international
component, does not make subtle evaluations as to whether a regime is serving
the long-term interests of capital. When there is political turmoil and popular
mobilization, business confidence will fall, and it will rise when there is a restoration of order, no matter how brutal. ...

A sharp decline in business confidence leads to a parallel economic down-turn. High rates of unemployment coexist with annoying shortages of critical commodities. The popularity of the regime falls precipitously. The only alternative to capitulation—eliminating controls and initial reforms—is sharp forward movement to socialize the economy. The government could put people back to work and relieve the shortages by taking over private firms. However, the political basis for this kind of action does not exist, even where the leaders of the government are rhetorically committed to the goal of socialism. Generally, the reformist government has not prepared its electoral supporters for extreme action; its entire program has been based on the promise of a gradual transition. Further, the government leaders themselves become immersed in the political culture of the state apparatus, militating against a sharp break with the status quo.

The outcome of this impasse is tragically familiar. The government either falls from power through standard parliamentary means—loss of an election, defection of some of its parliamentary support—or it is removed militarily. Military actions that violate constitutionality meet formidable obstacles in liberal capitalist nations, but when economic chaos severely diminishes the legitimacy of a regime, the chances of a military coup are enhanced. When the military intervenes, it does not do so as a tool of the ruling class. It acts according to its own ideas of the need to restore political order and in its own interests. Naturally, the removal of the reformist government leads to a rapid revival of business confidence simply because order has been restored. However, it should be stressed that this revival of business confidence might not be sustained, since there can be substantial conflicts between the interests of the military and the capitalists.

The key point in elaborating this scenario is that the chain of events can unfold without any members of the ruling class consciously deciding to act "politically" against the regime in power. Of course, such a scenario is usually filled out with a great deal of editorializing against the regime in the bourgeois press, much grumbling among the upper classes, and even some conspiratorial activity. But the point is that conspiracies to destabilize the regime are basically superfluous, since decisions made by individual capitalists according to their own narrow economic rationality are sufficient to paralyze the regime, creating a situation where the regime's fall is the only possibility.

RATIONALIZATION

The dynamic of business confidence helps explain why governments are constrained from pursuing anti-capitalist policies. It remains to be explained why governments tend to act in the general interests of capital. Part of the answer has already been suggested. Since state managers are so dependent upon the workings of the investment accumulation process, it is natural that they will use whatever resources are available to aid that process. In administering a welfare program, for example, they will organize it to aid the accumulation process, per-

haps by ensuring certain industries a supply of cheap labor. Unlike the individual capitalist, the state managers do not have to operate on the basis of a narrow
profit-maximizing rationality. They are capable of intervening in the economy
on the basis of a more general rationality. In short, their structural position gives
the state managers both the interest and the capacity to aid the investment accumulation process.

There is one major difficulty in this formulation—the problem of explaining
the dynamic through which reforms that increase the rationality of capitalism
come about. Almost all of these reforms involve an extension of the state's role
in the economy and society, either in a regulatory capacity or in the provision of
services. The difficulty is that business confidence has been depicted as so
short-sighted that it is likely to decline in the face of most efforts to extend the
state's role domestically, since such efforts threaten to restrict the freedom of individual capitalists and/or increase the tax burden on capitalists. If the state is
unwilling to risk a decline in business confidence, how is it then that the state's
role has expanded inexorably throughout the twentieth century?

Most theorists escape this problem by rejecting the idea that the capitalists are
as short-sighted as the idea of business confidence suggests. Even if many members of the class share the retrograde notions implicit in the idea of business
confidence, there is supposed to be a substantial segment of the class that is for-
ward-looking and recognizes the value of extending the state's power. Theorists
of corporate liberalism have attempted to trace many of the major extensions of
state power in twentieth-century America to the influence of such forward-look-
ing members of the ruling class. However, the position of these theorists ultimately requires an attribution of a high level of consciousness and understanding
to the ruling class or a segment of it, and assumes an instrumental view of the
state where state policies can be reduced to the input of certain ruling-class factions.

There is, however, an alternative line of argument, consistent with the view
of the ruling class and the state that has been advanced in this paper. It depends
on the existence of another structural mechanism—class struggle. Whatever
the role of class struggle in advancing the development of revolutionary consciousness, class struggle between proletariat and ruling class in Marx's view has
another important function. It pushes forward the development of capitalism—
speeding the process by which capitalism advances the development of the productive forces. This is conservative in the short term, but progressive in the long
term; it brings closer the time when capitalism will exhaust its capacity to develop the productive forces and will be ripe for overthrow. Class struggle produces this result most clearly in conflict over wages. When workers are able to
win wage gains, they increase the pressure on the capitalists to find ways to substitute machines for people. As Marx described the cycle, wage gains are followed by an intense period of mechanization as employers attempt to increase
the rate of exploitation; the consequence is an increase in the size of the indus-

trial reserve army, as machines replace workers. This, in turn, diminishes the capacity of workers to win wage gains, until the economic boom again creates a labor shortage. While this description applies particularly to competitive capitalism, the point is that workers' struggles—in Marx's theory—play an important role in speeding the pace of technological innovations. *Class struggle is responsible for much of the economic dynamism of capitalism.*

This pattern goes beyond the struggle over wages. From the beginning of capitalism, workers have struggled to improve their living conditions, which also means upgrading their potential as a labor force. For example, unbridled early capitalism, through child labor and horrendously long working days, threatened to destroy the capacity of the working class to reproduce itself—an outcome not in the long-term interests of capitalists. So working people's struggles against child labor, against incredibly low standards of public health and housing, and for the shorter day made it possible for the class to reproduce itself, providing capitalism a new generation of laborers. In each historical period, the working class struggles to reproduce itself at a higher level of existence. Workers have played an important role, for example, in demanding increased public education. Public education, in turn, helped create the educated labor pool that developing capitalism required. Obviously, not every working-class demand contributes to the advance of capitalism, but it is foolish to ignore this dimension of class struggle. ...

Once working-class pressures succeed in extending the state's role, another dynamic begins to work. Those who manage the state apparatus have an interest in using the state's resources to facilitate a smooth flow of investment. There will be a tendency to use the state's extended role for the same ends. The capacity of the state to impose greater rationality on capitalism is extended into new areas as a result of working-class pressures. Working-class pressures, for example, might lead to an expansion of educational resources available for the working class, but there is every likelihood that the content of the education will be geared to the needs of accumulation—the production of a docile work force at an appropriate level of skill. Or similarly, working-class pressures might force the government to intervene in the free market to produce higher levels of employment, but the government will use its expanded powers of intervention to aid the accumulation process more generally.

This pattern is not a smoothly working functional process, always producing the same result. First, working-class movements have often been aware of the danger of making demands that will ultimately strengthen a state they perceive as hostile. For precisely this reason, socialist movements have often demanded that expanded social services be placed under working-class control. However, working-class demands are rarely granted in their original form. Often, the more radical elements of the movement are repressed at the same time that concessions are made. Second, there can be a serious time lag between granting concessions to the working class and discovering ways that the extension of the state's power can be used to aid the accumulation process. There might, in fact, be continuing tensions in a government program between its integrative intent and its role in the accumulation process. Finally, some concessions to working-class pressure might have no potential benefits for accumulation and might simply place strains on the private economy. If these strains are immediate, one could expect serious efforts to revoke or neutralize the reforms. If the strains occur over the long term, then capitalism faces severe problems because it becomes increasingly difficult to roll back concessions that have stood for some time.

These points suggest that the tendency for class struggle to rationalize capitalism occurs with a great deal of friction and with the continuous possibility of other outcomes. Nevertheless, the tendency does exist because of the particular interests of the state managers. Where there is strong popular pressure for an expansion of social services or increased regulation of markets, the state managers must weigh three factors. First, they do not want to damage business confidence, which generally responds unfavorably to an expansion of the government's role in providing social services or in regulating the market. Second, they do not want class antagonisms to escalate to a level that would endanger their own rule. Third, they recognize that their own power and resources will grow if the state's role is expanded. If the state managers decide to respond to pressure with concessions,[2] they are likely to shape their concessions in a manner that will least offend business confidence and will most expand their own power. These two constraints increase the likelihood that the concessions will ultimately serve to rationalize capitalism.

MAJOR REFORMS

This argument suggests that while some concessions will be made to the working class, the threat of a decline in business confidence will block major efforts to rationalize capitalism. Since business confidence is shortsighted, it will oppose even pro-capitalist reform programs if such programs promise a major increase in taxes or a major increase in the government's capacity to regulate markets. This leaves the problem of explaining the dramatic increases in the state's role that have occurred in all developed capitalist nations during the course of this century. The explanation is that there are certain periods—during wartime, major depressions, and periods of postwar reconstruction—in which the decline of business confidence as a veto on government policies doesn't work. These are the periods in which dramatic increases in the state's role have occurred.

In wars that require major mobilizations, business confidence loses its sting for several reasons. First, international business confidence becomes less important, since international capital flows tend to be placed under government control. Second, private investment becomes secondary to military production in maintaining high levels of economic activity. Third, in the general patriotic climate, it would be dangerous for the business community to disrupt the economy through negative actions. The result is that state managers have the opportunity to expand their own power with the unassailable justification that such actions are necessary for the war effort. Some of these wartime measures will be rolled back once peace returns, but some will become part of the landscape.

In serious depressions and postwar reconstruction periods, the dynamics are somewhat different. Low levels of economic activity mean that the threat of declining business confidence loses its power, at the same time that popular demands for economic revival are strong. In such periods, the state managers can pay less attention to business opinion and can concentrate on responding to the popular pressure, while acting to expand their own power. However, there are still constraints on the state managers. Their continued rule depends on their capacity to revive the economy. As government actions prove effective in reducing unemployment, redistributing income, or expanding output, the political balance shifts. Pressure from below is likely to diminish: business confidence reemerges as a force once economic recovery begins. In short, successful reforms will tilt the balance of power back to a point where capitalists regain their veto over extensions of the state's role.

The increased capacity of state managers to intervene in the economy during these periods does not automatically rationalize capitalism. State managers can make all kinds of mistakes, including excessive concessions to the working class. State managers have no special knowledge of what is necessary to make capitalism more rational; they grope toward effective action as best they can within existing political constraints and with available economic theories. The point is simply that rationalization can emerge as a by-product of state managers' dual interest in expanding their own power and in assuring a reasonable level of economic activity. The more power the state possesses to intervene in the capitalist economy, the greater the likelihood that effective actions can be taken to facilitate investment.

Not every extension of state power will survive beyond those periods in which state managers have special opportunities to expand the state's role. After a war, depression, or period of reconstruction, the business community is likely to campaign for a restoration of the *status quo ante*. State managers in these new periods will be forced to make some concessions to the business community in order to avert a decline in business confidence. However, the state managers also want to avoid the elimination of certain reforms important for the stabilization of the economy and the integration of the working class. Self-interest also leads them to resist a complete elimination of the state's expanded powers. The consequence is a selection process by which state managers abandon certain reforms while retaining others. In this process, reforms that are most beneficial for capitalism will be retained, while those whose effects are more questionable will be eliminated. Again, the ultimate outcome is determined by intense political struggle.

CONCLUSION

The purpose of this essay has been to argue that a viable Marxist theory of the state depends on the rejection of the idea of a conscious, politically directive, ruling class. By returning to Marx's suggestions that the historical process unfolds "behind the backs" of the actors (including the ruling-class actors), it is possible to locate the structural mechanisms that shape the workings of the capitalist state. These mechanisms operate independently of any political consciousness on the part of the ruling class. Instead, capitalist rationality emerges out of the three-sided relationship among capitalists, workers, and state managers. The structural position of state managers forces them to achieve some consciousness of what is necessary to maintain the viability of the social order. It is this consciousness that explains both the reluctance of state managers to offend business confidence, and their capacity to rationalize a capitalist society. However, the fact of consciousness does not imply control over the historical process. State managers are able to act only in the terrain that is marked out by the intersection of two factors—the intensity of class struggle and the level of economic activity. ...

NOTES

1. Each of these categories requires some definition: "Capitalist class" or "ruling class" is used to refer to the individuals and families that own or control a certain quantity of capital. The cut-off point would vary by country or period, and it would necessarily be somewhat arbitrary, but the point is to distinguish between small businesses and large capitalist firms. The "managers of the state apparatus" include the leading figures of both the legislative and executive branches. This includes the highest-ranking civil servants, as well as appointed and elected politicians. "Working class" is being used in the broad sense. It includes most of those who sell their labor for wages, unwaged workers, and the unemployed.

2. They also have the option of responding to pressures through severe repression. The choice between concessions and repression is made by the state managers on the basis of their perceptions of the general environment and their political orientations.

27

The Potential Autonomy
of the State

THEDA SKOCPOL

Virtually everyone who writes about social revolutions recognizes that they begin with overtly political crises—such as the financial imbroglio of the French monarchy and the calling of the Estates-General in 1787–9. It is likewise apparent to everyone that revolutions proceed through struggles in which organized political parties and factions are prominently involved. And it is recognized that they culminate in the consolidation of new state organizations, whose power may be used not only to reinforce socioeconomic transformations that have already occurred but also to promote further changes. No one denies the reality of these political aspects of social revolutions. Nevertheless, most theorists of revolution tend to regard the political crises that launch revolutions either as incidental triggers or as little more than epiphenomenal indicators of more fundamental contradictions or strains located in the social structure of the old regime. Similarly, the political groups involved in social-revolutionary struggles are seen as representatives of social forces. And the structure and activities of the new state organizations that arise from social revolutions are treated as expressions of the interests of whatever socioeconomic or sociocultural force was deemed victorious in the revolutionary conflicts.

An assumption that always lies, if only implicitly, behind such reasoning is that political structures and struggles can somehow be reduced (at least "in the last instance") to socioeconomic forces and conflicts. The state is viewed as nothing but *an arena* in which conflicts over basic social and economic interests are fought out. What makes the state-as-political-arena special is simply that actors operating within it resort to distinctive means for waging social and economic conflicts—means such as coercion or slogans appealing to the public good. This general way of thinking about the state is, in fact, common to both liberal and Marxist varieties of social theory. Between these two broad traditions of social theory, the crucial difference of opinion is over which means the political arena distinctively embodies: fundamentally consensually based legitimate authority, or fundamentally coercive domination. And this difference parallels the different views about the bases of societal order held by each theoretical tradition.

One ideal-typical view is that the state is the arena of legitimate authority embodied in the rules of the political game and in governmental leadership and policies. These are supported by some combination of normative consensus and majority preference of the members of society. Of course this view resonates well with liberal, pluralist visions of society, which see it as being composed of freely competing groups and members socialized into a commitment to common societal values. In the theoretical literature on revolutions, one finds versions of these ideas about state and society especially in the arguments of the relative-deprivation theorist Ted Gurr and the systems theorist Chalmers Johnson. For them, what matters in explaining the outbreak of a revolution is whether the existing governmental authorities lose their legitimacy. This happens when socially discontented or disoriented masses come to feel that it is acceptable to engage in violence, or else become converted to new values wielded by revolutionary ideologues. Both Gurr and Johnson feel that governmental power and stability depend directly upon societal trends and popular support. Neither believes that state coercive organizations can effectively repress (for long) discontented or disapproving majorities of people in society. The state in their theories is an aspect of either utilitarian consensus (Gurr) or value consensus (Johnson) in society. The state can wield force in the name of popular consensus and legitimacy, but it is not fundamentally founded in organized coercion.

In contrast, Marxist theorists—and to a considerable degree the political-conflict theorist Charles Tilly, as well—do see the state as basically organized coercion. An important part of Tilly's polity model, recall, is a government defined as "an organization which controls the principal concentrated means of coercion within the population" (Tilly, 1978: 52). Similarly, Lenin, the foremost Marxist theorist of the political aspect of revolutions, declares: "A standing army and police are the chief instruments of state power. But how can it be otherwise?" (Lenin, 1975: 316). Neither Lenin nor (for the most part) Tilly see state coercion as dependent for its effectiveness upon value consensus or popular contentment. And both are quite aware that states can repress popular forces and revolutionary movements. Not surprisingly, therefore, in accounting for revolutionary success, both Tilly and Lenin place emphasis on the breakdown of the old regime's monopoly of coercion and the buildup of armed forces by revolutionaries.

It remains true, however, that Marxists and political-conflict theorists like Tilly are as guilty as Gurr and Johnson of treating the state primarily as an arena in which social conflicts are resolved, though of course they see resolution through domination rather than voluntary consensus. For, in one way or another, both Marxists and Tilly regard the state as a system of organized coercion that invariably functions to support the superordinant position of dominant classes or groups over subordinate classes or groups. ...

Thus, neither in classical Marxism nor in Tilly's collective-action theory is the state treated as an autonomous structure—a structure with a logic and interests of its own not necessarily equivalent to, or fused with, the interests of the dominant class in society or the full set of member groups in the polity. Within the terms of these theories, it is consequently virtually impossible even to raise the possibility that fundamental conflicts of interest might arise between the existing dominant class or set of groups, on the one hand, and the state rulers on the other. Society is characterized by intergroup domination and power struggles. And the state, based upon concentrated means of coercion, fits in as a form of instrumental or objective domination and as an object of struggle, but not as an organization-for-itself.

Yet what about the more recent developments in Marxist? Lately there has certainly been a renewed interest among Marxist-oriented intellectuals in the problem of the state. In critical reaction to what had become a widespread vulgarization—the notion that states were nothing but instruments manipulated consciously and directly by leaders and interest groups representing the dominant class—contemporary analysts such as Ralph Miliband, Nicos Poulantzas, Perry Anderson, Göran Therborn, and Claus Offe have raised the issue of "the relative autonomy of the state" from direct control by the dominant class. Interest in this possibility has been focused especially upon capitalist societies, but also upon the absolutist phase of European feudalism. Theoretical attention has been devoted to elucidating the broad structural constraints that an existing mode of production places upon the range of possibilities for state structures and actions. And, in a more innovative vein, the argument has been developed that state rulers may have to be free of control by specific dominant-class groups and personnel if they are to be able to implement policies that serve the fundamental interest of an entire dominant class. That interest is, of course, its need to preserve the class structure and mode of production as a whole.

Recurrently as this recent debate has unfolded, certain participants—especially those most concerned with understanding how states could act against dominant-class resistance to preserve an existing mode of production—have seemed on the verge of asserting that states are potentially autonomous not only over against dominant classes but also vis-à-vis entire class structures or modes of production. However, this possible line of argument has been for the most part carefully avoided. Instead, some analysts, such as Claus Offe, have simply hypothesized that although state structures and policies are causally important in their own right, they objectively function because of in-built "selection mechanisms" to preserve the existing mode of production. Others, especially the so-called structuralist Marxists, have replaced the discredited dominant-class instrumentalism with what might be labeled a class-struggle reductionism. According to this view, state structures and functions are not simply controlled by dominant classes alone. Rather they are shaped and buffeted by the class struggle between dominant and subordinate classes—a struggle that goes on within the objective limits of the given economy and class structure as a whole. Finally, a very recent contribution to the debate has been made by Göran Therborn in a ... book that focuses directly on state structures as such. Working in a related yet somewhat different vein from the class-struggle theorists, Therborn constructs and contrasts typological models of the different forms and functions of state organizations and activities in the feudal, capitalist, and socialist modes of production, respectively. He attempts for each mode to derive the state structure directly from the corresponding basic class relations. For, along with the "structuralist" theorist Nicos Poulantzas, Therborn maintains that "the state should be regarded neither as a specific institution nor as an instrument, but as a relation—a materialized concentration of the class relations of a given society" (Therborn, 1978: 34).

Thus the recent Marxist debate on the state stops short at the problem of the autonomy of the state, since most participants in the debate tend either to treat the state in a completely functionalist manner, or to regard it as an aspect of class relations or struggle. It is unquestionably an advance to establish (or reestablish, since this surely was the classical Marxist position) that states are not simply created and manipulated by dominant classes. Nevertheless, it is still essential for Marxists to face more directly the questions of what states are in their own right, and how their structures vary and their activities develop in relation to socioeconomic structures. So far, virtually all Marxists continue simply to assume that state forms and activities vary in correspondence with modes of production, and that state rulers cannot possibly act against the basic interests of a dominant class. Arguments remain confined to issues of *how* states vary with, and function for, modes of production and dominant classes. The result is that still hardly anyone questions this Marxist version of the enduring sociological proclivity to absorb the state into society.

Question this enduring sociological proclivity we must, however, if we are to be well prepared to analyze social revolutions. At first glance, a social–structural determinist perspective (especially one that embodies a mode of class analysis) seems an obviously fruitful approach. This seems to be the case because social revolutions do, after all, centrally involve class struggles and result in basic social-structural transformations. Nevertheless, the historical realities of social revolutions insistently suggest the need for a more state-centered approach. ... [T]he political crises that have launched social revolutions have not at all been epiphenomenal reflections of societal strains or class contradictions. Rather they have been direct expressions of contradictions centered in the structures of old-regime states. The political-conflict groups that have figured in social-revolutionary struggles have not merely represented social interests and forces. Rather they have formed as interest groups within and fought about the forms of state structures. The vanguard parties that have emerged during the radical phases of social revolutions have been uniquely responsible for building central- ized armies and administrations without which revolutionary transformations could not have been consolidated. Social revolutions, moreover, have changed state structures as much or more as they have changed class relations, societal values, and social institutions. And, the effects of social revolutions upon the subsequent economic and sociopolitical development of the nations that they have transformed have been due not only to the changes in class structures, but also to the changes in state structures and functions that the revolutions accom- plished. In sum, the class upheavals and socioeconomic transformations that have characterized social revolutions have been closely intertwined with the col- lapse of the state organizations of the old regimes and with the consolidation and functioning of the state organizations of the new regimes.

We can make sense of social-revolutionary transformations only if we take the state seriously as a macro-structure. The state properly conceived is no mere arena in which socioeconomic struggles are fought out. It is, rather, a set of ad- ministrative, policing, and military organizations headed, and more or less well coordinated by, an executive authority. Any state first and fundamentally ex- tracts resources from society and deploys these to create and support coercive and administrative organizations. Of course, these basic state organizations are built up and must operate within the context of class-divided socioeconomic re- lations, as well as within the context of national and international economic dy- namics. Moreover, coercive and administrative organizations are only parts of overall political systems. These systems also may contain institutions through which social interests are represented in state policymaking as well as institu- tions through which nonstate actors are mobilized to participate in policy imple- mentation. Nevertheless, the administrative and coercive organizations are the basis of state power as such.

Where they exist, these fundamental state organizations are at least poten- tially autonomous from direct dominant-class control. The extent to which they *actually* are autonomous, and to what effect, varies from case to case. It is worth emphasizing that the actual extent and consequences of state autonomy can only be analyzed and explained in terms specific to particular types of sociopo- litical systems and to particular sets of historical international circumstances. ...

State organizations necessarily compete to some extent with the dominant class(es) in appropriating resources from the economy and society. And the ob- jectives to which the resources, once appropriated, are devoted may very well be at variance with existing dominant-class interests. Resources may be used to strengthen the bulk and autonomy of the state itself—something necessarily threatening to the dominant class unless the greater state power is indispens- ably needed and actually used to support dominant-class interests. But the use of state power to support dominant-class interests is not inevitable. Indeed, at- tempts of state rulers merely to perform the state's "own" functions may create conflicts of interest with the dominant class. The state normally performs two basic sets of tasks: It maintains order, and it competes with other actual or potential states. As Marxists have pointed out, states usually do function to preserve existing economic and class structures, for that is normally the smoothest way to enforce order. Nevertheless, the state has its own distinct interests vis-à-vis subordinate classes. Although both the state and the dominant class(es) share a broad interest in keeping the subordinate classes in place in society and at work in the existing economy, the state's own fundamental interest in maintaining sheer physical order and political peace may lead it—especially in periods of crisis—to enforce concessions to subordinate-class demands. These concessions may be at the expense of the interests of the dominant class, but not contrary to the state's own interests in controlling the population and collecting taxes and military recruits.

Moreover, we should not forget that states also always exist in determinant geopolitical environments, in interaction with other actual or potential states. An existing economy and class structure condition and influence a given state structure and the activities of the rulers. So, too, do geopolitical environments create tasks and opportunities for states and place limits on their capacities to cope with either external or internal tasks or crises. As the German historian Otto Hintze once wrote, two phenomena above all condition "the real organization of the state. These are, first, the structure of social classes, and second, the external ordering of the states—their position relative each other, and their overall position in the world" (Hintze, 1975: 183). Indeed, a state's involvement in an international network of states is a basis for potential autonomy of action over and against groups and economic arrangements within its jurisdiction—even including the dominant class and existing relations of production. For international military pressures and opportunities can prompt state rulers to attempt policies that conflict with, and even in extreme instances contradict, the fundamental interests of a dominant class. State rulers may, for example, undertake military adventures abroad that drain resources from economic development at home, or that have the immediate or ultimate effect of undermining the position of dominant socioeconomic interests. And, to give a different example, rulers may respond to foreign military competition or threats of conquest by attempting to impose fundamental socioeconomic reforms or by trying to reorient the course of national economic development through state intervention. Such programs may or may not be successfully implemented. But even if they are not carried through, the sheer attempt may create a contradictory clash of interests between the state and the existing dominant class.

The perspective on the state advanced here might appropriately be labeled "organizational" and "realist." In contrast to most (especially recent) Marxist theories, this view refuses to treat states as if they were mere analytic aspects of abstractly conceived modes of production, or even political aspects of concrete class relations and struggles. Rather it insists that states are actual organizations controlling (or attempting to control) territories and people. Thus the analyst of revolutions must explore not only class relations but also relations of states to one another and relations of states to dominant and subordinate classes. ...

Yet not only does an organizational, realist perspective on the state entail differences from Marxist approaches, it also contrasts with non-Marxist approaches that treat the *legitimacy* of political authorities as an important explanatory concept. If state organizations cope with whatever tasks they already claim smoothly and efficiently, legitimacy—either in the sense of moral approval or in the probably much more usual sense of sheer acceptance of the status quo—will probably be accorded to the state's form and rulers by most groups in society. In any event, what matters most is always the support or acquiescence not of the popular majority of society but of the politically powerful and mobilized groups, invariably including the regime's own cadres. Loss of legitimacy, especially among these crucial groups, tends to ensue with a vengeance if and when (for reasons that are always open to sociological and historical explanation) the state fails consistently to cope with existing tasks, or proves unable to cope with new tasks suddenly thrust upon it by crisis circumstances. Even after great loss of legitimacy has occurred, a state can remain quite stable—and certainly invulnerable to internal mass-based revolts—especially if its coercive organizations remain coherent and effective. Consequently, the structure of those organizations, their place within the state apparatus as a whole, and their linkages to class forces and to politically mobilized groups in society are all important issues for the analyst of states in revolutionary situations, actual or potential. Such an analytic focus seems certain to prove more fruitful than any focus primarily or exclusively upon political legitimation. The ebbing of a regime's legitimacy in the eyes of its own cadres and other politically powerful groups may figure as a mediating variable in an analysis of regime breakdown. But the basic causes will be found in the structure and capacities of state organizations, as these are conditioned by developments in the economy and class structure and also by developments in the international situation.

The state, in short, is fundamentally Janus-faced, with an intrinsically dual anchorage in class-divided socioeconomic structures and an international system of states. If our aim is to understand the breakdown and building-up of state organizations in revolutions, we must look not only at the activities of social groups. We must also focus upon the points of intersection between international conditions and pressures, on the one hand, and class-structured economies and politically organized interests, on the other hand. State executives and their followers will be found maneuvering to extract resources and build administrative and coercive organizations precisely at this intersection. Here, consequently, is the place to look for the political contradictions that help launch social revolutions. Here, also, will be found the forces that shape the rebuilding of state organizations within social-revolutionary crises. ...

REFERENCES

Hintze, Otto. 1975. "Economics and Politics in the Age of Modern Capitalism." In Felix Gilbert, ed., *The Historical Essays of Otto Hintze*. New York: Oxford University Press.

Lenin, V. I. 1975. *The State and Revolution*. In Robert C. Tucker, ed., *The Lenin Anthology*. New York: Norton.

Therborn, Göran. 1978. *What Does the Ruling Class Do When It Rules?* London: New Left Books.

Tilly, Charles. 1978. *From Mobilization to Revolution*. Reading, Mass.: Addison-Wesley.

28

The Autonomous Power of the State

MICHAEL MANN

DEFINING THE STATE

The state is undeniably a messy concept. The main problem is that most definitions contain two different levels of analysis, the 'institutional' and the 'functional'. That is, the state can be defined in terms of what it looks like, institutionally, or what it does, its functions. Predominant is a mixed, but largely institutional, view put forward originally by Weber. In this the state contains four main elements, being:

1. A *differentiated* set of institutions and personnel embodying
2. *centrality* in the sense that political relations radiate outwards from a centre to cover
3. a *territorially demarcated area*, over which it exercises
4. a monopoly of *authoritative binding rule-making*, backed up by a monopoly of the means of physical violence.

Apart from the last phrase which tends to equate the state with military force (see below), I will follow this definition. It is still something of a mixed bag. It contains a predominant institutional element: states can be recognized by the central location of their differentiated institutions. Yet it also contains a 'functional' element: the essence of the state's functions is a monopoly of binding rule-making. Nevertheless, my principal interest lies in those centralized institutions generally called 'states', and in the powers of the personnel who staff them, at the higher levels generally termed the 'state elite'. The central question for us here, then, is what is the nature of the power possessed by states and state elites? In answering I shall contrast state elites with power groupings whose base lies outside the state, in 'civil society'. In line with the model of power underlying my work, I divide these into three: ideological, economic and military groups. So what, therefore, is the power of state elites as against the power of ideological movements, economic classes and military elites?

TWO MEANINGS OF STATE POWER

What do we mean by 'the power of the state'? As soon as we begin to think about this commonplace phrase, we encounter two quite different senses in which states and their elites might be considered powerful. We must disentangle them. The first sense concerns what we might term the *despotic power* of the state elite, the range of actions which the elite is empowered to undertake without routine, institutionalized negotiation with civil society groups. The historical variations in such powers have been so enormous that we can safely leave on one side the ticklish problem of how we precisely measure them. The despotic powers of many historical states have been virtually unlimited. The Chinese Emperor, as the Son of Heaven, 'owned' the whole of China and could do as he wished with any individual or group within his domain. The Roman Emperor, only a minor god, acquired powers which were also in principle unlimited outside of a restricted area of affairs nominally controlled by the Senate. Some monarchs of early modern Europe also claimed divinely derived, absolute powers (though they were not themselves divine). ...

But there is a second sense in which people talk of 'the power of the state', especially in today's capitalist democracies. We might term this *infrastructural power*, the capacity of the state to actually penetrate civil society, and to implement logistically political decisions throughout the realm. This was comparatively weak in the historical societies just mentioned. ... But it is powerfully developed in all industrial societies. When people in the West today complain of the growing power of the state, they cannot be referring sensibly to the despotic powers of the state elite itself, for if anything these are still declining. It is, after all, only 40 years since universal suffrage was fully established in several of the advanced capitalist states, and the basic political rights groups such as ethnic minorities and women are still increasing. But the complaint is more justly levelled against the state's infrastructural encroachments. These powers are now immense. The state can assess and tax our income and wealth at source, without our consent or that of our neighbours or kin (which states before about 1850 were *never* able to do); it stores and can recall immediately a massive amount of information about all of us; it can enforce its will within the day almost anywhere in its domains; its influence on the overall economy is enormous; it even directly provides the subsistence of most of us (in state employment, in pensions, in family allowances, etc.). The state penetrates everyday life more than did any historical state. Its infrastructural power has increased enormously. ...

TABLE [28].1   Two Dimensions of State Power

| Despotic Power | Infrastructural Coordination | |
	Low	High
Low	Feudal	Bureaucratic
High	Imperial	Authoritarian

But who controls these states? Without prejudging a complex issue entirely, the answer in the capitalist democracies is less likely to be 'an autonomous state elite' than in most historic societies. In these countries most of the formal political leadership is elected and recallable. Whether one regards the democracy as genuine or not, few would contest that politicians are largely controlled by outside civil society groups (either by their financiers or by the electorate) as well as by the law. President Nixon or M. Chaban-Delmas may have paid no taxes; political leaders may surreptitiously amass wealth, infringe the civil liberties of their opponents, and hold on to power by slyly undemocratic means. But they do not brazenly expropriate or kill their enemies or dare to overturn legal traditions enshrining constitutional rule, private property or individual freedoms. On the rare occasions this happens, we refer to it as a *coup* or a revolution, an overturning of the norms. If we turn from elected politicians to permanent bureaucrats we still do not find them exercising significant autonomous power over civil society. Perhaps I should qualify this, for the secret decisions of politicians and bureaucrats penetrate our everyday lives in an often infuriating way, deciding we are not eligible for this or that benefit, including, for some persons, citizenship itself. But their power to change the fundamental rules and overturn the distribution of power within civil society is feeble—without the backing of a formidable social movement.

So, in one sense states in the capitalist democracies are weak, in another they are strong. They are 'despotically weak' but 'infrastructurally strong'. Let us clearly distinguish these two types of state power. The first sense denotes power by the state elite itself *over* civil society. The second denotes the power of the state to penetrate and centrally coordinate the activities of civil society through its own infrastructure. The second type of power still allows the possibility that the state itself is a mere instrument of forces within civil society, i.e., that it has no despotic power at all. The two are analytically autonomous dimensions of power. In practice, of course, there may be a relationship between then. For example, the greater the state's infrastructural power, the greater the volume of binding rule-making, and therefore the greater the likelihood of despotic power over individuals and perhaps also over marginal, minority groups. All infrastructurally powerful states, including the capitalist democracies, are strong in relation to individuals and to the weaker groups in civil society, but the capitalist democratic states are feeble in relation to dominant groups—at least in comparison to most historical states.

From these two independent dimensions of state power we can derive the four ideal-types shown in Table [28].1.

The *feudal* state is the weakest, for it has both low despotic and low infrastructural power. The medieval European state approximated to this ideal-type, governing largely indirectly, through infrastructure freely and contractually provided and controlled by the principal and independent magnates, clerics and towns. The *imperial* state posseses its own governing agents, but has only limited capacity to penetrate and coordinate civil society without the assistance of other power groups. It corresponds to the term patrimonial state used by writers like Weber (1968) and Bendix (1978). Ancient states like the Akkadian, Egyptian, Assyrian, Persian and Roman approximated to this type. I hesitated over the term *bureaucratic* state, because of its negative connotations. But a bureaucracy has a high organizational capacity, yet cannot set its own goals; and the bureaucratic state is controlled by others, civil society groups, but their decisions once taken are enforceable through the state's infrastructure. Contemporary capitalist democracies approximate to this type, as does the future state hoped for by most radicals and socialists. *Authoritarian* is intended to suggest a more institutionalized form of despotism, in which competing power groupings cannot evade the infrastructural reach of the state, nor are they structurally separate from the state (as they are in the bureaucratic type). All significant social power must go through the authoritative command structure of the state. Thus it is high on both dimensions, having high despotic power over civil society groups and being able to enforce this infrastructurally. In their different ways, Nazi Germany and the Soviet Union tend towards this case. ... Nor is this to deny that such states contain competing interest groups which may possess different bases in 'civil society'. Rather, in an authoritarian state power is transmitted through its directives and so such groups compete for direct control of the state. It is different in the capitalist democracies where the power of the capitalist class, for example, permeates the whole of society, and states generally accept the rules and rationality of the surrounding capitalist economy.

These are ideal-types. Yet my choice of real historical examples which roughly approximate to them reveals two major tendencies which are obvious enough yet worthy of explanation. First, there has occurred a long-term historical growth in the infrastructural power of the state, apparently given tremendous boosts by industrial societies, but also perceptible within both pre-industrial and industrial societies considered separately. Secondly, however, within each historical epoch have occurred wide variations in despotic powers. There has been *no* general development tendency in despotic powers—non-despotic states existed in late fourth millennium BC Mesopotamia (the 'primitive democracy' of the early city-states), in first millennium BC Phoenicia, Greece and Rome, in medieval republics and city-states, and in the modern world alike. The history of despotism has been one of oscillation, not development. Why such wide divergences on one dimension, but a developmental trend on the other?

The Development of State Infrastructural Power

The growth of the industrial power of the state is one in the logistics of political control. I will not here enumerate its main historical phases. Instead, I give examples of some logistical techniques which aided effective state penetration of social life, each of which has had a long historical development.

1. A division of labour between the state's main activities which it coordinated centrally. A microcosm of this is to be found on the battlefields of history where a coordinated administrative division between infantry, cavalry and artillery, usually organized by the state, would normally defeat forces in which these activities were mixed up— at least in 'high intensity' warfare.
2. Literacy, enabling stabilized messages to be transmitted through the state's territories by its agents, and enabling legal responsibilities to be codified and stored. Giddens (1981) emphasizes this 'storage' aspect of state power.
3. Coinage, and weights and measures, allowing commodities to be exchanged under an ultimate guarantee of value by the state.
4. Rapidity of communication of messages and of transport of people and resources through improved roads, ships, telegraphy, etc.

States able to use relatively highly developed forms of these techniques have possessed greater capacity for infrastructural penetration. This is pretty obvious. So is the fact that history has seen a secular process of infrastructural improvements.

Yet none of these techniques is specific to the state. They are part of general social development, part of the growth of human beings' increasing capacities for collective social mobilization of resources. Societies in general, not just their states, have advanced their powers. Thus none of these techniques necessarily changes the relationship between a state and its civil society; and none is necessarily pioneered by either the state or civil society.

Thus state power (in either sense) does not derive from techniques or means of power that are peculiar to itself. The varied techniques of power are of three main types: military, economic and ideological. They are characteristic of all social relationships. The state uses them all, adding no fourth means peculiar to itself. This has made reductionist theories of the state more plausible because the state seems dependent on resources also found more generally in civil society. If they are all wrong, it is not because the state manipulates means of power denied to other groups. The state is not autonomous in *this* sense. ...

Two conclusions emerge. First, in the whole history of the development of the infrastructure of power there is virtually no technique which belongs necessarily to the state, or conversely to civil society. Secondly, there is some kind of oscillation between the role of the two in social development. I hope to show later that it is not merely oscillation, but a dialectic.

The obvious questions is: if infrastructural powers are a general feature of society, in what circumstances are they appropriated by the state? How does the state acquire in certain situations, but not others, despotic powers? What are the origins of the autonomous power of the state? My answer is in three stages, touching upon the *necessity* of the state, its *multiplicity of functions* and its *territorialized centrality*. The first two have often been identified in recent theory, the third is, I think, novel.

ORIGINS OF STATE POWER

The Necessity of the State

The only stateless societies have been primitive. There are no complex, civilized societies without any centre of binding rule-making authority, however limited its scope. If we consider the weak feudal cases we find that even they tend to arise from a more state-centred history whose norms linger on to reinforce the new weak states. Feudal states tend to emerge either as a check to the further disintegration of a once-unified larger state (as in China and Japan) or as a post-conquest division of the spoils among the victorious, and obviously united, conquerors (see Lattimore, 1957). Western European feudalism embodies both these histories, though in varying mixtures in different regions. The laws of the feudal states in Europe were reinforced by rules descending from Roman law (especially property law), Christian codes of conduct and Germanic notions of loyalty and honour. ...

In the long run, normally taken for granted, but enforceable, rules are necessary to bind together strangers or semi-strangers. It is not requisite that all these rules are set by a single monopolistic state. Indeed, though the feudal example is extreme, most states exist in a multi-state civilization which also provides certain normative rules of conduct. Nevertheless, most societies seem to have required that some rules, particularly those relevant to the protection of life and property, be set monopolistically, and this has been the province of the state.

From this necessity, autonomous state power ultimately derives. The activities of the state personnel are necessary to society as a whole and/or to the various groups that benefit from the existing structure of rules which the state enforces. From this functionality derives the potentiality for exploitation, a lever for the achievement of private state interests. Whether the lever is used depends on other conditions, for—after all—we have not even established the existence of a permanent state cadre which might have identifiable interests. But necessity is the mother of state power.

The Multiplicity of State Functions

Despite the assertions of reductionists, most states have not in practice devoted themselves to the pursuit of a single function. 'Binding rule-making' is merely an umbrella term. The rules and functions have been extremely varied. As the two-dimensional models recognize, we may distinguish domestic and international, or economic, ideological and military functions. But there are many types of activity and each tends to be functional for differing 'constituencies' in society. I illustrate this with reference to what have been probably the four most persistent types of state activities.

1. *The maintenance of internal order.* This may benefit all, or all law-abiding subjects of the state. It may also protect the majority from arbitrary usurpations by socially and economically powerful groups, other than those allied to the state. But probably the main benefit is to protect existing property relations from the mass of the property-less. This function probably best serves a dominant economic class constituency.

2. *Military defence/aggression, directed against foreign foes.* 'War parties' are rarely coterminous with either the whole society or with one particular class within it. Defence may be genuinely collective; aggression usually has more specific interests behind it. Those interests may be quite widely shared by all 'younger sons' without inheritance rights or all those expansively minded; or they might comprise only a class fraction of an aristocracy, merchants or capitalists. In multi-state systems war usually involves alliances with other states, some of whom may share the same religion, ethnicity, or political philosophy as some domestic constituency. These are rarely reducible to economic class. Hence war and peace constituencies are usually somewhat idiosyncratic.

3. *The maintenance of communications infrastructures:* roads, rivers, message systems, coinages, weights and measures, marketing arrangements. Though few states have monopolized all of these, all stages have provided some, because they have a territorial basis which is often most efficiently organized from a centre. The principal constituencies here are a 'general interest' and more particular trade-centred groups.

4. *Economic redistribution:* the authoritative distribution of scarce material resources between different ecological niches, age-groups, sexes, regions, classes, etc. There is a strongly collective element in this function, more so than in the case of the others. Nevertheless, many of the redistributions involve rather particular groups, especially the economically inactive whose subsistence is thus protected by the state. And economic redistribution also has an international dimension, for the state normally regulates trade relations and currency exchanges across its boundaries, sometimes unilaterally, sometimes in alliance

with other states. This also gives the state a particular constituency among merchants and other international agents—who, however, are rarely in agreement about desirable trade policy.

These four tasks are necessary, either to society as a whole or to interest groups within it. They are undertaken most efficiently by the personnel of a central state who become indispensable. And they bring the state into functional relations with diverse, sometimes cross-cutting groups between whom there is room to manoeuvre. The room can be exploited. Any state involved in a multiplicity of power relations can play off interest groups against each other. ...

And this is about as far as the insights contained within current two-dimensional theory can be expanded. It is progress, but not enough. It does not really capture the *distinctiveness* of the state as a social organization. After all, necessity plus multiplicity of function, and the balancing act, are also the power source and stock-in-trade of any ruthless committee chairperson. Is the state only a chair writ large? No, as we will now see.

The Territorial Centrality of the State

The definition of the state concentrates upon its institutional, territorial, centralized nature. This is the third, and most important, precondition of state power. As noted, the state does not possess a distinctive *means* of power independent of, and analogous to, economic, military and ideological power. The means used by states are only a combination of these, which are also the means of power used in all social relationships. However the power of the state is irreducible in quite a different *socio-spatial* and *organizational* sense. Only the state is inherently centralized over a delimited territory over which it has authoritative power. Unlike economic, ideological or military groups in civil society, the state elite's resources radiate authoritatively outwards from a centre but stop at defined territorial boundaries. The state is, indeed, a *place*—both a central place and a unified territorial reach. As the principal forms of state autonomous power will flow from this distinctive attribute of the state, it is important that I first prove that the state does so differ socio-spatially and organizationally from the major power groupings of civil society.

Economic power groupings—classes, corporations, merchant houses, manors, plantations, the *oikos*, etc.—normally exist in decentred, competitive or conflictual relations with one another. True, the internal arrangements of some of them (e.g., the modern corporation, or the household and manor of the great feudal lord) might be relatively centralized. But, first, they are oriented outwards to further opportunities for economic advantage which are not territorially confined nor subject to authoritative rules governing expansion (except by states). Economic power expansion is not authoritative, commanded—it is 'diffused', informally. Second, the scope of modern and some historic economic institutions is not territorial. They do not exercise general control of a specific territory, they control a specialized function and seek to extend it 'transnationally' wherever that function is demanded and exploitable. ...

Analogous points can be made about ideological power movements like religions. Ideologies (unless state-led) normally spread even more diffusely than economic relations. They move diffusely and 'interstitially' inside state territories, spreading through communication networks among segments of a state's population (like classes, age-cohorts, genders, urban/rural inhabitants, etc.); they often also move transnationally right through state boundaries. Ideologies may develop central, authoritative, Church-like institutions, but these are usually functionally, more than territorially, organized: they deal with the sacred rather than the secular, for example. There is a socio-spatial, as well as spiritual, 'transcendence' about ideological movements, which is really the opposite of the territorial bounds of the state.

It is true, however, that military power overlaps considerably with the state, especially in modern states who usually monopolize the means of organized violence. Nevertheless, it is helpful to treat the two as distinct sources of power. I have not the space here to justify this fully. ... Let me instead make two simple points. First, not all warfare is most efficiently organized territorially centrally—guerrillas, military feudalism and warrior bands are all examples of relatively decentred military organizations effective at many historical periods. Second, the effective scope of military power does not cover a single, unitary territory. ...

The logistics of 'concentrated coercion'—that is, of military power—differ from those of the territorial centralized state. Thus we should distinguish the two as power organizations. The militarist theory of the state is false, and one reason is that the state's organization is not coterminous with military organization. ...

If we add together the necessity, multiplicity and territorial centrality of the state, we can in principle explain its autonomous power. By these means the state elite possesses an independence from civil society which, though not absolute, is no less absolute in principle than the power of any other major group. Its power cannot be reduced to their power either directly or 'ultimately' or 'in the last instance'. The state is not merely a locus of class struggle, an instrument of class rule, the factor of social cohesion, the expression of core values, the centre of social allocation processes, the institutionalization of military force (as in the various reductionist theories)—it is a different socio-spatial organization. As a consequence we can treat states as *actors*, in the person of state elites, with a will to power and we can engage in the kind of 'rational action' theory of state interests advocated by Levi (1981).

The Mechanisms for Acquiring Autonomous State Power

Of course, this in itself does not confer a significant degree of actual power upon the state elite, for civil society groups, even though slightly differently organized, may yet be able largely to control it. But the principles do offer us a pair of hypotheses for explaining variations of power. (1) State infrastructural power derives from the social utility in any particular time and place of forms of territorial centralization which cannot be provided by civil society forces themselves. (2) The extent of state despotic power derives from the inability of civil society forces to control those forms of territorial centralization, once set up. Hence, there are two phases in the development of despotism: the growth of territorial centralization, and the loss of control over it. First function, then exploitation— let us take them in order. ...

[I]n all cases it is not economic or military necessity *per se* that increases the role of the state, for this might merely place it into the hands of classes or military groups in civil society. It is rather the more particular utility of economic or military *territorial centralization* in a given situation. There are other types of economy (e.g., market exchange) and of military organization (e.g., feudal cavalry or chariotry, castle defence) which encourage decentralization and so reduce state power. In all these above examples the principal power groupings of civil society *freely* conferred infrastructural powers upon their states. My explanation thus starts in a functionalist vein. But functions are then exploited and despotism results. The hypothesis is that civil society freely gives resources but then loses control and becomes oppressed by the state. How does this happen? ...

Provided the state's activities generate extra resources, then it has a particular logistical advantage. Territorial centralization gives effective mobilizing potentialities, able to concentrate these resources against any particular civil society group, even though it may be inferior in overall resources. Civil society groups may actually endorse state power. If the state upholds given relations of production, then the dominant economic class will have an interest in efficient state centralization. If the state defends society from outside aggressors, or represses crime, then its centrality will be supported quite widely in society. Naturally, the degree of centralization useful to these civil society interests will vary according to the system of production or method of warfare in question. Centrality can also be seen in the sphere of ideology, as Eisenstadt (1969) argues. The state and the interests it serves have always sought to uphold its authority by a claim to 'universalism' over its territories, a detachment from all particularistic, specialized ties to kin, locality, class, Church, etc. Naturally in practice states tend to represent the interests of particular kinship groupings, localities, classes, etc., but if they appeared merely to do this they would lose all claim to distinctiveness and to legitimacy. States thus appropriate what Eisenstadt calls 'free-floating resources', not tied to any particular interest group, able to float throughout the territorially defined society.

This might seem a formidable catalogue of state powers. And yet the autonomous power achievements of historical states before the twentieth century were generally limited and precarious. Here we encounter the fundamental logistical, infrastructural constraints operating against centralized regimes in extensive agrarian societies. ... [E]ven the most pretentious of despotic rulers actually ruled through local notables. All extensive societies were in reality 'territorially federal'. Their imperial rule was always far feebler than traditional images of them allow for. ...

So we have in this example contrary tendencies—militaristic centralization followed by fragmenting federalism. Combining them we get a dialectic. If compulsory cooperation is successful, it increases both the infrastructural and the despotic power of the state. But it also increases social infrastructural resources in general. The logistical constraints mean that the new infrastructures cannot be kept within the body politic of the state. Its agents continually 'disappear' into civil society, bearing the state's resources with them. This happens continually to such regimes. The booty of conquest, land grants to military lieutenants, the fruits of office, taxes, literacy, coinage all go through a two-phase cycle, being first the property of the state then private (in the sense of 'hidden') property. And though there are cases where the fragmentation phase induces social collapse, there are others where civil society can use the resources which the despotic state has institutionalized, without needing such a strong state. ...

Such a view rejects a simple antithesis, common to ideologies of our own time, between the state and civil society, between public and private property. It sees the two as continuously, temporally entwined. More specifically it sees large private property concentrations—and, therefore, the power of dominant classes—as normally boosted by the fragmentation of successful, despotic states, not as the product of civil society forces alone. So the power autonomy of both states and classes has essentially fluctuated, dialectically. There can be no general formula concerning some 'timeless' degree of autonomous state power (in the despotic sense). ...

Thus the impact of state autonomy on despotic power has been ambiguous. In terms of traditional theory, results might seem disappointing: the state has not consistently possessed great powers—or indeed any fixed level of power. But I have discussed interesting power processes of a different kind. In agrarian societies states were able to exploit their territorial centrality, but generally only precariously and temporarily because despotic power also generated its own antithesis in civil society. In industrial societies the emergence of authoritarian states indicates much greater potential despotism, but this is still somewhat controversial and ambiguous. In the capitalist democracies there are few signs of autonomous state power—of a despotic type.

But, perhaps, all along, and along with most traditional theory, we have been looking for state power ... [in] the wrong place. By further examining infrastructural power we can see that this is the case.

RESULTS: INFRASTRUCTURAL POWER

Any state that acquires or exploits social unity will be provided with infrastructural supports. These enable it to regulate, normatively and by force, a *given* set of social and territorial relations, and to erect boundaries against the outside. New boundaries momentarily reached by previous social interactions are stabilized, regulated and heightened by the state's universalistic, monopolistic rules. In this sense the state gives territorial bounds to social relations whose dynamic lies outside of itself. The state *is* an arena, the condensation, the crystallization, the summation of social relations within its territories—a point often made by Poulantzas (1972). Yet, despite appearances, this does not support Poulantzas' reductionist view of the state, for this is an *active* role. The state may promote great social change by consolidating territoriality which would not have occurred without it. The importance of this role is in proportion to its infrastructural powers: the greater they are or become, the greater the territorializing of social life. Thus even if the state's every move toward despotism is successfully resisted by civil society groups, massive state-led infrastructural reorganization may result. Every dispute between the state elite and elements of civil society, and every dispute among the latter which is routinely regulated through the state's institutions, tends to focus the relations and the struggles of civil society on to the territorial plane of the state, consolidating social interaction over that terrain, creating territorialized mechanisms for repressing or compromising the struggle, and breaking both smaller local and also wider transnational social relationships.

Let me give an example. ... From the thirteenth century onward, two principal social processes favoured a greater degree of territorial centralization in Europe. First, warfare gradually favoured army command structures capable of routine, complex coordination of specialized infantry, cavalry and artillery. Gradually, the looser feudal levy of knights, retainers and a few mercenaries became obsolete. In turn this presupposed a routine 'extraction-coercion cycle' to deliver men, monies and supplies to the forces. ... Eventually, only territorially centred states were able to provide such resources and the Grand Duchies, the Prince-Bishops and the Leagues of Towns lost power to the emerging 'national' states. Second, European expansion, especially economic expansion taking an increasingly capitalistic form, required (a) increased military protection abroad, (b) more complex legal regulation of property and market transactions, and (c) domestic property forms (like rights to common lands). Capitalistic property owners sought out territorial states for help in these matters. Thus European states gradually acquired far greater infrastructural powers: regular taxation, a monopoly over military mobilization, permanent bureaucratic administration, a monopoly of law-making and enforcement. In the long run, despite attempts at absolutism, states failed to acquire despotic powers through this because it also enhanced the infrastructural capacities of civil society groups, especially of capitalist property-holders. This was most marked in Western Europe and as the balance of geo-political power tilted Westwards—and especially to Britain—the despotically weak state proved the general model for the modern era. States governed with, and usually in the interests of, the capitalist class.

But the process and the alliance facilitated the rise of a quite different type of state power, infrastructural in nature. When capitalism emerged as dominant, it took the form of a series of territorial segments—many systems of production and exchange, each to a large (though not total) extent bounded by a state and its overseas sphere of influence. The nation-state system of our own era was not a product of capitalism (or, indeed, of feudalism) considered as pure modes of production. It is in that sense 'autonomous'. But it resulted from the way expansive, emergent, capitalist relations were given regulative boundaries by preexisting states. ...

In this example, increasing territoriality has not increased despotic power. Western states were despotically weak in the twelfth century, and they remain so today. Yet the increase in infrastructural penetration has increased dramatically territorial boundedness. This seems a general characteristic of social development: increases in state infrastructural powers also increase the territorial boundedness of social interaction. We may also postulate the same tendency for despotic power, though it is far weaker. A despotic state without strong infrastructural supports will only claim territoriality. Like Rome and China it may build walls, as much to keep its subjects in as to keep 'barbarians' out. But its success is limited and precarious. So, again we might elaborate a historical dialectic. Increases in state infrastructural power will territorialize social relations. If the state then loses control of its resources they diffuse into civil society, decentering and de-territorializing it. Whether this is, indeed, beginning to happen in the contemporary capitalist world, with the rise of multi-national corporations outliving the decline of two successively hegemonic states, Great Britain and the United States, is one of the most hotly debated issues in contemporary political economy. Here I must leave it as an open issue.

In this essay I have argued that the state is essentially an arena, a place—just as reductionist theories have argued—and yet this is precisely the origin and mechanism of its autonomous powers. The state, unlike the principal power actors of civil society, is territorially bounded and centralized. Societies need some of their activities to be regulated over a centralized territory. So do dominant economic classes, Churches and other ideological power movements, and military elites. They, therefore, entrust power resources to state elites which they are incapable of fully recovering, precisely because their own socio-spatial basis of organization is not centralized and territorial. Such state power resources, and the autonomy to which they lead, may not amount to much. If, however, the state's use of the conferred resources generates further power resources—as was, indeed, intended by the civil society groups themselves—these will normally flow through the state's hands, and thus lead to a significant degree of power autonomy. Therefore, *autonomous state power is the product of the usefulness of enhanced territorial centralization to social life in general*. This has varied considerably through the history of societies, and so consequently has the power of states. ...

REFERENCES

Bendix R. 1978: *Kings or People*. Berkeley: University of California Press.

Eisenstadt S. N. 1969: *The Political Systems of Empires*. New York: The Free Press.

Giddens A. 1981: *A Contemporary Critique of Historical Materialism*. London: Macmillan.

Gumplowicz L. 1899: *The Outlines of Sociology*. Philadelphia: American Academy of Political and Social Science.

Hintze O. 1975: *The Historical Essays of Otto Hintze* (ed. F. Gilbert). New York: Oxford University Press.

Lattimore O. 1957: 'Feudalism in history: a review essay', *Past and Present*, no. 12, pp. 47–57.

Levi M. 1981: 'The predatory theory of rule', *Politics and Society*, 10, pp. 431–65.

Mann M. 1986: *The Sources of Social Power*, vol. 1. *A History of Power from the Beginning to 1760 AD*. Cambridge: Cambridge University Press.

Poulantzas N. 1972: *Pouvoir politique et classes sociales*. Paris: Maspero.

Skocpol T. 1979: *States and Social Revolutions*. Cambridge: Cambridge University Press.

Tilly C. 1981: *As Sociology Meets History*. New York: Academic Press.

Weber M. 1968: *Economy and Society*. New York: Bedminster Press.

About the Book and Editors

An extensively revised and updated new edition of Olsen's *Power in Societies*, this book contains carefully selected and edited writings on the exercise of social power in contemporary societies. The essays cover four broad topics: power in social organization, theoretical perspectives on power, national power structures, and power and the state. Each of the book's sections is introduced with an essay by the editors. Designed as a text for courses in political sociology, social stratification, and power in society, the anthology offers classical and contemporary, theoretical and empirical, writings.

Marvin E. Olsen was professor of sociology at Michigan State University until his death in May 1992. **Martin N. Marger** is associate professor of sociology at Michigan State University.